Revolutionary Stagecraft

# Revolutionary Stagecraft

*Theater, Technology, and Politics in Modern China*

Tarryn Li-Min Chun

*University of Michigan Press*
Ann Arbor

Published in the United States of America by the
University of Michigan Press
Manufactured in the United States of America
Printed on acid-free paper
First published June 2024

A CIP catalog record for this book is available from the British Library.

Library of Congress Cataloging-in-Publication Data

Names: Chun, Tarryn Li-Min, 1984– author. | Michigan Publishing (University of Michigan),
    publisher.
Title: Revolutionary stagecraft : theater, technology, and politics in modern China / Tarryn
    Li-Min Chun.
Other titles: Theater, technology, and politics in modern China
Description: Ann Arbor : University of Michigan Press, 2024. | Includes bibliographical
    references (pages 273–308) and index.
Identifiers: LCCN 2023056317 (print) | LCCN 2023056318 (ebook) | ISBN 9780472076567
    (hardcover) | ISBN 9780472056569 (paperback) | ISBN 9780472903962 (ebook other)
Subjects: LCSH: Theater—China—History—20th century. | Theater—Political aspects—
    China—History—20th century. | Theaters—Stage-setting and scenery—China.
Classification: LCC PN2874 .C53   2024 (print) | LCC PN2874 (ebook) |
    DDC 792.0951—dc23/eng/20240122
LC record available at https://lccn.loc.gov/2023056317
LC ebook record available at https://lccn.loc.gov/2023056318

DOI: https://doi.org/10.3998/mpub.11555896

Publication of this book is made possible in part by support from the Institute for
Scholarship in the Liberal Arts, College of Arts and Letters, University of Notre Dame.

The University of Michigan Press's open access publishing program is made possible
thanks to additional funding from the University of Michigan Office of the Provost and
the generous support of contributing libraries.

Cover art by Jenna Rame and inspired by architectural drawings for a grand theater slated
for construction in central Beijing in the 1950s, but never built.

# Contents

Digital materials related to this title can be found on the Fulcrum platform via the following citable URL: https://doi.org/10.3998/mpub.11555896

# Illustrations

# Acknowledgments

In some sense, my journey to this project began more than two decades ago, the first time that I balanced on a catwalk above my high school auditorium with a lighting unit in hand and a wrench dangling from my belt loop. Years of experience huddled in the wings, perched on ladders, and calling cues from the lighting booth deeply impressed upon me both the beauty of a stage viewed from oblique angles and the precarity of each performance. That live theater can happen at all is nothing short of a miracle, and it's all the more breathtaking when it happens under challenging material and political conditions.

I owe the fact that I have been able to translate an early fascination with the stage into a career researching and teaching about Chinese theater to the mentors who first encouraged me to combine my creative and academic passions and then guided me in sharpening my ability to do so. In particular, I would like to thank Perry Link for my initiation into modern Chinese literary studies and scholarly writing, and David Der-wei Wang, Wilt Idema, Jie Li, and Martin Puchner for their intellectual inspiration, careful reading, and helpful feedback at the dissertation stage of this project. While at Harvard, I found my second home in the Drama Colloquium run through the Mahindra Center for the Humanities and owe a special debt of gratitude to Juyon Kim and Derek Miller for providing support throughout the latter years of my graduate studies. I also would like to thank my East Asian Languages and Civilizations scholar-family—especially Jingling Chen, Satoru Hashimoto, Casey Lee, Andy Rodekhor, Kyle Shernuk, Dylan Suher, and Ying Lei—and graduate school comrades Sam Adams, Einor Cervone, Sakura Christmas, Ariel Fox, Matthew Franks, Rebecca Kastleman, Shi-lin Loh, Elizabeth Phillips, and Qiaomei Tang for feedback on various versions of these chapters, intellectual compatriotism, and many an indulgent afternoon tea. Chapter 5 is dedicated to Lin, who first introduced me to *Atoms and Love* via materials she found and photocopied for me during fieldwork in Japan.

The project grew into its present form through the support of a postdoctoral fellowship at the Lieberthal-Rogel Center for Chinese Studies (LRCCS) at the University of Michigan and of several departments and institutes at my current institution, the University of Notre Dame. The LRCCS postdoc provided me with time to reconceptualize the project and the resources to conduct both data-driven research and follow-up fieldwork in the People's Republic of China (PRC). Colleagues Pär Cassel, S. E. Kile, Joseph S. C. Lam, David Rolston, Xiaobing Tang, Emily Wilcox, their graduate students, my fellow postdocs, especially Sonya Özbey, and the LRCCS staff made for a wonderful community during my year in Ann Arbor. I remain extremely grateful that my postdoc also enabled me to spend breaks at the University of Oxford and to find my current position in the Department of Film, Television, and Theatre at Notre Dame. At Oxford, Christopher Foster, Margaret Hillenbrand, and Pamela Hunt gave me opportunities to present sections of this book, invaluable feedback on draft chapters, and writing companionship. At Notre Dame, I would like to thank my colleagues in the FTT department for their unwavering support of my work and for their friendship, especially Chris Becker, Jim Collins, Don Crafton, Kevin Dreyer, La Donna Forsgren, Anne García-Romero, Peter Holland, Anton Juan, Michael Kackman, Mary Celeste Kearney, Carys Kresny, Olivier Morel, Susan Ohmer, Matthew Payne, Siiri Scott, and Pam Wojcik. I owe an immense debt of gratitude to Michel Hockx, not only for reading much of this manuscript and correcting many early *pinyin* errors in it, but more importantly for creating a thriving community of scholars through the Liu Institute for Asia and Asian Studies. One of the best parts of Notre Dame has been meeting and building relationships across departments, and I would like to thank Liang Cai, Korey Garibaldi, Alex Hsu, Jennifer Hyunh, Julia Kowalski, Iris Ma, Sarah Quesada, Jazmin Sierra, Sonja Stonjanovic, Joshua Tychonievich, Emily Wang, and Xian Wang for their feedback on pieces of the project and moral support.

In mainland China, I am indebted to colleagues at the Shanghai Theatre Academy, Shanghai Dramatic Arts Center, Central Academy of Drama, Beijing People's Art Theater, and Nanjing University. At the Shanghai Theatre Academy, a special thanks to Professor Ye Changhai for encouraging me to apply for a grant from the academy that enabled me to travel to Shanghai in 2013 to gather archival material and to Fei Yong for help with logistics and many stimulating conversations. I would like to thank Dong Jian, Li Chang, Liu Xinglin, Lu Xiangdong, Ma Junshan, William Huizhu Sun,

Wang Chong, Wang Xiang, Yu Rongjun, Zhang Fuhai, Zhao Shanlin, and the many other theater artists and scholars who helped me during fieldwork trips conducted between 2012 and 2017. I also spent several summers in Taipei, Taiwan, and a semester in 2014 conducting research at the Center for Chinese Studies at the National Central Library there. My eternal gratitude to Katherine Hui-ling Chou, Jascha Chung, Walter Ren-Hao Hsu, Lin Ho-Yi, Tsai Hsin-hsin, Tseng Yong-Yih, Wang An-Chi, Austin Meng-chao Wang, and many others for conversations that deeply shaped this project and for letting me sit in on classes at National Taiwan University, present work in progress, and accompany them to the theater.

I feel especially fortunate to be publishing this book at a moment when the field of English-language scholarship on modern Chinese theater has begun to flourish, not least because this has given me the pleasure of working closely with the senior colleagues responsible for this change. Xiaomei Chen, Claire Conceison, Xing Fan, Ruru Li, Siyuan Liu, and Emily Wilcox, in particular, have been scholarly inspirations, stimulating collaborators, and some of my greatest cheerleaders. I am indebted to Xiaomei, along with Jie Li, for reading and providing extensive feedback on the penultimate draft manuscript of this book. Meanwhile, in the broader realm of Asian theater and performance studies, Jyana Browne, Ellen Gerdes, Maggie Greene, Man He, and many other peers have been delightful fellow panelists and co-conspirators. I am grateful to have had your intellectual companionship and a reason to look forward to each conference.

Finally, I am grateful to LeAnn Fields, Haley Winkle, Kevin Rennells, and the entire team at the University of Michigan Press for their support of this project and patience with the process. The two anonymous reviewers provided valuable comments that helped to streamline and focus a sprawling draft manuscript. Over the years, librarians Xiao-He Ma at Harvard, Liangyu Fu at University of Michigan, and Hye-jin Juhn at Notre Dame helped me track down and acquire many obscure materials. My research assistants at the University of Michigan, Heshan Cui and Athena Chia-Yen Lee, devoted countless hours to mining data from local gazetteers. At Notre Dame, Yvonne Yu Feng and Xiyun Wu helped with both collecting additional materials and compiling the bibliography in the later stages of the project. An extra special thanks to my writing coach, Yael Prizant, for her encouragement and feedback as I worked to complete the manuscript and to Michael Gnat for his impeccable attention to detail.

Research for this project was supported at the dissertation stage by grants from the Center for Chinese Studies at the National Central Library (in Taipei) and the Shanghai Theater Academy, as well as the Fairbank Center for Chinese Studies, the Edwin Curley Fund, and a Graduate School of the Arts and Sciences Dissertation Completion Fellowship at Harvard University. At Notre Dame, generous course releases and a semester of leave provided by the College of Arts and Letters were essential to the completion of the manuscript, and a COVID Resilience and Recovery Grant from the Office of the Provost enabled me to hire research assistants and pay for editing services, which greatly reduced the time required for its final phases. Publication subvention and indexing have been made possible by grants from the Institute for Scholarship in the Liberal Arts.

Sections of chapters 1 and 2 appeared as part of my article "Revolutionary Illumination: Stage Lighting, Politics, and *Play* in 1930s Shanghai Theater," in *Modern Chinese Literature and Culture* 30, no. 2 (2018): 87–140, and an earlier version of chapter 4 was published as "Sent-Down Plays: *Yangbanxi* Stagecraft, Practical Aesthetics, and Popularization during the Cultural Revolution" in *Chinese Socialist Theatres of Reform: Rethinking Performance Practice and Debates in the Maoist Period*, edited by Xiaomei Chen, Tarryn Chun, and Siyuan Liu (University of Michigan Press, 2021). My thanks to the University of Edinburgh Press and the University of Michigan Press for permission to reuse and rework these previous publications.

I dedicate this book to Kyle and Hannah. Their love and unceasing support, along with that of my parents, siblings, and in-laws (Mia, Gene, Alyson, and Anthony; Jo, John, Peter, Brenna, and Kelsey) have made it possible to keep putting words onto paper, day after day. Kyle read nearly every sentence of the book manuscript, and readers may thank him for ensuring that many of the wordier ones did not make the final cut. It is not an exaggeration to say that, without my family, this book would not exist. True, it might have existed in a different form or perhaps a bit sooner—several years of a transatlantic marriage and parenting a toddler during a global pandemic did take a toll—but I am certain it would be less lovingly written.

# Note on Translation, Transliteration, and Chinese Characters

In this book, I take an unorthodox approach to transliteration and the inclusion of Chinese characters, in an effort to balance readability, usefulness, and fidelity to my source texts.

Many Chinese-language theoretical concepts and artistic terms are challenging to render succinctly in English, depend on context for precise translation, have a history of being biased or inaccurate in their most common English translations, or face a combination of the above. One example lies in genre names such as *jingju* 京劇/京剧, which in its usual translation as "Peking opera" or "Beijing opera" involves the adoption of an outdated place name (Peking) or Eurocentric musical term (opera) that does not accurately reflect the theatrical form in question. Another set of examples includes aesthetic terms such as *xu* 虛/虚 and *shi* 實/实, which have long histories of use and numerous possible English translations. For terms that I feel fall into these categories and that recur multiple times throughout the book, I provide *pinyin* romanization, Chinese characters, and an English translation on first mention. Subsequent mentions use only the *pinyin* romanization. For artistic terms or phrases that occur only once, but for which I feel having the original term would benefit Chinese-language readers, I provide an English translation followed by the Chinese characters.

Book, article, play, and film titles are provided in English and Chinese characters on first mention, then subsequently referred to in English translation for ease of reading. Where texts have been published in English, I adopt the most common title translation; when discussed for the first time in English, I provide my own title translation. Notes provide citations in English for English-language sources and *pinyin* for non-English sources. Chinese characters for all source authors and titles can be found in the bibliography.

Other proper nouns, such as the names of people and places, are provided in romanization and characters on first mention, then subsequently referred to using romanization for ease of reading. All use either *pinyin* or the most common romanizations where those differ from standard *pinyin*, as in Chiang Kai-shek.

Chinese-language sources referenced in this study vary in their use of *jianti* 简体 (simplified) or *fanti* 繁體 (traditional) Chinese characters; generally, sources from before 1949 use *fanti* characters in the original, and sources from after 1949 use *jianti* if published in the PRC, or *fanti* if published in Hong Kong or Taiwan. The body of the book therefore uses *fanti* characters in chapters that focus on the pre-1949 period and any notes that provide information (beyond bibliographic citations) on pre-1949 texts or figures. *Jianti* characters are used in chapters that focus on the PRC era. Similarly, bibliographic entries for pre-1949 or post-1949 sources published in Hong Kong or Taiwan provide *fanti* characters, while sources that were published under the PRC provide *jianti* characters.

Japanese and Russian names, titles, and key terms are also provided in both the original and translation.

Translations are my own unless otherwise noted.

# Introduction

## *Thinking Chinese Theater through Technicity*

The opening full-page photograph of the August 1933 *Theater Studies Monthly* sets the stage for a celebrity entrance: towering trees of stage lights, elegantly draped curtains, and rows of weighted pulleys hang expectantly around the playing space (fig. 0.1). To the left of the image, strip lights and footlights frame a proscenium opening, with ornate audience boxes and blurred, underexposed orchestra seating just beyond. Additional lights, border curtains, and perhaps flying scenery hover far above the stage. A metal cage around one light, positioned on the floor beneath a lighting tree, hints at the presence of actors whose misplaced limbs might otherwise jostle and displace the unit. However, neither actors nor audience members take the stage. Instead, the caption reads "美國紐約羅克西（Roxy）劇院之舞臺燈光設備"—"Stage lighting equipment at the Roxy Theatre in New York, USA." In this photograph, backstage technology itself is the star of the show.[1]

The theater depicted is Manhattan's Roxy Theatre, which opened to much fanfare in 1927 and housed both film screenings and live performances. The journal in which the photograph appears, however, was published thousands of miles away in the city that was then called Beiping (now Beijing). Titled *Juxue yuekan* 劇學月刊 in Chinese, *Theater Studies Monthly* was a journal that typically published articles on *xiqu* 戲曲 (sung drama, often called "Chinese opera"), penned by some of the most famous theatrical luminaries of the day. In addition to the detailed photo of the Roxy, the journal's special double issue on *huaju* 話劇 (spoken drama) also carried illustrations of an array of "modern" stage equipment, including a lighting unit manufactured by the New York–based Kliegl Brothers company, resistance dimmers, special effects devices for creating thunder and lightning, and photo spreads on

美 國 紐 約 羅 克 四 (Roxy) 劇 院 之 舞 臺 燈 光 設 備

Fig. 0.1. Photograph of backstage lighting equipment at the Roxy Theatre in New York City, as depicted in *Theater Studies Monthly*. The photo is uncredited, but was taken by N. Lazarnick Commercial Photographers; a print is held in the collection of the Theatre Historical Society of America. Source: *Juxue yuekan* 2, nos. 7–8 (August 1933): n.p.

Swiss lighting designer and theorist Adolphe Appia (1862–1928) and American scenographer Norman Bel Geddes (1893–1958). Article topics ranged from the history of *huaju*, to long treatises on directing and stage lighting, to a materialist theory of theater.

Why were photos of the Roxy Theatre, Kliegl Brothers lighting units, Appia, and a Bel Geddes set design published in a Chinese *xiqu* journal in the early 1930s? What were the motivations of the Chinese theater artists writing about foreign theaters and backstage technological modernization, and who was the intended audience? How did the transnational circulation of technical knowledge affect Chinese theatrical practice, especially in light of broader calls to "modernize" Chinese society and culture? These questions all point to the importance of the relationship between theater and technology in modern China, yet questions of this kind have rarely been addressed in Chinese theater scholarship. Nonetheless, beginning in the mid-nineteenth century, both theater and technology in China were important sites of cross-cultural encounter between Chinese and foreign entities; both areas saw local innovation and ingenuity, amid the transnational circulation of theory and practice; and both spoke to the intersection of economic and artistic interests, while also illustrating the political stakes of even the most technical decisions. Chinese emissaries to Europe and the United States in the 1870s and 1880s, for instance, were equally impressed by the steam engines of the Industrial Revolution and the monumental national theaters they encountered on the Continent.[2] From this late Qing dynasty (1644–1912) moment of "encountering the West" to the present, both theater and technology have been intimately connected to the social reforms, political revolutions, and epochal changes of modern China.

Theater and technology, however, do not merely run in parallel, but also intersect in the realm of stage technology, rendered most directly in Chinese as *wutai jishu* 舞台技術. At the time when *Theater Studies Monthly* was in circulation, the term itself was only just beginning to enter common parlance. Prior to the 1930s, elements of the stage apparatus were largely referred to individually and with a range of terms derived from older usage in *xiqu*, borrowed from Japanese, or translated from other foreign languages. Scenery, for instance, was discussed as *wutai bujing* 舞台佈景 (stage scenery), *wutai zhuangzhi* 舞台裝置 (stage installation/device), *wutai zhuangshi* 舞台裝飾 (stage decoration/ornamentation), and *wutai sheji* 舞台設計 (stage design).[3] However, in the 1930s, "stage technology" as *wutai jishu* emerged as a holistic category used to refer to stage apparatus such as backstage machinery and fly systems, scenery and props, lighting and sound equipment, and special effects devices, as well as the know-how required to build and operate them. It could also sometimes include costumes and makeup, or even playwriting. Some of these elements, such as mechanical scenery and special effects, already had a long local history on the palace stages of late imperial China. Others, like electric lighting units and the revolving stage, were initially imports from Europe, the United States, and Japan and, as such, were indelibly marked as novel, modern, and foreign.

It was also in the 1930s that Chinese theater artists began to experiment with stage technology both onstage and by encoding potential uses of the stage apparatus into their plays. In one scene in the *huaju* play *Thunderstorm* (雷雨, 1934) by Cao Yu 曹禺 (Wan Jiabao 萬家寶, 1910–96), for instance, a burst of thunder startles the two main characters into an embrace, while a crack of lightning illuminates a shadowy, rain-drenched figure watching them through a nearby window. Cao Yu's stage directions connect these special effects so closely to the play's dramatic action that they also raise questions about *how* scenic designers and technicians would have created a thunderstorm (or the semblance of one) onstage in the mid-1930s. In a world where a fully equipped proscenium stage was still a relative novelty, and theater artists may or may not have had access to the thunder and lightning devices depicted in *Theater Studies Monthly*, how were these effects achieved? Reviews of productions provide some answers to these questions, but often focus more on the quality of the script and the actors' performances than design and technology (unless exceptionally good, or exceptionally bad). Reading technical handbooks, how-to articles, and photo spreads like those in *Theater Studies Monthly* alongside plays and production reviews, however, enables an exploration of the potential uses of stage technology in performance and uncovers innovations that often go unnoticed in the historical record. Handbooks written by Chinese theater artists around the time that *Thunderstorm* premiered, for example, reveal a variety of methods for creating stage lightning that range from a simple lighting effect to touching two live wires together, in order to produce an actual spark.

Alongside material changes to the stage apparatus and their practical applications, Chinese theater artists began to frame theater discursively in relation to technoscientific developments and even to see theater *as* a science or technology. Also writing in the August 1933 issue of *Theater Studies Monthly*, for example, *huaju* director Jiao Juyin 焦菊隱 (1905–75) would take as a given direct connections among science, technology, and theatrical advances:

Every element of [the theater] is of equal use as its other sister arts, and in addition, is closely connected with science. For example, theater architecture belongs not only to the realm of aesthetics, but also to that of architectural studies; it even incorporates principles from the disciplines of acoustics, optics, and physics. In terms of the design of lights and colors, the result of deploying stage lighting is an art, but the principles of light and color, changes in the color of lighting and its application, the nature of electrical power and how to manage it, the construction of lighting instruments and their use—there is not one that is not pure science.[4]

Here, Jiao connects the aesthetics and artistry of the theater both to modern science in general and to a specific type of technology that physics and other fields had made possible: lighting instruments. Science and its technological applications lend legitimacy to the theatrical enterprise. More significant, this is not an instance of an idiosyncratic or unique perspective of one theater director; similar ideas can be found in the work of such contemporaries as Chen Dabei 陳大悲 (1887–1944), founder of the amateur theater (愛美戲劇) movement of the 1920s, and Yu Shangyuan 余上沅 (1897–1970), a prominent playwright, theater theorist, and educator.[5] Moreover, the basic concept that scientific and technological advancements are closely related to aesthetic developments in the theater, and that theater is as much of a science as an art, would be repeated in the Chinese discourse surrounding modern theater throughout the twentieth century.

As a whole, then, stage technology provides a set of material, dramaturgical, and epistemological connections between the theater and the broader waves of technological modernization that occurred in China from the mid-nineteenth century onward. Far from a simple matter of "how to" operate a light or create an effect onstage, the theory and practice of stage technology in modern China relates intimately to the political and aesthetic goals of the directors, designers, and technicians involved in generating, disseminating, and implementing it. Stage technology also links theater to realms of technical knowledge production and circulation, as well as to the larger technical systems of ideology, economics, and culture. The central argument of this book is therefore that modern Chinese theater must be thought through these layers of technicity: that questioning how humans make and interact with technical objects onstage and backstage, and how these interactions shift as technology itself changes, is fundamental to understanding what the theater is and what it means for specific actors, audiences, and historical contexts. In the chapters that follow, the history of modern Chinese theater is rethought through this framework, with specific stage technologies and their affordances as points of departure. Equal importance is given throughout to technology's materiality and to its historical contingency. Ultimately, this approach reveals stage technology to be neither neutral nor deterministic, but rather a site of powerful negotiations among technological potential, historical exigency, artistic aims, and human agency.

## Theater and Technicity

What does technicity mean in relation to Chinese theater? After all, the connection between theater and technology is not solely or even primarily a modern condition, nor is it unique to the Chinese context. As W. B. Worthen notes in his recent study of Shakespeare and technicity: "There's no essential theatre apart from its apparatus."[6] And, indeed, one might trace this truism much farther into the past than Shakespeare, to architectural details of temple theaters in the ancient Hindu *Nāṭyaśāstra* or the deus ex machina of Greek tragedy or even the simple technologies of early Chinese shadow puppetry. As the story goes, for instance, Chinese shadow puppetry was invented by a magician serving Emperor Wudi of the Han Dynasty 漢武帝 (156–87 BCE). When the emperor fell heartsick following the death of his favorite concubine, Lady Li (李夫人), he was revived only after the magician lit torches, set up curtains surrounding the lighting source, and created the shadowy likeness of Lady Li.[7] The anecdote may be apocryphal, but it appears both as one of the most commonly cited origin stories for shadow theater and in scientific histories of Chinese optics.[8] It thus demonstrates the long-standing importance of theater's technical apparatus to Chinese performance, as well as deep historical connections among the discourses surrounding science, technology, and the theater. Indeed, theater across cultures shares moments of what we might call, borrowing from Jacques Derrida and Bernard Stiegler, an "originary technicity" that speaks to a human and (simple) machine assemblage as fundamental to the art form.[9] Building on this concept, one of the main concerns of this book is to illustrate how the unique case of stage technology in modern China can shed light on broader questions concerning theater and its technics.

Technicity in theater, broadly writ, might be understood through previous scholarship in two main areas: historical studies that emphasize the material dimensions of theaters past, and studies that focus on media technologies in contemporary performance. In particular, the study of ancient Greek and Roman theater, as well as of early modern European theater, has long been rich with analyses of how architecture, stage mechanics, special effects, costumes, and props intersect with both dramaturgy and the theater's social, cultural, political, and economic contexts. When the object of study shifts to theaters postdating the Industrial Revolution, technology looms all the larger and becomes, as Chris Salter puts it, even more deeply "entangled" with the "form and operation of the work" itself.[10] Studies of melodrama, modernism, and the avant-garde accordingly delve into theater's response to technological modernization in both content and form. Similarly, there has been a material turn in theater studies, as exemplified by work like Andrew Sofer's *The Stage Life of Props*, and the new materialism of performance studies by scholars such as Robin Bernstein.[11] Materialist scholarship does not always focus on technology per se, but demonstrates the value of centering inquiry on objects, or things. The objects and apparatus of the theater, then, can encompass everything from the simplest handkerchief to complex systems of lifts, pulleys, and (increasingly) digital technologies onstage. Indeed, in twenty-first-century theater, materiality has become inseparable from mediality.[12] The ubiquity of behind-the-scenes computerized systems and new media onstage may be a contemporary phenomenon, but it nonetheless serves to remind us, yet again, that theater has never been without its technologies.

The technicity of *Chinese* theater, however, must be defined both through a similar attention to the theatrical technicity and within contextually specific understandings of both theater and technology. From an etymological perspective, the term that appears in *wutai jishu* (stage technology), for instance—*jishu* 技術—can mean technology in the sense of electronics, mechanics, or systems, but also carries connotations of technique, skill, art, and craft. Indeed, scholars of Chinese science and technology commonly note that the concept of "technology" per se did not exist in premodern China; the two terms *ji* 技 and *shu* 術 historically appeared separately with some overlap in usage, but rarely together as *jishu*/technology.[13] Early dictionaries glossed *ji* as "ingeniousness and skillfulness of craftsmen," as well as related to arts such as singing and dancing, and *shu* as "the ways or roads in town," with another meaning as "skill, method, procedure" in a range of areas.[14] There is, therefore, an etymological relationship between technics and the performing arts (especially given the predominance of sung drama in indigenous Chinese theater), as well as a strong focus on instances of the making and use of objects in the historical Chinese understanding of technology. The Greek term *technê* and its associated English terms "technics" and "technicity" aptly capture the constellation of concepts associated with these terms. At the same time, as Francesca Bray and others have shown, technical objects in late imperial China were deeply implicated in the construction and standardization of social practices and values.[15] The human element, then, rather than—or in addition to—the mechanical, has historically been central to Chinese conceptions of technics.

The human also figures centrally in dominant understandings of indigenous Chinese theatrical traditions, in both Chinese and foreign discourses. The image of the virtuosic *xiqu* performer on a bare stage, with at most a painted face and a hand prop, has inspired Euro-American theater artists searching for alternatives to spectacle and realism, as well as Chinese artists and intellectuals struggling to assert the uniqueness of their traditions against political hegemonies and cultural imperialisms. Even today, European and North American theater studies tends to value Chinese theater primarily for its classical dramatic texts and "traditional" performance forms, such as the Ming dynasty (1368–1644) *chuanqi* 傳奇 play *The Peony Pavilion* (牡丹亭) or *jingju* 京劇 (Beijing opera). Yet some of the earliest records of Chinese performances, like the shadow puppetry story cited above, root the form in interactions among actors, technical objects, and audiences. Given this, the material trademarks of "traditional" Chinese theater—its props, makeup, and costumes—might be more productively conceived of as theatrical prostheses, rather than exotic ornamentation. As seen in Stiegler's work, the prosthesis—that which is outside the human, but also is a mode of being for the human—is a defining element of technicity, even in its simplest forms.[16] Stage technology therefore may be differently articulated and create unique forms of assemblage in the Chinese context, but it is no less important. And if technicity is indeed fundamental to theater across a range of cultural contexts, then it is essential that our core understanding of the concept be built upon a range of case studies that expand beyond the familiar, Eurocentric theater canon.

To be clear, the intent of this study is not to project Euro-American theories of technology or questions about technology onto Chinese cases. Rather, it explores how a shared characteristic of the theater—its technicity—takes on and creates meaning in a context that is typically excluded from discussions of theater theory. In fact, the topic of this book is doubly marginalized. As Worthen notes, despite the intermedial turn, theater scholarship tends to sidestep deep engagement with the topic of technicity and to focus on "the uses of 'technology' in the theatre—as though those instruments operated within some larger, non-technological framework, as though theatrical performance *used* technologies but remained distinct from them."[17] One might also contend that theater studies scholarship too often divorces material stage equipment from social or political technologies, in the Foucauldian sense. In contrast, Worthen argues instead for study of "the instruments, objects, spaces, construction, and practices of performance as a *'technical system'* (Stiegler, 'Anamnēsis')" and "the ways theatre as an assemblage represents the human at the defining interface with technology."[18] Centering theater's technicity, then, gives equal weight to the materiality of technical objects, human interactions with those objects, and the broader technical systems in which both are implicated. Most important, it creates space for considering technology as culturally and historically contingent, rather than universal.

In agreement with Stiegler and Worthen, this book argues that technology is constitutive of Chinese theater and inseparable from how the theater operates as a whole, but that the precise nature of this imbrication varies over time. The relationship between theater and technology in China becomes especially important at the historical moment when technological *modernization*—of the theater apparatus and in society at large—took on new layers of meaning and new levels of perceived importance in relation to politics, economics, and social change. Technicity in modern Chinese theater therefore is defined by both how material technologies have been used and how theater itself functions as a technical system, intertwined with other technologies of power and characterized by a close relationship between knowledge and practice. It therefore also gestures toward the theater as a Deleuzian machinic assemblage or, as Salter puts it in his study of performances that use technologies, "as an immanent, collective entanglement of material enunciations that operate on, shape, and transform the world in real time."[19] As such a collective, modern Chinese stage technology is deeply invested in the process of transforming the world—and, as this book demonstrates, doing so in a revolutionary way.

## Technology, Modernization, and Theater in China

How and why technicity matters to modern Chinese theater cannot be separated from the broader historical context of the technological modernizations born of the Industrial Revolution and spread around the world by trade, empire, and colonization. Indeed, in late Qing dynasty China, technologies such as steam power, electricity, and the telegraph were seen not only as modern marvels and practical improvements but also as key examples of how the

Industrial Revolution had enabled Europe and the United States to surpass China in the realm of scientific and technological development. Even though this pervasive sense of "backwardness" has long since been challenged and problematized, the technological changes brought by the Industrial Revolution in Europe and late imperial modernization in China nonetheless deeply affected the materiality of the theater and the meaning of technology in the Chinese context. Changes to the apparatus of the theater, such as the introduction of gas and electric light, the proscenium arch, and the revolving stage, were made possible by advances in science and engineering that originated outside of China, and occurred amid controversies over whether and how China should "catch up" to Western nations. The material advances of the late Qing laid important groundwork for the later developments in stage technology discussed throughout this book, while the political connotations attached to modern, Western theater, technology, and technical knowledge would shadow the art form throughout the twentieth century.

Prior to the 1860s, missionaries—first Jesuit during the Ming dynasty (1368–1644) and then Protestant during the late Qing—had been the primary conduits for European and later American scientific and technological knowledge. The defeat of the Qing in the First Opium War (1839–42), however, heightened awareness of differences between Chinese and British military technologies, and galvanized Chinese interest in Western technology and industries. Beginning in the 1860s, the Qing government began to actively pursue Western technology through the purchase of European machinery, the construction of manufacturing plants, and the establishment of new translation bureaus and technical schools teaching subjects like chemistry, physics, and mechanics.[20] As the second half of the nineteenth century unfolded, the political stakes (and complexities) of scientific and technological modernization only increased. The late Qing faced multiple devastating military conflicts—including both domestic rebellions, such as the Taiping Rebellion (1850–64), and clashes with foreign powers—as well as the introduction and local development of military, transportation, industrial, and communication technologies that originated in Europe and the United States.[21] Thus, Western technology and industry became synonymous with modernization and civilizational advancement for some leaders, intellectuals, and artists of the time, while others associated them with predatory foreign political and commercial entities.

The crises of the late Qing contributed to calls for actively reinventing Chinese theater in terms of its content, form, and social function—in effect, to engineer a break with the past that would make it modern. In the latter decades of the nineteenth century, Chinese reformers focused their energies on technological and institutional modernization in the Self-Strengthening Movement (1861–95). However, with another defeat by a foreign power in the First Sino-Japanese War (1894–95) and the failure of the Hundred Days Reform, some prominent intellectuals turned their attention to culture. Perhaps the most famous of these was Liang Qichao 梁啟超 (1873–1929), who, in an influential essay published in 1902, called for the reform of fiction and drama as didactic tools.[22] One case that proved particularly inspiring for reformers like Liang was the role that theater had played in Japan's modernization, as Siyuan Liu has argued in his study of *wenmingxi* 文明戲 (civilized drama), a hybrid genre of Chinese theater that flourished in the first two decades of the twentieth century. Together, the successful reform of Japanese *kabuki* 歌舞伎 and the rise of *shinpa* 新派 (new drama) provided Chinese reformers with powerful precedents for culture as an instrument of national rejuvenation.[23] Liang Qichao's push for reform would be echoed widely in the following decades, as others took up the call for literature and the arts simultaneously to reflect a distinctly Chinese culture and to participate in the formation of modern subjects for a modern nation.

At the same time, the new material technologies and technical knowledge of the late Qing also had a direct effect on the practice and aesthetics of Chinese theater, namely through the introduction of gas and electric lighting, the proscenium theater, and the revolving stage. All three arrived in China as foreign imports; all three represented a significant departure from earlier modes of staging; and all three would continue to be of importance, both technically and politically, well into the twentieth century. The theatrical landscape on which they would leave a mark, however, was already complex, in flux, and technically sophisticated in its own way at the time of their introduction. Late Qing theatrical practice ran the gamut from traveling local and regional *xiqu* theater troupes who performed in towns, villages, and rural areas, often on temple or temporary stages, to urban commercial enterprises, to large-scale palace pageants.[24] As scholars such as Liana Chen, Andrea Goldman, and Colin Mackerras have shown, the nineteenth century was a particularly important period for court patronage of theater, the growth of theater as an urban entertainment industry, and the maturation of genres like *jingju*.[25] From the perspective of theater technicity, imperial patronage provided artists with access to elaborate three-tiered thrust stages, with backstage space and machinery that could be used for special effects, and encouragement to write panegyric plays that made use of these technologies.[26] It also, as Chen details, developed a complex institutional system for theatrical training and production.[27] Teahouse theaters, meanwhile, became the dominant venue for commercial *xiqu* in Beijing and then in Shanghai, where they first opened in 1867.[28] As the name suggests, the teahouse theater sold beverages and snacks alongside *xiqu* performances, with patrons seated at tables arranged around a small thrust stage. These theaters offered their own unique acoustic environments for performance and also would serve as the location for experiments with introducing early film technologies to Chinese audiences.[29]

Indeed, the introduction of modern lighting technologies and the proscenium theater occurred contemporaneously and alongside the rise of the teahouse theater. The Lanxin Theater (蘭心戲院, called the Lyceum Theater in English), for example, was built to house foreign theatricals in Shanghai's foreign concession in 1866, and was both the first proscenium stage in China and the first to be outfitted with gaslight.[30] Gaslight was likely added to the Lanxin in 1874 when it was rebuilt after a fire, and was used in play garden (戲園) performances beginning in 1875.[31] Electric stage lighting then first appeared in Shanghai theaters in 1884, only a few years after the Savoy Theatre in London debuted the technology.[32] In contrast, with the exception of the occasional evening performance or genres such as *dengcaixi* 燈彩戲 (lantern plays), which used artificial illumination for its characteristic brightly colored lanterns, Chinese theater of the nineteenth century was typically performed during the day, and venues were open air or had windows.[33] Both gas and electricity therefore constituted a significant departure from the typical practice of using natural light to illuminate *xiqu* performance, yet it would take until the early twentieth century for electric lighting (and the proscenium theater, for that matter) to become widespread.

The fact that the Lanxin opened only a year before the first teahouse theaters in Shanghai, and that the two types of venue were artificially illuminated within a year of one another, suggests that the teahouse and the proscenium theater may be thought of as equally "modern" forms of Chinese theater architecture. Yet, as Joshua Goldstein has shown, it was the proscenium arch that retained and benefited from a sense of newness well into the first decades of the twentieth century.[34] For example, the New Stage (新舞台), which was located on the Bund (Shanghai's outer-bank waterfront area) and constructed in 1908, proved popular in part due to its innovatively framed, half-moon-shaped thrust stage.[35] From the perspective of stage technology, the novelty of the proscenium theater came from its introduction of elements such as fly systems of battens (long pipes) hanging over the stage, which could be used to suspend curtains, large painted backdrops, and lighting or special effects units. The scenography that could be realized on such stages was far more complex that on a simple outdoor platform or the relatively unadorned teahouse stage. The difference between three-tiered palace stages and proscenium stages, meanwhile, is analogous to the difference between English Elizabethan playhouses or Spanish Golden Age *corrales* and eighteenth- or nineteenth-century European framed stages. The key development was not from the absence to the presence of stage mechanics or decoration, but rather a shift in amount, style, and degree of complexity.

In addition to electric lighting and fly systems, another technology associated with the introduction of Western-style theater architecture was the revolving stage (轉台), or turntable (磨盤). Generally, a revolving stage involves setting a large, circular segment of the stage floor on a pivot, which enables it to turn.[36] In contrast to individual rotating set pieces, which were sometimes used in popular forms like *dengcaixi*, the revolving stage could move entire preset scenes; it could be used both to facilitate set changes and for special effects. According to most historical sources, the aforementioned New Stage was also the site of the first "new-style revolving stage" (新式轉台) in China. It was inspired by the Japanese *kabuki* theater and was constructed in consultation with a Japanese scenic technician.[37] In contrast, the First Stage (第一舞台) in Beijing, which was constructed in 1914, was specifically said to have used a "Western-style revolving stage method" (西洋轉台法).[38] In Europe, revolving set pieces had been used on ancient stages and on occasion from the sixteenth century onward, but the particular technology referenced by Chinese sources was likely the mechanized revolving stage developed at the turn of the twentieth century in Germany, devised by Karl Lautenschläger for the Residenztheater in Munich in 1896.[39] According to early twentieth-century theater historians, the German revolving stage was in fact also inspired by the Japanese; its innovations included increasing the size of the stage, adding modern ball bearings for smoother turning, and operating by electric power.[40] European technologies were then later employed in the renovation and reconstruction of Japanese revolving stages in the early twentieth century.[41] Thus, like the proscenium stage and electric lighting, the revolving stage demonstrates a complex transnational process of technology transfer. Although marked as "new" and "Western" in media commentary, it was in fact simultaneously old and new, as well as a hybrid product of Japanese and European innovations that then would be turned to unique applications in the Chinese context.

One key shift that all of these new technologies brought was the development of more detailed and highly realistic scenery, and along with it, the potential for realism and naturalism in dramaturgy and acting styles. In

Europe, for instance, the introduction of modern lighting technologies to the theater initially had been closely tied to questions of how to illuminate interior spaces, which had posed a significant challenge to architects and scenic designers for centuries. Gas lighting, and later electricity, enabled far brighter illumination than oil lamps or other earlier forms of illumination and eliminated the extreme shadows created by the high angle of the footlights that had been popular during the baroque period. Theaters throughout Europe experimented with gaslight, arc lights, and limelight from the early to mid-1800s, and in 1881 the Savoy Theatre in London became the first public building in the world to be lit throughout by electricity.[42] As Wolfgang Schivelbusch writes, "The new light mercilessly exposed all the old methods of creating illusions."[43] Perspectival painted flats looked less natural once seen in the cold, bright glare of electric top and front light, and were gradually replaced by more three-dimensional sets. Color also looked different depending on the lighting source, and had to be adjusted accordingly.[44] Actors, meanwhile, were no longer forced to play only far downstage, nearest the audience and the lights, and the brightness of electricity made their expressions more visible.

At the same time, new lighting technologies were also bent to more expressive ends and displayed as novelties alongside other new inventions across Europe. There is a conventional narrative within theater history that scientific and technological advance gave rise primarily to naturalism and realism onstage. Yet the novelty of new technologies enticed theater artists to incorporate them within grand spectacles, such as in Appia's designs for Richard Wagner's operas. At times, technology itself *was* the spectacle. Schivelbusch, for instance, relates how both the gas "thermolamp" and the steam engine were exhibited in France and England, respectively, "as something like a circus act."[45] Terence Rees similarly notes how one of the earliest uses of gaslight in the theater was, in fact, a demonstration of a gaslight apparatus on the (London) Lyceum stage in 1803.[46] And as Ulf Otto observes, "the rise of the electrical industry was in its beginnings powered by spectacle," due to the demand for electricity in theaters, malls, and other entertainment venues, and resulted in a close link between theatricality and electricity, as well as between technics and aesthetics.[47] In other words, the spectacular application of new lighting technologies was not a rare or even secondary use, but rather as important as the realist trajectory.

It was this latter, more spectacular application of electric lighting that found a parallel in the technology's early use in Chinese theaters. As *xiqu* historian Jia Zhigang relates, many Chinese theater artists in the late Qing were eager for new lighting systems that would enable them to perform safely at night; at the same time, however, it would be decades before electrified theaters became the norm, even in semicolonial Shanghai.[48] The more immediate effect of new lighting technologies seems to have been in enhancing spectacle in the performance of certain *xiqu* genres and through special effects such as wind, clouds, thunder, lighting, the rising and setting sun, smoke, and fire.[49] A special type of scenic design called "electric lighting sets" (電光佈景) would even become popular in *yueju* 粵劇 (Cantonese opera) performances of the early twentieth century.[50] Likewise, the revolving stage was associated with both smooth scene-to-scene transitions and scenic effects in Japanese *kabuki* and with quick set changes in naturalist and realist European drama.[51] Yet initially the technology was most commonly used as an element of the spectacular mechanical stage sets (機關 佈景) popular in Shanghai-style *jingju* and other *xiqu* forms in the early decades of the twentieth century.[52] Furthermore, although mechanics such as lifts, pulleys, and water-pumping systems had been used in elaborate court pageants performed on three-tiered stages during the Qing dynasty, it was Shanghai-style mechanical stage sets that brought such spectacle to popular audiences.[53] Around the same time, teahouse theaters also began to feature magic lantern slides, "foreign shadowplay" (西洋影戲), and new sound technologies, like the phonograph, in variety show programs alongside live *xiqu*, acrobatics, and magic tricks.[54] Indeed, technology would bind theater and film together throughout the twentieth century via adaptation, attempts to create cinematic effects onstage, and an ongoing contest for the privileged position of most modern medium.

New styles of theater architecture, illumination, mechanics, and audiovisual display thus represent a number of competing (but not necessarily incommensurable) sets of possibilities for the modernization of Chinese theater. On one hand, in newspaper articles from as early as 1907, Western-style theater design and mechanisms were associated with specific theatrical styles and a broader theatrical culture seen to be a model for the modernization of Chinese theater.[55] As Goldstein has shown in the case of *jingju*, both theater architecture and technologies were associated with paradigm shifts in the realms of theatrical production and reception: while *jingju* actors ultimately moved from presentational to representational performance, audiences found themselves disciplined into new colonial-modern modes of spectatorship that demanded quiet attention and polite applause. By the time the "Western-style revolving stage" was installed at the First Stage in Beijing, genres such as realism and naturalism were attracting increasing attention from reform-minded Chinese intellectuals and theater artists. Even *xiqu* performers, such as the renowned *jingju* artist Mei Lanfang 梅蘭芳 (1894–1961), experimented with newly written plays featuring more contemporary (and realistic) settings and costumes. Changes in stage technology were thus entangled with the development of new modes of dramaturgy and performance that emphasized realistic detail. Yet, at the same time, many applications of new technologies were highly spectacular. In some cases, as in *jingju*, a distinction arose between the *jingpai* 京派 (Beijing school), which upheld a traditionalist approach, and the *haipai* 海派 (Shanghai school), which embraced new technologies and sensational special effects.[56] In other cases, there seemed to be a finer line between the titillation of a realistic contemporary costume and a pyrotechnic effect, and thus far less of a conflict between aesthetic modes.

## Revolution and Stagecraft

Contestation among different visions of "modern" Chinese theater continued beyond the end of the Qing dynasty in 1912, as did tensions over the practical uses and political implications of Western technologies (both theatrical and otherwise). Indeed, the stakes of technological development and of theater's role in shaping politics and society only increased as China moved into the period that historian of China Joseph Esherick has called the "century of revolution."[57] From the 1911–12 Xinhai Revolution (辛亥革命) that ended Qing dynastic rule to numerous highly political theatrical movements, to victory by the Chinese Communist Party (CCP) in 1949 and the later Cultural Revolution (1966–76), China's twentieth century would come to be defined by a succession of ideological, cultural, and epistemological paradigm shifts. Political revolution, however, did not forestall investment in technological advancement; if anything, politics and technology became even more closely connected after the founding of the People's Republic of China (PRC) in 1949. Mao Zedong 毛泽东 (1893–1976) began promoting a "technological revolution" (技术革命) as early as 1953, and both Mao and Zhou Enlai 周恩来 (1898–1976) spoke of technological and cultural revolution as closely linked.[58] To be accused of "counterrevolution" (*fan geming* 反革命), in contrast, became one of the greatest ideological crimes, and the moniker of "counterrevolutionary" was deployed across numerous political campaigns and party purges throughout the high socialist period.[59] The dominance of revolution as both an ideological concept and a guiding principle for policy making would then culminate in the Cultural Revolution. The epitome of Mao's calls for a "continuous revolution," the Cultural Revolution would demonstrate both the paradigm-destroying potential of political revolution and the dangerous cyclicality of endlessly revolving violence.

The "century of revolution" had a number of effects on the theater. On one level, periods of military conflict and political turmoil affected the material resources available to the theater. From the late Qing onward, Chinese theater artists remained interested in technologies like electric lighting, the fly systems of the proscenium theater, and the revolving stage. The availability of foreign imports, however, fluctuated depending on the status of geopolitical and commercial ties; for example, as is discussed in chapters 1 and 2, Shanghai saw a boom in the construction of well-equipped theaters during the 1920s–1930s, whereas artists in hinterland cities during the late 1930s–1940s faced material shortages due to the progression of the Second Sino-Japanese War (1937–45, also called the War of Resistance against Japan [抗日戰爭]). Similarly, after the founding of the PRC in 1949, the government prioritized the building of theaters so much that the government's First Five-Year Plan set a target of constructing 2,078 new venues by the end of 1957.[60] At the same time, however, the source of foreign technologies and knowledge transfer shifted to the Soviet Union and countries of the Soviet Bloc. When the Capital Theater (首都剧场) was built in 1954, its lighting equipment was imported from East Germany, and delegations of Soviet theater artists visited Beijing that same year to perform and deliver lectures (including on the topics of stage design and technology) for their Chinese peers. Western European and US technologies and technical knowledge, in contrast, became less available and more ideologically suspect.

One lasting impact of the fluctuating access to material resources and cross-cultural knowledge transfer was the development of a localized, *tu* 土 (homegrown, indigenous, or grassroots) ethos among Chinese theater designers and technicians. Indeed, as is demonstrated throughout this book, one of the things that distinguishes and defines modern Chinese stage technology is its homegrown, grassroots ethos; here, professionalism and slick, high-tech innovation are not necessarily privileged. Instead, as early as the 1930s, technical publications reveal a number of low-tech yet ingenious responses to the practical problems of the theater. Lightning, for example, might be created by cutting a zigzag shape out of a piece of plywood and positioning a lighting source behind it. During the PRC period, this theatrical ingenuity was then reframed with discourses of self-reliance and socialist independence from the capitalist West, with strong parallels in calls for localized progress in technical and scientific fields. One of the results of this localizing ethos, illustrated throughout this book, was a closer equivalence of artistry and craft, and of form and content: *how* theater was made became as important as, and integrally connected to, *what* was represented onstage. Stagecraft also became equally the purview of the expert artist and the amateur, with both contributing to knowledge production in the areas of playwriting, acting, directing, design, set construction, and even the engineering of lighting instruments.

Political revolution also affected the theater in terms of its social and ideological mission, which in turn intersected with content and form. The popularity of the hybrid, often spectacular *wenmingxi* declined in the 1920s, just as Chinese intellectuals and (some) theater artists were beginning to see other genres as more socially engaged and politically efficacious. Meanwhile, the genre of the "social problem play" (社會問題劇), modeled on the work of Henrik Ibsen, Bernard Shaw, and other European and American writers, became influential for the New Culture and the May Fourth Movements of the 1910s–1920s.[61] For intellectuals and theater artists alike, a wide range of European and American dramatic styles—from Shakespeare to Wagnerian opera to expressionism—influenced experimentation in writing and producing the genre that would become known as *huaju*, but realism in various modes ultimately emerged as the style seemingly best suited to representing and promoting social reform.[62] Meanwhile, the commercial ethos of urban theater persisted, while local *xiqu* forms also became seen as important tools for reaching broader audiences. During the Second Sino-Japanese War and beyond, theater functioned as a key mode of disseminating political messages and propaganda. The founding of the PRC and direct state involvement in the performing arts only accentuated the impetus for theater to become ideologically correct in both content and form, even as on-the-ground practice remained heterogenous and even heterodox.

Beyond these material, formal, and ideological realms, theater and technology also functioned separately and together as powerful political metaphors throughout the twentieth century. For instance, Mao's 1940 treatise "On New Democracy" (新民主主義論) opened by claiming that it had "the same purpose as the beating of the gongs before a theatrical performance," while devoting its final section to discussing the "national, scientific, and mass" (民族, 科學, 大眾) characteristics of ideologically correct culture.[63] This simultaneously framed the (printed) political treatise as an act of performance and connected the theater to Marxist ideas of the scientific. Mao also famously evoked Vladimir Lenin's description of literature as "a cog and a screw"[64] in the revolutionary mechanism in his 1942 "Talks at the Yan'an Forum on Literature and the Arts" (在延安文藝座談會上的講話):

Proletarian literature and art are a part of the whole proletarian revo-lutionary cause; as Lenin said, they are "a [cog and] screw in the whole machine," and therefore, the party's work in literature and art occupies a definite, assigned position within the party's revolutionary work as a whole. . . . Literature and art are subordinate to politics, and yet in turn exert enormous influence on it. Revolutionary literature and art are a part of the whole work of revolution; they are a [cog and] screw, which of course doesn't compare with other parts in importance, urgency, or priority, but which is nevertheless indispensable in the whole machin-ery, an indispensable part of revolutionary work as a whole.[65]

The Yan'an Talks crystallized Mao's theory of how art relates to politics and influenced the work of Chinese theater artists for decades to come. In partic-ular, his extended mechanical metaphor enabled the positioning of literature and art as simultaneously fixed in their relationship to political revolution and as subordinate but essential to other aspects of the revolution (not unlike a revolving stage, ambulatory but pegged to a pivot point below the feet of the actors).[66] The question of how to support the revolution became one that compelled theater artists, including designers and technicians, throughout the early PRC period, as is detailed in chapter 3. And as stagecraft became increasingly enmeshed with the resources and authority of statecraft, the stakes of how theater was made rose even higher.

At the same time, however, the idea that the relationship between theater and ideology was one of fixity created great tension for Chinese theater art-ists. On one hand, the theater-as-(political)-machine held the promise that, if done *just so*, a performance could convey a precise ideological message and create a specific response in its audiences. Under this rubric, stage technol-ogy, in its use of actual (not metaphorical) mechanisms and devices, therefore seemed especially predisposed to application as a tool of politics. A bright red wash flooding the stage surely could not but inspire a wave of revolutionary sentiment in the audience. Yet the liveness of theater also rendered a perfor-mance impossible to control completely, and technology is prone to failure and glitches. As the ensuing chapters show, one of the recurring conflicts in modern Chinese theater has been between the fantasy of control in the theory behind stage technology and the reality of contingency inherent in its practical application. In multiple senses then—paradigm shifts, cyclicality, and even the literal turning of the stage—technology would prove revolu-tionary throughout the twentieth century.

## Technics as Method

Approaching modern Chinese theater from the perspective of its stage technologies raises a number of methodological questions. Some of these are familiar to theater historians, whereas others will resonate with scholars and students focused on the Chinese context. All center on the tension between presence and absence engendered by foregrounding the materiality of historical technologies and human interactions with those technologies. Live theatrical performance is governed by immediacy and ephemerality; the textual and archival sources that persist beyond the moment of performance offer at best incomplete fragments of the actual event. Playwrights, directors, designers, actors, and technicians may be interviewed, if still living, but memory is notoriously subjective, selective, or even unreliable, and the work of technicians has rarely been deemed worthy of oral record.[67] This occurs despite the fact that design work typically involves more paperwork, in the form of blueprints, stage layouts, and equipment diagrams, than does the rehearsal process.[68] Meanwhile, modern Chinese history has been marked by a series of revolutions, which have entailed material destruction in moments of change and the selective preservation of sources afterward. Vast numbers of theater scripts, documents, spaces, and equipment no longer exist, and others have been erased from or diminished in the historical record for political reasons. Oral histories collected under repressive regimes must contend with censorship and self-censorship, as well as the vagaries of memory. How, then, to reconstruct specific historical productions in a way that facilitates understanding of stage technology and highlights human agency?

This study proposes that the answer lies in considering technics *as* method, focusing on actual stage technologies as its objects of engagement and exploring them in the context of a study on modern Chinese theater history. This approach entails situating objects equally in relation to their technical potential, their human use, and to the social, political, economic, and cultural forces that influence both. On one hand, each technical object holds a certain technical potential; its physical and mechanical properties create a range of possible uses for the object. A lighting unit, for instance, can shine only as brightly as the type of light bulb and strength of electrical current allow. Yet, at the same time, it does not have to shine at full brightness at all times. It can be dimmed. The color can be altered with the addition of gels. Its beam of light can be broken into patterns by placing a cut-out piece of material (a gobo, in today's technical terms) in front of its bulb. Its physical and mechanical properties therefore delimit but do not determine its precise use in the context of a given theatrical production. By proceeding from the technical object, then, technics as method raises and centers questions about design, construction, and use, as well as the transmission of knowledge in all of these areas. In addition, as Lewis Mumford writes in *Technics and Civilization:* "The world of technics is not isolated and self-contained: it reacts to forces and impulses that come from apparently remote parts of the environment."[69] Just as technical objects are not transparent, they are not created or used in a vacuum. To take technics as method is therefore to resist the impulse to see technology as something neutral or universal and instead to insist upon examining technical objects in situ. In this way, we shift our understanding of the technical object from that of the mere tool to that of a material conduit that, through use, embeds human agents in the broader reconfiguration of the relationship among technology, theater, and politics.

Finally, technics as method employs a mode of reading technically that departs from the prevailing tendency to approach theater semiotically—an approach that persists even as structuralism has long since been complicated by a myriad of other methodologies. Indeed, the very fact that stage technology typically remains offstage and largely out of sight renders it decidedly *un*semiotic. Even when stage technology is present onstage, it does not necessarily make meaning in the manner understood by semiotics. Reading technically therefore first approaches scripts (and especially their stage directions) from the perspective of how the text creates a set of technical challenges for production that then must be solved in a given performance. Performances are analyzed in light of how the extant stage technologies actually were used to create desired effects onstage, based on written documents and audiovisual recordings. The solution that a given scenographer or effects designer develops for a given production can fall anywhere on a spectrum of naturalistic to abstract, concrete to evocative, technically simple to technically complex. Reading a performance technically therefore requires attention to how a particular creative team has addressed the technical challenges posed by the script for a given production. How do the designers and technicians interpret the stage directions and the playwright's vision? What specific devices and techniques do they use to create the desired effects onstage? Why were these decisions made and how did they contribute to the meaning making of the play and production?

Crucially, reading technically also requires expanding beyond the script and the performance to include contemporaneous technical manuals, treatises, handbooks, and even scientific and technical materials and histories. Many of these documents themselves function as a kind of technology, with illustrations, texts, and paratexts working together to illustrate how to build and operate specific stage technologies. These sources can reveal connections between performance and technical documentation that enable the latter to shed light on the former. For example, when a lighting designer publishes an article on how to build a rudimentary dimmer in the same month that he designs a production that reportedly uses homemade dimmers, we can safely assume that the devices are similar, if not one and the same. The technical details absent from the archive suddenly become present.

To these ends, this study draws on a range of sources, including published material, theater archives, and interviews with dozens of theater practitioners and scholars. The plays and performances analyzed in each chapter were chosen not because of canonicity or popularity, but rather because their scripts pose significant, concrete technical challenges and their technicity is foregrounded in the historical record. I conducted fieldwork in Beijing, Shanghai, and Taipei at institutions such as the Beijing People's Art Theater (北京人民艺术剧院, aka BPAT), Shanghai Dramatic Arts Center (上海话剧艺术中心, formerly the Shanghai People's Art Theater 上海人民艺术剧院 and Shanghai Youth Huaju Theater 上海青年话剧团), National Theater of China (中国国家话剧院, formed in 2001 by the merger of the China Youth Art Theater 中国青年艺术剧院 and the Central Experimental Theater 中央实验话剧团), the Shanghai Theatre Academy (上海戏剧学院, aka STA), and the Shanghai Municipal Archive. I also extensively searched Chinese, Taiwanese, North American, and British library systems for forgotten books and periodicals. To my surprise, these libraries hold a trove of technical treatises, manuals, and other published texts about technical theater, many of which have only rarely been checked out or are available only in "archival copies" (保存本) in mainland Chinese libraries. In addition, this project was conducted during a period of rapid digitization of resources from the Republican era and early PRC. Online databases such as the Shanghai Library's National Index, Dacheng, Chinamaxx, Duxiu, digitized *Shenbao*, and Wanfang Data's Local Gazetteers collection made a large number of rare and local materials available. I relied heavily on these databases to gather specific texts and also to make more general observations about the types of material published during the periods covered by this study.

By taking technics as method, this book turns the decolonizing work of Chen Kuan-Hsing in *Asia as Method* and others toward theater studies methodologies, by questioning prevailing assumptions about how and why specific tools, devices, and instruments are used onstage.[70] The tendency to equate Chinese theater with the premodern perpetuates a hierarchy in which Western cultures figure always as more advanced; foregrounding the fraught processes of Chinese theater's technological modernization, in contrast, complicates the teleological assumptions and power imbalances undergirding that dominant framework. On a more concrete level, this study also extends and expands upon how existing English-language scholarship on modern Chinese theater has approached stage technology. In general, the importance of the stage apparatus is commonly acknowledged but rarely analyzed in any depth. In contrast, Chinese-language scholarship on modern theater often suffers from an *over*emphasis on technical detail, relayed in an encyclopedic manner at the expense of more theoretical interventions. Exceptions to this rule, and inspiration for this study, can be found in the recent work by scholars such as Xiaomei Chen, Xing Fan, Joshua Goldstein, and Siyuan Liu (in English) and Ma Junshan (in Chinese).[71] In particular, Goldstein's approach to *jingju* as "an object of a certain kind of knowledge production, enmeshed in the context of colonial modernity," as well as his attention to the ways institutions, spaces, and art forms themselves can and did function as modernizing technologies, has informed much of my analysis.[72] Similarly attuned to colonial modernity, Liu's study of *wenmingxi* as a thoroughly hybrid form provides a model for the integrated discussion of text, performance, and context, with close attention to the technical details of theatrical productions even when they are not the focus per se.

Beyond theater scholarship, the value of attention to technical details has also been well demonstrated by recent scholarship on Chinese film and media, music and sound, and visual culture. In particular, the work of scholars like Weihong Bao, Andrew Jones, Laikwan Pang, and Zhang Zhen demonstrates the intricate relationships among the technologies of cultural production, audience reception and engagement, and broader sociopolitical shifts.[73] Each of these studies is rooted in a close reading of the unique ways in which individual technologies like photographic and film cameras or gramophones connect to the social and economic apparatuses of popular culture, mass marketing, and commerce. These technologies then, in turn, play their parts in the creation of new scopic regimes or soundscapes and various subject formations—revolutionaries, citizens, consumers. The theatrical case studies in this book shed light on the fact that what is true for mechanically reproducible technologies is equally significant to arts of a more ephemeral and immediate nature: materiality matters.

## Chapter Overview

Ultimately, the narrative of this book is neither one of technological progress nor one of technological determinism. Instead, it is about an ongoing negotiation among technological potential, historical exigency, and human agency. In keeping with this book's attention to the connections among the theatrical, the technological, and the political, the chapters are loosely demarcated by dates and major events that structure canonical narratives of modern Chinese history. However, the danger of implying a teleology is equal to that of reifying technology as a motive agent, as described by Leo Marx.[74] Thus, although these dates (and associated technologies) provide convenient cornerstones, the content of the chapters demonstrates more continuities across historical moments than radical breaks.

Chapter 1 takes us to 1920s Shanghai, a time and place of significant technological, aesthetic, and political change for the Chinese theater and a formative moment for the genre of *huaju*. As detailed above, Shanghai had already been the site of China's first proscenium theaters and "new-style" revolving stages, as well as an early adopter of technologies like electricity, trams and trolleys, and sanitation systems. How did fast-paced changes to theater's infrastructure—construction of new theaters, equipped with modern stage technologies—in the 1920s and 1930s relate to shifts in performance practice? What was considered essential knowledge for the theater maker, amateur or professional? New journals, treatises, handbooks, and essays in the popular press introduced specific technologies, like theatrical lighting units, and techniques, like how to position a lighting unit, as essential components of a *modern* theater. Meanwhile, the translation of nineteenth-century realist plays and more stridently political works from the early twentieth century, along with new plays written by novice Chinese playwrights, provided opportunities for aspiring artists to put theory (and technology) into practice. One such play, Russian playwright and poet Sergei Tret'iakov's *Roar, China!*, proved famous for its anti-imperialist depiction of Chinese laborers rising up against foreign oppression, and infamous for how difficult the play's technical details made its actual staging. Analysis of a 1933 production of *Roar, China!* by the Shanghai Theater Society (上海戲劇協社) demonstrates how Chinese theater artists successfully mobilized scenography, lighting, and human labor in order to transform the theater into a technology of political revolution.

Chapter 2 then turns from the stage to the page, to explore how the circulation of technical theater knowledge and the maturation of *huaju* production influenced playwriting within that genre. Although foreign scripts continued to be performed, an increasing number of Chinese playwrights penned longer and more sophisticated *huaju* plays in the mid-1930s to early 1940s—a period that has been termed the first "Golden Age" (黃金時代) of *huaju*, but that also coincided with the escalation of the Second Sino-Japanese War and the turn of many theater artists to nationalistic propaganda. How did these playwrights negotiate the competing exigencies of professional performance and wartime conditions? How was playwriting envisioned in relation to technical areas of the theater, and how do scripts written during this period reflect playwrights' growing awareness of the technical capacities of the modern stage? This chapter reads stage directions alongside technical theater manuals to demonstrate how Chinese playwrights scripted plays in a manner that relied on specific stage technologies to propel dramatic action and create atmosphere. At the same time, as the war wore on, their scripts and production practices increasingly valued adaptability over precise execution, flexibility over standardization, thereby also demonstrating how the *lack* of technical capacity can equally influence playwriting and production practices. Applying the idea of "reading technically" to *huaju* scripts such as *Thunderstorm* (1934) by Cao Yu, *Under Shanghai Eaves* (上海屋簷下, 1937) by Xia Yan 夏衍(1900–1995), and *Foggy Chongqing* (霧重慶, 1940) by Song Zhidi 宋之的 (1914–56), this chapter sheds new light on how the material world of the theater relates to text and asks us to reimagine fundamentally how we read and understand dramatic literature.

In contrast to wartime chaos, chapter 3 examines what happened when both theater and technology became key elements of nation-building efforts and a new socialist state ideology during the Seventeen Years period of the PRC (1949–66). Initially, the PRC was the recipient of large-scale technology transfer from the Soviet Union in the form of expertise, equipment, and an ethos that privileged military, industrial, and agricultural technologies. By the Great Leap Forward (1958–62), however, a growing rift with the USSR and internal politics shifted the prevailing ideology toward self-reliance and homegrown technologies—in some cases, to disastrous effect. How did the ideological emphasis on Chinese (and socialist) approaches to technology and Mao's call for a "technological revolution" impact the development of *stage* technology? And how did the theater negotiate the tensions between problematic class background and ideological imperatives, between political conviction and expertise that characterized this period? This chapter looks at the popularization of technical theater knowledge via amateur handbooks alongside technological ingenuity in three professional productions: *Fantasia of the Ming Tombs Reservoir* (十三陵水库畅想曲, 1958) by Tian Han 田汉 (1898–1968), *Sentinels under the Neon Lights* (霓虹灯下的哨兵, 1963) by Shen Ximeng 沈西蒙 (1918–2006) and others, and the song-and-dance epic *The East Is Red* (东方红, 1964). Each production confronts a specific technical issue—a revolving stage, neon lighting, backdrop projection—that proved both essential to the play's message and difficult to execute. Production teams' homegrown (and at times even amateurish) responses to these challenges demonstrate how even the most technical elements of the theater were engaged in negotiating between ideology and artistry during this period.

Chapter 4 then explores what happens when the technical expression of ideology is taken to an extreme and codified in the *geming yangbanxi* 革命样板戏 (revolutionary model operas) of the Cultural Revolution. Often dismissed as mere propaganda, the *yangbanxi* were also unprecedented in their sophisticated scenography and the stage technology required to realize lighting, scenic, and properties design onstage. How did the narrowing of the cultural landscape and concentration of resources in this group of productions affect theatrical design and execution? What can a technical reading of the *yangbanxi* contribute to our understanding of a genre that is often seen as hegemonic and transparently propagandistic? Whereas a problem-solving, engineerlike mindset characterizes the approaches to stagecraft discussed in the preceding chapter, analysis of the *yangbanxi* demonstrates the privileging of technical detail shifting into the fetishization of technical perfection. Design decisions and their technical implementation made by specific theater troupes, for specific well-equipped spaces in urban areas, became codified into dramatic texts by way of published promptbooks. These efforts at extreme standardization, however, met an unintended form of resistance found in official movements to promulgate the *yangbanxi* in provincial cities and rural areas. Largely unable to reproduce the productions precisely, theater artists and amateur performers once again turned to grassroots ingenuity and reframed their efforts to produce sophisticated *yangbanxi* productions as narratives of revolutionary struggle. Focusing primarily on *The Red Lantern* (红灯记, 1970 production), this chapter explores how both the fantasy and the fallacy of technical control shaped the use of stage technology during the Cultural Revolution.

The final chapter expands from a focus on stage technologies per se to plays that feature science and technology as content from the post-Mao era. The 1978 revival of the "Four Modernizations" by Deng Xiaoping 邓小平 (1904–97) was a watershed moment for the reinvigoration of science and technology during China's Reform Era. How did this new ideological focus affect the theater? How did theater serve as an interface between representations of scientific research and its technological applications? During this period, a new technoscientific ethos for theater propelled interest in plays *about* science, as well as research and development in fields such as computerized lighting equipment, stage mechanics, and even so-called cybernetic acting. Well-established *huaju* director Huang Zuolin 黄佐临 (1906–94) even went so far as to argue for a direct equivalence between theater artists and scientists. Paradoxically, however, these shifts propelled a move *away* from more ostentatious uses of stage technology in performance. Through close readings of both the script and the staging of *Life of Galileo* by Bertolt Brecht, produced by the China Youth Art Theater in 1979, and *Atoms and Love* (原子与爱情) by Li Weixin 李维新 and others, produced by the General Political Department Huaju Troupe (总政话剧团) of the People's Liberation Army (PLA) in 1980, this chapter demonstrates how science and technology came together both onstage and off in a new era.

By thinking through technicity in each of these case studies, this book offers its readers a new perspective on modern Chinese theater. It emphasizes the importance of technics within theater's ability to make meaning in performance and transform the world beyond the stage. Overall, it makes an argument for the importance of considering those elements of the theater whose physical and temporal location behind the scenes too often relegates them to a subordinate position in relation to acting, directing, and playwriting. Instead, guided by stage technology, this book reveals the complex and at times surprising ways in which Chinese theater artists and technicians of the twentieth century envisioned and enacted their own revolutions through the materiality of the theater apparatus.

# ONE

# Mobilizing Illumination

## *Lighting, Scenography, and Affective Arousal in Early* Huaju

———————◆◆◆◆◆———————

The first act of *Roar, China!* (怒吼吧, 中國! or Рычи, Китай!), by Sergei Tret'iakov (1892–1937), ends in utter chaos: rioting Chinese dockworkers scuffle with the police, while their foreman makes a hasty exit and foreign tourists wander obliviously through the fray. The cause of the conflict came earlier in the act when Hawley, an American leather merchant, attempted to lower the wages of his Chinese workers and then to fire them for protesting. For patrons of performances that took place at the Hung King Theater (黃金大戲院) in Shanghai in September 1933, no curtain fell between scenes to stop the madness.[1] Instead, the lights only dimmed. Then, an army of stage-hands sprang into action, exacerbating the chaos by transforming several large set pieces—a wharf railing, gangplank, and nearly life-sized merchant ship—into the upper deck of a British gunboat, complete with protruding bridge and artillery (see figs. 1.1, 1.2). Even the lighting units had to be moved in full, if darkened, view of the audience, in order to be positioned to illuminate the next scenes. When the lights came up after only a few minutes, the audience found itself transported to a new and highly realistic setting. The crew had accomplished the first successfully executed scenic blackout quick change in the history of Chinese theater.

Historic firsts and points of origins must necessarily be treated with a healthy dose of skepticism. However, the idea that there previously had been few attempts at blackout quick changes seems credible, given that *huaju* with realistic sets, like *Roar, China!*, were still relatively novel in the early 1930s. In contrast, most Chinese genres of *xiqu* were traditionally performed without

Fig. 1.1. Wharf and merchant ship in act 1 of *Roar, China!* Production
photograph from Shanghai Theater Society performances in September
1933. Source: *Nuhou ba, Zhongguo!* (Shanghai: Liangyou tuhua yinshua
gongsi, 1935).

Fig. 1.2. Gunboat in act 2 of *Roar, China!* Shanghai Theater Society performances in
September 1933. Source: *Nuhou ba, Zhongguo!* (Shanghai: Liangyou tuhua yinshua
gongsi, 1935).

elaborate scene changes. The genre that would become known as *huaju* did not develop until the first decade of the twentieth century, beginning with the hybrid form of *wenmingxi* performed by Chinese students in Japan. These plays, some of which were based on European and US dramatic adaptations of novels such as *La Dame aux Camélias* (*The Lady of the Camellias*) and *Uncle Tom's Cabin*, soon made their way back to China. There, they fostered both the concept of nonmusical theater, in general, and the use of realistic scenery, lighting, and props on the Chinese stage. Early efforts in this vein attracted attention for their novelty, but remained rudimentary even as Chinese theater artists began to attempt more ambitious stagings of foreign plays and to write their own *huaju* in the 1920s. Meanwhile, many *wenmingxi* plays focused on topics such as national identity and oppression, giving the genre a political bent from the outset. With the publication of essays on Henrik Ibsen and translations of his plays in the prominent journal *New Youth* (新青年) in 1918, artistically inclined intellectuals also began to take an interest in the new genre. This further cemented links among *huaju*, realism, and the use of theater for sociopolitical reform.

*Roar, China!* and its purported "first" therefore sit at the nexus of two significant trends in the development of modern Chinese theater: one technical and one political. On the technical side, proud references to the first blackout quick change alongside discussion of *Roar, China!* in Chinese theater historiography speak to the importance of the technical achievements of this particular production. The timing of its performances also roughly coincided with another marker of the significance of theater technology: a sharp increase in both specialist and popular publications focusing on the mechanics of scenery, stage lighting, and special effects, which began in the late 1920s. The written pieces that the theater artists behind *Roar, China!*, such as director Ying Yunwei 應雲微 (1904–67) and members of the Shanghai Theater Society (上海戲劇協社), published about the production included set designs, lighting diagrams, and detailed descriptions of the production process, and therefore demonstrate that they were closely attuned to this technological trend. The journal in which these technical articles were published, *Play* (戲), was even edited by Yuan Muzhi 袁牧之 (1909–78), one of the lead actors in the production, and distributed to audience members at performances.

From a political angle, the work of the laboring stagehands required to mobilize the scenographic apparatus for the 1933 Shanghai production also mirrored the power of the masses displayed within the world of the play and thereby supported its strong anti-imperialist message. Organized in nine "chains," as the scenes were metaphorically termed by their author, the play shares its title with a futurist poem that Tret'iakov penned in 1924 and was inspired by his experiences living in China during 1920–21 and 1924–25.[2] Both poem and play chronicle the exploitation of Chinese labor by foreign capitalism and military power, but the play is more clearly tied to a specific historic incident that took place in 1924 in Wanxian, a town on the Yangtze River.[3] In the play, soon after the initial conflict described above, Hawley pays a visit to the captain of a British gunboat, the *Cockchafer*; on his way back to shore, Hawley falls overboard and drowns in an altercation with the boatman ferrying him.[4] Even though Hawley caused the accident by refusing to pay the man his due, the captain of the *Cockchafer* demands either the confession of the boatman or the execution of two other (innocent) Chinese. The captain refuses repeated appeals for mercy, threatening military action against the village if they do not comply. Two Chinese men are ultimately executed in front of a crowd of onlookers. The play ends with the irate crowd moved by these senseless deaths—and some choice words by a political agitator conveniently on the scene—to rise up and "roar" against the injustices perpetrated by their foreign oppressors.

This chapter explores the inextricable connections among the theatrical, the technical, and the political suggested by the 1933 Shanghai production of *Roar, China!* It begins by reconsidering the formative years of Chinese *huaju* from the perspective of theater construction, stage technology, and the discourse surrounding lighting and scenography. Theater texts published in the 1920s–1930s discuss not only practical applications of new, modern stage equipment but also how lighting, sound, and scenery could be deployed to accentuate revolutionary political messages and mobilize audiences. These texts, some translated and some penned by Chinese theater artists, demonstrate a prevailing desire to connect the technical elements of the theater with its political efficacy. Indeed, as this chapter shows, analysis of technical publications and how they relate to performance practice and dramatic literature reveals how theater technology—especially scenography and lighting—became a major component in theater's ability to arouse audiences affectively. What this suggests is a close alignment of theater technology per se and theater as a technology of revolution at a crucial moment in the development of modern Chinese drama. *Roar, China!* then provides a case study for examining how Chinese theater artists choreographed technical elements like scenography and lighting in a way that aligned with the political message(s) of a dramatic text. The theater artists involved with the production of *Roar, China!*, however, did not isolate their efforts behind the fourth wall. Instead, by providing audience members with printed, technical information via the journal *Play*, they also worked to render a highly technical critique legible to spectators. This in turn suggested the importance of specialized (modern) knowledge and contributed to a broader trend of educating audiences about stage technology.

## Modern Technology for a Modern Theater

In the first decades of the twentieth century, Chinese theater flourished against a backdrop of dynastic change, fast-paced modernization, and international conflict. Although the Xinhai Revolution of 1911 had led to the founding of a new Republic of China in 1912, the new government struggled to establish itself. President Yuan Shikai 袁世凱 (1859–1916) ruled from 1912 until his death in 1916, after which supporters of the Qing dynasty attempted (briefly and unsuccessfully) to reinstate imperial rule. Competing warlord factions controlled most of the territory in China until the Nationalist Party (Guomindang 國民黨 [GMD], also known in English as the Kuomintang [KMT]) established a stronger central government in 1928. Meanwhile, the territories and treaty ports that had been ceded during the Opium Wars of the preceding century remained largely under foreign control. This facilitated the continued foreign dominance of international trade routes and extraction of Chinese resources, which led to growing disquiet with the presence of foreign imperialism on Chinese soil. China sided with the Allied forces in World War I, but anger at the international community erupted when the Treaty of Versailles of 1919 ceded the German-held Shandong Peninsula to the Japanese Empire, not China. Student-led protests on May 4, 1919, then inaugurated the May Fourth Movement, a push for social, political, and cultural reforms that defined the next decade.[5]

Meanwhile, in the theater world, urbanization and the construction of new spaces equipped with "modern" stage technology propelled an explosion of new genres, forms, and styles of performance. Although new theaters and new forms sprang up in all major cities, it was the Shanghai metropolis that saw the largest boom in new theater construction and that also came to epitomize China's modernization.[6] The city's location near the mouth of the Yangtze River, China's largest and most important waterway, had propelled Shanghai to importance as a domestic and international commercial hub in the nineteenth century. Economic development led to exponential growth and urbanization, as well as the selection of Shanghai as the location for new state institutions devoted to technological development, like the Jiangnan Arsenal ironworks and shipyard. However, large swaths of the city had also been ceded to the British Empire, United States, France, and other powers as foreign concessions, with privileges such as extraterritoriality and consular jurisdiction. The incursion of foreign interests and political power into this city mirrored the state of the country as a whole. Meanwhile, however, investment from foreign companies, the availability of foreign products, and proximity to foreign culture all helped to vault Shanghai to fame as the "Paris of the Orient."[7] The city became emblematic of a new modern, urban lifestyle and served as a hub of literature, art, fashion, and entertainment.

The construction of a large number of new theater spaces designed with commercial interests in mind helped to cement the association between these venues and urban, bourgeois entertainments. By the time of the May Fourth protests in 1919, for instance, more than seventy "new-style" (新形式) proscenium theaters had been built in Shanghai, and dozens more—including some of the city's most iconic venues—would be constructed in the following decades.[8] The Carleton Theater (卡爾登劇院, later renamed the Yangtze Theater [長江劇場]), for example, was built in 1922–23 and became an important venue for *huaju* productions.[9] The rise of the film industry and need for film screening spaces also led to the construction of auditoriums that could double as theaters and cinemas. Meanwhile, entertainment complexes like the Great World (大世界) situated theater spaces and their performances in the context of a plethora of other leisure activities.[10]

A key element of what made such theaters "new" was being equipped with new-to-China stage technologies, such as the overstage battens, electric lighting, and revolving turntables discussed in the introduction. Chinese theater artists of all styles and forms eagerly experimented with these novel technologies, but, by the 1920s, different approaches to scenography, lighting, sound, and special effects also were becoming a means of distinguishing *among* genres. Specifically, the use of stage technology in conversation with Euro-American theater conventions and in a more realistic mode became a means of marking the nascent form of *huaju* as more "modern" and "scientific" than either indigenous *xiqu* forms or the hybridized *wenmingxi*. One key factor in the growing association of *huaju* with modern stage technology was the amateur theater movement helmed by theater artist and educator Chen Dabei, whose influential text on the topic, *Amateur Theater* (愛美的戲劇), was first published as a series of essays in 1921.[11] As is commonly acknowledged in related scholarship, Chen's choice of the term *aimei* 愛美 (lit. "for the love of beauty") for his title captured both the sound of the word "amateur" in English and the anticommercial ethos of his movement.[12] He defines the amateur as one who "loves art and doesn't do it for the purpose of earning a living" and "independently researches an art form."[13] Chen was inspired by amateur theater movements in the United States, Europe, and Japan, with his *Amateur Theater* citing sources by Sheldon Cheney, Emerson Gifford Taylor, and William Lyon Phelps.[14]

Chen's book, however, is far more than a treatise on theater as pure art; it includes theater history, theory, and practical guidelines for script selection, troupe management, rehearsal and production process, acting, makeup, and scenography. In an evolutionary mode, Chen also sees developments in playwriting and acting styles as intimately connected with architectural and technological shifts. For example, he argues that both the realist script and advances in lighting technology contributed to the rise of the proscenium stage in European theater. The dramatic style of realism necessitated a strict division between the world of the audience and the world onstage, while gas and then electric lamps made it possible for audiences to see actors positioned upstage of a picture-frame arch. As Chen writes, "All manner of advancements in theater art are related to science."[15] A specific connection to technological modernization is even emphasized by demarcating the opening sections of the book with text-free pages featuring sketches of modern modes of transportation, such as a dirigible, a speeding train, and a car. The implied teleology is clear from both content and print form: scientific progress on a Western model enabled technological modernization, which in turn transformed and elevated theater as an art form.

*Amateur Theater* was also one of the first Chinese texts to introduce modern, Western theater architecture, scenic design and construction, and stage lighting in a systematic way—an impulse that would become an important trend in the following decades. In doing so, it advocated the broader dissemination of backstage knowledge that was otherwise seen as the realm of professionals and, as Chen himself notes, often carried the elusive air of the "trade secret" (秘訣). A similar attitude can be found in a series of personal essays also published in 1923–24 by playwright and theater educator Yu Shangyuan, written during his time studying in the United States at Carnegie Tech and Columbia University.[16] These included topics such as his reflections on the relationship between theater and science, and detailed descriptions of stage lighting equipment.[17] Indeed, beginning in the 1920s, there was a slow but steady increase in the number of both publications that referenced technical theater topics and theater-specific periodicals.[18] The terms "stage technology" (舞台技術), "stage lighting" (舞台光 or舞台照明), and "stage effects" (舞台效果), for example, begin to appear after 1920, with increasing frequency in the 1930s and 1940s.[19] Moreover, while *xiqu* artists continued to woo popular audiences with supernatural subject matter and fantastical uses of lighting, mechanical sets, revolving stages, and special effects onstage, many of the publications on stage technology focused specifically on its applications in *huaju* performance.

This growing interest in technical theater and a cementing of the association between modern stage technologies and *huaju* in the mid-1920s–1930s was also driven by increased experimentation in actually staging *huaju*, the return of students who had studied abroad in Japan, Europe, and the United States, and the founding of theater organizations, including educational institutions. With its affinity for social reform-minded themes and lack of music and acrobatics, *huaju* initially appealed more to university students and intellectuals than to the average entertainment seeker, and in fact failed miserably at the box office on its first outings. For instance, one of the first full-length *huaju* productions attempted in Shanghai—Bernard Shaw's *Mrs. Warren's Profession*, staged in 1920—was famously a complete flop.[20] Similarly, Hong Shen's 洪深 (1894–1955) *Yama Zhao* (趙閻王, 1922), which was an expressionist piece inspired in part by Eugene O'Neill's *The Emperor Jones*, faced a lukewarm reception at its premiere in 1923.

By the mid-1920s, Chinese theater artists were gaining more practical experience staging *huaju*, and increased production quality drew more audience interest. Undeterred by his experience with *Yama Zhao*, for example, Hong Shen went on to stage a successful adaptation of Oscar Wilde's *Lady Windermere's Fan* with the Shanghai Theater Society at the Shanghai Vocational Educational Center (職工教育館) in 1924.[21] In addition to taking a more rigorous approach to the rehearsal process and foregrounding the role of the director—a significant difference from the star-centered production process of most *xiqu* genres—the production of *Lady Windermere's Fan* also contributed to technical advances in its attempt to use lighting to indicate the passage of time.[22] While quite rudimentary by today's standards, this literal lighting shift represented an important departure from earlier uses of lighting as either simple illumination or for crowd-pleasing special effects. During the mid-1920s, according to lighting designer and technician Ouyang Shanzun 歐陽山尊 (1914–2009), the Theater Society gained a reputation for being "extremely rigorous in their performances, valuing technology, requiring lighting to be closely connected to the plot, and producing a strong atmosphere of real life."[23] Ouyang specifically notes the role of their theater venue, which had a relatively large stage and was comparatively well equipped, in enabling this rigor. He also discusses how changes in the availability of lighting technologies provided new opportunities for their application. Lighting dimmers, which enabled operators to control the brightness of lights, for example, were not yet available at the time of *Lady Windermere's Fan*. By the 1930s, however, Chinese theater artists had access to dimmers, new equipment such as "focus lights" (聚光燈), and even colored gels (彩色玻璃紙).[24] These specific technologies could be used to create more natural shifts between lighting levels, more precise lighting areas, and a wider range of colors onstage, which in turn helped to propel developments in scenography.

As technology advanced and onstage application grew more sophisticated, the association between modern stage technology and *huaju* grew even stronger. This can be seen, for example, in the special "Spoken Drama Issue" of *Theater Studies Monthly* published in 1933 that was referenced in the introduction.[25] The issue's opening full-page photograph of the Roxy Theater in New York that highlighted rows of lighting equipment offstage, for instance, suggested a strong connection between the proscenium theater and a "modern" stage apparatus (see fig. 0.1). Similarly, a two-page spread featuring close-ups of foreign lighting equipment was labeled with the title "Tools of the Modern Stage," and an exhaustive sixty-four-page article on stage lighting by director Jiao Juyin made explicit links between science, technology, and theatrical modernization (fig. 1.3).[26] Even editor and renowned *jingju* actor Cheng Yanqiu's 程硯秋 (1904–58) article on *huaju* directing devoted several sections to a detailed discussion of lighting principles and equipment.[27] On one hand, the fact that a *xiqu* journal and *xiqu* practitioners were demonstrating interest in and knowledge of modern stage technology and *huaju* suggests that relationships among genre, technology, and modernity were still in formation. However, by drawing repeated, direct connections between the modern stage apparatus and *huaju* theory specifically, the articles ultimately made an implicit argument for the sophisticated use of backstage technologies being central to and defining of *huaju* as a genre.

The above examples also demonstrate how the general proliferation of theater societies, theater schools, and other professional organizations provided increased opportunities for experimentation and furthered new ways of thinking about theater technology and training. In addition to the Shanghai Theater Society, which staged *Roar, China!*, other important groups of this period that both produced theater and trained *huaju* theater artists included the Nankai School New Drama Troupe (南開新劇團) in Tianjin, the Theater Department of the National Beijing Academy of Arts (國立北京藝術專門學校戲劇系, est. 1925), and the Southern China Society (南國社) in Shanghai.[28] Returning students and their transnational educations played an important role in shaping the nature of these organizations. For example, the head of Nankai,

Zhang Pengchun 張彭春 (1892–1957), and key founders of the Beijing National Academy of Arts Theater Department, Yu Shangyuan, Zhao Taimou 趙太侔 (1889–1968), and Xiong Foxi 熊佛西 (1900–65), all had studied at Columbia University in New York.[29] At these institutions, scenography and stage technology were important curriculum components. In the summer of 1930, for example, the Shanghai Art Theater Society (上海藝術劇社) held a training program called the Theater Workshop (戲劇講習班) at the CCP-affiliated Chinese Arts Academy (中華藝術大學). It featured prominent theater artists and educators training actors, directors, designers, and sound/effects technicians, and was attended by more than a hundred participants.[30]

In addition to training students directly, these organizations also contributed to the aforementioned increase in theater-related publications during this period. Shanghai in the 1920s–1930s provided a particularly rich milieu for creative exchange and production of print material, as Michel Hockx has demonstrated in the case of literary societies and literary journals.[31] This proved equally true for the theater world. Two early examples include the Theater Society of the Masses (民眾戲劇社), which published six issues of *Drama* (戲劇) in 1921, and the Southern China Society, which published various periodicals beginning in 1924. It was a trend that would continue over the next two decades, with the many journals affiliated with professional theater schools, amateur theater troupes, and political drama societies offering readers an amalgam of introductory lessons and more sophisticated theories.

Production practice, theater education, and published technical articles further demonstrate that early *huaju* developed in conversation with a wide range of current theater styles and approaches to stage technology from Japan, Europe, the United States, and Russia. Beyond Chen Dabei's citation of sources and the large number of Chinese theater artists who studied abroad, newspapers and journals frequently referenced the work of foreign theater artists and theorists who were particularly invested in exploring the use of technology onstage. Newspaper databases and catalogs of Republican-era periodicals, for example, hold sporadic references to Western lighting theorists from as early as 1904. Edward Gordon Craig (1872–1966, transliterated as "Gedeng Kelei" 戈登克雷) and Adolphe Appia (transliterated as "A'biya" 阿比亞) were introduced to Chinese artists and readers along with the basics of lighting technology, with Chen Dabei referencing Craig in *Amateur Theater* and Appia mentioned as early as 1926 in a *Shenbao* 申報 article.[32] Similarly, a 1929 article on stage lighting in *Modern Drama* (現代戲劇), by *huaju* theorist and director Ma Yanxiang 馬彥祥 (1907–88), references an English-language text called "Modern Theater" by one "Irving Pickel" (likely Irving Pichel's

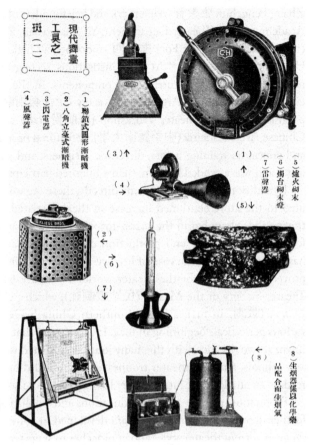

Fig. 1.3. (*right and facing page*) Photo spread entitled "Tools of the Modern Stage" published in *Theater Studies Monthly*. Source: *Juxue yuekan* 2, nos. 7–8 (August 1933): n.p.

*Modern Theatres*, published in 1925) and "The Book of Play Production by Smith" (likely referencing Milton Myers Smith's *The Book of Play Production for Little Theaters, Schools, and Colleges*, published in 1926). The same journal issue also contained photographs of productions by and translated articles about Austrian-born theater director Max Reinhardt (1873–1943, transliterated as "Laiyinhate" 萊因哈特), who was well known for his innovative and spectacular stagings.[33] The very foundation of China's modern technical theater knowledge therefore was laid with a keen awareness of the material technologies used and practices advocated by cutting-edge theater artists from around the world.

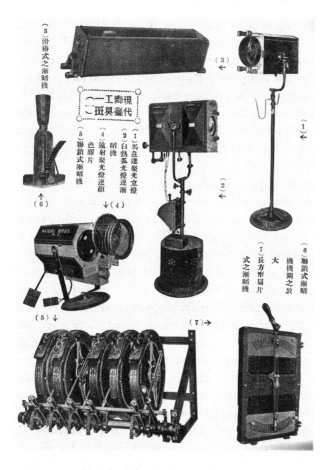

## *Roar, China!* and the Transnational Circulation of Radical Scenography

In the 1930s, the development of *huaju* and the transnational circulation of technical theater know-how began to collide and combine with more politically oriented theater practice, especially in service of a leftist agenda. To be sure, many *wenmingxi* plays were patriotic, and May Fourth intellectuals associated Western-style realist drama, one of *huaju*'s main sources of inspiration, with social reform. The late 1920s and early 1930s, however, saw many of the major figures in the Shanghai theater world, including several of those responsible for promoting a modernizing impulse in *huaju* scenography and stage technology, beginning to ally themselves overtly with leftist politics and projects. The League of Left-Wing Dramatists (中國左翼戲劇家聯盟), for example, formed as an umbrella organization for cooperation among these artists and with the Chinese Communist Party. In 1931, it called for new revolutionary content to be produced to promote "proletarian realism" (普羅列塔利亞寫實主義).[34] With the support of Communist agents in Shanghai, the League sent actors into factories to aid in strikes and raise class consciousness through dramatic productions, and the number of workers' theater groups increased dramatically.[35]

Extant historiography tends to highlight the proletarian theater movement's preference for activities such as street performance, yet even troupes focused on agit-prop theater and immediacy did not necessarily eschew interest in stage technology. The Shanghai Art Theater Society, for instance, emphasized movable stages, traveling performances, and student involvement.[36] They participated in activities organized by political organizations and performed in villages outside of Shanghai, as well as employing tactics such as planting leftist actors within variety programs and then co-opting the performances to incite the audience.[37] Yet, as noted above, they also ran a successful theater training program that included technical topics. Likewise, given the initial commercial orientation of many new-style theater venues and their association with what, in leftist ideology, was deemed "bourgeois" entertainment, one might expect to find critiques both of special effects and of their underlying technologies from those theater artists promoting political exigency as a driving force for art. However, as recent research by scholars such as Siyuan Liu and Liang Luo has shown, there was never so rigid a divide between the various spheres of the late Qing and Republican-era (1911–49) theater worlds.[38] Commercial success often went hand in hand with nationalist or leftist politics, and frequent cross-pollination occurred between the popular and the avant-garde, often because the same artists were working in both.

Attention to stage technology and technical training among politically activist theater artists was also reflected in theater publications. The journal *Modern Drama*, for example, was an organ of the nascent League of Left-Wing Dramatists and focused one of its only two issues on the practical and technical sides of the theater.[39] Edited by Ma Yanxiang and published in May–June 1929, the journal featured essays by several prominent Chinese actors and theater reformers, including Ma himself, Chen Dabei, Hong Shen, and future *Roar, China!* actor Yuan Muzhi. A brief introduction to stage lighting by Ma, written under his pseudonym "Ni Yi 尼一," covers the basics of stage lighting history, theory, and application. In it, Ma introduces four principles of lighting usage that would go on to become common tenets in later lighting handbooks:

1. to illuminate the stage and actors;
2. to suggest the degree of natural light in order to express time, season, and weather;
3. to expand the value of color, add light and shadow, as well as to harmonize the setting;
4. to bring out the meaning and psychology of the script, as well as to supplement the acting.[40]

The first three items on Ma's list represent fundamental, realist applications of stage lighting. The final tenet, however, when paired with the depth of technical detail of Ma's article and the agenda of *Modern Drama*, implied the advocacy of lighting to bring out the political meaning of the script. Indeed, with its various references to lighting theories and applications, Ma's journal as a whole made a clear connection between advances in theater technology and the modernization of drama under a leftist political umbrella. What this suggests is that leftist theater artists at the turn of the 1930s were beginning to draw connections between a working knowledge of the stage's more technical aspects and the political efficacy of theater. Moreover, they were making this connection by linking the ideas of artistically progressive European and American theater artists to their own politically progressive agendas.

Of all the theatrical elements, lighting held the most promise as a political-aesthetic tool and provided the biggest challenge to Chinese theater artists working in the 1930s. A key example of this can be found in many artists' interpretation and alteration of a well-known precept of Appia's lighting theory. Appia was perhaps best known for his design concepts for Wagnerian operas and for pioneering the theory that lighting could be used not only to illuminate the scenery but also to create and modulate the atmosphere and emotion of the action unfolding onstage.[41] In the 1930s, his famous claim that "lighting is the soul of the theater," paraphrased in various ways, became an often-repeated, almost totemic utterance in the writing of Chinese theater artists.[42] Moreover, Appia's lighting theory was linked directly to the idea of a "modern" stage and to specific technologies. Cheng Yanqiu, for example, writes: "We might say that the dimmer is the soul of lighting, just like lighting is the soul of the performance."[43] Cheng's emphasis on the dimmer was notable because, as detailed above, dimmers were a novel and relatively

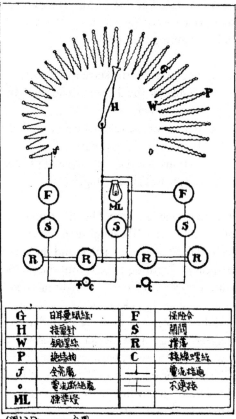

Fig. 1.4. Illustration of a dial dimmer accompanying article by Ouyang Shanzun published in *Play*. Source: Ouyang Shanzun, "Dianqi jian," *Xi* 1, no. 1 (1933): 43.

| G | 白耳愛跟絲' | F | 保險盒 |
|---|---|---|---|
| H | 捷電針 | S | 開閂 |
| W | 銅螺絲 | R | 燈泡 |
| P | 絕緣柄 | C | 接線螺絲 |
| ƒ | 全亮處 | — | 電流接通 |
| o | 電流斷絕處 | — | 不連接 |
| ML | 標準燈 | | |

(圖卜) Dimmer 全圖

rudimentary technology for most theaters at this time. While dimmers were already installed in cinemas for the practical purpose of lowering and raising the house lights at film screenings by the 1930s, they proved more of a challenge for theatrical productions and onstage lighting.[44] Designers often had to make their own makeshift devices in order to control lights above the stage. Ouyang Shanzun, for instance, experimented with a simple homemade dial dimmer that enabled different levels of brightness onstage, but did not allow for smooth transitions from one lighting level to the next (fig. 1.4).[45] Yet, despite the difficulty of obtaining or creating such dimmers, it is this particular piece of equipment that is foregrounded in Cheng Yanqiu's discussion of lighting principles.

Inspired by Appia's and Craig's innovative uses of stage lighting, Chinese theater artists went a step further to combine lighting theory with a basic understanding of modern psychology. One of the things that was appealing about a "scientific" approach to stage lighting was that it (in theory) could be systematically applied to achieve certain responses from audience members—a concept not dissimilar to what Weihong Bao has observed in the technics of Hong Shen's acting theory from this same period.[46] For instance, in the *huaju* special issue of *Theater Studies Monthly*, Jiao Juyin argues that lighting is important because it is "one of the greatest elements governing human feeling" and, when employed in the theater, colors the emotions of the characters onstage and those of the audience.[47] This property of light also proved the close interrelation of science and the arts, in which the technique is scientific but the effects (and affects) produced qualify as art.[48] Jiao's inclusion of a list of specific lighting colors that links each to a list of meanings and emotions in his article further suggests that, with careful calibration, a director or lighting designer might not only invoke but also provoke certain emotions in his or her audience. Jiao is, however, careful to qualify his theory with the caveat that audience members will not necessarily have a unified response to a given lighting effect onstage; symbolic associations are culturally contingent and affective response highly subjective.

Nonetheless, the idea of provoking a consistent psychological audience response appealed to those artists who were interested in mobilizing specific affects in the service of political revolution. Writing a few years after Cheng and Jiao, for example, dramatist and theorist Xiang Peiliang 向培良 (1905–59) extended Appia's notion that lighting is the soul of the stage to argue that it is colored light, specifically, that can directly control the emotions—and therefore color is the true lifeblood of the theater.[49] Director Wu Renzhi 吳 仞之 (1902–95) echoes this sentiment, though in blunter terms: "Using light to manipulate the emotions is one of the important applications of stage lighting today."[50] Another article by Zhang Geng 張庚 (1911–2003), a CCP member and later vice-president of the Central Drama Academy in Beijing, reveals why this particular theory of lighting design is so important: correctly employed, colored lighting could be used to "arouse the audience's revolutionary feeling."[51] Here, we might find another close parallel to the theory behind agitational events involving both cinema and theater, especially in the service of wartime propaganda, that Bao has also discussed.[52] For Zhang Geng's vision of the theater, it is only a small step from provocation of the senses and emotions to agitation of the people themselves, from reaction to action. He even suggests using red light at the climax of a play to build spectator emotion to a fever pitch, referencing Russian director Vsevolod Meyerhold's (1878–1940) radical stage experiments. And while Zhang's color choice may seem all too obvious in the context of Communist iconography, it is not insignificant: it demonstrates that Chinese theater artists were beginning to look to the technical elements of the theater as a means to inspire revolutionary passion and action in their audiences via a mixture of physiological and affective response.

Beyond the circulation, interpretation, and extension of foreign ideas about how scenography and lighting might be used for radical politics, reports on international productions were also an important source of inspiration, knowledge, and even proof of concept for Chinese theater artists. Among these, the many international productions of Tret'iakov's *Roar, China!* demonstrated that radical theatrical politics could succeed in practice and even take the world by storm. The play's premiere at the Meyerhold Theater in Moscow on January 23, 1926, was directed by Meyerhold's student Vasily Fyodorov (1891–1973) and received lukewarm critical reviews, but proved an incredible popular success and made international headlines.[53] Its fame grew as the Meyerhold Theater took the production on tour, and theater companies in Japan, Germany, the United States, and England tried their hand at translating and performing the play.[54] *Roar, China!*'s reputation hinged on both its political stance, which made it simultaneously a favorite of leftist theater troupes worldwide and a target of censorship, and the radical experimentation within its performance style. Indeed, from its first performance, the impressive execution of the play's scenic elements was a significant part of the discourse surrounding *Roar, China!* Long descriptions of the play's five main settings were included in the published script, and articles in the international press followed suit by printing photographs of the large, stylized "three-dimensional set" designed for the Moscow production.[55] As these images suggest, and as Robert Crane has argued, this production used the placement of key set pieces, like a massive gunboat, and of actors onstage to create greater sympathy for the oppressed Chinese among Russian audiences (fig. 1.5).[56] In other words, the scenery was not just for show, but rather was central to the political-aesthetic mission of the production.

At the same time, this seemingly radical scenography also proved easily transformable into spectacle, as in a production designed by Lee Simonson (1888–1967) for the New York–based Theatre Guild in 1930. Simonson covered his stage with a shallow tank of water and created the illusion of a Chinese riverscape by putting partial ships on casters in the water, so they looked as though they were floating and generated real waves when rolled back and forth (fig. 1.6).[57] In this instance, the extent to which descriptions of the sets dominated reviews may have been driven by an aversion to what

Fig. 1.5. Production photograph from Meyerhold Theatre production of *Roar, China!* in 1926, depicting angry dockworkers with fists raised in the air. Source: MS Thr 402 (Box 33: 1254), Houghton Library, Harvard University.

was seen as relatively flat, propagandistic content. For example, (Leola) Baird Leonard (1888–1941), the theater critic for *Life* magazine, writes that "since I firmly believe that propaganda has no place in artistic entertainment, whether printed or enacted, the things that pleased me most about the Theatre Guild's *Roar, China!* were its brevity (we were home by eleven o'clock) and its scenery," and then goes on to describe Simonson's design at length.[58] Whatever the various motivations, the common inclusion of detailed comments about the sets and photographs in reviews ultimately made the scenographic and technical aspects of *Roar, China!* as much a part of its international reputation as its strident anti-imperialist message.

It was the international success of *Roar, China!* and its reputation for combining stunning scenery with a decidedly left-leaning politics that would finally catalyze serious experimentation in the use of stage technology to further the revolutionary mission of Chinese theater. In China, the novel use of scenery in *Roar, China!* circulated via photographs from and descriptions of foreign productions, as well as publications of several translations of the script that included the playwright's original stage directions. Articles by

Fig. 1.6. Scene aboard the bow of the HMS *Europa*, with water-filled stage visible below. From the New York Theatre Guild production of *Roar, China!* in 1930, with sets by Lee Simonson. Photo by Vandamm Studio ©The New York Public Library for the Performing Arts.

dramatists Tian Han and Tao Jingsun 陶晶孫 (1897–1952) first introduced the play to Chinese readers in 1929, and three Chinese translations were published between 1929 and 1933.[59] Both the American Theatre Guild production and a Japanese production by Tsukiji Little Theater (Tsukiji shōgekijō 築地小劇場) in 1929 drew attention when a photograph from the New York performance was published alongside an overview of the play in *Literature and Art News* (文藝新聞) in 1931, and photographs of the Little Tsujiki Theater performance circulated in *Contradiction Monthly* (矛盾月刊) in 1933.[60] Several Chinese theater troupes announced plans to stage the play in the early 1930s, and the title alone became so symbolic that it was borrowed for a number of works of nationalistic visual art and literature.[61]

However, the radical scenography and revolutionary stagecraft of *Roar, China!* initially proved difficult to translate, given Chinese theater conditions. Early attempts to stage the play largely failed, including one particularly infamous production directed by Ouyang Yuqian 歐陽予倩 (1889–1962) in Guangzhou in 1930. Ouyang's production gained notoriety both for attracting the attention of the local KMT authorities and for its lackluster execution; despite the best efforts of the director, the play's scene changes took as long as the scenes themselves. In a later reflection, Ouyang would blame these failures squarely on the lack of appropriate stage machinery:

> A certain type of play requires a certain type of stage, and a certain kind of stage will have a certain type of play. Without the efforts of the New Romantics and the full use of machinery, the expressionists and the futurists would not have had a starting point for their performances. Many new forms of performance cannot be done without a well-equipped stage.[62]

Ouyang's comments illustrate an interesting, if somewhat counterintuitive, lesson drawn from his failed production. Rather than advocating for political theater to scale back its ambitions in light of technical difficulties, Ouyang insists on an essential connection between stage equipment and aesthetics that held no less true for radical leftist performance than it did for expressionism or the well-made play.

With *Roar, China!*, the transnational circulation of radical scenographic theory and the clear case of how that theory could translate into practice provided Chinese theater artists with a blueprint for the political mobilization of modern stage technology. Both types of source suggest that Chinese theater artists of the 1920s and 1930s perceived a strong connection between the stage apparatus and the success of a production on both artistic and political fronts. The many translations and early attempts at producing *Roar, China!* on Chinese stages, for Chinese audiences, further demonstrates how eager Chinese theater artists were to capitalize on these connections for their own agendas. Significantly, the failure of many of these early attempts—specifically, the simultaneous technical failure and political censorship of Ouyang Yuqian's production—did not deter future productions, but rather would galvanize Chinese theater artists to new levels of innovation.

## Mobilizing Technical Critique Onstage

In contrast to Ouyang Yuqian's failed production of *Roar, China!*, the successful attempt by the Shanghai Theater Society on September 16–18 and October 8–9, 1933 clearly demonstrates the combined influence of technical knowledge circulation, the increasing availability of "new-style" stages, and political conditions on Chinese theater artists' ability to put theories of radical scenography into practice. Indeed, the 1933 production of *Roar, China!* stands out as one of the most celebrated, as well as the most overtly political, productions of the decade. The production took place at the Hung King Theater, which was located in the "Eight Immortals Bridge" (八仙橋) theater district of Shanghai, not far from the Great World entertainment complex.[63] The Hung King Theater had opened to much fanfare only three years prior, on January 30, 1930, and had been billed as "the *newest* style theater in Shanghai."[64] One of its main selling points was that it was built as a multiuse space suitable for both theater and film. In celebration of its opening, one newspaper carried a rendering of its exterior, while another brief article praised its planning and the motivation of its founder, Huang Jinrong 黃金榮 (1868–1953):[65]

> This Mr. Huang, in light of the fact that Shanghai theater architecture is mostly of the old style, with none of them [i.e., extant theaters] able to satisfy one's desires in terms of equipment, thus decided to create a most complete, most exquisite Hung King Theater, considering it to be a harbinger of reform for all stages. In the future, this theater's architecture will not only be suited to singing *jingju*, but also will enable film screening, with full attention to both lighting and sound.[66]

And while the initial intent may have been to stage primarily *jingju* and film screenings, the Hung King also hosted important meetings and became one of the primary performance venues for the Shanghai Theater Society.[67] It would go one to become one of the key locations for *huaju* activities in the 1930s. As such, the theater's architecture and technical infrastructure would influence what theater artists were able to attempt and achieve onstage.

Finally, in a "well-equipped" theater and with an experienced creative team, Chinese theater artists could mobilize stage technology in a way that both drew lessons from prior productions and extended the anti-imperialist critiques of *Roar, China!* into the material world of the stage. From the production design article that director Ying Yunwei published, as well as production photographs, it is clear that his artistic vision indeed drew inspiration from previous productions in its use of large set pieces and well-choreographed transitions (figs. 1.7 and 1.8).[68] Set designer Zhang Yunqiao 張雲喬 (1910–2006) even recalls that the *Life* magazine review and photos of the Theatre Guild production, in particular, attracted Ying to the play.[69] As in foreign productions, the American merchant ship, British gunboat, wharf, and a radio tower filled the stage. Lighting designer Ouyang Shanzun had ten "spotlights" (聚光燈, also translated as "focus lights") at his disposal and three handmade dimmers to control them. Supplies for these set pieces and the lighting equipment required to orchestrate eight blackout scene changes, however, ran the budget up to two thousand yuan. The amount was so exorbitant that Ying felt the need to devote an entire section of his production design article to justifying his fundraising strategy. In short, the Shanghai Theater Society production of *Roar, China!* certainly did not imitate previous or foreign productions, but it was inspired by them and mobilized every resource in order to match their level of production quality.

Even with a large budget and a well-equipped stage, however, staging *Roar, China!* also required a good deal of artistic and technical ingenuity. As noted at the beginning of this chapter, one of the greatest aesthetic and technical interventions of the production was its successful use of the blackout quick change—a purported "first" for the Chinese theater world. In the words of one reviewer, the director's success at reducing the complex changes to only three to five minutes each "could be considered the dawning of a new era for *huaju*."[70] Yet it is not only the speed but also the mechanics of the set changes that deserve attention, especially for how they engaged and displayed theatrical labor. Set designer Zhang Yunqiao would later describe the sets as follows:

In order to facilitate thinking concretely about how to do a quick change of scenery, I built a set of small models, then Mr. Ying and

## 怒吼吧中國上演計劃

應雲衛

自從『怒吼吧中國』在中國有了第一個譯本直到現在，引起過不少人的注意，也有不少的劇團累次想把它搬上舞台，結果除了廣州以外，卻沒有第二次的實現。

廣州那次的成績我們沒有見到，但據朋友的口述及廣州戲劇雜誌的報告，我們知道他們那次是吃虧在怨促，不能有較完美的計劃。

因此，這第二次的上演，尤其是因為在上海，我們不得不格外的謹慎。第一要無論怎樣使它上演，不會期待了幾年的觀衆們失望；第二總想卽使上演也不會失敗，叫一般熱望的人們失望。

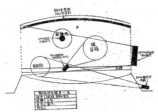

但是，我們不難保我們的計劃一定完滿，更不難保上演的成績一定美好；不過我們總盡了我們的力量。

以下我們且談談我們這次計劃的大概：

1. 關於劇本和導演

怒吼吧中國的劇本在中國有了不少的劇本，有從英文重譯的，有重日文重譯，這次我們是把所有的譯本集在一起，用英文本做參考而修正的。

導演方面雖然由我負擔，但事前有黃子布，孫師毅，沈西苓，席耐芳，顧仲彝，嚴工上

等幾位同志費了好多次的談話討論過的。

2. 關於經濟的預算

協社自從『威尼斯商人』劇折以後，累次想公演都困於經濟，因此足足有三年光景的消沉着，沒有一點供獻，這油不妨順便申明我們

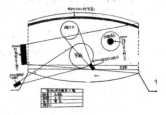

對愛護協社的觀衆們的歉意。

至於這次，也並不是受了或種協助而突然地富裕起來了，事實上，我們是冒險着來嘗試的。我們這次經濟的來源：

1. 借款
2. 預約券

好在有一部分的支出並不需要現款，我們就冒險拿上述兩項得來的款先把商船，兵艦，碼頭……都造起來了。

這次最費的自然是佈景，其次是燈景，因為人多，伙食的開支也隨之而多，連廣告等等，一起總需二千以上，也許還要稍爲超出一點。

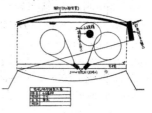

56

Fig. 1.7. Director Ying Yunwei's production design for the Shanghai Theater Society production of *Roar, China!* in 1933, including lighting diagrams by Ouyang Shanzun. Source: Ying Yunwei, "*Nuhou ba Zhongguo* shangyan jihua," *Xi* 1, no. 1 (September 1933): 56.

I fiddled around with them for several nights. Mr. Ying finally came up with the idea of dividing the entire warship into two parts, which could be joined together to form the ship or separated to form two ship berths. And after they were separated, they could be turned around to become the stairway for the exterior dock scene. During the blackout change, we would just need several stagehands to work together to turn the ship around, and we'd have the dock set. The other

戲劇協社演出怒吼吧中國的佈景圖樣
張　雲　喬

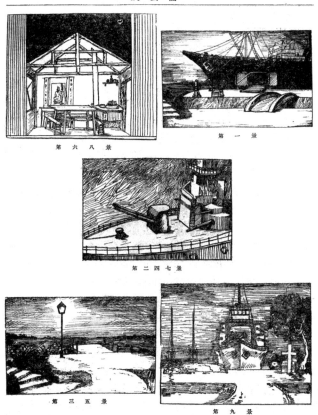

第　六　八　景

第　一　景

第　二　四　七　景

第　三　五　景

第　九　景

Fig. 1.8. Set renderings for the Shanghai Theater Society
production of *Roar, China!* in 1933, by Zhang Yunqiao. Source:
Ying Yunwei, "*Nuhou ba Zhongguo* shangyan jihua," *Xi* 1, no. 1
(September 1933): 57.

stagehands could determine how to split up the other tasks to return
the other parts (the ship railing, the gun turret hanging down from
overhead) to their original positions. When the lights came up, the
scene's lights would already be in place.[71]

Even the lighting units (which in a proscenium theater typically remain hidden) had to be quickly repositioned between each scene. In his detailed production design article, Ying Yunwei includes both set renderings (by Zhang

Yunqiao) and lighting plots (by Ouyang Shanzun), the latter of which show different positions for the ten lighting units in each scene. Ying glosses the diagrams with the following comment:

> Typically, the lights are installed after the sets have been put up (referring to the small elements, like wall lamps or table lamps), but that didn't work this time. The lights have to be changed during the blackout along with the sets. Our method is to hang the spotlights so that they can move, then use a rope of a certain length to guide it to a specific spot, and likewise with the dimmers. Once the blackout has reached a certain point, they are turned on again.[72]

Comparing the various diagrams published in Ying's production design notes with the number of lighting units he claims to have used, it does indeed seem that some of the "spotlights" switched location or direction between scenes. Ouyang Shanzun would also later comment that "moving the lighting units could only happen during the blackout," which he and a single assistant accomplished in fewer than fifty seconds.[73] The fact that the scene changes happened without closing the curtain also meant that the movements of stagehands and equipment alike happened in full, if dim, view of the audience.

The blackout quick change, however, was not achieved by a rotating stage (the Hung King Theater did not have one) or special effects, but rather through the concerted efforts of more than thirty stagehands. Indeed, the very term that Ying used for "quick change" throughout his published production design, *qiangjing* 搶景 (literally to "snatch" the "scenery"), simultaneously evokes the human agency required by these set changes and suggests an imperative of speed and force.[74] In addition, Ying Yunwei specifically calls attention to the stagehands' labor and praises them as the "unsung heroes" (無名英雄) of the production. Their heroism was further compounded by the need to do three performances each day in order to recoup the high production costs. Ironically, more advanced stage technology necessitated *more* human labor, not less. The technical advances achieved by the production were more a matter of ingenuity and mass coordination than of economy or efficiency.

The use of large-scale sets and quick changes in the Theater Society production therefore was not merely about impressing the audience or participating in an international mode of staging Tret'iakov's play. It was also about aligning the mobilization of theatrical labor *onstage* with the politics of the play itself. Recalling how the stagehands required a week of nearly all-night practice to perfect the transitions, Zhang Yunqiao further hints at a parallel between actor and stagehand at work in this production: the quick changes were a rehearsed performance.[75] The same could be said of the movement of the lighting units, making actors, technicians, and equipment equally performers. This elision of roles opens up the possibility of reading these quick changes not as technical details subordinate to acting, directing, and script, but rather as an integral part of the performance. As such, the transitions become actions that could be invested with meaning, by the director and designers, and open to interpretation by the audience and critics. What the Chinese cast of stagehands did, after all, was nothing less than deconstruct massive symbols of foreign imperialism—disassembling and reconfiguring an imposing hunk of British gunboat—directly in front of the audience. The labor of stagehands onstage thus simultaneously mirrored the characters who were laborers within the play and extended the critique of their oppression into the material world of the stage.

The Shanghai Theater Society production's active use of design and scripting of transitions therefore may be considered what Christin Essin has termed "scenographic activism": "a process of dramaturgical interpretation, visual representation, and material practice that meaningfully supports the actions and objectives of social movements or organizations dedicated to a progressive political agenda."[76] In particular, the dismantling of symbolic scenery onstage can be read as heightening the ways in which, within the play itself, these symbols are dramaturgically linked to a critique of the military and communications technologies that enabled imperialism and its oppression. The first and most obvious example of this can be found in the British military gunboat anchored in the Yangtze River, which many productions chose to foreground. In the Shanghai production, the design of the gunboat corresponded roughly to the kind of British naval vessel actually anchored in the Yangtze River in the 1920s and 1930s. Equipped with engines and artillery, these vessels—and their theatrical doppelgangers—represented not only imperialist expansion and oppression in general but also the specific incursions of mechanized military equipment in the post–World War I era. Modernization of this era is further represented by the radio tower, which could appear onstage in as many as four scenes. On one level, the station belongs to the same network of military technologies as the gunboat; in the final scene, the British captain of the gunboat receives (and disregards) an important message from his superiors via telegraph. At the same time, the term used—literally, "wireless radio station" (無線電

台)—and the actual large set piece suggests radio, rather than the simpler telegraph. This nod to radio, as well as several instances of photography used onstage, evokes the technological trappings of bourgeois modern life and offers a clear contrast to the conditions surrounding the play's main characters. As manual laborers and boatmen, they do not own such devices or participate in modern industrial production. The play therefore sets up technology itself as a marker of modernization and calls attention to the power disparities that technological modernization creates.

The play's representation of these technologies, however, is not purely symbolic or comparative, but rather critiques the specific ways that modern technologies aid and abet imperialism. Accordingly, their usage is subtly woven into the plot at key moments. The first instance takes place during the disagreement between Hawley and his workers. According to the text, when one laborer approaches Hawley menacingly, a nearby tourist and his wife snap a photograph. The gesture is intrusive and insensitive, but ultimately harmless, and guides quickly lead the tourists away from the scuffle and on to a nearby historic site. The play makes clear, however, that such naive voyeurism is an iteration of a much more troubling impulse; the next time we see a camera onstage is in scene 7, only moments after a young Chinese serving boy on the British gunboat has taken his own life. The stage directions script the suicide to happen onstage, and the boy's lifeless body to be found hanging from the captain's bridge by Cordelia, the daughter of Hawley's business partner and a guest onboard the boat. After recovering from her initial shock and calling the ship's lieutenant, she says: "I'm all right now. Do you think you could get me my camera and some magnesium? It would make a marvellous photograph!"[77] The camera becomes the apparatus by which Cordelia transforms unjust death into aesthetic pleasure, staging another level on which modern technologies function as implements of oppression.

This moment is mirrored only two scenes later, with an added reference to photography's role as an instrument of exploitation in modern print media. After two Chinese men are wrongly executed, a foreign journalist working at the radio station ushers grieving Chinese onlookers aside to take a photograph of the dead bodies. He quips: "It'll be quite a scoop!"[78] With a glib attitude, the photographer exceeds the ignorance of the tourists and Cordelia's morbid fascination. Instead, he directly instrumentalizes the deaths of the Chinese, attempting to transform them into a mechanically reproduced spectacle for the global news circuit. However, a political agitator from Canton (Guangzhou), who has been encouraging the local laborers to unionize throughout the play, physically blocks the journalist's lens. Here, the human body halts the workings of technologized oppression. And when the masses of Chinese boatmen and laborers begin to mobilize against the British military captain and his supporters at the end of the play, it becomes clear that the best weapon is, after all, pure and unmediated human resistance. The masses at once become a technology of revolution and exceed the power of mere mechanics.

What stands out about the scenographic activism of the Shanghai Theater Society production of *Roar, China!*, then, is the way it at once borrows the utility of technology and directly critiques the oppression perpetrated by means of technology. The chaotic violence that threatens at the end of the play, when its diegetic Chinese masses begin to rally against their foreign oppressors, contrasts with the tightly managed and controlled display of strength used to mobilize the physical pieces of scenery. Its performance thus presented two narratives of agency: one of masses rising up against their oppressors, designed to agitate viewers into action, and another of masses controlling the technologies that control them, enacted through the manipulation of stage elements. This dialectic echoes Xiaobing Tang's discussion of representations of *Roar, China!* in the Chinese woodblock print movement of the 1930s. The prints emphasized both the visceral aurality of the "roar" and the way in which literature, visual arts, and sound function as "mobilizing technologies" that transformed viewers and listeners into active agents of social and political change.[79] In the production of *Roar, China!*, both stage apparatuses and actors likewise become "mobilizing technologies." Where the Meyerhold Theater production had used scenic design to create sympathy between the audience and the action onstage, and where Lee Simonson had borrowed a propaganda piece to play with spectacular floating set pieces, the Shanghai Theater Society asserted the power of the masses by putting well-orchestrated theatrical labor on display.

## Rendering Technical Critique Legible

This reading of *Roar, China!* alongside its Shanghai staging raises crucial questions regarding audience: How receptive would its viewers have been to such a strident leftist critique of imperialism, and would they have been equipped to interpret the technical dimensions of its messaging? After all, while some members of the Shanghai Theater Society and the League of Left-Wing Dramatists may have advocated targeting proletarian audiences, the commercially oriented venue used for this particular production and its ticket distribution method suggest a more bourgeois orientation. To begin, the cost of tickets ran from five jiao (or one-half yuan) for open seating to one yuan for reserved seating. While not exorbitantly expensive, these prices were on the upper end of the spectrum for theater tickets at the time, despite efforts to sell as many tickets as possible at the lower price point.[80] Furthermore, as shown by advertisements in *Shenbao*, the production participated in a promotional scheme run by the Shanghai Domestic Products Company (上海國貨公司) on Nanjing Road (fig. 1.9).[81] For loyal customers who purchased either a pound of embroidery floss (絨線) or five-yuan worth of products, the store would give them a free five-jiao ticket to the play. Both the ticket prices and the giveaway suggest a certain level of affluence among targeted spectators and a commercial orientation to the entire enterprise. Insofar as the play is about laborers and criticizes elements of modern, bourgeois life, such spectators seem questionable receptors of its message.

Some leftist critics even expressed confused skepticism about the political orientation of the production, due to its audience makeup. For instance, one reviewer writes:

As for the production done by the Theater Society at the Eight Immortals Bridge Hung King Theater—the fact that the Theater Society chose this play is highly unexpected [lit. exceeded all expectations] and in some respects hard to understand, because it is *this* kind of a play, and the Theater Society to date has been *that* kind of a theater troupe.[82]

Here, the ambiguous "this" and "that" seem to refer to the highly political nature of the production and the previous reputation of the Shanghai Theater Society. As noted above, the troupe had staged plays such as the 1924 adaptation of *Lady Windermere's Fan* and was well known for its high production values, but not necessarily for a clear political mission. The critic also goes on to complain about the production's audience of "male spectators in Western-style suits and Sun Yat-sen suits, female spectators in high heels and cheongsams," including their affected responses to the play and misinterpretation of its message. These observations seem to confirm that the average patron of the Hung King Theater in 1933 was likely a petty urbanite (小市民)—apparently quite fashionable and likely more interested in middlebrow entertainment than hard-hitting anti-imperialist politics. In other words, they were similar to the kind of spectator who would enjoy Lee Simonson's floating sampans more than the message of Tret'iakov's play and might marvel at the onstage spectacle without necessarily questioning its mechanisms.

Fig. 1.9. Advertisement for a *Roar, China!* ticket giveaway run by the Shanghai Domestic Products Company on the front page of *Shenbao* (September 15, 1933). Image courtesy Bodleian Library, University of Oxford.

The likely audience demographic of the Shanghai Theater Society production of *Roar, China!* raises even greater questions about whether they would have been attuned to the highly technical dimensions of its political critique. Perhaps anticipating both political and technical misunderstandings among audiences, one of the lead actors in the production, Yuan Muzhi, decided to launch his own theater journal alongside the premiere of the play. As noted at the beginning of this chapter, his journal *Play* was rushed to press so that it could be distributed *at* performances of *Roar, China!*[83] The journal's revolutionary mission is clear from its leading article, which, in strident prose-poetry, decries the lack of a "pure" theater journal in China to date. It also champions the theater journal as an essential part of a rising theater movement, and announces, "This journal [stands] for all those who toil for the theater! It [stands] for all those who love the theater!"[84] Here, Yuan's rhetoric presages the labor-focused narrative of *Roar, China!*, as well as the production's emphasis on the labor of its stagehands. The remainder of the issue offers its readership a wide range of material, with articles on "drama for the masses" (大眾所需要的戲劇 or 民眾戲劇) by prominent members of the

Shanghai theater scene, exhortations to attract film audiences to the theater, and a special section devoted to *Roar, China!* that includes the production design article by director Ying Yunwei, discussed above.[85] Special sections on specific authors, texts, or cultural phenomena were a common feature of the many literature and arts periodicals in circulation in 1930s Shanghai, but this one differs from the norm in the depth of technical detail it provided its audiences.[86] It is also unique in that the entire journal issue is tied not to a theater society or institution, as was common at the time, but to the technical dimensions of a specific production, and that the audience of that production is its intended readership.

By lifting the curtain on backstage elements of the theater, the articles in *Play* could be seen as disaggregating and defamiliarizing the performance in order to create a distancing effect and provoke critical reflection among audience members. To be sure, one must not discount the possibility that *Play*'s emphasis on scenery and lighting might have been an attempt to impress its audience and gain notoriety by ratcheting up the novelty of the production, as was the case with many other theatrical innovations in Shanghai theater. However, with the exception of its introductory manifesto, the language in the journal is not that of a sales pitch, and the amount of detail provided far exceeds what would be necessary to impress the uninitiated. Thus, we may perhaps see in this provision of unfamiliar, technical details an impulse akin to the radical separation of theatrical elements advocated in Bertolt Brecht's (1898–1956) early writings on the epic theater.[87] Ying Yunwei's contribution in particular breaks down the production process into five discrete segments: script and director; budget; actors; scenery; and lighting. The lighting diagrams and set renderings further call attention to elements that are typically removed, spatially or temporally, from the audience; lighting units, with a few exceptions, remain hidden in the wings and fly space, and set renderings must, by necessity, precede the actual scenery that appears before the audience. Distributing highly technical material to audience members could also be aligned with Brechtian didacticism and his desire to forestall any sense of immersion in the world of the performance.

At the same time, the sense of agitation conveyed by both the play itself and the Theater Society's display of theatrical labor seem more aligned with leftist Chinese theater artists' goal of affective mobilization than with Brecht's cerebral politics. The Shanghai production therefore perhaps resonates more fully with the concept of a "theater of attractions" put forth by *Roar, China!* playwright Sergei Tret'iakov than with Brechtian estrangement. Penned in the same year as Tret'iakov's original *Roar, China!* poem, his theory borrows

the term "attraction" from the early theatrical experiments of Sergei Eisenstein (1898–1948), who wrote of the "montage of attractions" in 1923 as he
adapted the theory from theater to film.[88] According to Tret'iakov, Eisenstein
considered an attraction to be "any *calculated pressure on the spectator's attention
and emotions*, any combination of staged elements that is able to focus the
emotion of the spectator in the direction that the performance requires."[89]
The idea of mobilizing the materials—or, indeed, the technologies—of the
stage to provoke affective responses in audiences seems to have been the very
theory at work in the original Meyerhold Theater production of *Roar, China!*
And while Tret'iakov's writing on the theater of attractions does not seem to
have been translated and published in China at the time, it clearly shares a
conceptual framework with the lighting theories circulating in 1930s Shanghai, and echoes of its core tenets may have found their way onto the Chinese
stage via the influence of foreign productions.

Yet, whereas Tret'iakov's and Eisenstein's theory primarily concerns the
relationship between performance and audience, *Roar, China!* adds the key
dimension of printed technical text. Rather than either fully alienating or
fully manipulating, therefore, *Play* placed alongside the production of *Roar,
China!* invites its audience-readers to experience the live performance both
sensorially and cerebrally, combining the affective and the critical. It provides
background information that frames the content of the play and technical
information that guides attention to certain elements of the production. The
lighting plots indicate to a careful audience-reader which set pieces and parts
of the scene were deemed important enough to be illuminated and how the
lighting would shift between scenes. They are, in other words, a set of Cliffs-
Notes for reading the movement of scenery and lighting in the production.
These notes function as a decoding rubric capable of rendering legible the
message latent in the production's use of stage technology; without their issue
of *Play* in hand, audiences might be mesmerized or manipulated by the technical mastery, but with it, they were given the tools for a whole new level of
interpretation. Thus, the project of mobilizing stage technology in the service
of political texts and documenting this for audience members does not seem
to have been one of mere distancing from the play's realist premise. Rather,
it combines an affective and political project with an epistemological and
educational one, familiarizing audiences with new technical knowledge and
including them in the processes of artistic production and interpretation.

This goal of rendering scenographic activism legible to audience members, moreover, was not limited to one particular performance of one particular play, but rather extended to a broader epistemological and educational

project. Indeed, to return to the phenomenon of theater publications of the 1920s–1930s, it is clear that many of the articles and special journal sections on stage technology targeted a lay audience. Some were written for theater artists by theater artists, certainly, but advanced theories about lighting, color, and affect could be found even in otherwise introductory texts on the technical secrets of the theater. For instance, two compendia covering the fundamentals of theater practice, from playwriting to troupe management to technical theater, were published by the National Professional College of Theater (or National Theater College, 國立戲劇專科學校) and the Shanghai Commercial Press (商务印刷館) in 1935–36. The latter series included no fewer than twenty slim volumes: Zhang Geng opened the series with the sweeping *Overview of Drama* (戲劇概論), designer He Mengfu 賀孟斧 (1911–1945) contributed a volume on stage lighting (see chapter 2), and Xiang Peiliang delved into the realm of color theory with his *Color Studies for the Stage* (舞台色彩學). Their palatable size and low average price of two jiao per book suggest a mass market beyond the relatively limited sphere of active theater practitioners. A *Shenbao* advertisement for the series even claims that their clarity would "make professional researchers think them not ordinary or superficial, and make beginners not find them too difficult."[90] Blurring distinctions between amateur and professional, the accessibility of these volumes makes an argument for the general importance of specialized knowledge.

A similar impulse can be seen in articles in popular magazines, which introduced readers to modern theater through vivid photographs and basic introductions. A bimonthly pictorial called *Small World* (小世界), for example, carried a full-page spread illustrating the "technologization of the stage" (舞台機械化) in one of the its 1934 issues (fig. 1.10). Zhang Geng's comments on Meyerhold and inspiring revolutionary feeling through lighting, discussed above, were in fact published in a set of twelve short articles in *Life Knowledge* (生活知識) entitled "Theater Talks for the Audience" (為觀眾的戲劇講話), which was serialized in 1935–36. These articles were not sparing in their references to technical knowledge and foreign lighting theories.[91] Yet, the title clearly indicates that the contents are intended for audience members, not theater makers, and suggests that the modern theater aficionado might be one who is equipped to understand what happens behind the scenes. However, in contrast to the accessible yet detailed compendia, the glossy photos of lighting arrays and more superficial references to foreign theater toe a finer line between knowledge transfer and knowledge performance. Here, the specter of the spectacle arises, threatening to dazzle readers with impressive displays and cosmopolitan references rather than truly educate them.

Fig. 1.10.
Photo spread
entitled "The
Technologization
of the Stage"
published in
*Small World*.
Source: *Xiao shijie*
50 (1934): 12.

This tension hints again at the politically problematic association of onstage technologies with bourgeois entertainment, which would come to the fore as discussions of theater became increasingly ideological in subsequent decades. At the time, however, artists and audiences of all persuasions seem to have been eager to absorb and apply these novel areas of technical expertise—new "modern knowledge" that could be used to arouse audiences affectively, but that also offered the tantalizing possibility of scientific, rationalized mastery over even art and emotions.

In contrast to the fantastical uses of lighting and special effects in *xiqu* and *wenmingxi* in the preceding decades, the early 1930s saw the mobilization of stage technology in service of leftist politics and affective arousal, as well as the increased dissemination of technical theater details via print culture. The 1933 Shanghai Theater Society production of *Roar, China!* stands out as significant both because of its political message and its revolutionary staging, highlighted by the accompanying special issue of the journal *Play*. The production demonstrates, on one hand, how *huaju* artists, especially, were beginning to conceptualize theatrical know-how as part of both a distinctly modern theater and a distinctly modern epistemology, with a strong transnational dimension. The production was also a key catalyst in the broader creation of a new relationship between theater making and spectatorship wherein the message of the play depended equally on its narrative content, performance aesthetics, and technical effects. However, these changes might be intelligible only to an audience that had been primed with foreknowledge of the technical parameters of a particular production, or that was more generally knowledgeable about theater technology. The mode of politically engaged theatrical production that developed in 1930s Shanghai thus necessitated the technical training of theater makers and the development of a tech-savvy audience, educated through performance-specific publications, articles in the popular press, and compendia targeted at amateurs and professionals alike. Lifting the curtain on backstage trade secrets in turn contributed to a larger epistemological project of modernizing and standardizing knowledge in the interest of national reform and social progress.

Armed with this knowledge, theater artists and audiences alike could go forth to stage their own revolutions in the theater and in the world beyond. Indeed, beginning in the 1930s, an increasing number of Chinese playwrights were also putting pen to paper to write the plays that would later be lauded as the first Golden Age of *huaju*. Discussions about selecting plays, found in texts on producing modern theater, were transformed into how-to guides for playwriting technique and raised questions about the broader relationship between page and stage. As Chinese playwriting practice matured, how did playwrights envision what could happen on stage, not just between characters but in how their stage directions created atmosphere and affect? In particular, how did the scientific discourse that linked modern stage technology to the more general modernization of theater affect the craft of dramaturgy? As the political agitation of the early 1930s transitioned into full-blown war and foreign occupation with the advent of the Second Sino-Japanese War (1937–45), Chinese artists would have ample opportunity to explore the melding of theater, technology, and politics under material conditions that demanded ever-increasing levels of ingenuity and innovation.

# TWO

# Dramaturgical Technologies

## *Engineering Atmosphere in the First Golden Age of* Huaju

———◆◆◆◆◆———

The opening stage directions of *Foggy Chongqing* (霧重慶, 1940) by veteran theater artist Song Zhidi 宋之的 (Song Ruzhao 宋汝昭, 1914–56) describe an evocative and curious setting: an interior second-floor room that is oddly at eye level with the city street beyond. Through a small window that opens onto the street, the denizens of the room and the audience can see the scurrying feet of passersby. Spit, coal ash, and other detritus rain into the room from outside. The semisubterranean space is dark and humid, with water dripping down the walls and fog rolling in through its windows.[1] For readers and audiences in wartime Chongqing, where the play is set and where it premiered in 1940, the setting would not have been puzzling, but rather would have represented a type of hillside house characteristic of the city's rolling geography. The foggy atmosphere, meanwhile, alluded to the fact that Chongqing is as famous for being China's "fog capital" (霧都) as London is for its pea soup fog. During the Second Sino-Japanese War, Chongqing's climate took on further significance as the city's long foggy winter provided relief from near-constant Japanese aerial bombardment, since planes could not navigate or find their targets in the murky atmosphere. The cover of fog also enabled theater artists living and working in Chongqing to produce a full winter season of plays for enthusiastic audiences, then retreat to the safety of bunkers or the surrounding countryside in the spring and summer months.

Within the world of *Foggy Chongqing*, architectural structure and atmosphere create specific physical, social, and emotional relationships between interiority and exteriority. Song's description envisions the space as a liminal one that mirrors the conflicted psyches of the play's characters both in its structure and its meteorological characteristics. Taking place in 1938–39, following the outbreak of the Second Sino-Japanese War and the retreat of the Kuomintang government to Chongqing, the play centers on a group of educated young men and women who struggle to survive against the backdrop of protracted military conflict. Unlike many of the heroes of propaganda performances and wartime plays, the characters in *Foggy Chongqing* are not defined by their patriotism or commitment to the war effort. Instead, they are refugees who fled from the Japanese-occupied territories to Chongqing and, at the play's outset, struggle with basic subsistence and the acute stress of living under threat of bombings and blackouts. They exist in a state of mental and spiritual uncertainty—a civilian "fog of war"—that is externalized as the fog rolling into their living spaces. Onstage, however, the fog takes on an additional, metatheatrical level of meaning. From a practical and technical perspective, stage fog is notoriously difficult to control and, at the time, may even have been challenging to create.

In its dramaturgical style, narrative, and connection to current events, *Foggy Chongqing* is emblematic of Chinese *huaju* plays and theatrical productions of the Second Sino-Japanese War. This period has been heralded in Chinese theater historiography as the first Golden Age of *huaju*, when the relatively young form reached a point of maturity. On the one hand, this period witnessed an explosion of playwriting during which many now established classics of the *huaju* canon were written, published, and performed. The range of narrative content, nuance of characterization, and variety of dramaturgical styles greatly expanded, with plays increasing in both number and quality. At the same time, after the beginning of all-out war between China and Japan in 1937, many theater artists turned their creative energies toward mobilizing their fellow citizens to support the war effort and national salvation. Beijing- and Shanghai-based theater artists followed the KMT retreat inland, fled to the CCP-controlled base areas, or joined traveling troupes that promoted national salvation and support for the war in rural areas and the interior provinces.[2] Much of the theater produced by these brigades was street theater or drew on local *xiqu* forms, in order to better appeal to local audiences. Such propaganda efforts had little use for full-length *huaju* written for well-educated audiences and well-equipped theater venues.

These two paths in the development of *huaju* may seem to branch in different directions or even to be at odds with one another. However, they are in fact intimately connected through their indebtedness to broader trends within the theater world and, in particular, to the growing importance of technical knowledge and a technological mindset among theater artists. Prior to the war, the broader professionalization (職業化) of urban theater troupes meant that playwrights increasingly were commissioned to write for theatrical production (instead of or in addition to literary publication) and were able to earn a living from their plays. This direct connection to the stage in turn necessitated more familiarity with the material conditions of performance and the production process. Even during the war, many articles and handbooks on playwriting advised playwrights that both real-life experience and stage experience were essential to writing compelling drama. The rapid turn toward performance in support of the war effort also contributed to the immediate and urgent need for new scripts primed for quick production. Technical treatises and manuals once again played a role, both as a source of information on theatrical production and by directly addressing the craft of playwriting, or dramaturgy. The historical coincidence of these different trends invites us to look at plays and playwriting from a new angle: backstage. If playwrights were indeed writing with theatrical production in mind, how might an understanding of specific theater venues, available stage equipment, and changing performance standards have affected their dramaturgical practice? In particular, in what ways did advances in stagecraft and staging technology—key components of the overall theatrical professionalization—relate to the scripting of new plays?

This chapter explores the connections and tensions between the technical and the dramaturgical that emerge in Chinese plays written during this period of simultaneous artistic maturation and existential threat. It begins by examining how the standardization of the craft of playwriting contributed to the development of *huaju*, a trend that parallels the rise in attention to other technical elements of the theater. The positioning of playwriting as a kind of technology, which could be learned and practiced by amateurs and professionals alike, both drove the sharp increase in the number of plays written during this period and facilitated the reconceptualization of plays as "weapons" of propaganda. Like other military technologies, plays-as-weapons could be held to standards of efficacy and consistency in their contributions to wartime mobilization. At the same time, however, playwrights also began to rely on technology in another way: by scripting modern stage technologies into the fabric of the dramas themselves. Plays, and especially their stage directions, increasingly reflected a clear awareness of what would be required to make lighting, sound, and other special effects happen onstage. In plays like *Thunderstorm* (雷雨, 1934), *Under Shanghai Eaves* (上海屋簷下, 1937), and *Foggy Chongqing*, elements like thunder, lightning, rain, and fog become characters in texts and onstage, directly intervening in the play's action and more subtly engineering a suitable atmosphere in which that action could unfold. This use of stage effects parallels the provocations of *Roar, China!* in the early 1930s, as well as the observations made by film scholars such as Weihong Bao on the role of what cultural theorist Peter Sloterdijk calls "atmoterrorism" in the aesthetics and affect of wartime cinema.[3] Wartime plays likewise emphasized connections between environment and human psyche, but also reverberated with an awareness of the danger and precarity of gathering audiences and creating real effects onstage. This translated into a more diverse application of technology and a more indirect reflection of the atmosphere of war, which in turn allowed for more flexibility in how the page translated to the stage. Thus, during the first Golden Age of *huaju*, scripting technology became a central element of dramaturgical practice, but one that was far from homogenous in its application.

## Playwriting as Technical Knowledge

Although playwriting may seem to be a primarily literary endeavor, Chinese *huaju* playwriting was both inspired by literary models and inextricably connected to the development of theatrical production practices in the early twentieth century. Moreover, the origins of *huaju* playwriting do not precisely coincide with the birth of the genre itself. Rather, the productions typically cited as the "first" *huaju* performances—the 1907 Spring Willow Society productions of *The Lady of the Camellias* and *Black Slave's Cry to Heaven*—were not original plays, but rather, respectively, a translation of the play by Alexandre Dumas *fils* and an adaptation of Harriet Beecher Stowe's *Uncle Tom's Cabin*.[4] Some material written for *huaju*'s precursor *wenmingxi* was indeed original, but drama histories tend to point to Hu Shih's 胡適 (1891–1962) one-act *The Greatest Event in Life* (終身大事, 1919) as the first *huaju* script by a Chinese playwright to achieve widespread influence.[5] In the decade that followed its publication, Chinese writers began to experiment with the form of the spoken play in a number of modes, from Ibsenian realism (like Hu Shih's play) to neoromanticism, expressionism, and symbolism. Many of the *huaju* plays published during the 1920s, however, were one acts or experimental in form, and the genre was initially met with skepticism and confusion from audiences more accustomed to *xiqu* and *wenmingxi*.[6] The number of scripts by Chinese playwrights gradually increased, but a standardized approach to the craft of playwriting was slow to develop. Into the early 1930s, *huaju* performance often still relied on translations of foreign scripts (such as the production of *Roar, China!* discussed in chapter 1).

This developmental trend is evident in the difference between early treatises on *huaju* production, which emphasized script selection, and later articles and handbooks from the mid-1930s that introduced instructions for original composition. For example, Chen Dabei's *Amateur Theater* includes a chapter entitled "A Discussion on Selecting Plays" (選擇劇本底討論), but not one on writing plays, implying that amateur troupes, at least, would be working exclusively from preexisting plays.[7] A shift occurs in articles in theater periodicals and handbooks beginning in the mid-1930s, with an increasing number of pieces that focus on the process of *huaju* playwriting itself. For example, in the series published by the Shanghai Commercial Press in 1935–36, Xiang Peiliang contributed the volume "Script Theory" (劇本論), which included both a brief history of Western drama dating from the ancient Greeks and detailed recommendations on content, structure, character, dialogue, and style for the aspiring playwright.[8] This shift is significant on two levels: first, it shows an increased investment in the composition of Chinese plays by Chinese playwrights; second, the inclusion of playwriting, or dramaturgical, guidelines alongside acting and directing technique, stage design, and other production elements demonstrates a close connection among the literary, artistic, and technical sides of the theater.

This shift in attention to dramaturgical craft also coincided with the early years of the first Golden Age of *huaju*, a period characterized by more mature script composition, professionalized performances, and *huaju* popularization, especially as the genre was increasingly used to promote patriotism and national salvation during the Second Sino-Japanese War.[9] The beginning of the war is generally dated to the battle around the Marco Polo Bridge Incident, or Lugou Bridge Incident, on July 7, 1937. That battle catalyzed all-out mobilization against the Japanese and was even the topic of multiple plays hastily written to support the war effort. In the latter half of 1937, the Japanese moved steadily southward and inland, occupying first Beijing, then Shanghai and Nanjing.[10] The ruling KMT government was forced to retreat from Nanjing to Wuhan, and then further inland to Chongqing once Wuhan fell to the Japanese in October 1938. *Huaju* artists swept up in turmoil and military conflict came to see their medium as ideal for educating the masses and spreading patriotic sentiments, provoking a related need for the genre to expand in terms of both form and content. As they retreated from coastal cities to Wuhan, Chengdu, Chongqing, and Guilin, or migrated to the CCP revolutionary base areas (such as Yan'an) and rural areas, these artists faced the challenge of adapting what had been considered a primarily urban, bourgeois art form for new audiences.[11]

Wartime exigency thus propelled the development of *huaju* into more accessible forms, such as street theater, and encouraged a nationalistic move away from foreign scripts to those written by Chinese playwrights on Chinese topics. Street theater, which was already popular with leftist agitators, became the paradigmatic example of this new iteration of *huaju*. Its simplicity, flexibility, interaction with the audience, wartime themes, and incorporation of catchy songs aided in its appeal to broad audiences.[12] This form became so widespread that Chang-tai Hung, in his work on wartime popular culture, has argued that "the center of attention shifted from the play to the audience," and that an emphasis on collectively developed performance "conveyed an implicit yet unmistakable hostility toward literature and words."[13] However, while this may have been the case for certain forms of propaganda performance, it did not preclude the composition and performance of more sophisticated scripts by playwrights and troupes with access to proscenium theater spaces and audiences. As theater historians Chen Baichen and Dong Jian note in their seminal history of modern Chinese drama, the wartime period involved not only the increased political importance of *huaju* but also the penning of new scripts in greater numbers and of higher quality than in preceding decades.[14] Many of these would go on to become modern classics, such as the trilogy of *Thunderstorm* (1934), *Sunrise* (日出, 1936), and *The Wilderness* (原野, 1937) by Cao Yu; *It's Only Spring* (這不過是春天, 1934) by Li Jianwu 李健吾 (1906–82); *Under Shanghai Eaves* by Xia Yan; *Foggy Chongqing* by Song Zhidi; *Return on a Snowy Night* (風雪夜歸人, 1942) by Wu Zuguang 吳祖光 (1917–2003); and *Qu Yuan* (屈原, 1942) and *The Tiger Tally* (虎符, 1942) by Guo Moruo 郭沫若 (1892–1978).[15] Among these, many are multiact plays with complex dramatic structures and large numbers of characters. Narratives range from the more formulaic (a frequent critique at the time) to nuanced and original, and often speak to the historical moment both directly and indirectly. Main characters have complicated histories and motivations, they develop over the course of the plays, and they communicate in well-crafted, lifelike dialogue, whereas secondary characters still tend to be underdeveloped or at times even caricatures. Emotions and actions, as well as settings, environments, and atmospheres, are communicated through the use of stage directions that often seem novelistic in their length and degree of detail.

By invoking these commonly held perspectives, I note a distinctive shift in playwriting practice that took place at this time, without implying an evolutionary or teleological relationship between the writing of different periods. There is a tendency in some Chinese historiography, especially scholarship produced under highly politicized conditions, to frame dramaturgical developments as inevitably leading toward post-1949 socialist realism or, later, the more experimental work of the 1980s and early 1990s. However, neither socialist realism nor modernist-inspired, experimental forms are necessarily more mature than other dramatic styles; there were complex plays written before the 1950s and simpler, less sophisticated scripts penned afterward. Indeed, as will become clear from the discussion below, the body of work produced during the first Golden Age of *huaju* was far from uniform, and some of the plays that engage stagecraft in a highly technical way might otherwise be dismissed as short, simple, or even crude.

The maturation of Chinese dramaturgy during this period reflects an increased attention to the details of playwriting as a craft, which also can be seen from the continued increase in writing *about* playwriting—even among theater artists who had dedicated themselves to a political agenda. A number of handbooks on wartime theater that addressed playwriting, among other areas, were published, such as *Lectures on Wartime Theater* (戰時戲劇講座) compiled by the KMT-affiliated National Theater Academy (國立戲劇學院) in 1938, as well as a work entitled *The Performance Handbook* (演劇手冊) and a "Wartime Theater Theory Series" (戰時戲劇理論叢書) the following year.[16] Playwrights are instructed in how to select topics and titles, create structure and character, and write dialogue, while also being advised to gain some practical theater experience themselves. One handbook, entitled *On Playwrighting Methodology* (編劇方法論), which was part of the "Wartime Theater Theory Series," even included a specific chapter on how to script scenery.[17] Playwriting guides also often used terms such as *bianju shu* 編劇術 or *bianju jishu* 編劇技術—playwriting technique, technics, or technology— and placed playwriting essays alongside other technical and artistic areas of the theater. In the National Theater Academy lectures, for example, a chapter on "Playwriting Technique (編劇術)" by Cao Yu (writing as Wan Jiabao) parallels sections on "Directorial Technique (導演術)," "Acting Technique (表演術)," and "Makeup Technique (化妝術)."[18] As Man He notes in her study of the "technics of acting" (表演術) during this period, such a technical approach to performance at a time of crisis elicited critiques from theater artists more focused on action.[19] Nonetheless, widespread publication of texts on playwriting suggests an effort to standardize and popularize method and technique despite, or perhaps because of, the ongoing national chaos.

The terminology used in playwriting guides and their placement within larger published collections highlight the importance of technique in the playwriting process and link dramaturgy to technical aspects of the theater. This connection was not a mere coincidence. In fact, the dissemination of technical knowledge and guidelines for wartime theater practice was marked by a cross-pollination of theater artists who worked across different technical and artistic areas. Zhang Geng, for instance, whose lectures on stage lighting were referenced in chapter 1, also published multiple articles on playwriting in the late 1930s–early 1940s. Hong Shen trained as a chemical engineer before studying theater, and published handbooks on acting, directing, and scriptwriting for both theater and film, such as *Methods for Writing Film and Theater Scripts* (電影戲劇的編劇方法) in 1935.[20] Xia Yan, who wrote a number of plays including *Under Shanghai Eaves* and essays on playwriting, also had a background as an engineer and worked as a lighting designer and technician on several plays in the early 1930s. In fact, during this period, it was common practice for theater artists to have experience across the literary, artistic, and technical areas of the theater, as well as to move between the genres of theater and film.

The importance of the connection between theatrical production and dramaturgy can also be seen in some of the aforementioned articles about playwriting. One article, "The Writing of Plays (劇本的創作)" (1940) by Xia Yan, for instance, offers aspiring young playwrights advice on the importance of writing from one's own experience and chastises the theater industry for a lack of production opportunities for less seasoned writers.[21] Although he does not explicitly discuss the connection between stage technology and dramaturgy, Xia does link seeing one's work staged to the process of maturing as a playwright.[22] In the same article, Xia also complains that too much of the "responsibility for theater artistry" had come to rest on the playwright.[23] From the perspective of stage technology, the privileging of the playwright matters because authorial direction through devices like setting descriptions and stage directions then influences the work of designers and technicians. For Xia, this had a negative effect that extended to the director and actors, leading them mechanically to copy previous productions—an approach with which Xia emphatically does not agree, but that speaks to a desire among some to apply a more film-like mechanical reproducibility and artistic consistency to live performance.

The specific connection between playwriting and staging during this period was also influenced by what theater scholar Ma Junshan has termed a "professionalization movement" (演劇職業化運動) in *huaju* that began in the early 1930s.[24] As Ma argues, this movement was multifaceted: at its most fundamental, it had to do with a growing number of artists relying on theater as their livelihood or primary career/occupation. This was, in one sense, a continuation of common practice for *xiqu* and of the commercial orientation that characterized many *wenmingxi* troupes in the first two decades of the twentieth century. Professionalization, however, did not necessarily indicate commercialization, but rather an elevation of craft and related remuneration (just as a literary author may make money from fiction without being a "commercial" author). This professionalization therefore was a marked contrast to the student and amateur nature of troupes that performed *huaju* during the 1920s. For theater troupes, professionalization meant an increased financial dependence on ticket sales and, for playwrights in particular, the "performance fees" (上演税) that came with productions of their work.[25] Even those playwrights who were not fully dependent on their plays for a living often wrote for professional theater troupes.[26] Therefore, while many plays were published, *huaju* playwrights of the 1930s were largely writing for theater troupes and for performance.[27] This was especially significant as professionalization also involved a move into larger, better equipped theater spaces (for those troupes performing in urban areas like Shanghai) and a change in the standards for directing, acting, design, and stagecraft—shifts that also related to the marked uptick in publications on the technical elements of the theater that took place in the early 1930s. The influence of venues on production practice continued even after the Second Sino-Japanese War broke out, especially in urban areas like occupied Shanghai. There, as Edward Gunn has shown, Japanese restrictions on film screenings and the strong presence of CCP-backed underground organizations in fact opened more spaces for performance.[28] Thus, although some theater artists did face new challenges in adapting *huaju* to more mobile and rural forms, the impact of professionalization and the importance of writing for well-equipped stages did not disappear during the war.

Playwrights dictating production elements can also be linked to the rise of realism as a literary and theatrical style. As noted in the introduction, during the May Fourth Movement, dramatic realism occupied pride of place as both a literary and an epistemological model for Chinese modernity.[29] However, this is not to say that realism was the only style in circulation, nor to imply that the role of author or technology is diminished in nonrealist styles. As studies of literary realism have shown, the very concept of realism in Chinese literature, art, and theater was far from stable during the early decades of the twentieth century. Marston Anderson and others have discussed how the "revolutionary literature" debates of the early 1930s tasked literature with both representing reality and creating it, in order to reflect the experiences of the masses as well as educate and inspire them.[30] During the first Golden Age of *huaju*, the political leanings of theater artists were far from universally leftist, but the exigencies of war aligned many in the belief that plays needed to reflect wartime reality, speak to the masses, and spur them to action. The main difference between drama and other literary genres, as acknowledged in articles on playwriting from this period, lay in the fact that plays were written to be performed and therefore faced the challenge of materially representing their worlds onstage.[31] Different genres and styles of performance had differing implications for theatrical production; realism required realistic effects actually to be produced on the stage, from elements as concrete as putting a working lamp (or practical light) on the set to creating believable bursts of lightning. Variation in the availability of stage equipment thus directly affected dramatic realism's ability to be actualized onstage. *Huaju* playwrights were well aware of potential material limitations on performance, but did not regard them solely as restrictions. Instead, a major element of their dramaturgical maturation involved finding creative ways to envision uses of scenery, lighting, sound, and special effects in the service of creating realistic atmospheres, propelling dramatic action, and heightening affect.

## Experimenting with Stage Effects and Agency

The most direct evidence for *how* Chinese playwrights engaged with the technical and material sides of theatrical production can be found in their stage directions, or the typically unspoken sections of plays that describe setting, scenery, and special effects or suggest basic movements and emotional tone for characters. Indeed, one shared characteristic of many classics of Golden Age *huaju* is the extreme level of detail in their stage directions, which are often described as novelistic. The novelty of scenic realism in early *huaju* had already necessitated clear descriptions of what should appear onstage. For instance, Randy Barbara Kaplan has identified scenic realism as one of playwright Tian Han's key contributions to the development of the genre in the 1920s, as seen in his short plays calling for "numerous properties," "detailed, realistic . . . set pieces," and "realistic sound and lighting effects."[32] The trend was not, however, limited to realism. In Hong Shen's 1922 *Yama Zhao*, for instance, the playwright draws heavily on Eugene O'Neill's *The Emperor Jones* (1920) and directs sound, lighting, and scenery toward more expressionist ends. Over time, as *huaju* matured, the length and degree of detail that playwrights included in *huaju* stage directions expanded.

 *Huaju* stage directions also differed significantly from the historical practices of Chinese *zaju* and *chuanqi* playwrights. For example, as scholars such as J. I. Crump and Min Tian have discussed, Yuan dynasty (1279–1368) *zaju* 雜劇 uses only very concise stage directions to indicate actions and emotional states, which became conventionalized over time.[33] Yuan *zaju* stage directions have therefore been interpreted by most scholars as a guide for stage performers and perhaps imaginative readers, but little more. The case was even more extreme for the multitudinous varieties of regional *xiqu* in late imperial China, which often did not even rely on written scripts. Instead, performances were improvised based on scenarios or texts, and blocking transmitted orally from masters to disciples. Publication of *xiqu* scripts for professionals, aspiring amateurs, and general readership greatly increased around the turn of the twentieth century, leading to a process of "textualization" and a more fixed relationship between page and stage—as David Rolston has demonstrated in the case of *jingju*. For instance, Rolston discusses how a 1938 stand-alone edition of one play enabled inclusion of far more detailed stage directions than in earlier print editions of the same play.[34] By *huaju*'s Golden Age, then, stage directions were growing in importance across genres and styles of theater.

Increased attention to stage directions on the part of *huaju* playwrights perhaps also reflects the influence of foreign playwrights. According to Bess Rowen, there was a clear link between the rise of realism and naturalism in late nineteenth- and early twentieth-century European and American theater and an increased complexity in stage directions that "seemed to reach out from the page with the desire to do something more than simply dictate movements," especially in the work of playwrights such as Ibsen, O'Neill, Shaw, and Anton Chekhov.[35] Rowen claims that Shaw in particular has been widely recognized as the first European playwright to "change the stage directions from something written down in a promptbook to often fanciful and rich descriptions of the set, characters, and subtext."[36] In China, Shaw had an enormous influence both on theater and more generally. Grouped with John Dewey and others, Shaw was embraced by some New Culture intellectuals as a sympathetic anti-imperialist and pragmatist, whose ideas and literary works could contribute to modernizing Chinese society and culture.[37] He also holds the dubious honor of having written the play that is both lauded as the first full-length "Western" play produced in China (in 1920) and remembered as a famous flop: *Mrs. Warren's Profession*. Neither the play nor its quasi-realist performance style translated well for Shanghai audiences, who were more accustomed to the content and style of regional *xiqu* forms.[38] As Kay Li has argued, however, the experience of failure and Chinese theater artists' attempts to pinpoint what had gone wrong had an enormous influence on the subsequent development of *huaju* production, performance, and audience reception.[39]

Here, I do not mean to suggest that Chinese playwrights' approach to scriptwriting was a dramaturgy of imitation, but rather that their foreign interlocutors offered key dramaturgical models for stage directions. Chinese playwrights too had a desire for stage directions to "do something" beyond the minimum of suggesting basic blocking. In the Chinese case, however, that "something" included the specific and sophisticated ways in which playwrights integrated their knowledge and understanding of novel stage technologies into the fabric of their plays. Perhaps the clearest example of this phenomenon can be found in the work of Cao Yu, whose early plays became instant classics either when they were produced or upon their publication in the mid-1930s. Called the "reluctant disciple of Chekhov and O'Neill" by Joseph S. M. Lau, Cao Yu's use of stage directions travels well beyond the realm of movements, feelings, and tone.[40] Throughout his plays, he crafts key scenes whose atmosphere depends on specific visual and aural effects for their theatrical realization. These scenes, and their technical effects, in turn contribute to propelling each play's action forward and drawing the audience into its emotional world.

Cao Yu's first play, *Thunderstorm*, was published in 1934 and uses the titular metaphor of a building storm to drive a family drama filled with love affairs, jealousy, incest, illegitimate pregnancy, rebellion against tradition, and a workers' revolt. The play's dark portrayal of "feudal" society and patriarchal oppression has generally been interpreted as being in line with the enlightenment program of the New Culture Movement and May Fourth Movement, while its literary characterizations and narrative structure are often attributed to the influence of works from the Western canon.[41] In the play, the main character, Zhou Ping, is the scion of a wealthy family who has fallen in love with the maid, Lu Sifeng, despite differences in their backgrounds and social class. They plot to run away together, but their plans are foiled by the intervention of Zhou Ping's stepmother, Zhou Fanyi (with whom he was once romantically involved), and Sifeng's mother, Lu Shiping, who returns home to discover Sifeng employed by *her* former lover, Ping's father Zhou Puyuan, a mine owner. Meanwhile, Ping's younger half-brother, Zhou Chong, has also fallen in love with Sifeng, and her half-brother, Lu Dahai, becomes involved with workers' agitation at the Zhou family mine. This twisting plot takes a further turn when it is revealed that Sifeng is a half-sister to Ping and that she is pregnant with his child. Throughout the play, an actual storm first brews in the background and then rains down on its characters, with the air clearing only at the end of the play.

From a literary perspective, the use of a thunderstorm as a melodramatic metaphor hardly seems a subtle move. However, Cao Yu scripts his stage directions to suggest more than a general relationship between the thunderstorm and his plot. For example, in one iconic act 3 scene, Sifeng has just promised her mother that she would never see any of the Zhou family again. Lu Shiping retires to the next room with Sifeng's father, Lu Gui, just as Ping suddenly turns up at the Lu family house. As this transpires, the stage directions depict eerie flashes of light, sheets of rain, and the shivers of fear provoked by spectacular summer storms:

(*A crescendo of thunder, a deafening crash*)

LU SIFENG (*quietly*): Oh, Mom! (*Running into Ping's arms.*) I'm frightened!

(*The thunder roars and rain pours down in torrents. The stage darkens even more, and in the blackout can be heard*):

LU SIFENG: Hold me. I'm afraid.

(*The stage goes completely dark for a moment, with only the flickering light of the lamp on the table and eerie blue flashes of lightning outside the window.* Lu Dahai's *voice is heard outside shouting to be let in.* Lu Dahai *is heard entering the house. The lights gradually come on again.* Zhou Ping *is sitting on a stool, while* Lu Sifeng *stands nearby. The bed sheets are somewhat ruffled*).[42]

These stage directions are rendered all the more important by the fact that the playwright uses the storm not just to set the scene but also to carry it forward. Cao Yu invests the storm with so much agency that it functions, as he himself remarked, as an additional character: "There was originally a ninth character in *Thunderstorm*, who was in fact the most important, but I didn't write him in—a good fellow called 'thunderstorm.' He is nearly always onstage, and manipulates the other eight [characters like] puppets."[43] The thunderstorm here is envisioned as both god and ghost, a shadow character always present and invested with supernatural control over the human characters. In the scene cited above, we see this in the crescendo of thunder and deafening crash—onstage, two sound effects—that compel Sifeng to throw herself into her lover's arms, a moment that proves crucial to the development of the plot. Prior to this scene, Sifeng has promised her mother that she would break off her relationship with Ping, but frightened by the thunderstorm, she returns to him. The action then accelerates: Sifeng's mother and brother discover the two lovers together, prompting Sifeng to run off into the storm. In act 4, the entire cast of characters searches for her and finds themselves at the Zhou family manor, where the playwright finally reveals the incestuous truth of Sifeng and Ping's relationship. A power line, downed in the storm, then serves as a deus ex machina that suddenly and tragically resolves the plot: Sifeng, distraught by the news, runs offstage, collides with the wire, and dies by electrocution.

While on one level the thunder, lightning, and downed power line function as literary metaphors and plot devices, the fact that these details were written as stage directions also raises the question of how the effects actually could have been created in performance. After all, the responsibility for creating the proper atmosphere for the play's melodramatic web onstage fell not on social movements or cross-cultural intertextualities, but rather on stage technologies—namely, lighting cues and sound effects.[44] Indeed, if one imagines this scene in performance, it becomes immediately clear that lighting, sound, and some simulation of heavy rain would be necessary to bring its atmosphere to life (fig. 2.1). In other words, if we reread *Thunderstorm* from the perspective of its stage directions and stage technologies, we begin to see how the playwright's careful descriptions imply that the realistic onstage replication of the visual, aural, and affective dimensions of a thunderstorm are an essential part of its performance.

In fact, *Thunderstorm* was produced soon after its first publication, so that its literary metaphors quickly became practical problems for the actors, directors, designers, and technicians involved.[45] However, in a context where many of the technologies used to produce effects (especially lighting effects) were new and rudimentary, the very details that enliven the literary text with their complexity and precision constituted both technical challenges and a tantalizing opportunity for putting stage theories into practice. For example, articles from 1934—the very year *Thunderstorm* was first published—contain detailed descriptions of how to make "the sound of thunder" (雷聲), "a flash of light" (閃光), and "the sound of rain" (雨聲)—precisely the components needed to create the effect of a proper thunderstorm onstage (fig. 2.2). Thunder could be created by shaking a sheet of metal or with a soft drumroll; rain by rolling dry beans around inside a wooden box. A flash of light is suggested as follows: "Creating a flash of light requires collaborating with the lighting department. The method is to take two electrical wires, and on each end affix a metal shaft. Collide the two metal shafts together, and it will produce a

Fig. 2.1. Photograph from December 1935 production of *Thunderstorm* by the Fudan University Drama Society (復旦劇社), depicting the scene in act 3 discussed in this chapter. Source: *Shanghai bao*, December 19, 1935, 2.

flash."[46] In other words, technicians were instructed to create an actual, live electric current onstage. A thunderstorm, it seems, could prove as hazardous backstage as in literary text (or real life). The fact that technicians may have risked real electrocution while producing lighting effects for *Thunderstorm* was painfully apropos, given the plot twist at the end of the play.

One might imagine that the challenges—and potential failures—of risky special effects would deter playwrights from writing them into the script. Cao Yu, however, shows that this was far from the case. Despite an early aversion to writing *for* performance, he could not help but react to productions of his work, once complaining: "I've seen several productions of *Thunderstorm*, and I always feel that the stage is very lonely. There are only a few people jumping in and out, with some life missing among them. I guess this is probably because that good man 'thunderstorm' never takes the stage, and the people performing have unwittingly left him out."[47] Here, Cao Yu continues to anthropomorphize the thunderstorm and does not mention technical effects directly. Yet, around the same time he wrote the essay containing this quote in 1936, he also made revisions to the text of *Thunderstorm* that suggest this is precisely what he had in mind. Rather than add an actual new charac-

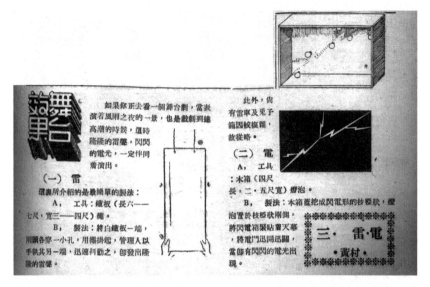

Fig. 2.2. Example of thunder and lightning special effects techniques published in 1948. Source: Huang Cun, "Wutai xiaoguo san (lei, dian)," *Zongyi: Meishu xiju dianying yinyue banyue kan* 1, no. 3 (1948): 6.

ter to the story, he increased the specificity of the stage directions related to the storm. Take, for example, the scene quoted above. The version published in 1936 significantly augments the stage directions as follows:

> (*Against the background of a crescendo of thunder there is a deafening crash overhead.*)

LU SIFENG (*in a subdued voice*): Oh, Mom! (*Taking refuge in* Zhou Ping's *arms*) I'm frightened!

> (*Runs to a corner to hide. As the thunder roars and the rain pours down in torrents, the lights are gradually dimmed. A gust of wind blows open the window. It is pitch-dark outside. A sudden blue flash of lightning lights up an eerie white face at the window. It is* Zhou Fanyi's. *She looks like a corpse as she stands there, heedless of the rain that pelts down on her disheveled hair, tears streaking down the corners of her eyes as she gazes at the couple in each other's arms. The lightning stops for a moment. The sky is pitch-dark again. A new flash of lightning shows her reaching her hand inside and pulling the window to, then fastening it on the outside.*)

*As the thunder crashes and roars louder than ever, the stage is plunged into complete darkness. Only* Lu Sifeng's *low voice can be heard.*)

LU SIFENG (*in a low voice*): Hold me tight. I'm afraid.[48]

Cao Yu does two things in this revision. First, he clarifies the jealous voyeurism of Zhou Fanyi—Zhou Ping's stepmother—who is standing outside the window. This is implied in the first published version, in a section preceding the lines quoted above, but not made explicit. Second, he increases the number of special effects in this scene. Whereas in the earlier version we have general storming, here we have flashes of light at specific moments that are necessary to illuminate and punctuate action happening onstage in the dark. The flashes of light allow Fanyi to observe the interaction between Sifeng and Ping. They also allow the audience members to see Fanyi and recognize her role in the unfolding events. And just as readers now better understand the scene from the stage directions, so too will the theatrical success of this scene depend, even more than before, on the technical execution of these moments of illumination. Revising with a greater awareness of performance, Cao Yu encodes his dramatic text with even more technical detail, mobilized in the service of his poetics and of the dramatic action.

A similar predilection for technical detail—and technical difficulty—can be found in Cao Yu's second play, *Sunrise*, which he wrote in 1936. *Sunrise* centers on the story of Chen Bailu, a "modern" young woman caught between her desire for independence, the allure of a decadent lifestyle, and the difficulties of making her way in a sexist and patriarchal society. As is the case in *Thunderstorm*, *Sunrise* features frequent paragraph-long descriptions of mise-en-scène.[49] These stage directions often focus on describing sets and costumes, but in the final act, they shift to emphasizing lighting and sound. For instance, the stage directions note Bailu first opening the windows in her room to gaze at a predawn cityscape, then "the morning light gradually seeping through the window, with the glow of the sun at first only reflecting on the eaves" of nearby buildings (fig. 2.3).[50] A few pages later, she "opens the curtains, and the sunlight shines on her face," prompting her to "suddenly turn off the interior lights and close all of the curtains, so that the room goes dark and only a few beams of light quiver through the openings in the heavy curtains."[51] In fact, the act as a whole can be read as a delicate choreography of lighting: as the sun gradually rises outside the hotel room window, characters open and close the curtains multiple times, and the interior lights turn on and off. The brightening and darkening of the room vacillate along with the

Fig. 2.3. Production photograph from the 1937 China Traveling Theater (中國旅遊劇團) production of *Sunrise*. Note the low height of the interior walls and building flats behind, which would allow the lighting shifts to fill the backdrop and make dimming all the more important. Source: *Zhonghua*, no. 54 (1937): 41.

mood of protagonist Chen Bailu, who is deeply in debt and unable to support the bourgeois lifestyle to which she has become accustomed. This mapping of lighting shift to mood demonstrates the pervasiveness of the idea that lighting animates the emotional core of the theater. When Bailu eventually swallows a handful of sleeping pills to end her life, dawn breaks outside the window and the chanting of construction workers (offstage) heralds a new day. The juxtaposition of the darkness and light, both literally and symbolically, in this final moment emphasizes the starkness of the contrast between the negative and positive sides of modern urban life.

Here again, the lighting and sound scripted into Cao Yu's play relied on stage technology that, although basic today, was challenging and even dangerous for technicians at the time. For example, the brightening of sunlight described in the final act of *Sunrise* required the use of a dimmer capable of smooth, gradual lighting shifts. Today, the technology known as a solid-state dimmer is common on both theatrical lighting boards and for household use: a turning knob or sliding switch enables one to control the lighting level

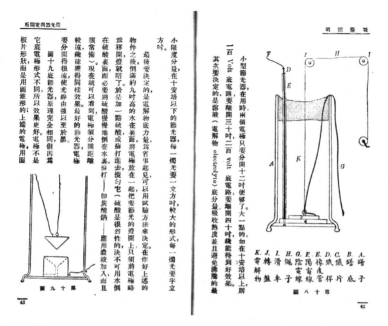

Fig. 2.4. Illustrations and explanation of how a liquid rheostat (saltwater) dimmer functions. Source: He Mengfu, *Wutai zhaoming* (Shanghai: Shangwu yinshu guan, 1936), 42–43.

onstage or in a room. In the 1930s, however, the semiconductor technology needed for this type of dimmer had not yet been invented. Lighting manuals describe slider and dial dimmers that jumped abruptly between different preset lighting levels, as well as an apparatus called a "saltwater" or "fluid" dimmer (鹽水節電器 or 液體節光器).[52] The saltwater dimmer, also known as a liquid rheostat dimmer, was essentially a vat of ionized water with two pieces of pig iron and electrical cables forming a circuit inside the solution. When the two pieces of iron touched, the circuit was closed and the attached light was at full brightness; to dim the lights, the stagehands used a pulley to move the pieces of metal apart. With the help of the ionized solution, electricity would still flow between the two pieces of metal and their attached cables, but the current weakened and the light dimmed as the distance increased (fig. 2.4). As with the mechanism for creating theatrical lightning, this technology simultaneously advanced the creation of realistic atmospherics onstage and posed a potential danger for its operators backstage (due to the presence of electrified vats of water).

In *Sunrise*, the shifts in lighting levels, and therefore a functioning dimmer, are essential to communicating the play's central message: the interior of the set darkening slowly at the end of the play, while the scene outside the window brightens, is a metaphoric indication that the lights are waning on a bourgeois and corrupt way of life and rising on the new society beyond. Cao Yu was not so strident a leftist as many theater artists of his time, but the political message of a new day dawning at the end of *Sunrise* is unambiguous. The rising sun and proletarian soundscape outside the window herald the coming of a new era for China, one in which the hold of superficial, parasitic middle and upper classes gives way to the reign of workers. Ultimately, neither the effect of a gradual sunrise onstage nor the successful communication of this message could be achieved without the close cooperation of technology and script.

There is, of course, a question as to whether stage directions can or should be read as the voice of the author. Work on early modern English theater, for example, has highlighted the difficulty of attributing authorship of stage directions when extant editions vary in their inclusion.[53] Stage directions often reflect notes from promptbooks, added to published plays only *after* performances, or are the work of editors attempting to rectify textual discrepancies or make scripts more reader-friendly. Similar concerns exist for early modern Chinese drama. Ming dynasty editors of Yuan dynasty *zaju*, for instance, are known to have heavily edited texts and added stage directions to their collections.[54] For early twentieth-century *huaju*, it was common practice to publish the first version of a play (often in a literary periodical) in advance of, or at the same time, that the play was being rehearsed and staged—in other words, *before* it was even possible to know the details of its first performance. As was the case with Cao Yu, playwrights also frequently published prefaces and notes alongside their plays (a common practice in the Chinese literary tradition) that clearly claimed the following work as their own. These documents often commented on the playwright's writing process and even provided details on the theater troupes and spaces for which they wrote a particular play. In Cao Yu's notes for the third act of *Sunrise*, he goes so far as to acknowledge openly the difficulty that his highly technical stage directions might cause the director:

> I had no choice but to use who knows how many backstage sounds to help create ambience in this act. This difficulty is a great headache for the director. If it [i.e., the play] should have the good fortune to be performed, these special effects must have specific timing, duration,

strength, speed, and all kinds of tone and perspective. Each sound must make sense and be adjusted according to the atmosphere, as well as calling to mind and emphasizing just the right meaning.[55]

Given such a statement, Cao Yu's stage directions clearly can be read as the voice of the playwright—one who is both highly aware of the practical implications of his script and insistent on the importance of the successful execution of stage effects.

The significance of the specific ways in which Cao Yu scripts technology in *Thunderstorm* and *Sunrise* thus cannot be underestimated. Both plays became highly influential as soon as they were published, with a number of performances in the 1930s–1940s and a lasting impact in the repertoires of major theater companies after the founding of the PRC. These plays also set an immediate example for the penning of sophisticated multiact dramas; what might seem to us today to be transparent metaphors and melodramatic plotting were not necessarily received that way at the time. Cao Yu's plays were included as exemplary texts in theater training programs, and articles on playwriting from the 1940s would mention *Thunderstorm*, in particular, as a dramaturgical model for aspiring writers, especially in reference to the playwright's success at dramatic realism.[56] Scenic designer and scholar Li Chang even goes so far as to claim that Cao Yu's dramaturgy impacted performance practice directly: "In terms of scenographic art, the playwright gives exhaustive descriptions; regardless of whether sets, lighting, props, costumes, or the atmosphere of the period, it is as if Cao Yu were writing a scenographic textbook, and through this educates directors and designers, leading them toward realism."[57] Stage directions thus serve multiple functions: as an imaginative guide for the reader, a practical blueprint for production, and an educational tool.

## Scripting Technology as Dramaturgical Mode

Where Cao Yu's stage directions may have offered a primer for how to draw direct connections between atmospheric effects and narrative development, the work of other theater artists at this time demonstrates an even more complicated relationship among stage technology, playwriting, and knowledge production. One key example of this can be found in the work of Xia Yan, who wrote several significant plays in the 1930s, worked as a lighting designer and film screenwriter, and went on to serve as deputy minister of culture of the PRC from 1955 to 1965. Like many of his contemporaries in the theater world, as noted above, Xia had a background in engineering; before his career as a theater artist began, he attended the Zhejiang Industrial Academy (浙江省立甲種工業學校) and studied abroad at the Meiji College of Technology (明治專門學校) in Kitakyushu, Japan, where he concentrated in electrical engineering. Xia Yan's background in engineering affected not only his design and technical work but also the way he envisioned and wrote plays such as *Under Shanghai Eaves* (1937).

Like Cao Yu, Xia constructs the world of *Under Shanghai Eaves* through intricate and lengthy stage directions, and draws a clear connection between atmospheric effects and the emotions of the characters. The play centers on the interwoven lives of several tenants of a Shanghai "lane house," whose architecture is essential to the relationships among the play's characters and the unfolding of its plot.[58] The scenery is so thoroughly planned and the architecture of the house so important to the play's plot that later editions of the play printed an image of the set alongside the opening stage directions.[59] Atmospheric effects are also carefully wrought, as in this section of the opening stage directions:

> From the opening curtain to closing curtain the fine rain rarely stops. When the rain is heavy, its "ding dong" [sound] can be heard pouring off the eaves, but then, a minute later perhaps, a pallid sun may thread its way through the clouds. The barometer is low and the air is very heavy, which has its effect on the emotions of the tenants. Their actions and speech reveal the depression, irritability, and anxiety they all share, so that the slightest provocation can at any moment trigger an outburst of excessive pent-up anger.[60]

Similar techniques to those used in productions of *Thunderstorm* could be employed for the "sound of rain" or for lighting effects to match descriptions such as that in act 2, when "the sun appears and casts a dazzling beam of light into the house, long soaked with humidity."[61] Xia even notes the specifics of what type of practical light to use onstage, as in the placement of "a five-watt light bulb, with only half its shade remaining" in one room of the house.[62] In addition to descriptions of details like this one, however, the script also specifies temporal settings for each act—morning, noon, and evening—that have implications for lighting design. Both the suggestion of a continuous sound of rain throughout the play and the specific lighting levels required throughout each act created new degrees of technical difficulty as well as a different, durational role for lighting and sound effects. Rather than a one-off bolt of lightning or clap of thunder, the rain and lighting levels functioned more like a painted backdrop, ever present and essential to the underlying mood and meaning of the entire play.

The importance of Xia Yan's technical interventions can be substantiated by two types of source: by performance reviews that reference specific elements of the scenery, lighting, and sound effects, and by the frequent use of *Under Shanghai Eaves* as an example in practical and theoretical articles on stage technology. Multiple reviews of a 1940 production by the Shanghai Theater Art Society (上海劇藝社), for example, call the play's scenery "unprecedented" and cite the fact that the theater company spent two whole days constructing its lane house set.[63] One of the reviews also dwells specifically on the morning–noon–evening lighting effects and how "the atmosphere of the scenes places strict demands on the lighting," noting the novelty of the Shanghai Theater Art Society's purchasing two lighting dimmers (燈光變壓器) in order to control the lighting levels.[64] What is most significant about these reviews, however, is that they frame these technical details not just as production design decisions made by theater troupes but also as scripted elements attributable to the playwright. As one article on preparations for the play's premiere production in 1937 phrased it: "The playwright asked Amateur Experimental [i.e., Amateur Experimental Theater Troupe (業餘實驗劇團)] scenic designer Xu Qu 徐渠 to move an entire house onto the stage."[65] Later in life, Xia Yan would reflect on this particular set piece as a marker of impractical, youthful exuberance, but at the time it was heralded as a bold innovation in the scripting of scenography.[66]

This dramaturgical trend of scripting stage directions with close attention to the technical elements of theater extended even to shorter plays that were written for much less ideal material conditions. *Under Shanghai Eaves* was set and staged in Shanghai, where resourceful theater troupes managed to negotiate access to modern theater venues and equipment even while under Japanese occupation.[67] In contrast, theater artists who fled the occupied areas, followed the KMT as it retreated to Wuhan and then Chongqing, or joined traveling national salvation propaganda troupes faced different material landscapes, audiences, and demands on their art. Yet even short propaganda pieces could be—and were—written with a reliance on stage technology. One example is *This Era* (這一代), written by He Mengfu and published in the journal *War of Resistance Literature and Art* (抗戰文藝) in 1939. Only five pages long and with only three speaking characters (an Old Man, his daughter, and a county squire), *This Era* nonetheless devotes a disproportionate amount of its text to stage directions. For example, fully a third of the script's first page is devoted to setting the action in an unnamed village in Shanxi Province:

> A village in northern Shanxi. By the time enemy forces entered, it was long after the county seat had fallen. The peaceful villagers were suddenly subjected to an incursion from the outside, and were able to escape the enemy's piercing attack only by hiding deep in the mountains. However, the enemy occupied the village, without any possibility that they would retreat. Those hiding deep in the mountains waited patiently for a long time, but finally their provisions ran out, so when the enemy publicized a conciliatory policy, one after another they returned to save their lives—but, what they really got was death. . . .
>
> The setting: a cave house of the kind found in Shanxi and Shaanxi. Other than a clay *kang* [heatable sleeping platform] and the coal oven connected to it, there is nothing in the room but a messy pile of papers. Clearly, the enemies have searched here. The window sills have already become sticks of withered charcoal. Because the cave was made of earth, it has fortunately avoided being incinerated, but even the earthen walls have been blackened by smoke and corroded. The shafts of light in the room are very dim, with only light from outside coming in through the window, shining on the earthen walls—the desolate, bleak atmosphere following a battle.
>
> On the earthen wall, shadows collide. It is the Old Man and his daughter, returning carrying cloth bundles. They haven't been home in many days, and everything seems different upon their return. They seem to think someone is following them, glancing behind themselves anxiously.[68]

Beyond giving the location and immediate context for the play's action, He Mengfu's stage directions also describe in great detail the smoke-blackened earthen walls, dim shafts of light, and shadows colliding. In the scenes that follow, the Old Man and Girl are visited by the Squire, who informs them that the Girl will be conscripted to entertain the enemy soldiers. He Mengfu continues to include references to practical effects onstage, such as the coal brazier being lit and used to cook food, and specific lighting changes, such as the sun setting and darkness falling. As discussed above in relation to *Sunrise*, the effect of a gradual lighting change was one that required specific equipment—a lighting dimmer. This was a challenge that He Mengfu clearly understood, as he had already described the mechanics of dimmers in detail in his book on stage lighting.[69] Yet, despite his awareness of the complexities of stage technology, He Mengfu does not shy away from including them in even the simplest of plays.

The technical specificity of *This Era* provides yet another example of how a playwright's understanding of stage technology influenced the scripting of stage directions. He Mengfu was a designer, director, and playwright who worked in both theater and film and published widely on technical theater topics. He studied scenic design under Yu Shangyuan and Xiong Foxi in the theater department of the Peking University Academy of the Arts (國立北平大學藝術學院) in the late 1920s, then worked for film companies in Beijing and Shanghai.[70] While in Shanghai, he served as lead screenwriter for a number of films, including Fei Mu's directorial debut *Night in the City* (城市之夜, 1933), and was a founding member of several "amateur" theater troupes.[71] After the war broke out, he followed the Amateur Theater Society (業餘劇人協會) inland and continued to work in both film and theater in Chengdu and Chongqing, directing and designing well-received productions for a number of prominent theater troupes while also teaching scenic design at the National Theater Academy.[72] In addition to his volume on stage lighting for the Shanghai Commercial Press series (see chapter 1), He also contributed essays on scenic design drawings to *The Performance Handbook*, and wrote and translated a number of theoretical works and technical treatises. He was one of the first Chinese translators of Konstantin Stanislavski, for instance, and of *The Theatre of To-day* by Harvard-educated American theater critic Hiram Kelly Moderwell (1888–1945).[73] He Mengfu thus provides yet another example of a theater artist well versed in technical theater who contributed to the body of knowledge about these areas *and* translated that knowledge into dramaturgical practice.

At the same time, He Mengfu's stage directions for *This Era* also illustrate new uses of stage technology that simultaneously capture the atmosphere of the wartime era and adapt to its material conditions. Beyond setting the scene and describing basic lighting effects, He Mengfu relies on the use of lighting, or rather, shadows, in a manner directly related to dramatic action. As seen above in the opening stage directions, the image of shadows colliding on an earthen wall precedes the entrance of the Old Man and the Girl. On three other occasions, shadows are used in a similar fashion to announce the entrance of the third character (the Squire) and to gesture to offstage events that the characters see and discuss, but that the audience otherwise does not see. He Mengfu pairs the shadows with sound effects that further heighten the emotion of what is happening onstage and indicate offstage action. In the play's final moments, for instance, the Girl announces her intention to stand her ground until the Japanese soldiers come to take her away by force. A menacing crowd of soldiers gathers outside but, according to the stage directions, is represented onstage only by the frenetic movement of shadows and the sound of a roar from the wings.

The use of shadows is particularly ingenious because they simultaneously gesture to the psychology of wartime terror and make accommodations for the variable material conditions of wartime performance. The dread caused by the shadows in *This Era* comes both from what they imply—capture by Japanese soldiers—and from the extent to which they leave the details of those horrors to the imagination. Whereas thunder and lightning, as in *Thunderstorm*, provoke an immediate, visceral response, shadows play more on individual psychology and the unknown. The image of chiaroscuro shadows on the wall also parallels a similar phenomenon in transnational expressionist wartime film. In a recent article, for example, Tim Shao-Hung Teng identifies several cinematic examples from the 1930s in which "terror emerges as an environmental experience shaped by the dynamic choreography of shadows, air, and female bodies" and which can mobilize spectators to become "motivated agents taking part in national defense."[74] He follows Weihong Bao's work in linking this phenomenon to Sloterdijk's concept of "atmoterrorism" and a broader concern with the design of atmosphere in works of literature, art, film, and theater that gained particular urgency in the early 1930s, when Japan began its aerial attacks on China.[75] The menacing atmosphere in He Mengfu's *This Era* seems similarly motivational, especially at the end of the play.

Moreover, as with all stage effects, shadows also have a practical dimension and, in contrast to a lighting dimmer, are relatively easy to create. All one needs is a steady lighting source and an object as simple as a piece of paper or cardboard to block some of the light. And unlike Xia Yan's five-watt bulb, the lighting source can be large or small, natural or artificial, as long it is bright enough to cast a perceptible shadow onstage. Thus, although He Mengfu clearly wrote with an awareness of what complex stage technology could contribute to text and performance, he also scripted elements that enabled flexibility in their execution. This flexibility was especially important as the military confrontations and atmoterrorism of the Second Sino-Japanese War continued, creating increasingly difficult conditions for theatrical performance.

## Engineering Atmosphere under Wartime Conditions

The effects of atmoterrorism and the material limitations of protracted war were acutely felt in Chongqing, which served as the wartime capital, KMT base of military operations, and home to refugees who had fled occupied areas from 1938 on. As such, Chongqing became the main target of Japanese aerial attacks, with more than 21,600 bombs dropped on the city in at least two hundred separate attacks between February 1938 and August 1943.[76] The city was literally on fire throughout much of the year—a condition that became a dominant image used for "affective mobilization" in the wartime films produced in Chongqing, as Weihong Bao has argued.[77] Residents of Chongqing lived in perpetual fear of bombings, spending much of their time in bunkers or retreating to the nearby countryside.[78] For theater artists, the increased danger of large gatherings meant a near halt to performances, with one exception: the annual "foggy season" of plays that they were able to mount in the winter months, when a thick blanket of fog covered the city and made aerial attacks too dangerous and difficult to attempt.[79] Theater's fate and flourishing during this period was thus intimately connected to, even dependent on, fog.[80] This helps to explain why fog came to be one of the most evocative (and popular) atmospheric metaphors in wartime Chinese theater. Wartime literature, in general, abounds with references to Chongqing fog, but there is a special emphasis on fog in plays like Song Zhidi's *Foggy Chongqing* and Lao She's 老舍 (Shu Qingchun 舒慶春, 1899–1966) *Lingering Fog* (殘霧, 1939).[81] Beyond serving as a setting, fog in these dramatic texts also metaphorically represents the psychological condition brought on by protracted trauma; rather than acute terror, it is the "brain fog" brought by unrelenting stress and uncertainty. And on a practical level, creating fog onstage presented yet another unique technical challenge for wartime theater artists.

Song's *Foggy Chongqing* offers an example of how the scripting of stage fog invokes these different layers of atmospheric meaning. Originally titled *The Whip* (鞭), the play was retitled *Foggy Chongqing* for its premiere—a change that not insignificantly emphasizes its atmospherics. Its Chongqing debut in 1940 was directed by Ying Yunwei (who had also directed the 1933 production of *Roar, China!*) and made a particular impression on Chongqing audiences before going on to performances throughout China and in Hong Kong (fig. 2.5).[82] In this play, the "fog of war" takes on a different meaning from its original European context; rather than the uncertainties encountered in military combat, it describes the ennui felt by those outside of, but affected by, the war.

Fig. 2.5. Production photograph from performance of *Foggy Chongqing* by the Long-Life Theater Troupe (中國萬歲劇團) in December 1941, depicting the semi-underground setting of act 1. Source: *Liangyou*, no. 128 (1941): 25.

As Constantine Tung has noted, the play reflects a change in the dramatic zeitgeist as the Second Sino-Japanese War wore on: "patriotic passion eventually gave way to a more reflective state of mind as the war prolonged and hardship became more intense," and drama began to offer a more nuanced "awareness of defects of the social, political and economic systems that had affected the conduct of the war and that were factors which caused increasing suffering of the people in their daily life."[83] The titular fog thus reflects the characters' inability to discern moral paths forward for their lives, while their ultimate failure to commit fully to the war effort has been read as a critique of mismanagement and corruption on the part of the KMT government. Chen Baichen and Dong Jian link the murkiness of the play's setting to intentional obfuscation, arguing that *Foggy Chongqing* indirectly references (and criticizes) attempts by the KMT to shroud its developing plans to launch a second purge against suspected CCP members in its ranks.[84] Only one character in *Foggy Chongqing*, a young woman named Lin Juanyu 林卷妤, consistently strives to find meaning in life and contribute to society. The others find their sense of purpose muddled by the promise of wealth from illegal business deals, financial dependence on romantic relationships, and incurable illness.

Yet again, the playwright also takes the literary metaphor beyond the text and scripts it into the material world of the stage. Analysis of *Foggy Chongqing* tends to focus on the circumstances its characters face and fog as a metaphor. This may be due in part to the fact that, at first glance, the stage directions in *Foggy Chongqing* do not seem as voluminous or technical as those of

Cao Yu and Xia Yan. However, as in Xia Yan's *Under Shanghai Eaves*, Song Zhidi uses scenographic architecture to establish specific physical and social relations among the characters, and like Cao Yu, he challenges production teams to create a specific and technically complex stage effect. The opening stage directions describe the setting of the first act as follows:

> This second floor is on the same level as the main street, and because of this, there is a small window that opens onto the side of the street. Frequently coal ash and even spit from people on the street come in. Through that small window, you can see the rapidly moving feet of pedestrians.
>
> There are two other windows in the left corner of the room, facing the steps of the alley house. People go up and down via those stairs, up to the street or down underground. The steps are very narrow, and very dark. This room on our stage, year-round practically never sees sunshine, and instead, sometimes fog rolls in through the windows. This makes the already dark room even seem humid—this room is dark and humid. Water even has the nerve to drip down along the walls.[85]

In Song's description, Chongqing's fog physically permeates the interior space and creates an oppressive atmosphere. One could almost imagine a similar effect in the theater itself, during the foggy season. Sound and light, too, bleed into the room:

> When the curtain rises, it is already dusk. The room is very quiet, but the street noisy. Nighttime Chongqing is lively. There are no lights on in the room, with only dim light from the street lamps giving off a faint outline. Outside the windows by the stairs, two sedan chairs have just gone by, with a mouthful of their mutterings, like: "Lift your head and look," "Heading up the mountain!," "Uh, how slippery!," "What's the rush?," "On the left, on the left!" As if there were someone intentionally walking by on the right and there was a very minor dispute, then finally the phrase "Let him pass!" is uttered, and everyone goes on their way![86]

These visual, material, and aural incursions establish that, in effect, there are no safe spaces in this world. Rather, the interior space is constantly at risk of being breached by uncontrollable outside forces, just as the residents of wartime Chongqing faced the ever-present possibility of a Japanese aerial attack.

In subsequent acts of the play, the setting shifts to a small restaurant started by the main characters and then to a more opulent villa in the (safer) city suburbs, even as the fogginess of the opening scene continues metaphorically to envelop the characters. However, what we find is not a direct relationship between stage effect and emotion, as seen in Cao Yu, but rather an equally close, but more amorphous, relationship between atmosphere and affect.

Indeed, rather than propelling action forward, the stage directions in *Foggy Chongqing* focus on creating environmental conditions that mirror and metaphorize the themes, message, and emotions of the characters. This use of atmosphere aligns with what Gernot Böhme has called its "quasi-objective" property, quoting Hermann Schmitz—sitting somewhere between object and subject, capable of being produced by and also of producing experience in those who experience it.[87] As Böhme notes, the critical potential of atmospheres lies in their ability to engage affectively, that is, to change minds, manipulate moods, and evoke emotions.[88] In the theater, atmosphere (like fog) spills over the edge of the stage, suffusing both the playing space and audience. This in turn transmits affect not just from playwright to actors as instructions or suggestions but also from the world of the play to the world of the audience.

Much like the thunder and lightning in Cao Yu's *Thunderstorm*, stage fog must have posed a series of challenges for staging. As a technical effect, fog is notoriously difficult to control. Today, theater technicians distinguish among smoke, haze, and fog, each of which has its own properties and production techniques. All three are often used in tandem with lighting to create atmospheric and supernatural effects onstage. Smoke and haze are typically created by machines that diffuse a chemical fluid into the air; smoke fills the stage space and then quickly dissipates, whereas haze particles linger in the air. Fog, in contrast, hovers close to the ground, and can be created simply by adding dry ice (solid carbon dioxide) to hot water. The carbon dioxide vapor produced is dense and colder than the ambient air temperature, so the resulting substance does not rise and dissipate, but rather rolls along the ground.[89] The machines and chemical substances common today were not developed until the mid-twentieth century, but the use of dry ice dates much earlier. First produced in a lab by French inventor Adrien-Jean-Pierre Thilorier (1790–1844), solid carbon dioxide was introduced in China as "dry ice" (乾冰) during the early- to mid-1930s.[90] Initially, it seems to have been used primarily for food storage, air conditioning, and experiments in cloud seeding, but at least one article makes reference to the use of dry ice and fans to create fog in Hollywood film productions.[91] It is also possible that dry ice may have been used by military scientists, as in the United States, Great Britain, and Japan, for experiments that helped design aeronautical navigation systems.[92]

Did Chinese theater artists in wartime Chongqing, then, use dry ice to create actual fog for their production of *Foggy Chongqing*? How essential is the effect—does fog actually *need* to roll in through the windows during the play? Likewise, how might a production transmit the highly tactile feeling of humidity from stage to audience, or engineer a continuous drip of water without damaging the set pieces? Fog differs from thunder, lightning, and even rain and snow in that it is by nature more amorphous. A crack of thunder or bolt of lightning is sudden and sharp. A sunrise is gradual but distinct, moving clearly from darkness to light. Fog is more diffuse. It permeates the atmosphere and changes it in sometimes imperceptible ways. At other times, it can be so dense as to obscure vision and conceal the material reality in front of one's very eyes. Fog also appears less frequently than thunder and lightning in technical articles on stage effects, and when it does appear, it is grouped with clouds. He Mengfu's stage lighting book, for instance, refers to fog along with clouds and fire as effects that could be created with an "effects projector" (效果放映機), as well as other techniques for using lighting for "clouds and fog" (雲霧) or waves.[93] The fact that many of the articles on theatrical special effects published around this same time do *not* describe fog, however, suggests that the materials for making dry-ice fog may have been less commonly available or used for the stage. And unfortunately, performance reviews from the time do little to shed light on these particular questions, though they do record general praise for the stage design and technology involved in productions of *Foggy Chongqing*, both in Chongqing and beyond. The mystery of precisely how, or even if, Chinese theater artists were able to make stage fog in wartime Chongqing may remain obscure. Yet the fact that a playwright scripted a difficult technical effect into his play, even under adverse wartime conditions, once again underscores the importance of the relationship among stage technology, atmosphere, and affect in *huaju* of this period.

The puzzle of wartime stage fog also points to a bigger issue that undergirded many of the theoretical discussions of the period: the ultimate difficulty of controlling live theater. This question of control surfaces both in their heightened investment in the one theatrical element that seems the most stable—the script—and in debates over the extent to which performances ought to rely on lighting, sets, and other technical elements. In the late 1930s–early 1940s, Chinese theater artists wrote frequently and vociferously about a perceived "script wasteland" (劇本荒)—a term used at the time to refer to a lack of new, original plays by Chinese playwrights and a perception that runs counter to the way in which later historiography has labeled this very era a "Golden Age" of *huaju*. Oftentimes, such discussions were embedded in how-to guides for aspiring playwrights, as in the Xia Yan essay cited earlier in this chapter, or alongside references to the role of theater as a weapon of war. Theater-as-military technology was tasked primarily with mobilizing audiences in support of the national war effort and against the Japanese, which required consistent and precise messaging. The necessity of getting the script just right was in turn motivated by the widespread perception that a script could and did impose clear and specific requirements on theatrical production. As Zheng Geng wrote of politically oriented realist plays, "The script is content and the performance is the form; here, the script first of all *requires* theater workers in all areas to carry out the realist line" (emphasis added).[94] In other words, a play *must* be staged the way it was written. Control of the script would therefore translate into control of the performance and, ultimately, its effect on the audience. The dissemination of consistent and at times even mechanically prescriptive sets of instructions for all areas of the theater was thus essential for theater's efficacy as it increasingly took on the role *of* a technology—specifically, a technology of war—as conflict with Japan escalated.

In this, wartime theater theory also suggests far-reaching acceptance of the concept of theater as an "art of control," which Bao has identified and discussed within the wartime writing of dramatist and theorist Hong Shen. Drawing connections to Hong's training as a ceramic engineer at Ohio State University and his interest in behavioral psychology, Bao argues that Hong Shen developed a "technics" of theater that emphasized the "social effects" of performance and prioritized results, efficiency, procedural control, and the elimination of waste. However, as she notes, Hong's theory also allowed for a more dialectical relationship between control and freedom in the creative process, even as the perceived need for control over its "social effects" increased.[95] In addition, while Hong Shen's work may offer one of the clearest articulations of the complex relationship among technics, performance, and social efficacy, he was far from unique in his attempts to theorize their connection. As this chapter shows, this was in fact a widespread concern, and one that influenced all elements of theater making.

Stage technology created a particular conundrum for the art of control: on the one hand, control of stage technology (like control of the script and the acting) could enable greater control of its effect on the audience; on the other hand, resource scarcity that limited access to well-equipped stages and spectacular effects could distract from the political work at hand. According to a history of scenography written by Li Chang, Hong Shen wrote in 1938:

> Those who only understand how to quibble over scenographic and lighting conditions, as of today have already been proven to be impossible and unnecessary. They are those who argue that the weapons win the war, and this is very different from our position. When we talk of the level [of performance], it is to show that under extremely difficult conditions, we can do away with the help of stage conditions, even leave the stage itself, and [instead] use theater with real plots and honest performances to move people.[96]

Notably, Hong Shen *did* believe design and technology to be important components of theater, and wrote sections on topics such as scenery and lighting in his introductory guide for directors, published in 1943. However, he also highlights the fact that "technique is the means and not the end."[97] Moreover, in the quote displayed above, Hong Shen deemphasizes the elements of the theater that he perceived as less consistently controllable under wartime conditions—notably, scenic and lighting elements.[98] In contrast, theater artists such as Song Zhidi and He Mengfu advocated a more middle-ground approach that suggested adapting, rather than doing away with, "stage conditions."[99] Indeed, it was perhaps the tension among these positions, as well as the material conditions of performance, that most shaped the plays written as the war raged on, especially those composed in the hinterland cities of Wuhan, Chengdu, and Chongqing.

In light of contemporaneous debates, we can reread Song's *Foggy Chongqing* as an attempt to bridge the gaps between reliance on and eschewal of stagecraft and stage technology. Rather than doing away with scenery and lighting in the face of poor material conditions and the resulting difficulty of fully controlling the stage space, Song uses fog to build fluidity and flexibility into the technical elements that his stage directions stipulate. With actual fog onstage, his script would be fully realized; without it, however, the proper oppressive, suffocating atmosphere could still be created through other technical effects like lighting and scenography. These foggy atmospherics also add layers of nuance to the idea of theater as a wartime "art of control." The flexibility of fog necessarily relinquished some degree of the playwright's control over the text, but it also enabled more widespread production and political efficacy under wartime conditions.

Playwriting may seem like the least technical, or rather, the least *technological* component of theatrical production. Indeed, while many playwrights do compose with some imagination of the stage in mind, it is rarely if ever their responsibility to determine *how* their vision will be transformed into material reality. The case of Chinese theater artists from the 1930s–1940s, however, demonstrates an alternative understanding of the relationship between page and stage. *Huaju* playwrights including Cao Yu, Xia Yan, He Mengfu, and Song Zhidi clearly wrote with a grasp of staging and stagecraft, but, more important, they made key elements of their plots, character development, and the overall atmosphere of their plays dependent on stage effects. In the development of stage directions and playwriting theory from the mid-1930s to the early 1940s, then, we can trace an arc of how awareness about the technical potential of the stage affected dramaturgy. When playwrights like Cao Yu and Xia Yan first began to write with production and well-equipped theater venues in mind, they scripted effects and architectures that maximized the potential of lighting, sound, special effects, and scenography. As the Second Sino-Japanese War gained momentum and altered both the mission and the material conditions of the theater, there was a shift to plays that still reflected this heightened awareness of production and sophisticated stage technology, but that also built in the flexibility needed to accommodate greater degrees of uncertainty and variation in performance circumstances. This shift provides further evidence for a general maturation of *huaju* dramaturgy during this period, but in an area that has been less acknowledged in previous theater historiography.

The close connection between dramaturgy and stage technology seen in the stage directions of wartime *huaju* plays is, moreover, indicative of a much broader and deeper connection between theater and technology in modern Chinese drama. During the Second Sino-Japanese War, this relationship developed in several significant ways. First, wartime conditions prompted new discussions of content and form, in which form was often discussed in relation to stage technology and theater was explicitly positioned *as* a type of military technology. Second, the fervor with which many theater artists answered the call to transform theater into a weapon of wartime mobilization (and, in the CCP base areas, political conversion) cemented the importance of theater as an ideological tool across political lines. As discussed in the introduction and chapter 1, the use of Chinese theater for ideological and didactic purposes has a long history, and social reform was one of the main goals of early *huaju* in China. And, although the presence of other artistic, commercial, and personal motivations should not be discounted, it is significant that the artists most concerned with writing, and writing about, *wartime* theater were also engaged in the publication of practical and technical guides for theatrical production. In other words, the technical details of theatrical production became a key component of both its aesthetics and its politics. Finally, continued attempts at broad dissemination of practical how-to guides, as both stand-alone volumes and in wartime periodicals, speaks to the ongoing relationship between theater technology and knowledge production. However, whereas the late 1920s–early 1930s saw theater technology framed as an essential component of modern common knowledge, publications in the late 1930s–early 1940s started to reframe the same topics as elements of political propaganda.

The increasingly similar terms with which Chinese theater artists wrote of playwriting—as well as design, directing, acting, and other theatrical elements—also suggests a movement toward standardization of theatrical practice, or at least a growing desire for consistency in some areas. Lively debates over the purpose, content, and form of theater continued, however, and any real standardization was rendered impossible by the vast variation in individual perspectives and wartime conditions across China. Both ideological divides and material conditions only worsened as the Second Sino-Japanese War concluded and conflict turned inward during the Chinese Civil War (1945–49) between the KMT and the CCP. During the Civil War, the importance of military metaphors to the theater increased and took on additional meanings. In the CCP-controlled areas, for instance, the idea of militarized theater invoked more of a guerrilla-style attack and emphasized adaptability over standardization.[100] After the CCP emerged victorious and established the People's Republic of China in 1949, it then fell to theater artists to untangle these mixed metaphors and reconceptualize all aspects of the theater, from the most practical to the most theoretical, for a new socialist state. Ironically, the driving ethos that would emerge in the realm of stage technology also was not solely one of rigid control, but rather a dialectic between standardization and ingenuity that inherited both concerns over control and a spirit of flexibility from wartime theater.

# THREE

# Socialist Utopian Special Effects

*Technological Fantasy on the Seventeen Years Stage*

————◆•▶◀•◆————

The final act of Tian Han's *Fantasia of the Ming Tombs Reservoir* (十三陵水库畅想曲, 1958)[1] ends with a vision of the future: twenty years after the play's main events, Chinese society has been fully transformed into a socialist utopia, marked by a harmonious blending of traditional Chinese aesthetics and modern technology. In this utopian imaginary, the Ming Tombs Reservoir, which was an actual construction project completed in June 1958, has become a site of leisure, education, and artistic creation. Elderly tourists and children learn the history of humans overcoming nature through story and song (see fig. 3.1). Residents wear clothing that evokes the styles of historic costume drama, while they eat and drink the hybrid fruits of agricultural science. Telecommunication devices bear striking similarities to laptop computers or tablets, with screens that enable users to video chat with friends and family.[2] And while recent scholarship has demonstrated the popularity, influence, and importance of science writing and science fiction from the founding of the PRC in 1949 to the beginning of the Cultural Revolution in 1966—known as the Seventeen Years period in the historiography of the PRC—*Fantasia of the Ming Tombs Reservoir* remains relatively unique in bringing the future to life onstage during this period.

*Fantasia* brings together several different realms of offstage and onstage technology by depicting the future of the Ming Tombs Reservoir alongside the initial construction of the reservoir itself, in 1958, and by valorizing disciplined voluntary participation in a public works project. The main arc of the play follows a group of writers and artists who visit the reservoir work site in order to gain inspiration for literary and artistic pieces about the project, as well as to participate in manual labor. The context, characters, and plot clearly

Fig. 3.1. Production photograph from the final futuristic scene of *Fantasia of the Ming Tombs Reservoir* by China Youth Art Theater. From the family collection of Xiaomei Chen.

reflect the top-down modernization, infrastructure projects, and bureaucratic reorganization that characterized the early decades of the PRC. On another level, the play's twelve acts, multiple locations, and quick temporal shifts also provided theater artists with an opportunity to experiment with stage technologies and special effects in new ways. This process—in particular, the development of a "homegrown" revolving stage (土转台) to facilitate scene changes—in turn brought theater making into alignment with the broader experimental spirit, efforts at self-reliance, and emphasis on *tu* 土 (local, indigenous, or homegrown) technologies that characterized the early PRC and especially the Great Leap Forward (1958–62).

In one sense, the scripting and application of stage technology in this period continued the trajectory begun in the late Qing and Republican eras. However, Republican-era stage technologies were primarily seen as Western imports and incorporated into a body of common knowledge targeted at an urban petite bourgeoisie (see chapter 1). Wartime know-how focused on atmospherics and the flexible deployment of stage technology in the service of national salvation. In contrast, the early PRC saw an expansion in the target audience for technical know-how and a shift to a multidirectional mode of knowledge production. The reach of theater handbooks, trade journals, and popular periodicals was extended, with the publication of simple "how-to" handbooks for the masses (群众) significantly increasing in the 1950s and

1960s. At the same time, the experimental spirit of the age and the call to "learn from life" (体验生活) prompted theater artists to seek inspiration from the grassroots. Well understood in relation to the content of theater produced during the early PRC, this ethos also extended to professional artists creating rough-and-ready solutions to technical problems in the theater.

This chapter examines the role of stage technology during the Seventeen Years period, with a focus on the Great Leap Forward and the subsequent Socialist Education Movement (1962–66). First, it examines the discourse surrounding theater technology in the early PRC, an area where theater intersected on a material level with other major areas of state-driven development, such as industrial and agricultural technologies. Whereas previous scholarship has focused largely on the reform of dramatic content and acting practice in this period, I argue that the industrialization of professional arts organizations and dissemination of technical knowledge were equally important elements of attempts to remake theater into a tool of the socialist state. The Great Leap Forward, in particular, saw a concerted effort to improve stage technologies in the name of a broader "technological revolution" (技术革命). Then, in order to demonstrate how theater artists translated these abstract ideological frameworks into practice, I analyze production-specific innovations in stage technology in three seminal plays of this period: *Fantasia of the Ming Tombs Reservoir* (1958), *Sentinels under the Neon Lights* (霓虹灯下的哨兵, 1963), and *The East Is Red* (东方红, 1964). Despite differences in content and genre, these plays all presented theater artists with specific—and difficult to achieve—technical requirements. In overcoming these challenges, theater artists both displayed their prowess at *tu* innovation and developed a new aesthetics of *technological fantasy* that invited audiences to imagine both the world of the play and the stage technologies used to create it. Through such fantasies, socialist utopian visions of the past, present, and future operated not only on the level of content but also through the material, technical world of the stage and its audience.

## Technology, Culture, and a New Nation

The foundational importance to the PRC of the relationships between industry and culture and between technology and art can be illustrated by its most iconic moment: Mao Zedong standing atop Tiananmen in Beijing to declare the birth of the new nation on October 1, 1949. Looking out over crowds of thousands, China's new leaders saw both a sea of willing spectators and visions of what Tiananmen Square—and the city surrounding it—could become. Mao Zedong imagined that a forest of chimneys would dominate

Beijing's skyline, while Premier Zhou Enlai saw the potential of a large open space flanked by imposing edifices. According to anecdotes recorded by Zhou Enlai's head bodyguard at the time, Cheng Yuangong 成元功 (1925–2012), the premier remarked that "the largest square in the world should also be the most beautiful, and that it should be the heart of the nation, with a monument, a history museum, and a grand national theater at the centre, the east, and the west respectively."[3] The visions attributed to Mao Zedong and Zhou Enlai are indicative of the two-pronged approach taken to development in the first decade of the PRC, which emphasized both industrial growth—to be facilitated by improvements in industrial technology—and cultural development. Smokestacks and grand theater spaces, both real and imagined, would become key visual and material symbols of China's transformation into a modernized socialist nation.

From the beginning, the practical aspects of establishing a new nation were intertwined with the cultural and symbolic. In the years immediately following the CCP's victory over the KMT in the Civil War, the new government faced tasks such as constructing the bureaucracy necessary to govern a large nation and rebuilding an economy devastated by decades of war and disorder. Early efforts at socialist transformation focused on the development of industrial capacity and land reform, as well as shifting from private to joint private–public or state-owned enterprises. A key element of these advances was technological development, largely with the aid of industrial and agricultural technology transferred from the Soviet Union.[4] On the first anniversary of its founding, the country found itself again at war when Chinese troops joined the Korean War (1950–53) on October 1, 1950. Yet, despite these urgent political, economic, and military concerns, the new PRC government also prioritized setting guidelines and creating infrastructure for cultural production across different fields such as visual art, literature, theater, and film.

Along with film, theater was especially central to the cultural dimensions of socialist construction, and served as a meeting ground for technology, science, and the arts. By 1949, the belief that theater could play an active role in the creation of a modern Chinese society was well established in both Communist and non-Communist circles. As noted in previous chapters, intellectuals of the May Fourth Movement had advocated the use of Ibsenian social problem plays and realism more broadly as a means of revealing and correcting the ills of contemporary society. In the early 1940s, Mao Zedong articulated the role of literature and the arts (文艺) in the Communist revolution and emphasized the "national, scientific, and mass" (民族，科学，大众) characteristics of ideologically correct culture.[5] The "Talks at the Yan'an Forum on Literature and the Arts" in May 1942 made a similar connection among politics, culture, and technology by positioning literature and the arts as cogs and screws in the revolutionary machine (in reference to Lenin).[6] After the founding of the PRC, the idea that a scientific approach was essential to the arts persisted, and as the political importance of technological development increased, so too did the importance of technology to the theater.

The cultural concerns of the early 1940s carried over into the new state, and groundwork for a new cultural bureaucracy was laid even before the PRC was officially founded. In July 1949, 753 representative "culture workers" (文艺工作者) gathered at the former imperial garden of Zhongnanhai in Beijing for the First All-China Literature and Arts Workers Representatives Meeting (第一次全国文学艺术工作者代表大会). There participants formulated a series of broad regulations for the arts and selected members for an All-China Federation of Literature and Arts (中国文学艺术界联合会).[7] The federation, referred to as "Wenlian" for short, was an umbrella organization for individual associations organized by cultural field, such as the Chinese Dramatists Association (中国戏剧家协会). After 1949, these organizations and their members answered to the newly formed Ministries of Propaganda and Culture, which also established a number of professional and training institutions such as the Central Drama Academy (中央戏剧学院, est. 1950), the China Youth Art Theater (中国青年艺术剧院, est. 1949), and the Beijing People's Art Theater (北京人民艺术剧院, or BPAT, est. 1952).[8]

The results of creating a cultural bureaucracy and state-sponsored institutions were far from uniform, but nonetheless brought a greater degree of systematization to the world of literature and the arts than previously had been instituted.[9] Moreover, beyond arranging creative practices within a rationalized system with government and party oversight, the establishment of a cultural bureaucracy in China specifically aligned literature and the arts with an industrial logic of organization and production. This association between the arts and industry is made clear in a speech given by Zhou Enlai on July 6, 1949, in which he emphasized the national task of "developing production":

> Not only do we need to found an All-China Federation of Literature and Arts, we also need to model it on the federation of trade unions, with all kinds of industrial unions beneath it. We need to separate into divisions and establish leagues of literature, theater, film, music, fine arts, dance, etc. Only in this way will we be able to facilitate the progress of our work, facilitate the training of people with talent, facilitate promulgation, facilitate reform.[10]

In Zhou's formulation, literature and the arts are imagined as industries, with each art form figured as a trade, subject to standards of efficiency and dissemination that value the logic of the factory over spontaneous creativity. Industrial institutionalization brings writers and artists one step closer to being cogs and screws in the service of socialist transformation.

The regime was also interested in controlling, on a more concrete level, the technical parameters of the arts. For the theater, this meant codifying (at least in theory) all levels of production, from content to acting technique to theater management, venues, and equipment. Ideological correctness of content was one major area of concern, especially in popular repertoire carried over from before the founding of the PRC. For instance, the Ministry of Culture formed a Committee for Opera Reform (戏曲改进委员会) under the direction of Zhou Yang 周扬 (1908–89), then deputy minister of the Ministry of Culture.[11] This committee both banned specific titles and characterized other plays as either in need of revision or acceptable for performance.[12] All-China Cultural Administrative Conferences (全国文化行政会议) were also held annually beginning in 1951. Measures passed there included "Provisional Regulations for the Management of Theaters" (剧场管理暂行条例) in 1951 and a "Directive Regarding the Reorganization and Strengthening of Theater Troupes throughout the Country" (关于整顿和加强全国剧团的指示) in 1952.[13] As is discussed in chapter 4, the national, provincial, and local governments also invested heavily in renovating and constructing theater venues, as well as multipurpose spaces such as cultural palaces and workers' clubs that could also host performances.[14]

The state also financed the production and dissemination of new knowledge related to stage technology and theatrical design. One early example of this can be found in the China Youth Cultural Troupe (中国青年文工团), a delegation sent to participate in the Third World Youth and Students Festival in East Berlin in August 1951. This delegation included nine set designers and technicians, in addition to performers, cadres, and staff. Following the festival, the group staged exhibition performances and participated in cultural exchange throughout the Soviet Bloc.[15] The designers' purpose was not solely to provide technical support for the troupe's performances, which largely took place outdoors or on stages with simple backdrops, but also to spend time working in and studying with the staff of famous theaters in the Soviet cities visited. Upon their return, two members of the delegation, Li Chang 李畅 (1929–2021) and Qi Mudong 齐牧冬 (1922–2004), compiled a record of their experiences and many of the materials collected on the tour into a 1954 volume entitled *Theater and Stage Technologies* (剧场与舞台技术) (figs. 3.2

Fig. 3.2. Cover from *Theater and Stage Technologies.* Source: Li Chang et al., *Juchang yu wutai jishu* (Wuhan: Zhongnan renmin wenxue yishu chubanshe, 1954).

and 3.3). It includes photographs, diagrams, and detailed descriptions of both stage machinery and set construction techniques.[16] As the afterword notes, the book was specifically meant to transmit foreign expertise to professional theater troupes throughout China.[17] Likewise, theater experts from Moscow traveled to the PRC along with touring theatrical productions and participated in knowledge exchange, especially in technical areas. In December 1954, for instance, artists from the Stanislavski and Nemirovich-Danchenko Music Theatre performed several pieces at the Tianqiao Theater (天桥剧场) in Beijing and lectured on scenic design and stage technology. Transcripts of their lectures and technical materials were then published as a special "internal study document" (内部学习资料) in 1957.[18]

The early 1950s also saw the publication of technical theater handbooks

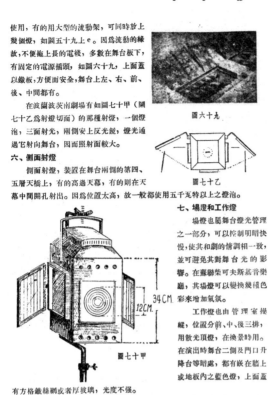

Fig. 3.3. Representative page illustrating lighting equipment from *Theater and Stage Technologies.* Source: Li Chang et al., *Juchang yu wutai jishu* (Wuhan: Zhongnan renmin wenxue yishu chubanshe, 1954), 37.

that were much more widely accessible than professional manuals or internal study documents. Some of these were reprints of materials that circulated in the 1930s–1940s, such as a journal called *New Performance* (新演劇) that had originally circulated in Wuhan and Chongqing from 1937 to 1940 and was republished in 1951. This particular journal largely consisted of translations of Soviet materials and included articles on scenic design principles under the broad heading of "stage technology."[19] This suggests a direct line of continuity between wartime theater artists and the early PRC, as well as a capacious, even blurry, conceptualization of "stage technology" that included design within its parameters. In the latter half of the 1950s, state-sponsored publishing houses also began to print new technical theater how-to guides that were directed at general audiences. These volumes explicitly targeted the "people" (人民) or the masses, discussed technical topics in colloquial language, and featured highly accessible titles.[20] *How to Organize Amateur Spoken Drama Performance* (怎样组织业余话剧演出, 1956) by the Guangdong People's Press, for instance, covers the basics of scripting, directing, acting, and stage technology in only twenty pages. The Chinese Theater Press, which is the national-level publishing house for the subject area, also issued an entire series on the topic of rural performance in 1958, with titles like *How to Tour a Performance* (怎样做好巡回演出工作) and *How Rural Amateur Troupes Can Put Up a Stage and Construct a Theater* (农村业余剧团怎样搭台和建筑剧场).

In contrast to professional manuals and pre-1949 reprints, these handbooks were not direct translations of foreign texts or compilations of foreign knowledge, but rather were either written by self-described amateur (业余) artists or collectively authored, and heavily emphasized self-reliance. One representative example published by the Liaoning People's Press, for instance, frames the content of its *Introduction to Scenography* (舞台美术入门) with reference to amateur theater troupe experience and specific technical theater areas (figs. 3.4 and 3.5). Author Zhang Yaoqing's 张耀卿 brief content description before the main text states:

> This book follows my own work experience and combines it with the actual circumstances of amateur theater troupe(s) to explain colloquially: typical stage equipment, scenery construction, and the flipped-picture method for the perspectival stage; lighting and costumes, sound, and other basic knowledge. In order to facilitate study and illustrate problems, simple and easy-to-understand figures are also included. In addition to being perused and used by amateur theater troupes, it can also be used as a textbook for literature-and-arts training classes.[21]

The brief description gives a sense of the extent to which stage technology and literacy in technical figures were considered essential elements of basic theater knowledge, even for amateurs.[22] Moreover, through its emphasis on work experience and training, the handbook's content description also highlights human agency in knowledge production and transmission. Not only were handbooks meant to be read and the skills within them applied, they were also meant to inspire further person-to-person sharing of information and expertise.

This emphasis on amateur knowledge production and transmission coincided with the broader promotion of amateurism in neighborhood and work unit "cultural troupes" (文工团), as well as collaborations between professional and amateur theater makers. Colin Mackerras, for instance, quotes a *People's Daily* (人民日报) report of 283,000 amateur and worker drama troupes nationwide in 1959 (compared with 3,513 professional troupes), and *Drama Monthly* reported 14,000 amateur troupes comprising 400,000 actors in Heilongjiang Province alone during that same year.[23] In the late 1950s, large state-sponsored *huaju* companies like BPAT, the Shanghai People's Art Theater (上海人民艺术剧院, or SPAT), and the China Youth Art Theater also began to recruit and collaborate with playwrights unaffiliated with their theaters (院外专业作家) and amateur worker and peasant writers (工农业余作家).[24] The Shanghai People's Art Theater similarly claimed that a full third of the performances they sponsored in 1958 were performed by workers, peasants, and soldiers.[25] In this context, theater handbooks written by and for the amateurs suddenly had widespread significance.

In addition to illustrating the kinds of technical theater know-how deemed important in the early PRC, theater handbooks also matter for what they reveal about the very nature of theatrical knowledge. First, handbooks suggest a technical level of interconnection among arts and culture, science and technology, and ideology during this period.[26] The handbook or how-to guide grew to be an important genre of popular literature during the 1950s, across a wide range of topics including literacy, literature and the arts, science and technology, and Marxist ideology. In the theater, handbook topics included technical and design elements such as scenography, lighting, costume and makeup, and so on, as well as the basics of theatrical production, performance technique for specific *xiqu* genres, and playwriting. Similar handbooks exist for film projectionists, which mirror theater handbooks in their technical orientation and, in addition to the basic skills for running film projectors, include such details as how to build and maintain slide projectors.[27]

The technical orientation of these handbooks also directly connects them to science and technology proper, and specifically to the "science popularization" (科学普及 or 科普) movement that began shortly after the founding of the PRC. Indeed, if science popularization and science fiction of the 1950s worked in concert to inculcate what Nicolai Volland has termed a "scientific mindset" in socialist readers, then the popularization of stage technology handbooks and increased amateur participation in theatrical production likewise fostered a budding *technical* mindset as the basis for artistic production.[28] While it has long been acknowledged that the arts, literature, and culture of

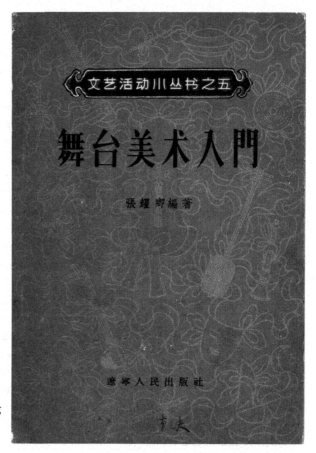

文艺活动小丛书之五

舞台美术入門

張耀卿編著

遼寧人民出版社

Fig. 3.4. Cover from *Introduction to Scenography.* Source: Zhang Yaoqing, *Wutai meishu rumen* (Shenyang: Liaoning renmin chubanshe, 1956).

the PRC played central roles in disseminating ideas and information—be that a party directive or basic scientific knowledge—the handbooks do more than deliver content.[29] They demonstrate an overarching concern with cultivating technical skill across different, seemingly unrelated areas via similar methods of knowledge transmission.

There was also an overlap in the personnel employed in efforts to popularize technical knowledge, in the arts and other fields, as well as the aforementioned increase of connections between professional and amateur theater artists. Cultural centers and arts workers participated in the process of disseminating science and technology to the masses, and, in turn, arts and cultural workers absorbed both political ideology and a technical mentality into their own creative processes. In the other direction, intellectuals who had been

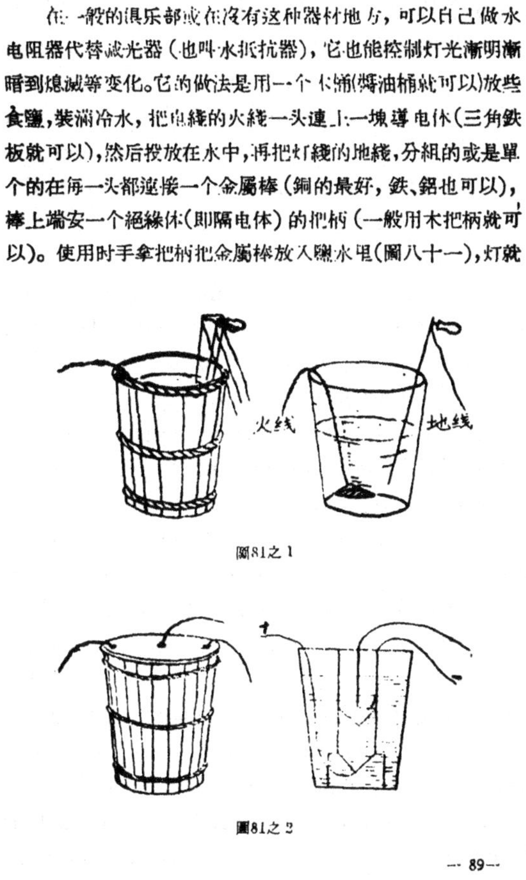
在一般的俱乐部或在沒有这种器材地方，可以自己做水电阻器代替减光器（也叫水抵抗器），它也能控制灯光漸明漸暗到熄滅等变化。它的做法是用一个木桶（醬油桶就可以）放些食鹽，裝滿冷水，把电綫的火綫一头連上一塊導电体（三角鉄板就可以），然后投放在水中，再把灯綫的地綫，分組的或是單个的在每一头都連接一个金屬棒（銅的最好，鉄、鋁也可以），棒上端安一个絕緣体（即隔电体）的把柄（一般用木把柄就可以）。使用时手拿把柄把金屬棒放入鹽水里（圖八十一），灯就

火线
地线
圖81之1
圖81之2
—89—

Fig. 3.5. Representative technical drawing from *Introduction to Scenography*, which shows how to make a liquid rheostat dimmer using techniques similar to those found in manuals from the 1930s. Source: Zhang Yaoqing, *Wutai meishu rumen* (Shenyang: Liaoning renmin chubanshe, 1956), 89.

active in the theater world took leadership positions that reached into science and technology. One key example is Guo Moruo, who was known for his work in archaeology as well as in literature and drama. Between the 1940s and 1960s, Guo wrote a number of influential plays, such as the historical dramas *Qu Yuan* (1942) and *Cai Wenji* (蔡文姬, 1959). In 1949, he became the head of the Chinese Academy of Sciences (中国科学院) and an advocate of science popularization, as well as the first chairman of the All-China Federation of Literature and Arts.[30] This trend echoed the case of many Republican-era theater artists who received training in engineering or science before working in the theater (see chapter 2). However, whereas the field of theater (in the Bourdieusian sense) before the founding of the PRC was geographically dispersed and politically diverse, close connections among theater and other arts industries in the early PRC took place under the umbrella of state control.[31] To be sure, as recent scholarship has demonstrated, top-down policies were far from hegemonic in practice, and experience at the grassroots level varied widely.[32] State-directed systematization of knowledge dissemination, the application of a techno-industrial ethos to nonindustrial fields, and an emphasis on scientific method as ideologically correct shaped theatrical practice, but also resulted in a variegated relationship and porous boundaries among art, industry, and technology.

Finally, handbooks (theatrical and otherwise) reflect larger tensions between expertise and popular knowledge that rose to the fore under socialist construction. In particular, the framing of the manuals and handbooks discussed above reveals a desire to recast foreign knowledge for a Chinese audience and technical expertise for nonexperts. The emphasis on amateur-*produced* knowledge in mass handbooks also parallels what Sigrid Schmalzer has called the "class politics of knowledge" in reference to science dissemination, or an emphasis on creating a two-way flow of knowledge between intellectuals and the masses that originated in Mao's 1942 "Talks at the Yan'an Forum."[33] The class politics of knowledge pervaded literature, culture, and scientific and technological development throughout the high socialist period, and related tensions perhaps most famously rose to the fore during the Hundred Flowers Campaign (1956) and Anti-Rightist Movement (1957).[34] Under the directive of "letting a hundred flowers bloom and a hundred schools of thought contend," for instance, Mao and other CCP leaders called for intellectuals and artists to use their expertise to critique both government policies and the progress-to-date of socialist construction. Mao's speeches during the Hundred Flowers period also emphasized the need to be "both red and expert" (又红又专), or to balance political consciousness and intellectual contributions.[35] The subsequent Anti-Rightist Movement, however, quickly suppressed dissenting political opinions and harshly persecuted a large number of intellectuals and artists, many of whom had foreign ties, elite backgrounds, or both.[36] Playwright Wu Zuguang, for instance, had been celebrated for wartime plays such as *Return on a Snowy Night*, but was persecuted during the Anti-Rightist campaign by the Dramatists Association, then under the direction of Tian Han.[37] Scientists were also condemned for expertise that contradicted politically driven campaigns, as in the case of hydrologist Huang Wanli's 黄万里 (1911–2001) opposition to the Three Gorges Dam project.[38] In the wake of purging high-profile intellectuals across fields, Mao then began more actively to advocate the bottom-up production of folk knowledge and "mass science."[39] Ultimately, this reflected the ongoing and contentious negotiation of what kind of knowledge was ideologically correct and how to position expertise that extended across fields in both art and science.

## Socialist Utopian Plays and Technological Fantasy

In the theater, the complexities of the relationships between industrialization and cultural production, between experts and the people, and between the technical and the artistic were reflected in the content, production process, and even the material technologies of the plays produced during this period. The play referenced at the beginning of this chapter, *Fantasia of the Ming Tombs Reservoir*, for example, showcased human creativity, effort, and engineering in equal measure. It served as the catalyst for an enthusiastic, though short-lived, trend of "socialist utopian plays" (社会主义乌托邦戏剧) about technological innovation and material production that were written and staged from 1958 to 1960.[40] The production of *Fantasia*, meanwhile, served as a site for *tu* innovation in the service of the special effects that playwright Tian Han envisioned and scripted. It provided an example for negotiating how foreign technologies, *xiqu* aesthetics, and audience imaginations could be made to work together in the theater of socialist construction.

From its very conception, *Fantasia* was imbricated in the logic of industrial production in that it was one of ten new plays that Tian Han pledged to write for the Great Leap Forward. Begun by Chairman Mao in February 1958, the Great Leap Forward was a period of mass mobilization in industry and agriculture, with the goal of surpassing the production levels of the United States and the United Kingdom. Slogans such as "more, faster, better, cheaper" (多快好省) inspired attempts to increase crop yields, the smelting of steel in backyard furnaces, the tireless labor of construction teams, and, in the theater, pledges of exponential increases in the number of plays to be written and produced. Tian Han, for example, published a manifesto in April 1958 that promoted the Great Leap ethos and listed astronomical script production and performance quotas for various city and regional professional troupes.[41] The Shanghai People's Art Theater pledged to increase its planned number of new scripts from 30 to 82; BPAT pledged to create 120 scripts within their organization and to advise external playwrights on an additional 60 scripts. The China Youth Art Theater set their goal at 366 scripts.[42] Projected increases in performances were on a similar scale, with SPAT, for example, reporting a 262 percent increase in the number of performances from 1957 to 1958.[43]

As noted above, *Fantasia* also connected to the Great Leap Forward on a narrative level, as the play was based on the actual project to create a dam and reservoir at the site of the Ming Tombs, on the outskirts of Beijing, that took place between January and June 1958. Its massive movement of earth and feats of engineering involved more than 400,000 people, and it was portrayed in the media as a triumph of collective labor and of man over nature, with the project's successes widely remediated through literature, drama, and visual art. Tian Han's play focuses on a delegation of writers and artists visiting the Ming Tombs work site and is, as Paola Iovene has argued, "concerned not only with assessing the correct handling of the relationship between technical expertise (*zhuan*) and political conscience (*hong*) on one hand, and manual and intellectual laborers on the other, but also with the problem of how to write such a play."[44] As a document about *how to* write about labor, the play thus parallels the how-to orientation of the many handbooks published in the 1950s, but with a literary twist. The solution Tian Han proposes to this problem is that artists and intellectuals must willingly and actively participate in manual labor in order to be able to portray it, as the characters in the play demonstrate. They offer a blueprint for this process by touring the work site, interviewing leaders and model workers to find the best stories to retell, and finally rolling up their own sleeves to help with the construction efforts.

However, if the play's diegesis focuses on human labor and a "poetics of practice,"[45] as Iovene terms it, actual theatrical production also required attention to material technology and technics. From the beginning, *Fantasia* was a collaboration with the China Youth Art Theater, with production meetings and rehearsals taking place as Tian was drafting the script. As Tian Han's secretary Li Zhiyan 黎之彦 records, daily conversations involving Tian Han, director Jin Shan 金山 (1911–82), and Xiong Wei 熊伟, who served as assistant to the head of the China Youth Art Theater, covered not only plot and character development but also specific stage effects that Tian Han wanted to script into his stage directions. For instance, in one scene, a character (modeled on Guo Moruo) stands in front of the reservoir workers with a bright light on his face, as if in a thunderstorm, and sings a tune entitled "Ode to Thunder and Lightning" (雷电颂). As Li Zhiyan explains, Tian Han believed that "the beauty of the play should be expressed in the scenography and lighting, and also used to sculpt the personalities and behavior of the characters, like in Chinese *xiqu*."[46] Moreover, as in experiments with scripting atmosphere in wartime drama, scenography and lighting were considered components of dramatic form that also had affective dimensions. The work of a play about socialist labor was, therefore, to unite both scenery and sentiment with the narrative—or, in Tian Han's words, as recorded by Li Zhiyan: "Labor produces new emotions, and those emotions are in search of a new form to express themselves."[47] The new structure of feeling that Tian Han sought to reflect through his play therefore was both a matter of poetics and of the technics required to represent and evoke feeling onstage and in his audiences.

The greatest technical challenges posed by Tian Han's script were not, however, the thunder, lightning, or night scenes, but rather the sheer number of set changes required to move between its many acts. Tian Han specifically envisioned these scene changes taking place with the use of a revolving stage, like the ones he had observed when attending performances during an October 1957 trip to Moscow and had used in productions of his 1958 play *Guan Hanqing* 关汉卿 by BPAT at the Capital Theater (首都剧场).[48] He was particularly impressed by the equipment at the Soviet Army Theater (now the Central Academic Theater of the Russian Army). Built in the shape of a five-pointed star, the theater was constructed in the late 1930s and is a prime example of Stalinist monumentality. Its mainstage featured two embedded turntables, which were large enough to accommodate six interior sets and one exterior set, and had the ability to rise and lower.[49] According to Tian Han, most theaters in Moscow were outfitted with similar technology. In contrast, only a few theaters in Beijing (such as the Capital Theater) had mechanized revolving stages. Tian Han raised the issue of a revolving stage with the China Youth Art Theater production team during the writing and rehearsal process, and knew from their response that the troupe did not have access to a space with the appropriate technology. *Fantasia* would premiere on an outdoor stage in Sun Yat-sen Park in Beijing in June 1958, then perform again at the actual Ming Tombs Reservoir site as part of celebrations of the project's completion.[50] Yet, these realities did not deter Tian Han. He wrote the play as he envisioned it, including blackout changes (暗转) and even a reference to the stage "turning" (转到) into the play's final act. While *zhuan* 转 can be used in Chinese theater terminology to refer to scene shifts in general, here the root of the word in literal "rotation" evokes the specific type of scene change enabled by a revolving stage (转台).

In the face of the playwright's dramaturgical demand for "turning" quick changes, the China Youth Art Theater scenographic team might have searched for an alternative venue or way of bringing such a mechanized stage into their space. Instead, however, they invented a *tu*—i.e., "homegrown"—revolving stage that was portable, human-powered, and required no permanently installed equipment. It operated quite simply: a very long piece of cloth was painted with backdrop images for each act. The first background painting was hung across the upstage edge of the playing space, with the rest of the cloth spooled up offstage. A pulley attached laterally to the top edge of the backdrop fabric then allowed stagehands to reel the cloth across the stage (from stage left to stage right) to change the backdrop (fig. 3.6). Meanwhile, other scenic elements—such as cut-out flats shaped like a pile of rocks or the outline of a small house—were placed on wagons and casters. During the scene changes, stagehands hidden behind these pieces moved them offstage in the opposite direction from the moving backdrop (from stage right to stage left), while new wagons entered from offstage right. (Ironically, the stagecraft for a play that celebrated human labor purposefully obscured the bodies needed to power the scene changes.)[51] The backdrop and set pieces moving in opposite directions at the same time created the illusion of the stage rotating, even as the floor remained entirely stationary.[52] As Sun Haoran 孙浩然 (1910–95), who was himself a scenic designer, stated in a review of the production, the device "made use of the audience's visual misapprehension in order to produce the effect of the entire stage revolving."[53] Despite the slight deception, the device seems to have been quite the success, as most reviews mentioned the *tu* revolving stage and specifically praised the innovation for both its aesthetic power and, in keeping with Great Leap values, its economy.[54]

The lengths to which the theater troupe went to create the effect of a revolving stage in the absence of actual equipment raises the question of why the technology was seen as so important. On one level, the time and effort devoted to developing the *tu* revolving stage speaks to the importance of artistic collaboration during this period, or perhaps even to a carryover of privileging playwrights' visions from the 1930s and 1940s. The reasons why the *playwright* insisted on realizing this particular vision, in turn, had practical, dramaturgical, and aesthetic dimensions. Practically speaking, a revolving stage can reduce the transition time between scenes, and both the revolving stage and the blackout quick change had long been recognized as important elements of modern theater. From the perspective of the play as a whole, then, the seamless movement between locations and temporalities enabled by revolving can heighten the sense of connection between them, much like the transitions in film. Chinese director Xu Xiaozhong 徐晓钟 (b. 1928), for example, has compared the turning of the stage to the fade-in and fade-out of cinematic editing, especially when it is used to carry actors onstage and off.[55] Xu also links the revolving stage to aesthetics, differentiating between productions pursuing a *xieshi* 写实 (realist; lit. "writing reality") and *zaixian* 再现 (representational) aesthetic and those with a *xieyi* 写意 (suggestive; lit.

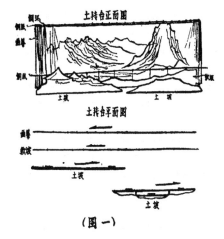

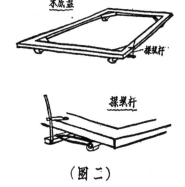

Fig. 3.6. Illustrations of the *tu* revolving stage used for *Fantasia*, with (*top*) arrows indicating direction of movement of spooling backdrop and set prop wagons and (*bottom*) mechanism for moving the wagons. Source: Zhang Fuji, "Jieshao Qingyi chuangzao de tu zhuantai," *Xiju bao*, no. 15 (1958), 35. From the collection of Maggie Greene.

"writing meaning") and *biaoxian* 表现 (expressive) aesthetic. For the former, the simple change of location matters most, whereas for the latter, the revolving stage could be used to externalize characters' emotions and materialize those of the actors; the ultimate goal was to use the technology in a way that inspired both thought and emotion in the audience.[56] Tian Han theorized the revolving stage in a similar manner. For example, he argued that the highly fantastical application of the revolving stage in a production of Vladimir Mayakovsky's *Mystery-Bouffe* (*Мистерия-Буфф*, translated as 滑稽的神秘剧) by the Moscow Satire Theater (now, Moscow Academic Satire Theater) heightened its "artistic truth" (艺术的真实性).[57] Moreover, to Chinese audiences, the use of multiple acts and locations, smooth transitions between settings, and suggestive aesthetics were as reminiscent of *xiqu* as they were of cinema. It thus was precisely a *non*realist use of the revolving stage that could create a bridge from traditional to modern dramaturgy, stagecraft, and aesthetics.

The issue of how to make the stage revolve furthermore illustrates the way in which theater technology paralleled and extended the broader debates about technical and scientific expertise of this period. To begin, Tian Han's source of inspiration for the revolving stage provides an example of how Sino-Soviet knowledge and technology transfer permeated the artistic world and how technology was inseparable from dramaturgy and aesthetics. As Tian Han related, Soviet stagecraft had convinced him that "playwrights should be very familiar with and have a good grasp of the stage, and make full use of modern staging conditions."[58] In reflecting on his trip to Moscow, Tian Han even made an explicit connection between theater and other areas of science and technology: "Just as they have advanced in leaps and bounds in science and technology, in recent years, scenography in the Soviet Union has also had amazing developments."[59] This echoes observations made by Liang Luo, drawing on Volland, that the pervasive understanding of "experimentations" (实验) in the 1950s "took on distinctive scientific qualities" that were related to both science education and the translation of Soviet science fiction.[60]

At the same time, the fact that the device used for *Fantasia* was not a blind copy of Soviet stage technology speaks to the shift toward emphasizing local innovation and technological production that took place in the late 1950s to early 1960s—not coincidentally, as political tensions between the PRC and the USSR rose in the buildup to the Sino-Soviet split. Indeed, beginning in 1960, the theater world began to respond to official calls for a new movement in "technological innovation and technological revolution" (技术革新和技术革命), as in this lead editorial from a 1960 issue of *Theater Gazette* (戏剧报):

All areas of theater work certainly have the potential to advance technological innovation and technological revolution. For example, in the area of scenography, the equipment, maintenance/storage, management, and use of sets, props, costumes, sound effects, lighting equipment, projectors, broadcast systems, etc. all could be revamped. . . . In the area of actor training, the methods and equipment for basic training, methods for practice of different kinds of special acting techniques, methods for vocal work, etc., all can be made more scientific and effective; rehearsal methods and the distribution of time, the writing of and technologies for projected surtitles, curricula, methods[,] and the making and use of teaching tools for theater education can all have new creativity; even the design of theater machinery and stage layout could have new research.[61]

The editorial also alludes to disagreements in the theater world as to whether this maxim could indeed be applied to theater, but criticizes any reluctance to do so as "conservative thinking and suspicions"—that is, a retrograde and ideologically incorrect perspective. Moreover, while elements of theatrical production with the closest relationship to other forms of technology take precedence in the enumeration of potential targets for innovation and revolution, the general perception of an overlap between artistic *technologies* and artistic *techniques* persists. In other words, a scientific approach was seen as equally important to backstage equipment and to the training of the performing body.

The naming of the device a *tu* revolving stage, meanwhile, drew a connection to the general promotion of vernacular knowledge production and vernacular technologies at this time, such as the "indigenous iron" (土铁) produced in backyard furnaces.[62] Technician Zhang Fuji 张傅吉, for example, published an article with detailed drawings in *Chinese Theater* (中国戏剧) shortly after the premiere of *Fantasia* (depicted in fig. 3.6). Framed as written in the interest of "exchanging experience" (交流经验), the article's description of how to make the device work was meant to be used and improved upon by other theater troupes.[63] The article thus participated in the broader practice of technical knowledge exchange that involved the publication and circulation of technical manuals during this period. The article's emphasis on homegrown innovation also echoed other Great Leap technological advances reported by major theater troupes in Beijing, Shanghai, Nanjing, Fuzhou, and Wuhu. BPAT, for instance, adopted a policy of "getting to work with homegrown methods, rebuilding through self-reliance" (土法上马，自力更生) that resulted in the invention of completely new stage lighting equipment.[64] The *tu* revolving stage in *Fantasia* therefore was not a unique case, but indicative of a much broader trend in homegrown theatrical innovation. As the pursuit of "technological innovation and technological revolution" in the theater gained momentum, theater troupes devoted more and more effort to reflecting *tu* values both onstage and behind the scenes.

This emphasis on homegrown methods and self-reliance also brought technological revolution in the theater into conversation with ideological debates surrounding the nature of scientific experimentation and technological development. In particular, *tu* methods were often juxtaposed with *yang* 洋 (Western) approaches, which were associated with elite professional expertise. The conception of *tu* and *yang* as binary gained increased prevalence during the Great Leap Forward across different fields of cultural production.[65] As Schmalzer has noted, this contrast formed "a radical vision of science in Mao-era China, that is, a science produced by the broad masses for the fulfillment of socialist revolutionary goals."[66] The emphasis on the *tu* and "its associated values of self-reliance, mass mobilization, and practical application," as Chenshu Zhou writes, also was highly influential in relation to film of the 1950s–1960s.[67] The same implicit contrast between the homegrown and the foreign troubled the theater world, where certain genres— namely, *huaju*—and nearly all modern stage technologies were associated with Western theater and their early history as foreign imports. The article reporting BPAT's advances, for instance, specifically pinpoints a problematic tendency of privileging the foreign over the indigenous as the target of their homegrown approach.[68] Part of the work of the *tu* revolving stage, then, was implicitly to transform a device with ideologically dubious foreign origins, in Japanese and European stage technologies of the late nineteenth century (see introduction), and a more ideologically correct corollary in Soviet stage technology, into a fully Chinese, grassroots innovation.

Finally, the visual and temporal connections between scenes created by the *tu* revolving stage in *Fantasia* demonstrate how stage technologies worked to embed the socialist utopian vision of the Great Leap Forward in the materiality of the stage itself. In addition to the sheer number of scenes in *Fantasia*, another notable element of its structure is the fact that it includes flashbacks (another quasi-cinematic technique) to scenes set in the Yuan (1271–1368) and Ming (1368–1644) dynasties and ends with a flashforward to around twenty years in the future. The historical scenes draw a stark contrast between the socialist present and the conscripted labor used to power massive engineering projects during China's imperial past, whereas the futuristic scene envisions the wildest successes of the socialist project. In his stage directions, Tian Han writes the transition into this final scene as a grand reveal: the stage turns (as noted above) and "smoke dissipates slowly to reveal the Ming Tombs Reservoir more than twenty years in the future."[69] Here, the smoke adds a visual cue that the audience is moving into the space of dream or fantasy—in other words, the very *fantasia* evoked by its title. Due to the futurism of this final scene, the cinematic adaptation of the play has even been referred to as China's first "science fantasy" (科幻) film.[70] The fantasy is clearly that of a socialist utopia, in which a combination of technological advancement, human labor, and the socialist political system create a perfect society.

The *tu* revolving stage in the China Youth Art Theater production of *Fantasia* also invited audiences into another act of fantasy: it asked them to imagine, or allow themselves to be deceived into believing, that a specific stage technology was moving the backdrop and set pieces from scene to scene—to imagine a revolving stage where there was none. The production thereby mobilized a kind of technical imagination that paralleled the socialist utopian imaginary within the play (and film)—or in other words, a layer of what we might call *technological fantasy* alongside its socialist utopianism and science fantasy. Whereas Chinese science fantasy literature and film most often portrays the struggle to attain technological advancement or the fruits of scientific successes, as in the final scene of *Fantasia*, here technological fantasy relocates the audience imagination to the mechanisms by which the world onstage (or onscreen) is produced. With the *tu* revolving stage, for example, imagining that the scenographic effect worked *just like* a mechanized revolving stage was as important as what it represented in terms of time and setting change. This technological fantasy was primed by the circulation (and echoed in the content) of technical theater handbooks and articles, which themselves asked readers to imagine certain stage technologies as they learned about them. At the same time, the *tu* nature of the device implied that anyone present could themselves participate in similar technical theater experimentation. Technological fantasy, then, added a material dimension to the socialist utopian imaginary, and paralleled mass science in its promise that "the people" could become the true drivers of innovation.

## Technological Fantasy as Ideological Critique

Ultimately, the Great Leap Forward would fail spectacularly and undermine the utopian spirit of *Fantasia*, but the importance of technological fantasy and homegrown innovation would only increase as the ideological winds shifted in the early 1960s. This trend is well illustrated by *Sentinels under the Neon Lights*, by Shen Ximeng 沈西蒙 (1918–2006), Mo Yan 漠雁 (1925–2009), and journalist Lü Xingchen 呂兴臣, which stands out among the new plays of the early 1960s for the fact that its driving metaphor[71]—the *nihongdeng* 霓虹灯 or "neon lights" in its title—simultaneously evokes an issue of political importance and (once again) implies a specific technical challenge that had to be solved by stagecraft. The story of *Sentinels* centers on the struggles of a military unit assigned to guard Nanjing Road in Shanghai after the People's Liberation Army (PLA) captured the city on May 25, 1949. Nanjing Road, which to this day remains one of Shanghai's main thoroughfares, was famous in the early twentieth century for being a center of cosmopolitanism, commerce, and entertainment. In the play, the sights and sounds of Nanjing Road serve as temptations for the soldiers stationed there; a few succumb to the siren song of Hollywood film screenings and dance halls, while the struggle against such decadence ultimately unites the rest of the unit and solidifies their political commitments. The play was so successful that it was performed by theater troupes throughout the nation and adapted as a film in 1964, featuring many original cast members.[72]

Premiered by the Nanjing Military Command Frontier Theater Troupe (中国人民解放军南京部队前线话剧团) in 1963, Sentinels reflects widespread efforts to translate the ideological emphases of the Socialist Education Movement for the stage. The Socialist Education Movement followed on the heels of the Great Leap Forward, which after initial seeming successes resulted in the "three bitter years" of 1959–61 during which famine ravaged the countryside and caused the deaths of tens of millions.[73] Overplanting exacerbated by drought destroyed crops throughout the country, backyard furnaces yielded useless pig iron instead of steel, and massive engineering projects had disastrous environmental consequences. Even urban theatrical production slowed down notably during 1961–62, as many theater artists were sent to the countryside for reeducation and manual labor.[74] A more pragmatic leadership took charge with the Eighth Plenum of the CCP Central Committee in 1961 and attempted to ease the famine, exercise more moderate governance, and espouse a liberal attitude toward literature and the arts.[75] However, Mao soon reasserted power with calls for a Socialist Education Movement that reemphasized class struggle and elevated the importance of mass scientific experimentation.[76] Mao's invocation of class struggle also signaled a new round of ideological tightening and an attempt to reinvigorate faith in his radical revolutionary project. In the theater world, as Xiaobing Tang has noted, the early 1960s saw a more concerted effort to produce new plays about contemporary life or revolutionary heritage. These plays were aimed toward "staging of the nation in the form of theatrical spectacle" and were performed throughout the country for maximum national impact.[77] The rhetorical and ideological shifts of the early 1960s also influenced production processes, including the ways in which design and technology were envisioned to relate to narrative and character development.

*Sentinels* demonstrates how this ideological focus translated into both dramatic narrative and production process, beginning with its emphasis on military history and its negative portrayal of the pre-PRC entertainment industry. Indeed, previous scholarship largely has analyzed the play and its film adaptation in relation to urban culture and the remediation of revolutionary historical narratives.[78] Throughout the play, examples of foreign-inflected bourgeois capitalist decadence are critiqued specifically by juxtaposing them with ideologically correct arts and entertainment. In the second scene of the play, for example, the stage directions describe advertisements for both the 1944 Hollywood movie musical *Bathing Beauty* (translated as 出水芙蓉) and a performance of the Chinese revolutionary musical *The White-Haired Girl* (白毛女).[79] Local hawkers try to entice passersby to buy tickets to both, and a conflict arises between one of the PLA soldiers and a man selling movie tickets when it seems the latter also has been involved in spreading "counterrevolutionary" leaflets criticizing *The White-Haired Girl* as "brainwashing propaganda."[80] Like the depiction of intellectuals and artists in *Fantasia*, the conflicts between foreign and Chinese, petit bourgeois and revolutionary entertainment options in *Sentinels* raise questions about the roles of literature, art, and leisure in the PRC's new socialist society.

However, whereas *Fantasia* offers a handbook or blueprint for *how* to make new art that extols the accomplishments of socialist construction, *Sentinels* interrogates and more clearly condemns certain artistic forms for distracting from the revolutionary project. The ideological problem of urban art forms, and specifically those originating in Shanghai, had been identified as early as the 1940s, which put theater in a particular bind.[81] The modern theater genres that had developed in the early twentieth century, such as *huaju*, largely had indisputably Western origins or influences. Meanwhile, various *xiqu* forms were alternately praised as representative of national culture (e.g., *jingju*), lauded for their roots in local folk culture (e.g., regional forms), and criticized for their exploitative institutional structures and perpetuation of problematic superstitions in their narrative content. Even stagecraft itself came under fire for decadence, with *xiqu* troupes in the 1950s frequently criticized for excessive use of lighting effects or mechanized stage sets.[82] In the new socialist society, therefore, even the technical details of *how* theater was made took on new political connotations.

In *Sentinels*, it is neon light that most clearly symbolizes and materializes these ideological conflicts through its associations with Shanghai nightlife and foreign influence. As Yomi Braester has discussed in detail, neon lights are ever present in films about Shanghai, and the title of *Sentinels* even "comes to represent a fundamental conflict, as if the sentinels are physically under attack by the neon lights."[83] The technology attained this iconic status through its widespread use as advertising for shops, cafes, dance halls, cinemas, and theater venues. The first neon signs in China, for instance, were foreign imports installed in the window of the Evans Book Company (伊文思图书公司) on Nanjing Road in 1927.[84] The luminescent properties of neon and other noble gases had been discovered three decades earlier, in June 1898, by British scientists William Ramsay and Morris Travers, and the earliest neon advertising signs were installed in Paris in 1912.[85] Early neon lights typically consisted of tubes of hand-blown glass that contained stable gases such as neon or argon. Electric current passed through electrodes in the tubes and caused the gaseous atoms to glow: red, orange, or pink if the gas was neon, or blue, yellow, green, violet, or white if argon. When neon light came to Shanghai, as in other metropolises worldwide, it joined a host of other electrified signage already illuminating the night sky. Workshops in China (largely in Shanghai) began to produce their own neon signage in 1927, although the companies were largely under foreign ownership. Chinese-owned neon lighting companies developed over the course of the 1930s in Shanghai, Tianjin, Chongqing, and other major cities throughout the country. After the founding of the PRC, new scientific and technological breakthroughs in the early 1950s allowed Chinese producers to make neon lights without any imported materials for the first time, but the industry ultimately declined during the high socialist period due to the "common perception" that neon lights were synonymous with capitalism.[86]

Likewise, the connotations and use of neon lights as a metaphor in literature, film, and drama shifted over time. In well-known examples from the 1930s, neon lights represented both the draw and the danger of the modern metropolis, most often with an underlying ambivalence. For instance, as Leo Ou-fan Lee has argued, writer Mao Dun "inscribes a contradictory message" in his novel *Midnight* (子夜, 1933) by describing an alluring sign reading "LIGHT, HEAT, POWER!" at the outset of what is otherwise a critical realist story of life in modern Shanghai.[87] Representations of the city in 1930s Chinese films similarly pair dazzling images of the city's lights and skyscrapers with narratives that question the impact of foreign influence and modernization on city residents. *City Scenes* (aka *Scenes of City Life*, 都市风光, 1935) and *Street Angel* (馬路天使, 1937) for example, both directed by Yuan Muzhi (star of *Roar, China!* and editor of the theater journal *Play*), are often cited for a sequence that features a series of quick cuts between shots of illuminated signage advertising entertainments in both Chinese and English. In the former film, this sequence appears via a traveling peepshow (西洋鏡),

and in the latter, beneath the film's opening title sequence.[88] Meanwhile, the casting of popular singer Zhou Xuan 周璇 (1920–57) in *Street Angel* as the down-on-her-luck female lead, Xiao Hong, lends a romantic air to the film's tale of exploitation. Indeed, female sexualization often was linked to the city itself and its neon lights. For instance, Zhang Yingjin has argued that in the film *The Goddess* (神女, 1934; dir. Wu Yonggang 吳永剛), "Shanghai is fantasized as an alluring prostitute smiling directly at the audience against a background of skyscrapers and flashing neon lights."[89] In contrast, films made in the 1950s–1960s that were set in Shanghai moved toward a fuller and more overt vilification of the city, as Braester has demonstrated. The film adaptation of *Sentinels*, in particular, "presents itself as the antithesis of the 1930s Shanghai films, in which the city is identified with—if not outright celebrated through—neon signs. The city lights, as well as Shanghai's spaces, are remolded to comport with the New China, not only overcome but also incorporated into the PLA's display of power."[90] In both the play and the film, this is most obviously represented by the replacement of neon advertisements with signs flashing "Long Live the People's Republic of China!" (中国人民共和国万岁) and "Long Live Chairman Mao!" (毛主席万岁) in the final scene.

Once again, however, the driving metaphor of *Sentinels* also presented a specific challenge for theatrical production, especially given that Chinese production of neon signage was in decline by the early 1960s. More fundamentally, the benefits of neon for stationary, semipermanent advertising—namely, its bespoke design and energy efficiency relative to equally bright incandescent or fluorescent bulbs—were counterbalanced by other concerns in the theater. For theatrical productions that have a limited run, the cost–benefit calculation of purchasing a handcrafted glass sign is quite different than for a business wishing to advertise its company name or a particular product indefinitely. Moreover, while neon glass tubing is relatively durable, it is not impervious to the elements or improper handling, and a tube breaking would release hazardous, flammable gasses. In Hong Kong, for instance, the authorities banned the use of outdoor neon lighting during typhoon weather after a sign caught fire in 1938.[91] A piece of signage that needed to be moved onstage and off between acts, either attached to a large set piece on wheels or using a fly system, would be even more vulnerable to mishap and even higher in its immediate risk to stagehands, actors, and audience members. Finally, neon lighting requires a very high voltage of electricity and a specific type of transformer designed to convert average electrical current for use in neon. China began producing such transformers (霓虹灯电源变压器) as early as

1930, but to have such a device backstage posed an electrocution risk to stage-hands and actors.

The question thus became: How does one produce the effect of neon lights without actual neon lights? The challenge was, of course, not unique to *Sentinels*; many other plays set in Shanghai or wartime Chongqing featured city streets and night scenes, which made theatrical neon lights a conundrum for amateurs and professionals alike. One handbook for amateur theater troupes from 1957, for example, suggests cutting the desired shapes into a piece of plywood, then mounting colored silk and a light source to the back of the plywood. Seen through the holes in the wood, the light shining through the colored silk would look like a neon sign and a flickering effect could be achieved with a simple on–off switch.[92] Meanwhile, when the China Youth Art Theater produced *Sentinels* in 1963, not long after its premiere by Frontier Theater Troupe, they experimented with slightly more complex construction techniques in advance of their performances. The production team developed two different methods: welding thin steel tubes into the proper shapes and painting them white, or affixing small pieces of yellow plastic tubing to a piece of clear netting to create letters or characters. For either, bright, colored light shone onto the tubing would then give the illusion of a lit sign.[93] It is also significant that all of these techniques mimic the specific look of neon lighting—smooth tubes or lines of brightly colored light—despite the fact that the Chinese term *nihongdeng* at times was used for illuminated signage more generally.[94] Indeed, production photos from the play's premiere, which were widely circulated in newspapers, magazines, journals, and print editions of the play, depict a number of signs that had the characteristic look of neon (see figs. 3.7–3.8). In one, it is even possible to see the steel pipes on which the "neon" tubing was hung for the "Long Live!" signs in the play's final scene.

One final technique used for imitation neon may have been slide projections. Fengzi 风子 (pseudonym for Feng Fengzi 封风子, 1912–96), a prominent actress, writer, and critic, writes of the successful use of "lighting and projections (灯光和幻灯)" in *Sentinels*, and, indeed, the *Bathing Beauty* sign has the hazy-edged look of a poorly focused projected image in some production photographs.[95] Fengzi's article unfortunately seems to be the only concrete reference to the use of projection in the original production of *Sentinels*, but it nonetheless offers the glimmer of an alluring connection between the scopic regimes of cinematic Shanghai of the 1930s and revolutionary theater of the 1960s. Whereas the other methods for creating stage versions of neon lights relied on material technologies that were noticeably physically present onstage, using a projected image for neon—or any other element of stage

Fig. 3.7. Production photograph from scene 2 of *Sentinels under the Neon Lights* by the Nanjing Military Command Frontier Theater Troupe in 1963, depicting several different neon light advertisements on Nanjing Road (including for performances of *The White-Haired Girl* and *Bathing Beauty*). Source: Shen Hsi-Meng et al., *On Guard Beneath the Neon Lights* (Beijing: Foreign Language Press, 1966), n.p.

Fig. 3.8. Production photograph from scene 9 of *Sentinels* by the Frontier Theater Troupe, with partial depiction of the new "Long Live Chairman Mao!" and "Long Live the PRC!" neon signs. Note that the imitation neon signs are clearly mounted on metal pipes. Source: Shen Hsi-Meng et al., *On Guard beneath the Neon Lights* (Beijing: Foreign Language Press, 1966), n.p.

design—substituted a cinematic technology for the theatrical. Projected signage would not have looked like other theatrical representations of neon, but rather like an image of neon mediated by celluloid and screen, as seen in the many films made and set in 1930s Shanghai.

As with the revolving stage in *Fantasia*, the goal of these innovative techniques was to create the impression of neon lights in the absence of the technology itself. Plywood cutouts, painted piping, and projected images asked their audiences to imagine one form of (stage) technology to stand in for another kind of (real-life) lighting technology, again invoking a theater-specific mode of technological fantasy. Moreover, in the case of *Sentinels*, this approach to stage technology was not merely the accidental effect of a creative response to adverse material conditions. Rather, the replacement of real neon lights with ersatz signage was a deliberate aesthetic and ideological choice. Mo Yan, the play's coauthor and director of its premiere, wrote the following in a piece on his directorial concept for the production:

> Only the *White-Haired Girl* and *Bathing Beauty* [signs] should stand out, in order to suggest the conflict between the culture of the two classes; the others should only be hung in darker spots, in order to avoid competing for the audience's attention. In the last scenes, the two very large neon signs with the slogans "Long Live the People's Republic of China" and "Long Live Chairman Mao" should overpower all of the other lights. The change in the neon lights suggests the change of Nanjing Road. It is absolutely unsuitable to use actual light bulbs for the neon lights, [they] absolutely should not dazzle the eyes and steal the show, and absolutely must not display neon light for the sake of displaying neon light. Otherwise, the "neon lights" will leave a deep impression on the audience, [but] the "sentinels" in contrast will not exist.[96]

In other words, even had neon lights been a practical and accessible choice for the production, the director still would have preferred the imitation lights precisely because they were not as powerful, bright, or attractive as the real thing. Mo Yan sees in real neon an overwhelming allure, investing the material technology with humanlike agency and the capacity to steal the show. The danger of the sentinels, and by extension the audience, succumbing to the power of neon—another reading of being literally *under* (the spell of) the lights—was thus too great. Indeed, avoiding this trap and succeeding in delivering the play's ideological message depended on the neon lights being nothing more than a special effect.

Beyond direct ideological implications, the director's preference for imitation over real neon also reflects how theater technology mediated the transmutation of key concepts from classical Chinese aesthetics into socialist discourse and practice. In his directorial concept piece, Mo Yan discusses at length his attempts to balance a key dyad in Chinese aesthetics, that of *xu* 虚 (empty) and *shi* 实 (solid) and, in particular, his belief that scenography should "use the empty to support the solid" (以虚托实).[97] Likewise, multiple reviews and later essays on scenography specifically praised the production for its successful combination of *xu* and *shi* (虚实结合).[98] This praise generally refers to the overall scenographic design of the production, but ersatz neon lights illustrate the principle well: real neon would be far too *shi*, and replacing the lights with something completely unlike neon would be too *xu*. The techniques developed by the production teams, in contrast, found an ideal middle ground.

The importance of balancing *xu* and *shi*, empty and solid, onstage relates not to the literal translations of the terms, but rather to the connotations that arise from their long history of use in classical literature, theater, and visual art as what Tina Lu calls "one of the most important binaries in Chinese thought."[99] In his explication of key terms in classical Chinese poetry, for example, Stephen Owen defines *xu* as "'empty' or 'plastic,' referring to substances like air or water that conform to 'solid' shapes; it is extended to refer to the changing fluidity of the emotions and the way they may be 'invested' in solid things."[100] Similarly, when writing of *The Peony Pavilion*—one of the most well-known *chuanqi* dramas of the late imperial period—Lu calls attention to the fact that "*xu* implies not only what is imaginary and unrooted but also what is purposeless and in vain."[101] *Xu* aesthetics thus can have a negative connotation associated with the abstract, the false, or even the virtual, and often arise in contradistinction to the term *shi*, which can mean concrete, true, or real. At the same time, the two exist in concert rather than in pure opposition, with the false able to illuminate elements of the true and vice versa.

Under the influence of Maoist ideology, then, the balancing of *xu* and *shi* became a matter of realist aesthetics and Marxist dialectics. Indeed, discussion of *xu-shi* as a dialectical (rather than binary) pair appears frequently during this period in discussions of theater reform, dramaturgy, stage aesthetics, and performance reviews. At times, the balancing of *xu* and *shi* seems more a practical question of how to reflect life as it was experienced by the privileged classes of workers, peasants, and soldiers in the material world of the stage (e.g., via sets and costumes). When Mo Yan speaks of balancing *xu* and *shi*, however, he does so in a way that theorizes the two as existing in a state of contradiction, in a clear reference to Mao's interpretation of dialectical materialism, and also as each representing certain sets of social contradictions that were prominent in Maoist discourse. The practical solutions for neon lights in *Sentinels* thus demonstrate how technical details also could play an important role in this ideological balancing act, not just in creating stage realism.

Finally, the concepts of *xu* and *shi* were also intertwined in how the production's aesthetics and technics worked together to engage the audience. In Chinese theater aesthetics, *xu* relates to the concept of "suppositionality" (虚 拟性 or 假定性), which captures the techniques by which *xiqu* performers create the world of the play through gesture, movement, and audience imagination.[102] The term derives from *xiqu* performance practices in which the stage remains almost "empty" (*xu*) or largely devoid of material (*shi*) objects, yet, as Ruru Li writes, "through the 'empty' (stylized dance sequences on an empty stage), audiences imagine the 'solid' (real actions and scenes)."[103] In other words, the *xu* elements of a production function as a kind of outline to be filled in through audience imagination. The fake neon lights function in a similar way, inviting the audience to imagine the reality of neon lights; the same effect was noted by reviewers in relation to the production's backdrop of skyscraper silhouettes, which were illuminated in certain night scenes. The building silhouettes were even referred to specifically as "outline scenery" (衬 景), invoking the aesthetic concept of stage design providing an outline for audience fantasy to fill in.

By evoking real neon through an alternative technology and creating scenery largely through outlines, productions of *Sentinels* added a layer of complexity to the operations of technological fantasy. The *tu* revolving stage in *Fantasia* had required audiences to imagine one specific theater technology in place of another, to the ends of creating a quasi-cinematic aesthetic for the theatrical production. In contrast, the fake neon and outline scenery of *Sentinels* not only invited audiences to imagine neon from its imitation and buildings from their outlines but also (via those substitutions) to imagine Shanghai as it had already been mediated by earlier cinematic representations. Indeed, the illuminated outline of Shanghai's skyline in *Sentinels* even seems to be a direct reference to the iconic scene from *City Scenes* that depicts rural audiences experiencing images of Shanghai's night skyline through a traveling peepshow (figs. 3.9–3.10). By using *xu* (fake) neon and *xu* (empty) scenery, the production suggested that the representations themselves were also *xu* ("purposeless or in vain"). On the one hand, then, theatrical and cinematic mediation itself could be seen as fundamentally *xu*, in reference to the "emptiness" of bourgeois pursuits and capitalist entertainment. But, at the

Fig. 3.9. Production photograph from *Sentinels* by the Frontier
Theater Troupe, depicting a night scene with illuminated building
outlines. Source: Shen Ximeng et al., *Nihong deng xia de shaobing*
(Beijing: Renmin wenxue chubanshe, 1964), v.

same time, that emptiness was also literally an outline that could be filled
in again, by the audience, with revolutionary or socialist utopian fantasies.
Thus, beyond the goals of not diverting audience attention from the message
of *Sentinels* and of critiquing Shanghai's urban entertainments, the various
technical mechanisms for creating imitation illumination also rehearsed a
form of technology-enabled fantasizing that drew audiences into the co-
creation of a shared socialist imaginary.

Fig. 3.10. Peephole show scene from the film *City Scenes* (Denton Film Company, dir. Yuan Muzhi, 1935), which provides an iconic and representative example of how the nighttime Shanghai cityscape was depicted in 1930s film.

### *Tu Dianying* Onstage and Theater as Socialist Mass Medium

The visual reference to cinema drawn by the scenic design of *Sentinels* points to another significant development in theater of the Seventeen Years period: a growing connection between the media of theater and film. This connection is most obvious from the number of plays that were adapted from theater to film almost immediately after their stage premieres—of which *Fantasia* and *Sentinels* were two of many. Yet, once again, this connection was not only a matter of the adaptation of content, but also took place on a material, techno-logical level through the use of projected backdrops (幻灯) onstage.[104] During the 1950s–1960s, the use of slide projection in the theater, and especially for backdrop projection, grew significantly and culminated in the use of a complex array of overlapping projection units for the large-scale "song-and-dance epic" (音乐舞蹈史诗) *The East Is Red* in 1964. Ultimately, however, the primary appeal of theatrical projections was that they—like their cinematic equivalent, *tu dianying* 土电影 (homegrown film, i.e., slide projector shows)—could be easily transported to and used in rural settings.

To be sure, the 1960s were not the first time that Chinese scenic designers had attempted to use projections of some kind onstage. In fact, projection provides yet another example of continuity between applications of stage technologies in the 1920s–1930s (see chapter 1), the dramaturgical scripting of technology (chapter 2), and experimentation in the context of socialist nation building and technoindustrial development. For example, Xia Yan's script for *Sai Jinhua* (賽金花, 1936) called for the projection of a short film, which established the play's setting, as a prologue to the first act.[105] *Jingju* productions from the 1930s likewise used projected images on occasion.[106] Technical articles and handbooks from the 1930s, many of which were based on foreign texts and described foreign technologies, also described the use of rudimentary projections for some special effects. In his stage lighting book, for instance, He Mengfu discusses an "effects projector" (放映機) that could be used to create images of clouds and fire on the backdrop curtain (天幕, aka cyclorama/cyc) and the suggestion that a "common projector" (尋常的幻燈) and slides might also be used to similar ends.[107] Special effects remained a key area of theatrical application for common projectors in the 1950s, and many *xiqu* troupes began to use projectors to create surtitles for performances.[108]

By the early 1960s, experimentation with theatrical projection had expanded from effects and surtitles to include replacing entire painted backdrops with projected images. Some descriptions of scenic design suggest that there was experimentation with projected backdrops as early as the mid-1950s. For example, Liu Lu 刘露 (1911–79), a scenic designer and educator who also authored technical manuals, notes that a 1956 production of *Spring Underground* (地下的春天) combined projections and painted backdrops.[109] However, Ou Zaixin 欧载欣 (b. 1929), the author of one of the first technical manuals for stage projections, credits himself with the invention of backdrop projections (幻灯投映衬景) in the early 1950s. According to Ou's account, he began to work in scenic design as a member of a *wengongtuan* 文工团 (cultural troupe) dispatched to support soldiers during the Korean War. After the war ended, demand for cultural activities and a higher quality of entertainment increased, but the logistics of transporting set pieces remained challenging. In response, Ou began to experiment with retrofitting a lighting unit that created the effect of moving clouds (跑云灯) to instead project images of static set pieces (景物) onto the backdrop curtain.[110] His first projections were made by taping painted cellophane or glassine paper (玻璃纸) onto glass slides and using a single light source, and he continued to experiment to create larger-scale and more sophisticated projections. While working on the design and tech for his cultural troupe's "homecoming" production of *Song of the Volunteer Soldiers* (志愿军战歌) in 1957, Ou was surprised to find that large theater troupes in metropolitan areas such as Beijing, Shanghai, and Guangzhou had yet to develop similar technologies. Later, when he was transferred to the General Political Department Cultural Troupe Scenography Team (总政文工团舞台美术队), Ou's use of projection for their song-and-dance performances garnered attention and imitation from other directors in Beijing.[111]

Backdrop projections were appealing and worthy of imitation for a number of reasons. First, creating projected backdrops was more cost-effective, in terms of both money and materials, than painted backdrops.[112] In general, plays with multiple locations would need different backdrops for each. Painted backdrops required large pieces of cloth, large quantities of paint, and a large amount of human labor; projected backdrops, in contrast, required only one white backdrop curtain. Individual slides were comparatively small, which meant a smaller surface to paint, and could be made from a range of materials, such as glass, cellophane, or acetate film (醋酸纤维薄膜). Second, many articles refer to the improved "artistic effect" (艺术效果) of projected backdrops, including such desirable qualities as implied meaning (含蓄), transparency (透明), and depth (深远).[113] Finally, projections made productions more flexible and facilitated faster set changes. The size of the backdrop image could be calibrated to fit different size stages by adjusting the distance between the projector unit and the backdrop curtain, and changing the backdrop image required only switching the slide itself. Moving between scenes was thus much simpler than flying large backdrops in and out, or operating a horizontal pulley system as stagehands had done in *Fantasia*, and could be done even faster than with a revolving stage. A projector and set of slides were also much easier to transport than painted backdrops or large flats.

The principles of economy, artistic effect, flexibility, and portability associated with projected backdrops resonated with the precise historical moment at which they gained popularity: between the end of the Great Leap Forward, through the Socialist Education Movement, and up to the stirrings of the Cultural Revolution. While all origin stories—especially self-authored ones—must be taken with a grain of salt, the timeline of Ou's narrative, at least, accords with other sources that suggest widespread experimentation with backdrop projection did indeed gain momentum in the late 1950s and early 1960s. For instance, an article by the Shanghai Experimental Opera Theater Lighting Group (上海实验歌剧院灯光组) begins by describing "using projectors to project large backgrounds and create more complex atmospheres on the cyc" as a "very recent thing" in 1960.[114] At that time, cost- and material-saving measures, in particular, would have upheld the Great Leap emphasis on economizing. A few years later, when many Great Leap slogans fell out of fashion in the face of widespread famine and mis-directed industrial production, the fact that the Leap had caused financial and material hardships only made the value of "economizing" all the more important in its wake. Similarly, the terms used to describe the "artistic effect" of backdrop projection also can be connected to the specific aesthetic dis-cussions that surrounded *Fantasia* and *Sentinels*. For instance, the idea of implied meaning is one that director Mo Yan also used when describing his approach to the scenography of *Sentinels*.[115] Finally, flexibility speaks to the needs of artists who were increasingly encouraged to perform in factories and rural locations, while simultaneously learning from their worker and peasant audiences. While this was an ongoing practice throughout the high social-ist period, official publications such as *Theater Gazette* especially encouraged "going down to the countryside" (下乡 or 上山下乡, lit. "going up to the mountains and down to the countryside") at the beginning of the Great Leap Forward and during the Socialist Education Movement.[116]

Theater artists' attempts to bring projector technology onto the stage speaks to another underlying goal of this period: the explicit melding of art and technology. In the phrasing of the Shanghai Experimental Opera Theater Lighting Group, "slides are a hybrid of art and technology."[117] The importance of this idea of technoartistic hybridity can be seen both in the broad interest in stage technology discussed throughout this chapter and in the fact that slides, in particular, were put on display in one of the most prom-inent theatrical productions of the early PRC: *The East Is Red*. Titled after and featuring a 1942 song of the same name, *The East Is Red* was a large-scale celebration of CCP and PRC history that was first performed at the Great Hall of the People in Beijing on October 2, 1964, in honor of the Fifteenth Anniversary of the Founding of the PRC, and then adapted into a film the following year.[118] As Xiaomei Chen has argued, the creation of *The East Is Red* simultaneously harkened back to the collaborative creative spirit of the Great Leap Forward and prefigured the theatrical production processes of the Cultural Revolution, which would involve both heavy intervention from cultural authorities and grassroots circulation. As "massive propaganda," to borrow Chen's term, *The East Is Red* was an unqualified success.[119]

In the memories of designers and technicians, *The East Is Red* stands out for its unprecedented application of backdrop projection in a theater with

9,770 fixed seats in three tiers and a proscenium opening 32 meters wide by 18 meters high.[120] In order to fill the cyc, designers and technicians created an array of seven projector units that each projected a slice of the overall image. The individual slide images had to be carefully composed so that there would be no distortion to the images and that the overlapping projections would give the impression of a single seamless image (figs. 3.11–3.12). Projections were also used for images of Karl Marx, Lenin, and Mao, and stage technology became a particular point of pride for the production. Alongside numerous reviews praising its music, dance, and overall effect, designers and technicians also penned articles on participating in the design process and working backstage.[121] As one *People's Daily* piece by scenic design team members Li Yegan 李也甘 and Han Linbo 韩林波 notes, the projections' success was due in part to the fact that they conducted "scientific experiments" (科学实验) to find the best painting techniques for the slides, and that the projections were used for scenic elements that "possessed distinguishing characteristics that were both real and virtual."[122] A new type of light bulb was even developed by the Beijing Light Bulb Factory that enabled bigger projections without losing the clarity of the image.[123] Later technical manuals on projection, such as Ou Zaixin's book and a simpler volume entitled *Stage Projection and Special Effects* (舞台幻灯和特技), cite *The East Is Red* as significant both for its technical success and its role in promoting wider use of backdrop projection technology.[124]

With its emphasis on experimentation and new techniques, *The East Is Red* speaks once again to the ongoing importance of *tu* innovation in the theater. In this particular instance, however, the nature of the experiments also draws a connection between the theater and another important "homegrown" mass medium and propaganda vehicle: slide projections shown as part of (or sometimes in lieu of) film exhibition and in educational settings. Recent work by scholars such as Tina Mai Chen, Jie Li, and Chenshu Zhou has called attention to the importance of slide projection—called both *huandeng* and *tu dianying*—to the media ecology of the high socialist period, when troupes of mobile film projectionists commonly performed slide shows as a preamble to, or even in place of, outdoor film screenings.[125] Zhou's scholarship, in particular, demonstrates that values such as economic efficiency, portability, and adaptability enlivened experimentation in slide projection and were inseparable from the impetus for self-reliance, mass mobilization, and practical application behind *tu* science.[126] Moreover, according to Zhou, the grassroots *tu* ethos and "elevated status" of slide projection reached a high point in 1964–65—in other words, at precisely the moment when pro-

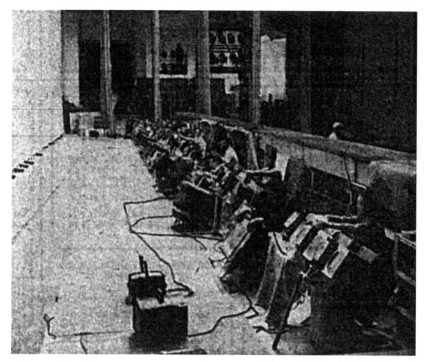

Fig. 3.11. Lighting and projection units backstage for performances of *The East Is Red* in October 1964. Photograph by Cheng Zhining. Source: Li Yegan and Han Libo, "Canjia *Dongfang hong* wutai meishu gongzuo de tihui," *Renmin ribao*, October 15, 1964, 5.

jection also rose to prominence in its application as a theatrical backdrop technique.[127]

Certainly, on a technical level, theatrical backdrop projections were not exact imitations of other projection technologies: units had to be set close to the cyc and angled upward, which required a shorter throw distance and correction for image distortion, and slides remained in place for the duration of an entire scene or act, which exposed the slide plates to high temperatures for extended periods of time. Yet all projectors operated by using a light source, a painted slide made of glass or other transparent materials, and from one to three lenses to condense the light and focus the image. Moreover, according to the theater artists who used them, theatrical projectors' "underlying principles were entirely the same" as common slide projectors.[128] Theater artists also drew close comparisons between their work and that of mobile projection teams and sometimes even used the same equipment as projectionists.

Fig. 3.12. Projected backdrop of Tiananmen (Gate of Heavenly Peace) from stage production of *The East Is Red* in October 1964. Source: *Renmin huabao*, no. 12 (1964), n.p.

One article from 1965, which summarizes a meeting wherein Beijing scenic designers discussed scenography for rural areas, mentions the difficulty of using backdrop projections when the cyc moved in heavy winds, and specifically notes that this was also a challenge faced by mobile projection units.[129] Another article in the same issue of *Theater Gazette* notes how the Rural Culture Work Team of the National Song and Dance Theater (中国歌剧舞剧院农村文化工作队) would use a generator intended for film screenings to power their stage lights, backdrop projector, and sound system.[130]

The overlap in technology, terminology, and performance demonstrates one key way that Chinese theater of the early to mid-1960s actively participated in the process of defining a socialist mediascape for the PRC that included both theater and film as a homegrown mass media. Significantly, the connections among these different media were not based solely or even primarily on the level of content, but rather on material connections in the technologies engaged and the spirit of grassroots experimentalism that animated them. Slide projections, of differing formats, appeared in the context of science and technology education, in performances by mobile projectionist teams, and as backdrops to theatrical productions.[131] Stories of *tu* experimentation and innovation in all of these areas accompanied reports of their successes in official publications. Technical articles and manuals rendered reproducible both the technologies themselves and an ideologically correct attitude toward their application. The result was a convergence of the visual, technical, and ideological regimes across different mass media, which brought together art and science on both concrete and theoretical levels.

At the same time, much like the *tu* revolving stage and ersatz neon lights, projected backdrops in the theater ultimately relied on a kind of technological fantasy—in this case, an optical illusion as well as the replacement of one stage technology with another. On one level, the projected images themselves were meant to replace and, to an extent, *look like* painted backdrops, which were in turn artistic representations of locations (some real, some fictitious). Via the numerous publications that describe the behind-the-scenes work of engineering the projections, the audience could (in theory) come to appreciate both the (voluntarist) labor of the technicians and understand the projections as an innovative improvement upon the core stage technology of painted backdrops. The projections also operated on the same aesthetic logic of blending *xu* and *shi* that appeared in *Sentinels*, but here the projections filled a literally empty, blank white curtain with fantastical images of the history of communism and of the nation. Simultaneously, the necessary angling of projector units means that any flat image will end up not only magnified but also distorted.[132] Scenic artists therefore had to employ techniques to counter that distortion as they painted slides and calibrated projectors. Without this human intervention, the projections would become warped images, as unreal and unattainable as the idealized histories and imagined futures they were meant to depict. The irony of the technology, then, was that both the ideals *and* the impossibility of the socialist utopian vision were embedded in the very apparatus used to project that vision onstage.

Ultimately, this chapter's survey of experimentation with homegrown stage technology by many prominent theater companies and in important theatrical productions during the Seventeen Years period demonstrates how the Chinese socialist utopian vision operated on a material level in the arts. At first glance, the history of industrial and agricultural technologies under the socialist state may seem only tangentially connected to the history of theater reform and cultural policy under the same regime. However, as this chapter has shown, these areas of development were two sides of the same coin. Parallel processes of technology transfer, knowledge production, and practical experimentation established similar values across technology, science, and the arts, while broad directives like the Great Leap Forward imperative to produce "more, faster, better, cheaper" shaped both factories and theater workshops alike. The case studies of the *tu* revolving stage, imitation neon lights, and projected backdrops further demonstrate both the continuation of dramaturgical practices that emphasized scripting technology into playtexts and the significant investment of labor in "technological innovation and technological revolution" in the theater.

These innovative homegrown theater technologies also created a new aesthetic of technological fantasy, which paralleled (on a material level) the impulses of both science fantasy and the utopian strain of socialist realism. As technological fantasy, *tu* revolving stages and imitation neon lights asked their audiences to imagine the workings of other, specific technologies onstage, while also fully acknowledging the material reality in front of them. No one was meant to be fooled into thinking that a horizontally rotating curtain was the same thing as a revolving stage, or a piece of painted pipe, a neon light. Instead, audiences (in theory, at least) were equipped, via widely circulating stage technology handbooks and articles that specifically described the inner workings of those devices, to appreciate the ingenuity of close approximation developed under material constraints. The technology behind backdrop projections was likewise celebrated, but, in contrast to the *tu* revolving stage and neon lights, this final homegrown technology ironically was less transparent in its inner workings. Scenic artists proudly described their efforts to overcome technical challenges, such as distortion, in written articles, but they did their jobs so well that any distortion was all but invisible in performance. Instead, what was projected onstage was a seamless technicolor setting for the staging of an idealized historical narrative. This, along with the portability and flexibility of projections, paved the way for the development of the model works and theater technology well beyond the proscenium stage during the Cultural Revolution.

The Cultural Revolution is not a period known for emphasizing the arts, or technology. If anything, the opposite is true; in the popular imagination and standard historical narrative, it is remembered as a time of persecution for artists and scientists alike and of the denigration of technical expertise. However, as the following chapter will show, the extreme politics of the period did not in fact sever ties between technological innovation and theatrical production. The industrializing ethos of the 1950s and early 1960s carried over into a technocratic approach to the creation of the Cultural Revolution's "model works." Stage technology continued to play an essential role, even in the production of propaganda theater with carefully scripted ideological messages. Indeed, the idea that the aesthetics and ideology of a theatrical production could be controlled through the codification of how technology was used in scenic, lighting, and property design became its own kind of technological fantasy—in essence, a fantasy of technological determinism turned to political ends. Yet, as has been the case throughout this study, stage technology would prove as prone to mishap as to success. Narratives of how technical failure was overcome and averted, or of how stage technology was actually implemented, then add nuance to our understanding of the culture of the Cultural Revolution. These descriptions also further demonstrate the ongoing importance of technical innovation and ingenuity in the making of modern Chinese theater.

FOUR

# Model Ingenuity

*Technical Mentality and Practicality in Cultural Revolution* Yangbanxi

———◆◆✕◆●———

In the opening scene of *The Red Lantern* (红灯记, 1970), protagonist Li Yuhe 李玉和 enters a darkened stage carrying the play's iconic red signal lantern. Spotlight #1 turns on at full brightness, illuminating the actor with a large, hard-edged circle of white light.[1] He turns to face the audience, resolute, and begins his first aria with a reference to the lantern's symbolic power for Chinese Communist revolutionaries defying the Japanese military. Set during the Second Sino-Japanese War in northern China, the play (and its film adaptation) follows Li Yuhe, a railway worker and underground Communist operative, as he attempts to deliver a secret code to a band of Communist guerrillas. Throughout, the lantern functions as an almost coequal protagonist, reappearing and interacting with various characters in key scenes. When Li Yuhe's adoptive daughter, Li Tiemei 李铁梅, learns of her own revolutionary family history from her adoptive grandmother, Granny Li 李奶奶, for example, the scene ends with one of the most famous tableaux of all the *geming yangbanxi* 革命样板戏 (revolutionary model operas or model works, hereafter *yangbanxi*): Tiemei and Granny Li together holding the red lantern high (fig. 4.1). In these scenes and others, the lantern repeatedly functions as both essential prop and central symbol, at times taking on an agency akin to that of the human characters.

As a "revolutionary model opera," *The Red Lantern* was one of a limited number of ideologically correct theatrical works permitted to be performed during the Cultural Revolution. It may seem all too obvious that a red lantern would figure prominently, with political significance, in a party-sanctioned

140

Fig. 4.1. Li Tiemei (*left*) and Granny Li (*right*) holding aloft the red lantern in the film version of *The Red Lantern* (August First Film Studio, dir. Cheng Yin, 1970).

play and film of the same name. Indeed, previous scholarship has already gone far in addressing the political co-optation of performance during the tumultuous Cultural Revolution and, in particular, in unpacking the many layers of signification embedded in the lantern's narrative use and visual iconography.[2] Reconsidering the red lantern from the perspective of theatrical production, however, transforms it into a different kind of cipher: one that poses the question of how the behind-the-scenes, technical aspects of the *yangbanxi* functioned. Onstage, after all, the lantern is a "practical," or a lighting unit that belongs to the world of the play and therefore must work onstage. Yet as we see in the scenes described above, its narrative function suggests that it should have the power to illuminate far beyond the throw of a single small bulb. It is simultaneously a simple stage prop and much more, bearing the dual burden of fulfilling a scenographic function and conveying ideological meaning. As such, it places unique demands on production design and application.

Focusing on the red lantern as a lighting practical and stage prop shifts focus from the message of the *yangbanxi* to the material technologies necessary to bring them to the stage and to the question of how the two dimensions intersected during a time of extreme politics. Notionally aimed at reviving Communist revolutionary spirit among Chinese citizens, the Cultural Revolution devastated the lives of millions and took an especially harsh toll on those associated with the "bourgeois old society"—like theater artists.[3] For these artists, the Cultural Revolution meant the suspension of theater troupes' regular activities, exile to labor camps, and punishment for past affiliations with "feudal" or foreign performance styles. Creativity was stymied and entertainment prescriptive. For a time, the *yangbanxi* were even perceived as so ubiquitous that the phrase "eight hundred million people watching eight model operas for eight years" (八个样板戏被八亿人看了八年) became a popular—and derisive—shorthand for describing the destructive effects that the Cultural Revolution wreaked on the production and reception of theater.

At the same time, the *yangbanxi* also represent years of concerted artistic efforts by some of the best performing artists in the country. The so-called eight model operas included five modern revolutionary *jingju* (现代革命京剧), two ballets, and a symphony, plus several later additions to the repertoire. All of the pieces featured revolutionary narratives, all promoted idealized revolutionary heroes, and all were crafted by leading state-sponsored theater troupes, initially for performance in proscenium theaters equipped with the best stage equipment. However, the *yangbanxi* functioned as more than representations of history, heroics, and artistic excellence. As Xiaomei Chen has noted, the popular slogans of "acting a revolutionary character in order to become a revolutionary person" and "watching a revolutionary model play in order to become a revolutionary man or woman" make clear that the *yangbanxi* were meant to produce a nation full of model citizens through audience identification with model heroes and actual participation in productions.[4] Or in other words, as Laurence Coderre argues, the *yangbanxi* were envisioned as a "technology of transformation," whereby the ordinary masses could (in theory) mold themselves into exemplary socialist citizens.[5] To achieve these goals, the government actively encouraged widespread performance and adaptation of these plays, especially with its 1970 campaign to "widely popularize the *yangbanxi*" (大力普及革命样板戏) and a second wave of campaigns focused on adapting *yangbanxi* into regional and local *xiqu* genres. Several of the *yangbanxi* were also filmed in the early 1970s, further increasing their reach and accentuating their status as the representative cultural works of the period.[6]

With the red lantern prop as a point of departure, this chapter reexamines the *yangbanxi* from the perspective of stage technology and with particular attention to how materiality and practicality intersected with fantasies of control in their scripting, staging, and popularization. While revolutionary plots and characters often seem to take precedence in scholarly and theoretical treatments of the *yangbanxi*, creating the correct environment for these characters via the practical dimensions of the stage was in fact a core component of the aesthetic theory driving them and central to their perceived ideological efficacy. As this chapter demonstrates, both a technical attention to craft and distinctive modes of dissemination tied the *yangbanxi* closely to actual, material technologies and infused them with a technical mentality at every level of production. Indeed, the *yangbanxi* represent a culmination of trends in the interaction among theater, technology, and politics that this study has been tracing from the 1920s onward. The creators of the *yangbanxi* fixated on the technical detail—and even fetishized it—precisely because technology and technique seemed to ensure a high level of control over an art form that is otherwise corporeal, ephemeral, and prone to unexpected events (both onstage and in the audience). When the *yangbanxi* were then "sent down" to locations such as factories, mines, rural villages, and army bases, the confrontation with less-than-ideal stage conditions became a matter of ideological urgency. Once again, theater artists, especially amateurs, met these challenges with revolutionary fervor and grassroots innovation, and transformed potential technical failure into the triumph of revolutionary struggle. Through *yangbanxi* popularization, the technical and practical elements of theatrical production thus became key components of revolutionary narratives lived out in real life.

## Theater and Technology during the Cultural Revolution

If the Seventeen Years period demonstrates the importance of technology in creating new forms of theater for a socialist nation, the Cultural Revolution reveals a more complete transformation of theater into a tool of politics through the creation and dissemination of the *yangbanxi*. As the most prominent official artworks of the Cultural Revolution, the *yangbanxi* were meant to embody and inculcate audiences with the values of what scholars Roderick MacFarquhar and Michael Schoenhals have termed "Mao's Last Revolution." Launched in May 1966, the Cultural Revolution was a political movement motivated by a number of factors: the failures of the Great Leap Forward; Mao's dissatisfaction with the Socialist Education Movement and desire to reassert power; deteriorating relations with the Soviet Union; and personal vendettas among top leaders.[7] On one level, the Cultural Revolution involved purges of high-ranking party officials, beginning in May 1966, and a radical reconfiguration of top leadership. On another level, it entailed the fomentation of violent student activism and grassroots campaigns against "counterrevolutionary" elements among local cadres and ordinary citizens. One of the key campaigns during this period targeted the "Four Olds": old ideas, old culture, old habits, and old customs. School and university classes were suspended as of June 1966, and bands of student Red Guards destroyed property and beat, maimed, and even killed individuals who had been targeted in class struggle.[8] Violent rebellion and factional fighting among different Red Guard groups raged from 1966 to 1968, when the government began to reassert control and millions of youths were dispersed to the countryside. By the early 1970s, there were attempts to reinvigorate industry, agriculture, and scientific research, and there was a limited renewal of cultural production in areas such as film. Waves of mass campaigns, persecutions, and purges, however, continued until the death of Chairman Mao on September 9, 1976.

Among those most severely persecuted during the Cultural Revolution were "class enemies" who had connections to either the "bourgeois" endeavors of Western education and culture—including scientific and technical fields—or the literary and artistic traditions of China's own "feudal" past. Intellectuals and artists alike were sent to rural areas in droves, where they performed manual labor under the premise of learning from the workers, peasants, and soldiers. Scientific establishments related to industrial and agricultural production were somewhat protected, but the closure of educational institutions hindered research, and indiscriminate punishment of intellectuals for bourgeois inclinations did not spare scientists.[9] Physicist Fang Lizhi 方励之 (1936–2012), for instance, who played a central role in the development of Chinese nuclear physics, astrophysics, and cosmology (and would later go into exile for political activism after 1989), was sent to do hard labor in a coal mine in the late 1960s.[10] The placing of authority over manufacturing and other areas requiring technical expertise in the hands of revolutionary committees made up of Red Guards, PLA soldiers, and party cadres further devalued certain forms of expertise.[11] In the artistic realm, *huaju* artists were attacked for the genre's connections to bourgeois Western culture, and *xiqu* artists for their links to the elite ruling classes of previous Chinese dynasties. Actors were forced to confess to "crimes" like maintaining a bourgeois individualist mentality (especially in the case of celebrity performers) or staging "counterrevolutionary" plays, such as those from the traditional canon featuring scholar-beauty romances or contemporary plays that did not toe the party line.[12] Playwright Tian Han (author of *Fantasia of the Ming Tombs Reservoir*), for example, faced criticism that his play *Xie Yaohuan* (谢瑶环, 1961) used historical content to critique Chairman Mao and was later imprisoned.[13]

Yet despite the clear antipathy toward technical expertise that pervaded the Cultural Revolution and the persecution of artists and scientists, both art and science remained active throughout the decade. Moreover, as recent scholarship on this period has demonstrated, artistic and cultural activity was far from monolithic. Work by Xiaomei Chen, Paul Clark, Laurence Coderre, Xing Fan, Barbara Mittler, Laikwan Pang, and others has proven otherwise in a number of areas: the creativity of sent-down youth, the myriad ways in which material culture simultaneously perpetuated and transformed official culture, the aesthetic value of the theater of this period, the unique cultural experiences of individuals who lived through the PRC's "ten years of turmoil," and even the complexities of propaganda itself.[14] As Pang writes, "Propaganda was both a carefully deliberated means to control the people and a range of everyday practices among the people that would necessarily evade that control."[15] Similarly, the experience of scientists and technicians was not solely one of suppression and stymied development.[16] Some genuine advances were made even in the midst of political turmoil.[17] For example, China tested its first thermonuclear bomb in 1967 and launched its first satellite in 1970, both during the Cultural Revolution. A continued emphasis on *tu* technologies (see chapter 3) also gave rise to widespread grassroots innovation in agricultural science and pest control, as well as to legions of "barefoot doctors" (赤脚医生) who delivered basic modern medical practices to rural areas.

Connections between theater and technology can be seen from the very name of the propaganda pieces promoted during the Cultural Revolution: the *geming yangbanxi*. On the surface, this name seems primarily to emphasize the revolutionary (*geming* 革命) ethos of the time and what Pang has called the "culture of models and copies" that characterized artistic production of this period.[18] However, as Pang reminds us, the very concept of the "model" or *yangban* 样板 in the *yangbanxi* derived from its use in scientific agricultural strategies in the early 1960s and may have been chosen precisely because of its association with scientific pedagogy and technical precision.[19] Indeed, from their inception, the *yangbanxi* relied heavily on what might be termed a "technical mentality," borrowing from Gilbert Simondon, as well as actual stage technology itself. In one sense, this technical mentality was essentially a matter of technocracy, and the result of tasking the artists having the strongest skill sets and best training with the systematic development of the *yangbanxi*. In this, artistic development paralleled the rise of "red engineers" during this period, as described by Joel Andreas.[20] At the same time, however, the technical mentality of the *yangbanxi* also accords with Simondon's use of the term. For Simondon, "technical mentality" encompasses "cognition, affect and will" and is "endowed with a 'collective dimension'" that enables a bridging "between technicity and culture, in the process of constituting the 'technical culture.'"[21] The *yangbanxi*, in both name and practice, likewise bridge between technicity and culture, but with the goal of constituting a new *revolutionary* culture.

This technical mentality can be seen first and foremost in the yearslong process of methodically perfecting both script and stagecraft of the works that would become the *yangbanxi*. All were based on preexisting scripts, and work by the teams that would produce the official performance versions of the *yangbanxi* began as early as 1963.[22] As discussed elsewhere in this book, efforts to reform Chinese theater had been ongoing since the early decades of the twentieth century, and state-directed *xiqu* reform became more pervasive and institutionalized after the founding of the PRC. Jiang Qing 江青 (1914–91), Chairman Mao's wife, played a particularly important role in shaping the *yangbanxi* by personally participating in the revision of several plays by prominent state-sponsored theater troupes: *The Red Lantern* by the National Jingju Troupe (中国京剧团); *Morning on the Docks* (海港的早晨, later titled *On the Docks* [海港]) and *Taking Tiger Mountain by Strategy* (智取威虎山) by the Shanghai Jingju Troupe (上海京剧团); and *Sparks amid the Reeds* (芦荡火种, later titled *Shajiabang* [沙家浜]) by the Beijing Jingju Troupe (北京京剧团).[23] The success of these revised plays then led to the formulation of artistic directives, issued by Jiang Qing in speeches such as "On the Revolution in Peking Opera" (谈京剧革命), that inspired a rush of *jingju* modernization and became prescriptive after the Cultural Revolution began in 1966.[24] Jiang Qing's personal involvement in the *yangbanxi* and her directives reveal an effort to standardize the process by which plays were written, revised, rehearsed, and performed, as well as to control their content. In other words, the *yangbanxi* represented not just model plays but also a model playmaking process that involved a systematization of craft.[25]

Jiang Qing played a central role in directing this creation process: in addition to suggesting scripts to specific theater troupes, she attended rehearsals and made detailed suggestions for their revision. Other top leaders, including Chairman Mao himself, also provided feedback following public performances that the theater troupes were expected to incorporate into further refinements of the script and production.[26] Troupes convened meetings both internally and with audiences throughout the production process to gather suggestions for improvement, which were then incorporated into further script revisions, rehearsals, and performances. Jiang Qing identified precisely this pattern as the ideal scriptwriting process in "On the Revolution in Peking Opera," using the example of a play called *The Great Wall on the South China Sea* (南海长城):

> This is how they did it: First, the leaders provided a topic. Then, the scriptwriters went down several times to experience life with the masses and participate in a military mission to destroy the special agents of the enemy. When the script was finished, many comrades from the Guangzhou army unit joined the script discussions. After rehearsals, the scriptwriters asked for comments from the public and revised accordingly. In this way they constantly sought responses and kept revising so that they could speedily produce a good play that reflects real struggles.[27]

This feedback practice was, in fact, not unique to the *yangbanxi*—playwrights of the 1950s frequently worked closely with directors and performers to revise during the rehearsal process, and the praise or critique of top leaders such as Chairman Mao and Premier Zhou Enlai strongly influenced the success of individual productions. Similarly, the idea of playwriting as a teachable craft suitable to standardization echoed the many handbooks and articles on the topic published during and after the wartime era. Jiang Qing's personal involvement in *yangbanxi* development and the publication of "On the Revolution in Peking Opera" effectively codified and made prescriptive a specific version of a process that had already been developing in the preceding decades. However, the degree of involvement of political authorities in the creation of the *yangbanxi* was even greater than it had been in the 1950s, and the plays' official designation as "model" works in 1966 heightened the importance of perfecting and standardizing both the process and product.

Moreover, the theatrical creation and production process as standardized via the *yangbanxi* placed particular emphasis on technical details in relation to heroic characters, as well as in relation to production design and performance technique. This fact is often obscured in scholarship on the *yangbanxi*, which tends to emphasize both Jiang Qing's invocation of the adage that "the script is key" (剧本，剧本，一剧之本) and the primacy of characterization represented in the dramatic theory behind the model works. Central to this theory was the idea that the "basic task" (根本任务) of literature and art was to create typical (典型) revolutionary heroes. A key term in Marxist literary theory, the concept of the "typical" as a cornerstone of realism originated in a letter written by Friedrich Engels in 1884, which promoted the idea of "typical characters under typical circumstances" (典型环境中的典型人物)—a phrase that was often quoted in theoretical discussions of art and literature during the Mao era.[28] Raymond Williams describes Marxist typicality, at its most generalizable, as "based on the recognition of a constitutive and constituting process of social and historical reality, which is then specifically expressed in some particular 'type.'"[29] The main character in *The Red Lantern*, for example, can be considered a "typical" hero constituted by the "typical" environment of Communist revolutionaries struggling against imperialist oppression. At the same time, Li Yuhe was also explicitly positioned as an exemplary or emblematic hero, which reflects the influence of another key framework—"The Theory of the Three Prominences" (三突出)—that gained importance in 1968. According to this theory, literary and dramatic narratives should construct a hierarchy of increasing importance among characters, "positive characters," and "heroic characters."[30] The fixation on characterization in these theories meant that, to some extent, all other elements of dramaturgy and stage production did work to serve it.

Yet Engels's oft-quoted formulation of "typicality" placed equal emphasis on typical characters *and* their circumstances, and the Chinese term chosen for "circumstances"—*huanjing* 环境—is more commonly translated as "environment." Thus, even in theory, creation of the world around the *yangbanxi*'s heroic characters was just as important as the characters themselves. In the script, environment exists in the realm of carefully scripted stage directions and, in performance, requires the mediation of design and stage technology to come to life. The creation process of the *yangbanxi* therefore incorporated close attention to design and technology, including significant revisions to the stage directions throughout the script development process. Textual modifications happened before and during the rehearsal process, as well as after public performances. This demonstrates that comments on the performance technique and blocking, stage and lighting design, and technical effects were incorporated alongside feedback on narrative, character, and themes. A reflection on an October 1964 performance of *The Red Lantern* published in the *People's Daily*, for instance, comments on changes that the First Troupe of the National Jingju Theater (中国京剧院一团) made after their performance at a festival earlier that year and specifically notes adjustments made to the scenery.[31] These comments demonstrate the concrete effects of feedback received and adjustments made in design areas even in early versions of the *yangbanxi*. Perhaps the most oft-repeated story in this vein recalls how Jiang Qing requested that *On the Docks* be filmed three times, because she did not approve of the particular shade of red fabric initially used for the heroine's scarf.[32] This anecdote may be interpreted as a troubling reflection on the extent of authoritarian influence over the arts or perhaps even an example of the terrifying pettiness that underlay some of the politics and persecutions of the Cultural Revolution. From the perspective of stage technology, however, it also demonstrates an extreme attention to detail that suggests a belief both that craft mattered to the message of the model works and that the latter could be controlled through the former.

## The Technicity of the Model Works

The technical mentality behind the *yangbanxi* not only shaped the dramaturgical development process but also affected the relationship between script and stage at a fundamental level. To begin, the specific theater venues where the *yangbanxi* received their highest-profile performances directly influenced scenographic design and stagecraft for the productions. While all of the *yangbanxi* were performed in multiple venues throughout their development process, the highest-profile performances in the capital city all took place in large proscenium-style theaters that had been renovated or newly constructed in the 1950s. According to performance notices printed in the *Beijing Daily* (北京日报) newspaper, for example, May 1970 performances staged in commemoration of the Twenty-eighth Anniversary of Mao's "Talks at the Yan'an Forum on Literature and Art" took place in large Beijing theaters.[33] All of these spaces were equipped with a large cyclorama, modern electric lighting and sound, and fly systems of up to thirty pipes that could be used for hanging instruments, scenery, and curtains.[34] As Xing Fan notes, the use of large proscenium theaters had a major impact on the aesthetics of the *yangbanxi*—especially the five *jingju* pieces, given that the use of elaborate scenery and "close-to-realistic" style that they enabled was a significant shift for this *xiqu* genre.[35] In the case of *The Red Lantern*, the fact that the May 1970 run was codified in print as a "performance edition" further suggests the influence of a specific theater venue on the officially sanctioned version of the play (table 4.1).

At the same time, these venues also connect *yangbanxi* development and performances to another technologically inflected local history: the construction and equipping of theater spaces in the first Seventeen Years of the PRC

Table 4.1. May 1970 *Yangbanxi* Performance Venues in Beijing

| Title | Venue | Construction / Renovation Dates | Seats | Stage Size |
|---|---|---|---|---|
| *Taking Tiger Mountain by Strategy* | Capital Theater 首都剧场 | 1954 | 1,227 | 26.7m w × 19.5m d × 18.5m h |
| *The Red Lantern* | People's Theater 人民剧场 | 1955 | 1,476 | 25.5m w × 17.5m d × 17m h |
| *Red Detachment of Women* (ballet) | Tianqiao Theater 天桥剧场 | 1953/1954 | 1,564 | 23.5m w × 16.5m d × 16.5m h |
| *Shajiabang* | Workers' Club 工人俱乐部 | 1955 | 1,485 | 22m w × 16.45m d × 20m h |
| Piano-accompanied arias from *The Red Lantern* Piano *Yellow River* Orchestral *Shajiabang* | Cultural Palace of the Nationalities 民族宫剧场 | 1959 | 1,102 | 22m w × 16.8m d × 18m h |

*Source:* Data from *Beijing Daily*, May 11, 1970, 3.

and, specifically, what architectural historian Lu Xiangdong has identified as a budding "technology worship" (技术崇拜) among Chinese theater designers and technicians of that period.[36] In the first decade of its existence, the PRC government directed significant resources to theater renovation and construction. From 1953 forward, the theater was recognized as a profession requiring a professional space with certain technical specifications. Some theater professionals even became convinced that the key to theater development was the installation of the proper "hardware."[37] This was a matter both of constructing a new socialist culture and of national pride. In a memoir recounting his experiences in the early 1950s, scenic designer Li Chang, for example, recalls his keen sense of a need to construct theaters in Beijing "that could match up to contemporaneous European theaters, like Tianqiao Theater, Capital Theater, People's Theater, Beijing Workers' Association, etc., in a short time."[38] The Capital Theater, for example, seated an audience of 1,227 and featured hidden speakers and a climate control system in the house. It also had a mechanically contracting proscenium and a revolving stage 16 meters in diameter, more than sixty hanging pipes and the newest in lighting control technology, wireless headsets linking different parts of the stage, and a stage feed in every dressing room.[39] Much of the equipment was imported and installed with the help of a team from East Germany.[40] Indeed, all of the theaters listed in table 4.1 were built in the 1950s, and all were outfitted with what was at the time the best in stage technology.

One of the results of performing the *yangbanxi* in these specific spaces was that scenic and lighting designers had access to the best possible equipment and therefore could actualize more sophisticated designs. In accordance with *yangbanxi* theory, this necessarily involved using design to aid in the creation of revolutionary heroes via scenery, costumes and makeup, and lighting.[41] *The Red Lantern*, for example, was praised for drawing an effective contrast between the world of the first nine scenes, which suffers under the oppression of the enemy and is dimly lit with cool colors, and the last two, when the characters reach the revolutionary base area, and the entire stage brightens, becoming more colorful to reflect a change in setting and spirit. Likewise, in *Taking Tiger Mountain by Strategy*, the scenography was seen to represent "the fundamental nature of the struggle situation at the time" and offer "a typical environment in order to mold the figure of the proletarian revolutionary hero."[42] Couched in the Marxist terminology of the "typical," reviews described features of the set and lighting design in relation to the play's central revolutionary hero, Yang Zirong 杨子荣. In the fifth act, for instance, the relative placement of distant snowy mountains projected onto the backdrop curtain, pine-tree set pieces, and the actor's blocking work together with his aria lyrics to draw connections between the near and the far, between the Communist revolution at home and the greater world revolution.[43] The use of projected backdrops, in particular, draws clearly on the *tu* technologies developed for the performance of *The East Is Red* in 1964. In the *yangbanxi*, however, the technology developed from a singular instance of innovation to a codified means of representing backgrounds that was systematically applied across all of the productions.

The published versions of *yangbanxi* scripts also feature changes in stage directions over time, which had direct implications for scenography, lighting, and sound design. For example, the opening stage directions of the 1968 version of *The Red Lantern* read:

> *A night in late autumn during the War of Resistance against Japan.*
> *A railway switch area near the Longtan Station in the northeast. A long slope in the foreground, mountains in the distance.*
> *The curtain opens: A dark autumn night, with the north wind howling madly, making everything blow about noisily. Four Japanese military police officers on patrol cross the stage.*
> *Li Yuhe carries the signal lantern in his hand, enters calm and composed.*[44]

In contrast, in the version of the script published widely beginning in 1970, the opening stage directions read:

> *During the War of Resistance against Japan. A night in early winter.*
> *Near Longtan train station somewhere in the northeast. The railway bed can*
> *    be seen. Rolling hills in the distance.*
> *The curtain opens: A piercingly cold north wind. Four Japanese military police*
> *    officers on patrol cross the stage.*
> *Li Yuhe carries the signal lantern in his hand, enters walking with vigorous*
> *    strides, full of energy and spirit, calm and composed.*[45]

Comparing these two stage direction excerpts reveals significant changes: first and most noticeably, several adjectives are added to help direct the movements of the actor playing Li Yuhe. These relate directly to Li Yuhe's designation as a heroic character according to the Theory of the Three Prominences. At the same time, however, there are also changes made that directly affect different areas of design and stage technology: first, the north wind is no longer "howling madly"; now it is "piercingly cold" and only howls later, *after* Li Yuhe sings the opening lines of his first aria. The sound effect thus competes less directly with the sound of the human voice, allowing the music and singing to open the scene. Second, the shift of setting from "late autumn" (深秋) to "early winter" (初冬), while seemingly minor, has implications for the quality and angle of light, as well as the color of the mountains and the potential need for special effects like snow. The fact that the later script is specifically subtitled "May 1970 performance edition" (一九七〇年五月演出本) further demonstrates that these changes were written into the script alongside or following production, and therefore likely reflect design decisions made for a specific venue. These examples thus illustrate how *yangbanxi* scripts encoded production decisions made by specific design teams into their dramatic texts.

On an even more technical level, each of the *yangbanxi* relied heavily on lighting and sound effects that required specialized equipment or construction techniques. As with examples discussed in previous chapters, these effects and properties were woven into the fabric of the play in a way that made them essential to plot and character development, and therefore, according to *yangbanxi* theory, to the communication of ideologically correct messages. For instance, the lighting instrument schedule (布光说明) for *Taking Tiger Mountain* lists no fewer than twelve types of special effects lighting units, such as "running cloud lights" (跑云灯) used to produce the

布 光 说 明 （二）天幕 灯

| 编号 | V、W 数 | 灯 型 | 色 彩 | 灯 具 说 明 与 使 用 场 次 | |
|---|---|---|---|---|---|
| A 1 | 220 V 2 KW | 投景幻灯 | | 物镜 450°+450° | 灯后距天幕 3m，标高 3m，灯与灯距 3m |
| A 2 | " | " | | " | " |
| A 3 | " | " | | " | " |
| A 4 | " | " | | " | " |
| A 5 | " | " | | " | " |
| A 6 | " | " | | " | " |
| A 7 | " | " | | " | " |
| B 1 | 110 V 1 KW | 投景幻灯 | | 物镜 900°+450° | 灯后距天幕 3m，标高 3m，灯与灯距 3m |
| B 2 | " | " | | " | " |
| B 3 | " | " | | " | " |
| B 4 | 220 V 1 KW | " | | " | " |
| B 5 | " | 特技幻灯 | | 第二场天幕幻灯树丛火烧受光面，第七场天幕加亮补光 | |
| C 1 | 220 V 1 KW | 跑云灯 | 红 | 第二场天幕火烧效果光 | 转速每分钟 1 周 |
| C 2 | | 长雪球×3 | | 天幕下雪效果 | 转速每分钟 2 周 |
| C 3 | | 圆雪球×4 | | " | 转速每分钟 2—6 周(可调速) |
| C 4 | 10 V 7.5 A×18 | 凸聚 | 白 | 天幕下雪效果光源，投射雪球，反射至天幕 | |
| C 5 | 1KW×2 | 跑云灯 | 白 | 第一场天幕风云效果光 | 转速每分钟 3—4 周 |
| C 6 | 110 V 1 KW | 土跑云 | 白 | 第八场山雾效果光 | 转速每分钟 ½ 周 |
| C 7 | " | " | 浅蓝 | 滑雪天幕跑云效果光 | 转速每分钟 3 周 |
| C 8 | | 凸聚 | 橙 | 第八场树网山头受光面 | 树网背后投光 |
| C 9 | 110 V 1 KW | 跑云灯 | 白 | 第五场蓝灰纱幕前跑雾效果光 | 转速每分钟 4 周 |
| C10 | 110 V 2 KW | 特技幻灯 | 白 | 第五场蓝灰纱幕前光束 | |
| C11 | 110 V 1 KW | " | 白 | 第五场光束 | |
| C12 | 220 V 2 KW×2 | " | 橙 | 第八场天幕朝霞效果光 | 倾斜物镜加波纹玻璃 |
| D 1 | 220V 500W×6 | 天幕顶光 | 红 | | |
| D 2 | " | " | 深蓝 | | |
| D 3 | 220 V 1KW×6 | 映钨灯 | 中蓝 | | |

Fig. 4.2. Lighting instrument schedule for July 1970 production of *Taking Tiger Mountain by Strategy*, including special effects equipment. Source: Shanghai jingju tuan *Zhiqu Weihushan juzu*, *Geming xiandai jingju* Zhiqu Weihushan (*yijiu qiling nian qi yue yanchuben*) (Beijing: Renmin chubanshe, 1971), 367.

effect of smoke from a burning fire or fog, and two different "snow balls" (雪球) used to project falling snow on the cyc.[46] In scene 2, when bandits set fire to a small village, both the running cloud light and a moving light (流动 灯) equipped with a red gel are used to create the effect of light and smoke from the large conflagration burning just offstage (fig. 4.2).[47] The burning of the village and the bandits' murder of railway worker Li Yongqi's 李勇奇 wife provide key motivations for Li's later antipathy toward the bandits and eventual embrace of the PLA when they arrive in his village (in scene 6). In *On the Docks*, atmospheric stage effects play an even more direct role in the plot: at the beginning of the play, news of an impending typhoon provides the impetus for a group of dockworkers to accelerate the process of loading grain onto a freighter bound for Africa before the storm can delay the shipment. Thunder and lightning are used at several points throughout the play to signal the impending storm and build tension, such as at the very end of scene 3 and in the second half of scene 5.[48] In scene 5, in particular, the stage directions indicate thunder and lightning effects in between lines about the time before dawn running out quickly. Interrupting the dialogue with these effects heightens the scene's sense of urgency, and the enhanced importance of the lightning is evident from the inclusion of a specific "lightning light" (闪电灯) in the instrument schedule.[49]

Lighting practicals and technically sophisticated set props also play a prominent role in creating atmosphere, driving plot, and conveying central metaphors in the *yangbanxi*. In *The Red Lantern*, for instance, the eponymous object functions similarly to the neon lights in *Sentinels under the Neon Lights*—albeit with positive, not negative, symbolism. As noted in the opening of this chapter, the lantern appears throughout the play, perhaps most famously at the end of one scene when the characters Granny Li and Li Tiemei hold it aloft and a red wash covers the stage. It functions on multiple levels, as Braester has shown: on the one hand, it is an obvious and direct reference to Chairman Mao, who was often described and depicted as a bright red sun. Mao, as sun and red lantern, illuminates the correct revolutionary path. The red lantern also is a literal materialization of the Cultural Revolution aesthetic mandate to be "red, bright, shining" (红光亮).[50] It further functions as an heirloom, possession of which designates the next generation of revolutionaries, and exists within a system of revolutionary codes wherein recognition of the lamp indicates one's membership in a community of guerrilla Communist soldiers.[51] From the perspective of stage technology, however, the red lantern also must operate correctly within the physical world of the performance. Simply put: as an onstage source of illumination, it should actually turn on and shine light onto the stage. Design schematics from performances by the National Jingju Troupe show that the prop lantern was indeed designed not only in terms of how the prop would look but also in terms of technical details such as the type of light bulb (small 6.2V), power source (two "number 2" batteries, held in place by a rubber band), and casing (a curved piece of red glass) (fig. 4.3). Clearly, the red lantern was intended to serve as more than a symbol.

This level of detail can be found across the various model plays, even when there is a less obvious connection between title and technicity. In *Taking Tiger Mountain*, for instance, a brazier used for heat and light in the bandits' cave in two scenes was created by placing a small motorized fan in a basin and surrounding it with four small 40-watt light bulbs. The basin was then covered by a screen to which pieces of dyed silk were attached. Turning on the light bulbs and fan illuminated the silk and made it flutter to look like flames.[52] The design and construction details of the brazier gave it a "close-to-realistic" look (as Xing Fan describes the overall aesthetic of the *yangbanxi*), but, more important, created a source of low-level directional

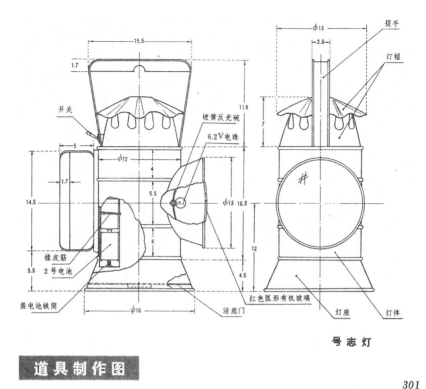

号 志 灯

道 具 制 作 图

*301*

Fig. 4.3. Red lantern prop schematic for May 1970 production of *The Red Lantern*
Source: Zhongguo jingju tuan, *Geming xiandai jingju* Hongdeng ji (yijiu qiling nian
wu yue yanchuben) (Beijing: Renmin chubanshe, 1970), 301.

lighting onstage that contributed to the characterization of the bandits' space
as dark and therefore antiheroic. When hero Yang Zirong enters the space,
he does so with a burst of bright white light that suddenly illuminates the
cave and provides a stark contrast to the villains' environment (and nature).
The first scene of *On the Docks* features much larger functional set props,
with dockworkers operating winches to load cargo onto small carts in their
opening choreography (figs. 4.4 and 4.5).[53] In the film version, the carts are
even motorized, although the performance edition scripts do not specify this
detail. The technical components of these props become even more important given their role in choreography, as the movements of the actors occur in
conjunction with the movement of the winches and carts.
    Indeed, given the functionality of these stage props and the mechan-
ics required to build them, one might even conceptualize working lanterns,

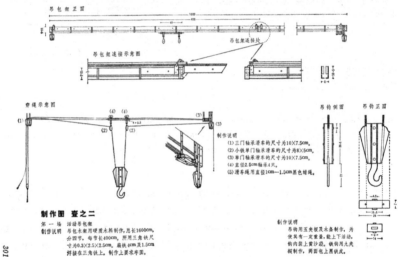

Figures 4.4–4.5. Example of how working winches were used in choreography and schematic for winch prop design from the 1972 production of *On the Docks*. Source: Shanghai jingju tuan *Haigang* zu, *Geming xiandai jingju* Haigang (yijiu qi'er nian yi yue yanchuben) (Beijing: Renmin wenxue chubanshe, 1974), 225, 301. Images courtesy Harvard-Yenching Library, Harvard University.

braziers, and winches as kinds of simple machines. Onstage, these simple machines were not set dressing or decorations, but rather animated by their interaction with human actors and made integral to atmosphere, plot, and ideological message. Li Yuhe, Li Tiemei, and Granny Li lift the red lantern; bandits gather around the "burning" brazier; dockworkers raise and lower winch cables. This human–prop interaction recalls what Tina Mai Chen has argued of the human-machine continuum in the Maoist imagination, wherein "the tempering of new bodies did not necessarily require advanced technology, specialized knowledge, or an inventor's genius."[54] Instead, under Maoism, the "assemblage of human bodies with instruments or gadgets" was central, and "machines were considered an extension of the body to realize a qualitative transformation."[55] This human–machine (or actor–prop) continuum is most apparent in *On the Docks*, wherein the winches are most literally components of a semimechanized maritime industry. They also represent the PRC's advanced place in economic development relative to the African nations to whom they are sending aid—a position that has been made possible by the successful industrial assemblage of willing socialist citizens and new technologies. Onstage, too, the working props found throughout the plays function as a kind of "extension of the body" through simple mechanics. In other words, the stage prop–performing body assemblage becomes a central part of the performer's revolutionary experience.[56] And if interaction with props and practicals was indeed part of the revolutionary transformation that one was meant to undergo through participation in the *yangbanxi*, then the technical details and appropriate construction of these elements were all the more ideologically important.

Set, lighting, and prop design—and the proper technical execution of those designs—therefore played not a subordinate but rather a fundamental role in the *yangbanxi*. It might even be argued that their potential ability to provoke the senses and emotions of audience members was precisely what made leaders see them as such valuable aesthetic and political tools. A passage in the article on *Tiger Mountain* referenced above, for example, notes a moment at the end of the play when the melody of the song "The East Is Red" swells and the lights gradually brighten to illuminate the entire stage.[57] As Xing Fan observes in her discussion of the same scene, the combination of music, acting, and lighting enables audience members to "witness the morning sun" in protagonist Yang Zirong's heart, "made manifest through the visual effect produced by lighting instruments" and in such a way that design predominates over the stage space and character alike.[58] Nor was the importance of these aspects of scenography limited to the world bounded by the proscenium opening. Discussing the model ballet *The Red Detachment of Women* (红色娘子军), for example, critic Ren Yi 韧宜 describes how the design in each act made the production's audiences feel, imbuing sets and lighting with the power to engender revolutionary fervor, comradery, and respect for revolutionary martyrs.[59] Another article on *The Red Detachment* likewise notes how a quick change into scene 4 parallels the speed of the main character Wu Qinghua's enlightenment to the revolutionary cause and praises the scenography of a particular moment in scene 5 for its "soul-stirring affective power."[60] Thus, although the *yangbanxi* were anchored by revolutionary characters, the successful execution of impressive scenic, lighting, and sound effects also created a sublime, often emotional response in audience members.

While discussions of *yangbanxi* scenic design are generally couched in Maoist terminology, this relationship between affect and mise-en-scène, in particular, is articulated by invoking one of the core concepts of classical Chinese poetics, "the blending of scenery and sentiment" (情景交融).[61] Classical poetics may seem out of place in Cultural Revolution aesthetic discourse, given the strict prohibitions on "old culture," but references to blending scenery and sentiment appear frequently in articles on *yangbanxi* scenography and even in some article titles.[62] One theoretical work by Fang Yun, for example, makes a claim for the fundamental importance of the concept in revolutionary performance:

> Scenery and sentiment, the environment for struggle and the mental activity of the characters, have always had a close relationship. The task of scenic designers is to manage properly the relationship between the two, taking the expression of the main theme and the molding of proletarian heroic figures as the point of departure, following the development of the plot, and providing characters with the typified environment for struggle.[63]

As explained by Li Zehou 李泽厚 in his work on Chinese aesthetics, this fusion of internal and external worlds in traditional poetics can be likened to a kind of empathy that consists of "the melding of the appreciating (or creating) self with the appreciated (or created) object" and the unification of subjective emotions with an objective form.[64] Li is, admittedly, discussing this principle in relation to early Chinese poetry. However, the way he describes it is illuminating for the case of the *yangbanxi*, in which the subjective emotions of the characters are unified with and externalized through the objective components of stage scenery and lighting. The tight coordination among the various production elements of the *yangbanxi* therefore seems to have enabled a reconfiguration of this particular concept to conform to Marxist and Maoist aesthetic principles and politics, with "blending" (交融) transforming into a "dialectical unity" (辩证统一) of elements.[65] And, indeed, in the Cultural Revolution era discussions of the concept mentioned above, the relationship between scenery and sentiment is often specifically framed as a dialectical one. Successful scenic design was thus also imbricated in demonstrating, much more generally, that classical aesthetic principles could be transmuted into ideals better aligned with party ideology, and that those principles could be translated to the stage through the mediation of specific stage technologies. The level of detail included further suggests that one underlying principle of the *yangbanxi* may well have been a form of technological determinism that paralleled the historical determinism of Marxist dialectal materialism. This determinism operated through the technical elements of the production: once perfected, proper mobilization of the stage apparatus would guarantee the successful creation of a "typical" environment onstage, which in turn would support the portrayal of the idealized revolutionary heroes of the *yangbanxi* and prompt the ideal audience response.

## Disseminating Technical Detail and Rendering the Technical Typical

Given the centrality of technicity to the *yangbanxi*, questions of how to construct set pieces and props or rig lighting equipment, as well as how to disseminate that knowledge to aspiring performers, directors, designers, and technicians, once again rise to the fore. As with previous periods discussed in this study, the spread of technical theater knowledge to theater professionals and the general public was a central part of how theater intersected with politics, but the mechanisms of dissemination differed greatly during the Cultural Revolution. In contrast to the 1930s or the Seventeen Years period, the Cultural Revolution in general did not see widespread production and dissemination of technical knowledge through specialized journal articles and handbooks. Instead, across all fields of knowledge, official publication ground to a near halt. *Theater Gazette*, which had published many of the articles on stage technology in the 1950s, paused publication after only three issues in 1966 and did not resume until 1976. Likewise, many scientific and technical journals ceased publication during the late 1960s, dropping from more than 400 titles in circulation in 1965 to only 20 in 1969.[66] To be sure, as recent scholarship has shown, this downturn in state-sponsored publication for general audiences did not mean a total knowledge blackout, but rather a shift to increased "internal" (內部) publication and underground circulation of ideologically questionable reading material.[67] However, the overall trend was a constriction of publishing outlets and narrowing of the materials in public circulation, especially in fields that had ideologically suspect histories—like the theater.

The increased attention to certain forms of theater as "models," however, led to widespread discussion of the *yangbanxi* in the limited official journals and newspapers that did circulate during the Cultural Revolution, as well as publication of *yangbanxi*-specific material. Most *yangbanxi* articles published in official outlets focused on dramaturgy, aesthetics, and ideological messages in the plays, but many of these discussions also included technical details discerned through processes of "putting into practice" (实践), "learning through experience" (体会), and performance "viewing notes" (札记).[68] Major publications such as the *People's Daily* also frequently printed commentary on the scenography of the *yangbanxi*.[69] These articles were then reprinted and circulated via provincial-level newspapers and essay collections.[70] They typically included detailed descriptions of the use of sets and lighting at specific moments in the productions, grounded in ideological and theoretical discussions of the function of scenography. Toward the latter half of the Cultural Revolution, singing and performance guides for amateur actors also circulated.[71] While one cannot imagine that every reader fully understood these details or that every audience member necessarily read these articles, their wide circulation does suggest an effort to equip theatergoers and amateur performers with more advanced awareness of technical theater and design, as well as performance techniques.

The emphasis on learning and experience in the titles of many published essays on *yangbanxi* performance and production further adds a participatory element to the circulation of technical knowledge. Indeed, both model stage technology and performance technique were also disseminated through pedagogical structures that encouraged "learning from" (学习) the *yangbanxi* through imitation, replication, and person-to-person knowledge transmission. Official state-sponsored troupes at the provincial and city levels facilitated the learning and performance of these pieces: the troupes that originated the *yangbanxi* were sent around the country to lecture and demonstrate, and prominent regional troupes traveled to Beijing or Shanghai to attend performances and participate in tutorials.[72] Meanwhile, many cities held large performance exhibitions (调演) or conferences (会演) wherein smaller local troupes from surrounding counties and villages would come to the city to perform and study the *yangbanxi*. While on one hand the top-down structuring of training speaks to a desire to standardize and control the process, person-to-person teaching and learning also resulted in diverse and idiosyncratic experiences on the ground.

The process of "learning from" the *yangbanxi* was further aided by the dissemination of "performance editions" (演出本) based on approved official performances. These scripts appeared in full in the *People's Daily* and other newspapers and journals, and state-sponsored publishing houses produced various editions that included dialogue and librettos, music, and illustrations.[73] *Yangbanxi* material even came to comprise an outsized proportion of all publishing in the field of literature and the arts: 245 out of 393 newly published arts and literature books in 1970, for example, were related to the model works.[74] Beginning that same year, full performance manuals—or "production bibles"—were published for five of the *yangbanxi*: *The Red Lantern* (published 1972), *Taking Tiger Mountain by Strategy* (published 1971), *The Red Detachment of Women* (published 1970), *Shajiabang* (published 1976), and *On the Docks* (published 1974).[75] Each marks itself as based on a specific model performance by attributing collective authorship to a given state-sponsored troupe and noting a date of performance on the front cover. Like a stage manager's promptbook or production bible, these volumes run many hundreds of pages and contain a script (based on a particular performance), descriptions and diagrams of blocking and choreography, musical notation, production photographs, set design sketches and blueprints, full-color costume and makeup renderings, prop illustrations and set lists, lighting plots, and cue lists for lighting, spotlights, and special effects. All of the technical elements are recorded in painstaking detail; the production bible for *The Red Lantern*, for example, includes a single, full-color master plot of almost a hundred and fifty lighting units, ranging from strips of footlights to 2,000-watt Fresnel lights to specials for projected backdrop images, followed by black-and-white drawings that indicate locations and focus directions for each act, and the follow spot cue list that instructs operators which characters to follow and what colors/level of brightness to use (fig. 4.6).[76] Schematics for important props and practical lights, as described above, are also included in these tomes. The production bibles thus further confirm that the scripts were indeed key to the *yangbanxi*, as Jiang Qing famously claimed, but also that the concept of a "script" was expanded to enfold all of the design and technical dimensions of theatrical production.

The completeness, level of detail, and standardized format of the production bibles also seem to suggest that their main purpose was to "fix" a specific

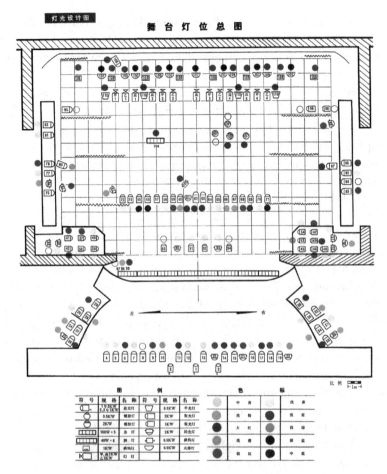

Fig. 4.6. Lighting plot from May 1970 production of *The Red Lantern*.
Source: Zhongguo jingju tuan, *Geming xiandai jingju* Hongdeng ji (yijiu
qiling nian wu yue yanchuben) (Beijing: Renmin chubanshe, 1970), 323–24.

version of each of the *yangbanxi*, as Paul Clark has written of their filmed
versions, and to facilitate reproduction of that ideal form.[77] Clark writes,
for instance, that the production bibles (along with scripts and scores) were
"designed to enable standardized live performances of extracts or complete
operas," while Chinese scholar Shi Yonggang similarly argues that they were
designed and disseminated to ensure "completeness" (完整性) and "standardization" (标准化).[78] This theory is further supported by the fact that the
production bibles were published as a part of the movement to popularize

the *yangbanxi* that began in July 1970. Professional troupes, like those that created the *yangbanxi*, traveled to factories, mines, rural villages, and army bases to perform for the workers, peasants, and soldiers there, while members of these classes also were encouraged to form their own amateur cultural troupes or Mao Zedong Thought Propaganda Brigades (毛泽东思想宣传队) and to study the *yangbanxi*. The creation and dissemination of filmed versions of the *yangbanxi* was also a key element of this popularization movement. These worked in tandem with *yangbanxi* print materials, with some described directly in relation to the original stage productions as "live television broadcast screen reproductions" (电视实况传播屏幕复制片) and "televised documentaries" (电视纪录片).[79] Indeed, with all citizens, regardless of their levels or even lack of theater training, encouraged to participate in *yangbanxi* activities, there does seem to have been an imperative to transform live performance itself into something reproducible on a grand scale via the dissemination of models for all elements of the productions.

Looking at the production bibles in detail, however, raises questions as to their utility as tools of pedagogy and reproducibility. On the one hand, the books do include sections that seem structured as how-to guides. Music is in basic notation (简谱), and the production bible for the *Red Detachment of Women*, for instance, provides details on choreography that include how to perform basic ballet positions and movements such as pirouettes. Yet, while the technical information in the production bibles may seem to the untrained eye to be a viable pattern for reproduction, these sections are actually missing essential details that would be necessary to accurately reproduce the designs and effects described. For example, as mentioned above, each of the *yangbanxi* used backdrop projections and special lighting units to create effects such as snow and cloud cover. From lighting schedules in the *yangbanxi* production bibles, it is clear that multiple lighting units were used for each backdrop image. We know from the history of backdrop projection discussed in chapter 3 that this would therefore have required the use of several overlapping slides, with the image painted on each adjusted to mitigate distortion. Yet the images of the backdrop projection provided in the guides show only one seamless image designed to fill the entire backdrop; no details on how to break the image into sections or adjust it for distortion are provided. Similarly, in lighting and special effects handbooks in earlier periods, entries on devices such as "running cloud lights" were accompanied by descriptions and diagrams of how to construct these special effects lighting units. In contrast, the *yangbanxi* production bibles mention only the names and positioning instructions for such units, not how to make or operate them. The schematics

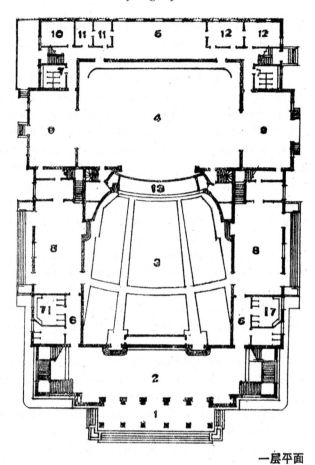

Fig. 4.7. Blueprint of the People's Theater, where *The Red Lantern* was performed in May 1970. Source: Qinghua daxue tumu jianzhu xi juyuan jianzhu sheji zu, *Zhongguo huitang juchang jianzhu* (Beijing: Qinghua daxue tumu jianzhu xi, 1960), 59.

一层平面

seem almost to be representative of a *type* of technical detail, rather than fully usable as guides for how to re-create the *yangbanxi*.

In other words, anyone attempting to reproduce *yangbanxi* by the book would have needed access to specific stage equipment, as well as the know-how to operate that equipment and translate technical information for the stage. The production bibles assume a level of technical theater knowledge that may have been possible because of the dissemination of handbooks and how-to guides in the preceding decades, as well as *yangbanxi*-related training programs. Yet they also presume a level of material sophistication (in terms of equipment) that was limited to the largest proscenium theater spaces in urban areas (like those discussed above). Furthermore, the ground plans and lighting plots included in the production bibles are not actually as standardized as they first seem; each features a slightly different stage shape and, in the case of the lighting plots, different hanging positions for over-stage, wing, and over-house lighting units. The individual stages featured in the production bibles in fact correspond to the specific theaters in which the troupes were performing at the time the design and technical details were recorded for publication—that is, the dates noted on the cover of each book. For example, the production bible for *The Red Lantern* is dated May 1970, when performances were taking place in the People's Theater in Beijing, and the lighting plot clearly reflects that theater's blueprint (fig. 4.7). If the production bible was meant primarily to function as a record of a given performance, then this specificity seems only logical; as a guide for reproduction, however, it creates the issue of how to translate the specific into something that could be more generally copied. Today, this type of design translation is common in professional theater productions that tour to different venues across the nation and internationally. The production conditions of the 1970s, however, raise the question of whether the *yangbanxi* as recorded in the production bibles could even have been widely reproduced, especially beyond the well-equipped spaces indicated in these books or by designers and technicians with lower levels of expertise. Indeed, the very standardization and reproducibility implied by the production bibles may be yet another form of technological fantasy, with the ideal form ultimately unrealizable by anyone other than the most well-resourced theater troupes.

The relationship between specific and general in documentation and implementation also suggests a deeper connection between the technical and the typical in the *yangbanxi*. As mentioned above, the idea of "typicality" or "typical characters under typical circumstances" was one of the cornerstones of *yangbanxi* narrative and character, and in many ways drove the elevation of scenic design from a subordinate to essential role in their staging. On another level, however, the tension between specificity and generalizability found in the technical drawings of *yangbanxi* production bibles also parallels the conflict between the "exemplary" and the "representative" that Richard King has observed in contending Chinese definitions of typicality. Whereas Engels's original formulation of "typical characters under typical circumstances" leaned toward the representative, King argues that "typical characters, in their Cultural Revolution manifestation, were entirely exemplary, the embodiment of the qualities of strength, wisdom, loyalty, and courage attributed to the working classes as idealized (or fantasized) by Jiang Qing and her associates."[80] Similarly, the stage technology of the *yangbanxi* is exemplary and idealized. Yet, at the same time, a central element of *yang-*

*banxi* typicality was that exemplary characters were touted as models for the masses; likewise, their ideal stage technology was presented as that which could become widespread if reproduced. The fact that venue names are not even mentioned in the production bibles confirms that the ground plans and lighting plots were meant to be seen as something that could be generalized, rather than specific—a model or pattern as well as a record of a unique event. In other words, one of the things that the *yangbanxi* did, through the production bibles, was attempt to render the technical typical and thereby align modern stage technologies with revolutionary aesthetic theory.

## Sent-Down Plays and the Potential for Technical Failure

The high theory of aesthetic dialectics and the typicality of stage technology were, however, also in constant dialogue with the practicalities of putting on actual stage productions. Within the reified environments of the state-sponsored troupes that originated the *yangbanxi*, resources, expertise, and political support enabled the creation of the model works. The necessity of sophisticated design and technology established in this context was then put to the test when the movement to popularize the *yangbanxi* began in July 1970. When the *yangbanxi* were sent to more remote areas, they confronted conditions far different from their points of origin. On a practical level, where *did* the majority of *yangbanxi* performances take place, and were these venues able to provide space for majestic sets and equipment for high-powered, colored stage lighting? Were there even enough domestic factories to produce the kind of lighting equipment required by the *yangbanxi*, and were local electrical systems able to handle upward of a hundred high-wattage lights? And what happened when the *yangbanxi* were sent down to the factories and the countryside without these necessities? When put into practice under varying circumstances, how did the technical details of production fare, and how did this affect the realization of a properly dialectical relationship between scene and emotion?

Indeed, if we look beyond Beijing and Shanghai, the locations of performances quickly begin to shift. A combined survey of newspapers, essay collections, and local gazetteers (新方志) gives a clearer picture of the range of performance locations and varying calibers of performers who were involved with popularizing the *yangbanxi*.[81] Individual production troupes often formed Mao Zedong Thought Propaganda Brigades, as did units of the PLA. Many of these troupes labeled themselves amateur;[82] almost all of them traveled, often "up to the mountains and down to the countryside" (上

山下乡), attempting to bring *yangbanxi* performances to underserved areas. Heilongjiang Province's Shuangyashan City Mao Zedong Thought Literature and Art Propaganda Troupe (双鸭山市毛泽东思想文艺宣传队), for example, first sent their key members to major cities across the country to learn *yangbanxi*, then later rehearsed and put on performances, including at Zhenbao Island for border guards and at Qiqihar for garrison troops.[83] Even in the provincial capital of Shandong, Jinan, the municipal *jingju* troupe performed *Shajiabang* not in the city's primary venue, the Shandong Theater (山东剧场), but in an assembly hall at the Shandong Chemical Plant (山东化工厂礼堂).[84] The wide range of performers and performance venues suggests an equally wide range in types of audience and in the basic material conditions for theatrical production.

The difficulty of performing full productions of the *yangbanxi* under varying conditions was acknowledged in the original calls for their popularization. The *People's Daily* editorial that launched the popularization movement even stated this explicitly:

> In popularizing the *yangbanxi*, pay attention to suiting measures to local conditions and proceeding from the practical. There are differences in the individual conditions between professional theater troupes and amateur cultural propaganda troupes, between provincial-level troupes and regional or county-level troupes, and among factory, village, production brigade, and school amateur cultural propaganda troupes. Under different conditions, you may perform the full production, or only select scenes, or excerpts, or certain songs. As long as you do not do harm to the *yangbanxi*, you can follow your own conditions and flexibly take control of areas such as orchestra organization, costume materials, lighting and sets, props, and more difficult movements (especially combat and dance techniques).[85]

The directive issued in the *People's Daily* seems to contradict the technical specificity emphasized throughout the development process of the *yangbanxi* and encoded in the production bibles. However, it does conform more closely to the ways in which the *yangbanxi* were already being circulated. Local, semirural theater troupes in Shouguang and Juxian, Shandong, for example, had rehearsed and locally toured *The Red Lantern* as early as 1966.[86] Far from achieving the harmony of scenery and sentiment or technical perfection, the Shouguang troupe members carved mock guns out of wood, borrowed costumes, and fashioned the titular prop in *The Red Lantern* from a bicycle light covered with red paper—hardly the meticulously crafted props documented in the *yangbanxi* production bibles.

Official absolution and clear precedent did not, however, fully allay anxieties over the need to meet the standards set by the model versions of the model operas. Another local *jingju* troupe in Anqiu County, Shandong, for instance, struggled greatly with the tension between the imperatives to maintain the quality of performance and to spread the *yangbanxi* to more remote locations:

> After we had understood and elevated our [ideological] thinking, there were still some practical problems with actually moving forward. At the time, our party cadres thought that although we had performed small plays before the Cultural Revolution and gone to the mountains and countryside pulling small carts and carrying shoulder poles, nowadays performing *yangbanxi* required us to have some new achievements. So, they used an entire month's time to design a "large-scale movable stage" that would cost 20,000 yuan and be pulled by tractors. Since this design was a cart made behind closed doors, it was very wasteful, and simply wouldn't be able to make it up into the mountain areas. So, it was quickly rejected by the county party committee. After this, our theater troupe created a set of scenery, props, and lights suitable for use in a commune assembly hall, and used a car to carry them to the Jingzhi commune, which was convenient to get to, for a performance. At the time, it was midwinter, so many poor and lower-middle peasants brought rations more than 10 *li* [ca. 5 km] in strong winds, even through snow in the middle of the night, to struggle to see the performance, and this kind of fervor was truly moving. At Jingzhi, we did nineteen performances in a row, and we still couldn't meet the needs of the masses. After seeing the performance, one poor old peasant who came from a mountain village tugged on the hand of an actor and said in excitement: "Seeing such a wonderful large play made this old man truly happy. Those of us who live in the mountains hope you'll come soon!" We felt the old man's heartfelt words, and his hopes for us, would be better taken as a criticism. We all felt that our own thought and work was really unsuited to the needs of the many poor and lower-middle peasants. The current sets and props were only suited for a commune assembly hall, and wouldn't even be able to go out to a village in the plains. How would we take them up the mountains, or down to the remote countryside?[87]

Similarly, another theater artist writing immediately after the Cultural Revolution, when the *yangbanxi* were subjected to severe criticism, recalls how some villages and factories had to stop production in order to divert enough electricity to power their stage lights.[88] In both cases, the practical demands of spreading the *yangbanxi* required the transportation of a massive amount of material and equipment to the locations of performances; in the latter case, the electricity available could barely support the lighting requirements. The more remote the location, the more dire the situation.

The specter that looms over these discussions is that of failure, on both a personal and a technical level. On the one hand, performers felt the burden of failing their audiences, due to a combined lack of ideological correctness and technical ability; on the other, even with the necessary equipment, they might be only a lighting instrument away from overloading the local generators. This issue of potential technical failure is significant on a theoretical level as well as a practical one. To return to the treatise penned by Fang Yun and the "blending of scenery and sentiment," we find that Fang's discussion of aesthetics is in fact paired with a caution against the mechanical or superficial application of scenic design principles. For Fang, "issues of methodology and technique" are "fundamentally problems of ideology and feeling."[89] In other words, in areas such as scenery, there was a close connection between the technical and the ideological, with a failure in implementation directly linked to an underlying failure in revolutionary spirit. This fear of technoideological failure in turn parallels Coderre's discussion of the "fear of the misfire" in *yangbanxi* acting and what Jason McGrath has called the "formalist drift" of stylized performance in *yangbanxi* film.[90] Across all areas of technics, then, *yangbanxi* stagecraft was at pains not to become mechanical and superficial, nor to fail completely.

This direct correspondence between technical and ideological failure, however, did not hold true in all cases. At times, the challenge of reproducing the *yangbanxi* actually contributed to raising the quality and ideological level of a given performance. The *Lanzhou Xiqu Gazetteer* (兰州戏曲志), for example, notes:

> During this period [the Cultural Revolution], the strengthening of activities to promote the model operas, from an objective standpoint, propelled each of the theater troupes in Lanzhou to raise their quality. This in turn led to some clear advances in form, compared to the past. First, in terms of scenography, modern lighting started to be used widely. Each troupe brought in cutting-edge sound and effects equip-

ment, and we used more scientific and advanced techniques and materials in design, scenery painting, props, set flats, costumes, makeup, etc. This made our performances produce a stronger artistic impact in the areas of visual and aural effects.[91]

While the stilted revolutionary narratives of the *yangbanxi* would eventually go out of style—and then resurface as objects of nostalgia—the technical advances achieved by attempting to reproduce their scenography led to lasting improvements in the technical areas of the theater. In more extreme cases, the imperative to meet the technical standards of the *yangbanxi* even directly spurred technological development. In Kunming, for instance, the Yunnan Provincial Spoken Drama Troupe (云南省话剧团) collaborated with the Kunming General Mechanical Plant (昆明市通用机械厂), Yunnan University (云南大学), the Yunnan Instrument Factory (云南仪表厂), and others to develop a new kind of semiconductor-based dimmer, used to control and modulate the strength of stage lighting.[92] As documented by the production bibles and discussed above, the ability to shift smoothly between different lighting levels—from dim for the environs surrounding negative characters to a bright wash illuminating revolutionary base areas, for example—was one of the fundamental tasks required of stage lighting equipment used for the *yangbanxi*. The dimmer devised in Kunming was far smaller, lighter, and more energy efficient than extant technology and, moreover, was designed specifically in order to "create better conditions" for "cultural troupes sent down to the countryside and up to the mountains to perform the *yangbanxi*."[93] In this case, then, the technical imperatives of the *yangbanxi* led not only to innovation, but to innovation in a collaborative, collective mode that aligned with the ideology of the times.

In other cases, such as that of the Anqiu County Jingju Troupe cited above, technical challenge bred not technological advancement, but rather low-tech, *tu* (i.e., homegrown) ingenuity. Faced with the practical problem of being unable to reach mountain villages with sets built for an assembly hall, the Anqiu County Jingju Troupe began to rethink their approach:

We got advice from all of the masses, split up and went into the factories, villages, and production brigades to do fieldwork research, and looked for every way possible to reinvent the stage, scenery, props, and lighting. After several days of continued struggle, we successfully made an iron casing pipe "mobile stage," "dual use lights," "seven-piece sets," and "folding props" that were convenient to carry, conformed to the standards, and were sturdy and durable. The sets and props for *The Red Lantern* and *Shajiabang*, which used to need four cars to move, now fit into fourteen small pushcarts.[94]

Here, the values of mobility and efficiency are as important as in the case of the Kunming dimmer, but the troupe focuses on simplicity (a stage made of iron piping) and economy (lights that could be used for multiple purposes) instead of relying on scientific advances. Another report by the Qu County Mao Zedong Thought Literature and Art Propaganda Troupe (衢县毛泽东思想文艺宣传队) published in 1970 offers a strikingly similar story of how, in the absence of electric lights, these productions made do with old-fashioned gas lamps.[95] Cast in the Maoist language of study and struggle, these troupes succeeded not by reproducing the most advanced sets and lighting, but rather by learning from the masses and engineering homegrown solutions without harming the quality of performance.

In other accounts, narratives of failure turn even more directly into stories of revolutionary sacrifice. An amateur propaganda troupe of the PLA Shanghai Garrison Command (中国人民解放军上海警备区), for instance, published a report that first recounts their difficulties establishing a troupe (given concerns over the ability of soldiers to perform), then proudly details their efforts in staging not one, but two full *yanbanxi* productions.[96] They detail how their lead actor rehearsed through physical exhaustion and how the entire troupe worked around the clock to finish building the props after their dress rehearsal date was suddenly moved up. The tone of the tale extends into their description of one touring performance, scheduled to take place on an island: their boat missed high tide, leaving them stranded far from shore, and the actors had to jump into the water, form a human bridge, and ferry the sets and props across. Another time, they erected a makeshift stage on a beach and hung their spotlights in nearby trees.[97] Here, a more complex relationship between the ideal performance and the actual emerges: a desire to bring the performance to fruition, spotlights and all, drove the amateur performers, yet what was celebrated in the telling is their dedication and ingenuity, not their success (or failure) at reproducing the model form.

These accounts ultimately highlight difficulty, perseverance, and ingenuity. In this, they demonstrate how the lack of proper conditions paradoxically allowed the troupe members to put into practice the lessons they had learned from the revolutionary heroes of the *yangbanxi*. At times, technical failure drove experimentation and innovation, resulting in new forms of homegrown stage technology and echoing the practices of theater during the Seventeen

Years period. At other times, failure spurred low-tech ingenuity and enabled the theatrical production process more closely to resemble revolutionary narratives of struggle and self-sacrifice. On yet another level, then, stage technology played an essential role in connecting the specifics of theatrical practice to a more generalizable revolutionary narrative that united the representative and the exemplary, or the two poles of typicality.

Ultimately, reexamining the *yangbanxi* from the perspective of theatrical technicity reveals how the Cultural Revolution was not a sudden break from previous trends in this area, but rather a continuation and an apotheosis of mobilizing stage technology for political and aesthetic ends. The standardization of theatrical composition and production processes involved theater artists who were among the best trained in the nation and accommodated a continuous feedback loop from political leaders. This emphasized technocratic professionalism and proximity to power even as specialized skills were ostensibly downplayed in favor of grassroots knowledge and cultural production. Meanwhile, creating productions to suit recently built proscenium theaters gave designers and technicians access to large stages and technically sophisticated lighting, sound, and stage equipment. The scenographic design of the *yangbanxi* made full use both of this equipment and of newer techniques, like backdrop projection, to align the technical dimensions of the productions closely with their ideological messages and to (attempt to) provoke specific emotional responses in their audiences. The "blending of scenery and sentiment" in the *yangbanxi* demonstrates not only a close coordination of aesthetic, technological, and political elements but also a systematization of this technical coordination across the entire corpus.

Tensions arose, however, with the imperative for the *yangbanxi* to function not only as propaganda performances to be viewed by mass audiences but also for the masses to become both performers and producers of technically sophisticated theater. By focusing on the technical and material dimensions of *yangbanxi* popularization, this chapter shows how the texts created to promote widespread performance (especially by local theater troupes and amateurs) created the fantasy of mechanical reproducibility, but did not provide enough information *actually* to re-create the *yangbanxi* fully. Instead, they make typical, in the Marxist sense, even the most technical details. Thus, whereas the examples from the Seventeen Years period demonstrate how the use of stage technology asked audiences to imagine other forms of technology onstage, Cultural Revolution technological fantasy asked would-be theater artists to imagine that they themselves could create the effects of sophisticated stage technology even in its absence. Faced with this challenge, local theater troupes and propaganda brigades responded with ingenuity, innovation, and collective action, engineering solutions that ran the gamut from simple stage props to a homegrown semiconductor.

What would happen, then, when the Cultural Revolution concluded and its many excesses came under the scrutiny of a new era? On one hand, the narratives and characters of the *yangbanxi* would fall out of fashion for a time, and new historical narratives would use their supposed hegemony as an argument against the extreme political co-optation of art and culture. At the same time, however, the technical advances made via theatrical practice were not so easily rolled back; progress, and especially scientific and technological progress, after all, was to become the driving ethos of the Reform Era (1978–89). Stage technology was therefore faced with a new set of tensions as it grappled with the legacies of the Cultural Revolution, theater's role as the political terrain shifted, and fast-paced developments in related fields of science and technology.

# FIVE

# Theater as Technoscience

## *Research, Design, and Nuclear Physics in the Post-Mao Era*

————————

At a key moment in act 2 of the play *Atoms and Love* (原子与爱情, 1980), the stage dims. A voice counts down "5 . . . 4 . . . 3 . . . 2 . . . 1 . . . fire!" and the stage flashes with a dazzling light, followed by the sound of an enormous explosion in the distance. A huge burst of fire appears on the horizon, then turns into a mushroom cloud of smoke that ascends to the sky. Cheers erupt and a joyous celebration follows. The team of scientists depicted in the play has just completed one of the most important experiments in modern Chinese history: the successful detonation of China's first atomic bomb on October 16, 1964 (fig. 5.1).

Already memorialized across a wide variety of media, this seminal moment of scientific achievement was resurrected and re-created for the *huaju* stage at a moment when science and technology had returned to the forefront of Chinese national consciousness. After the death of Chairman Mao Zedong and the end of the Cultural Revolution in 1976, new state leaders shifted national priorities from continuous revolution to modernization, with an emphasis on science and technology. This ideological sea change signaled the beginning of what would come to be known as the Reform Era (1978–89) and affected all areas of political, economic, social, and cultural life in the PRC, including the performing arts. Indeed, only a month before the premiere of *Atoms and Love*, aerospace engineer and physicist Qian Xuesen 钱学森 (1911–2009)—who himself had worked on nuclear research in the 1960s and is known as the father of China's space program—gave a speech at the Second National Representative Congress of the Chinese Science and

Fig. 5.1. Photograph of a mushroom cloud (*top*) and production photograph (*bottom*) used to illustrate the moment of the successful atomic bomb detonation in a comic book-style (连环画) adaptation of *Atoms and Love*. Source: *Yuanzi yu aiqing* [lianhuanhua] (Beijing: Zhongguo xiju chubanshe, 1980), 75–76.

Technology Association (中国科学技术协会第二次全国代表大会) urging that "science and technology modernization should lead the modernization of literature and the arts."[1] Consequently, during the late 1970s and early 1980s, the Chinese theater world turned its attention toward establishing "stage science and technology" (舞台科学技术), or "stage technoscience" (舞台科技, where the latter two characters are an abbreviation for "science and technology," i.e., 科学技术), as a legitimate field of theatrical research and development.

Unlike British warships, a threatening thunderstorm, neon lights, or a red signal lantern, however, a nuclear explosion cannot be represented even remotely realistically onstage—no matter how advanced the technology. Lighting and sound effects, even projections of images from the corresponding historical event, can reference and remediate the explosion, but the scale (and actual danger) of the technology far exceeds the capacities of the stage. More advanced stage technologies can perhaps create closer approximations of the effect, but only as their underlying mechanisms concurrently become more complex. At the time *Atoms and Love* premiered, for example, SCR (silicon-controlled rectifier) lighting dimmers that relied on semiconductor technology were becoming more widespread across the PRC; these developments were part of a broader push for technoscientific research in areas such as stage technology and theater architecture. Scenographers and technicians experimented with new stage technologies, translated and discussed recent foreign advances, conducted foreign study tours, and published increasingly professionalized technical materials throughout the 1980s. However, while high-tech devices like SCR dimmers were easier to operate and enabled innovations in lighting effects, their underlying engineering also became far more difficult to understand than the more homegrown tech of earlier decades. In a sense, then, the theater of the Reform Era drew closer to science through the research and implementation of high-tech devices onstage. At the same time, however, these advances made theater artists confront anew both the potentials and limits of live performance and their own technical knowledge.

One might expect plays produced under the Reform Era ethos of modernization and amid high-tech innovation to flaunt their technological sophistication, yet, paradoxically, this was not the case. The tradition of state-sponsored song-and-dance epics in the grand style of *The East Is Red* certainly continued. However, rather than generating a marked increase in theatrical productions that foregrounded advanced stage technology, stage technology research instead led to a diversification of theatrical form that included both spectacle and a strong trend toward a more abstract, suggestive aesthetics. The latter trend was motivated by a number of factors, including a desire among Chinese theater artists to distance themselves from the aesthetics and politics of the Cultural Revolution *yangbanxi*. They also had renewed access to modernist, experimental, and avant-garde work from outside of the PRC.[2] For example, Bertolt Brecht (1898–1956, transliterated as "Bulaixite" 布莱希特) provided one important source of inspiration for Chinese theater artists, who were particularly compelled by his strong stance against illusionistic theatrical realism. Brecht himself had a lifelong interest in Chinese theater and his work had been introduced to the PRC as early as the 1950s, but later fell out of ideological favor. A revival of interest was catalyzed by an April 1979 production of *Life of Galileo* (*Leben des Galilei*, translated as *Jialilüe zhuan* 伽利略传) by the China Youth Art Theater. Brecht's emphasis on exposing the stage apparatus, eschewal of an immersive experience, and critical audience engagement resonated with Chinese theater artists searching for a new aesthetics in an era of both scientific progress and ideological disillusionment.

This chapter explores what I term a "technoscientific" shift in the theater of this era of progress and disillusionment, specifically during the immediate post-Mao period from 1978 to the early 1980s. This technoscientific shift occurred through an increase of plays that focused diegetically on science and technology, as well as via efforts to develop advanced stage technologies through scientific research and development. Topics such as nuclear experiments and the natural sciences took on new urgency with the implementation of renewed modernization initiatives in the late 1970s. This is evident from the two cases discussed in this chapter: the celebrated 1979 production of Brecht's *Life of Galileo*, codirected by Chen Yong 陈颙 (1929–2004) and Huang Zuolin 黄佐临 (1906–94), and the lesser-known *Atoms and Love*, which was premiered by the General Political Department Huaju Troupe (总政话剧团) of the PLA in April 1980.[3] Both plays represent a turn toward small-scale experimental work in a Brechtian vein and may be read as a backlash against the theatrical style and the political trauma of the Cultural Revolution. At the same time, how these works stage the scientific process—and especially, their emphasis on the connections between pure and applied science—is linked with broader questions surrounding the theater's role in making science and technology legible for a lay audience. Alongside these representations, as this chapter demonstrates, theater artists were also engaged in theoretical debates about the relationship between theater and "technoscience." Scenography and stage technology became key topics of discussion, research, and experimentation, with the conclusion that advances in both areas should lead to a diversification of form and practice rather than a reification of technologized performance.

## Chinese Theater in the Age of Science and Technology

At the first National Conference on Science (全国科学大会) in March 1978, Premier Deng Xiaoping 邓小平 (1904–97) inaugurated a new era for the

PRC when he pronounced the modernization of science and technology to be key to all other aspects of development.[4] Prior to 1978, as noted in previous chapters, science and technology had been seen as national priorities for the PRC, but ones that ultimately served socialist goals in agriculture, industry, and national defense. While mass science and grassroots technology had been encouraged under Mao and even during the Cultural Revolution, the fraught status of intellectuals and Western, "bourgeois" scientific inquiry had also made certain types of research and researchers ideologically suspect. However, the death of Chairman Mao Zedong on September 9, 1976 and the October 1976 arrest of the "Gang of Four" (四人帮)—Jiang Qing and the radical clique that had been in power—ultimately led to the end of the Cultural Revolution and its policies. The more moderate leaders who subsequently took power gave pride of place to a vision of science and technology that did not sideline basic science or learning from Euro-American models. Disillusionment with Marxism–Leninism–Mao Zedong Thought created an "ideological vacuum that the leadership and intellectuals again sought to fill with the idealization of advanced science and technology," as Merle Goldman and Denis Fred Simon argue.[5] Resurrecting the concept of the "Four Modernizations" (四个现代化, i.e., modernization of agriculture, industry, military, and science and technology), first introduced in 1954, offered an opportunity for the new leadership to connect with the socialist project while moving away from the radical politics of the Cultural Revolution.[6] Moreover, Deng Xiaoping took the vital steps of redefining science and technology as "forces of production" (rather than elements of the superstructure) and intellectuals as "part of the working class," which significantly eased any lingering ideological issues related to the class nature of scientific inquiry or the class status of scientists.[7] The state reprioritized research and development in fields such as energy resources, computers, laser and space technology, high-energy physics, and genetics. Technical experts, vilified and persecuted during the Cultural Revolution, saw their fates reversed, and programs were even established to send thousands of researchers in science and technology to the United States for training.

In standard narratives of Chinese theater history, meanwhile, the immediate post-Mao moment is most often associated with the rehabilitation of persecuted theater artists, a general liberalization in content and form, and the allowance (albeit temporary) of criticism of Cultural Revolution excesses. The conclusion of the Cultural Revolution also heralded an end to the hegemony of the *yangbanxi* and the return to work of many artists who had suffered during the preceding ten years. Playwright Xia Yan, for instance, was imprisoned for eight years and then rehabilitated in 1978.[8] Cao Yu was also initially imprisoned, but later released into medical care when he fell seriously ill.[9] He, too, was rehabilitated after 1976 and returned to his post as head of BPAT. Scores of other theater artists returned from hard labor sentences and forced rural sojourns to major theater troupes in urban centers. Institutes such as BPAT and the Shanghai People's Art Theater had shut down for several years or shifted focus to propaganda troupe activities during the Cultural Revolution; after 1976, they returned to producing regular seasons in their home venues. In fact, as Xiaomei Chen has noted, the abundance of plays staged in 1978–79 led many to see the period as a "Chinese dramatic renaissance."[10] Many classics from the Seventeen Years period and earlier were revived, such as Cao Yu's plays *Thunderstorm* and *Sunrise*.[11]

At first, newly written plays cautiously focused on producing hagiographies of Communist Party leaders. Yet by 1978–79, directives issued by the Central Committee of the Eleventh Congress of the CCP (mid-August 1977) and the promise of new freedoms under a new Constitution (adopted March 5, 1978) encouraged artists and writers to experiment with politically critical and formally innovative new work.[12] As these artists, especially playwrights, reflected on the past decade and responded to the changed circumstances, many followed the broader literary trends of "scar literature" (伤痕文学) and "root-seeking literature" (寻根文学).[13] Scar literature, named after a short story published in August 1978, processed the trauma of the Cultural Revolution and condemned its ideological extremes by portraying the suffering of those unjustly persecuted during that period. Root-seeking, or exploring the significance of indigenous cultural roots to literary work, became an important theoretical debate and literary theme in the mid to late 1980s. Meanwhile, newly reinvigorated newspapers, periodicals, and publishing houses embraced the general spirit of "opening up" to the outside world by printing foreign theater theory and descriptions of a range of styles, including what has since been termed the "postdramatic theater."[14] An influx of translated texts that had been banned and largely unavailable, such as the work of Brecht, Antonin Artaud (1896–1948), and Jerzy Grotowski (1933–99), among others, led to wide-ranging theoretical debates and formal experimentation by playwrights, directors, and designers. Theater artists eagerly traded Great Leap slogans of "more, faster, better, cheaper" and Cultural Revolution dictums of "red, bright, shining" for an ethos of exploration (探索).[15]

As this chapter argues, there was both a general ideological alignment between the arts and sciences in this period, as well as a more specific connection between changes in official attitudes toward science and technology and a technoscientific shift within the theater. On one level, the Chinese theater's technoscientific shift was visible in how theater education and professional organizations' activities were conducted in the immediate post-Mao era. Most generally, along with the reinstatement of professional theater troupes, arts education institutions reopened and political-professional organizations like the Chinese Dramatists Association resumed activities in the late 1970s. Almost as if countering the emphasis on amateur performance during the Seventeen Years period and the Cultural Revolution, the post-Mao era saw increased attention to specialized areas of professional craft, including in the areas of design and stage technology. Indeed, as Colin Mackerras has noted, the early 1980s saw a marked reduction in amateur theater activities and a push for higher standards and professionalization in state-sponsored troupes like BPAT—in short, efforts to apply the ethos of "modernization" to the theater as well as to agriculture, industry, science, and the military.[16] In parallel to what Joel Andreas has observed of PRC political structures, however, this emphasis was not entirely new: the rise of a "technocratic class order" among theater professionals was propelled both by the groundwork laid during the preceding period (as discussed in chapter 4) and by the new policy emphases of the Reform Era.[17] Practically speaking, this involved concerted efforts to elevate production value in both an economic and a material sense. Many theater troupes that had been entirely dependent on the government for funding saw the level of support decrease and move toward a partial profit-sharing model. The logic behind this institutional shift was that if salaries depended on ticket sales, theater troupes would need to raise the quality of their performances in order to attract larger and higher-paying audiences.[18] For the troupes, this meant improving all areas of production from acting and directing to stage design and technology.

On another level, this period also saw an increase in the number of plays that focused on science and scientists in their content—and, specifically, scientists for whom experimentation was as much a matter of developing new technologies as it was of furthering basic science research.[19] This paralleled a broader trend in literature, film, and popular culture. As Hui Faye Xiao has noted, the assertion by Guo Moruo of a "springtime for science" (科学的春天) in his closing speech for the National Conference on Science in 1978 encouraged alliances between scientists and the cultural elite. Literature also began to popularize figures of scientists as "*the* national heroes of a new era who unswervingly dedicated themselves to the advancement of human knowledge and the development of scientific research despite economic difficulties and political adversity."[20] Recent scholarship by Xiao and others has demonstrated the specific flowering of science fiction literature, especially during the years between the National Conference on Science in 1978 and the Anti-Spiritual Pollution Campaign (反精神污染运动) in 1983.[21] Amid this climate, theater even played a minor role in science popularization efforts, with scripts published among essays, comics, short stories, and other content in science magazines for young readers. An excerpt of Brecht's *Life of Galileo*, for example, appeared in the magazine *Knowledge Is Power* (知识就是力量) the same year that the China Youth Art Theater staged their production of the play.[22]

Science plays occupied a significant place both onstage and as important catalysts for discussions of content, form, and theater's role in this new climate. While still not the most dominant theme among plays produced in the Reform Era, science plays generated strong audience interest and critical response to their innovations in both content and form. In terms of content, these plays divided roughly into two categories that paralleled contemporaneous literary trends: plays that reflected on key moments in the history of science and technology, which resonated with the scar literature genre, and plays that imagined moments in China's near future, which followed in the vein of much of the science fiction produced during this period. Both plays featured in this chapter belong to the first category; *Galileo* depicts the life of the historical Galileo in a way that resonated with experiences of Chinese scientists during the Cultural Revolution, whereas *Atoms and Love* eulogizes scientists' contributions to China's first successful detonation of an atomic bomb in 1964. The Central Experimental Drama Troupe (中央实验话剧院) production of *The Future Is Calling* (未来在召唤, 1979), in contrast, was nominally set in the present, but actually imagined a near future in which the Chinese space program successfully launched a manned spacecraft. The children's theater play *The Strange 101* (奇怪的101) is also set in a near future where Cultural Revolution trauma lingers, but China has advanced by technological leaps and bounds. Notably, all of the aforementioned plays also focus decidedly on elements of applied science; even Brecht's *Galileo*, which narrates the Italian scientist's contributions to proving Copernican theory, foregrounds his contributions to improving the telescope and other technoscientific devices.

On a formal level, science plays also repeatedly appear in reviews of scenographic design and related theoretical discussions. Articles on scenography by Hu Miaosheng 胡妙胜 (b. 1936) and Luan Guanhua 栾冠桦 (b. 1937), for example, both specifically highlight innovative scenic design in *Galileo* and *Atoms and Love*, as well as *The Future Is Calling* and another scientist play, *Mountain Spring* (山泉, 1978).[23] As is discussed later in this chapter, the need to represent laboratory spaces and scientific equipment onstage posed a significant technical and artistic challenge for scenic designers. Once again, technical difficulty fostered scenographic ingenuity, but it also catalyzed an influential debate over scenographic realism that continued and further developed the discussion of aesthetic concepts such as the *xu/shi* binary from previous decades (see chapter 3). Examination of science plays and their production histories therefore sheds light on the complex ways in which technoscience pervaded all layers of theater making during this period.

## *Galileo* in '79: Theater, History, and Technoscience

*Life of Galileo* was simultaneously a surprising and an entirely logical choice for a high-profile theatrical production in China in 1979. The production was surprising because, at the time, Brechtian plays and performance style were largely unknown to Chinese audiences, and Brecht had been deemed ideologically suspect during the preceding decades. At the same time, the revival of Brecht and an embrace of diverse theatrical styles aligned with broader trends in post–Cultural Revolution rehabilitation, artistic revival, and cultural liberalization. Brecht's play, which he revised several times between 1937 and his death in 1956, portrays the historical Galileo Galilei's efforts to prove Copernican theory through scientific observation, including his struggles with the restrictions of the Catholic Church and his eventual recanting of his scientific beliefs under threat of torture during the Inquisition. Codirector Chen Yong, as Xiaomei Chen has noted, envisioned the play's portrayal of the dawning of a new age in Renaissance Italy as paralleling both the promise and the conflicts of the post-Mao Reform Era.[24] Or, as *Galileo* translator Ding Yangzhong 丁杨忠 (b. 1932) phrased it, "Brecht uses the image of Galileo to expound upon the relationship between life and society, science and politics, reactionism and progress, darkness and light, obviously reflecting the spirit of the twentieth century."[25] Brecht also foregrounds Galileo's dual roles as both a technological innovator and a natural scientist, as well as his struggle to balance the two. This made the play all the more attuned to questions surrounding the relationship between pure and applied sciences that arose in the PRC's push toward modernization. The bid to capture the zeitgeist of the moment seems to have paid off: when the China Youth Art Theater premiered their version of *Galileo* on March 24, 1979, ticket buyers lined up around the block, and the production sold out for eighty straight performances.[26]

From the outset, the key artistic personnel involved with the production explicitly connected its mission to the Four Modernizations and Deng Xiaoping's emphasis on science and technology. In an article written to introduce the play to Chinese audiences, for example, *Galileo* codirector Huang Zuolin writes that the play's main point is a celebration of "scientific truth" (科学的真理) that all, even the most powerful, must follow. His emphasis on the search for and belief in scientific truth, in turn, makes performing the play resonate for him "at a time when our country is turning its focus to economic construction and moving toward a new historical period of advancing the Four Modernizations."[27] Like his codirector and the play's translator, Huang attempts to connect to the feeling of a new era. Yet he was perhaps even more specifically inspired by the prominent role assigned to science and technology within Deng's vision of the Four Modernizations. This is apparent in a *People's Theater* (人民戏剧) notice announcing the production, which quoted a letter from Huang: "At present we've come to the springtime for science, and the spirit of a scientist like Galileo who fights against conservative forces should be spread widely!"[28] In using the phrase "springtime for science," Huang makes direct reference to the title of Guo Moruo's famous speech.[29] And in the final sentence of his essay introducing the play, Huang enthusiastically praises *Galileo*'s contributions to discussions of science and experimentation (lit. practice, or *shijian* 实践) and the creation of "theater for a scientific age" (科学时代的戏剧)—a simultaneous nod to Brecht's repeated assertions of the need for theater for a scientific age and also to the precise moment at which China found itself.[30]

At the same time, discussions of Brecht's play also framed *Galileo* in a way that negotiated between a desire to retain some continuity with the Maoist era and the impulse to move away from the radical politics of the Cultural Revolution. In explaining the decision to stage *Galileo*, for example, Chen Yong connects Brecht directly to key tenets of socialism and Marxist philosophy such as class sympathy, dialectical thought, and dialectical materialism.[31] She claims that "the real hero of the play is not Galileo, but the people" and discusses the way Galileo's relationship to the people shifts over the course of the play.[32] As Kirsten Shepherd-Barr has argued, tension between the desires of the individual and responsibility to the community is in fact a common theme in a number of science plays in the Western dramatic canon (such as *Doctor Faustus* and *Galileo*).[33] From a Marxist perspective, elements of *Galileo* can even be read as a critique of the individualistic intellectual. However, at the same time, Brecht portrays the popularization of Galileo's theories among the common people and highlights the subsequent elite backlash against Galileo for advocating the popularization of scientific knowledge in vernacular languages. These elements of the play resonated well with Chinese communism's focus on historically undereducated rural masses and the CCP's many literacy campaigns, as well as the popularization of technical know-how.

Another significant way that the play valorizes "the people" lies in the role assigned to Andrea, the commoner son of Galileo's housekeeper. From the play's first scene, Brecht's Galileo takes an active interest in educating Andrea, who eventually becomes one of his star pupils. Dramaturgically, Andrea functions as a stand-in for the audience; his questions and confusion inspire Galileo to explain his theories simply onstage, and by extension, to the watching audience. Andrea's quick grasp of scientific concepts suggests that each audience member, too, could become initiated into new realms of knowledge. Andrea also becomes disillusioned with Galileo when he seemingly abandons his scientific commitments and social responsibility, yet he ends the play by smuggling Galileo's greatest and final work—the *Discorsi*—out of Italy to the Netherlands, where it could be freely printed and disseminated. Thus, through Andrea as a representative of "the people," the play models making scientific knowledge accessible to the uninitiated, while also reflecting the tension between disillusionment with an individual and dedication to science.

For many Chinese audience members and critics, the persecution of Galileo at the hands of the Church offered a powerful analogy to the plight of scientists during the Cultural Revolution. Huang makes this connection explicit when he writes, "When we were working on the character of Galileo, we couldn't but think of how the 'Gang of Four' persecuted the great science workers of our country."[34] Huang goes on to discuss how the play critiques systems in which, quoting Engels, science "had but been the humble handmaid of the Church."[35] Galileo's story, then, enabled theater artists and their audiences to appreciate the play's critique of the Church as an analogy for—and implicit criticism of—the way that science had been controlled under Mao's leadership, while also feeling a resonance with both Galileo's plight and his eventual capitulation to the pressures of the Church.[36] The play also generated a conversation surrounding whether the character of Galileo was a hero or a wrongdoer—with many critics taking the stand that he was both simultaneously, or "a dialectical character," as Lin Kehuan asserts.[37] This idea of a flawed, human hero who both pursues scientific truth and betrays his own principles was, as Xiaomei Chen discusses, an important departure from the "typical" heroes and villains of Cultural Revolution–era literature and art.[38] Galileo's specific flaws, moreover, might have recalled for many audience members "the painful memory of their own cowardice for not standing up for their principles against Maoist excesses."[39] The capacity of *Galileo* to be read as analogous to Chinese experiences, on multiple levels, ultimately enabled the production to function as a kind of mediating technology for both the history of science and the trauma of the recent past.

The strong sympathy for scientists felt by theater artists working on *Galileo* also constructed a close equivalence between art and science, via both their shared pursuit of truth and the shared experiences of artists and scientists during the Cultural Revolution. Chen Yong, for instance, recounts a particularly warm reception to the play from scholars and scientists; the theater troupe received a deluge of letters from the Institute of the History of Natural Science, the Institute of Electrical Science, the Higher Energy Institute, the Beijing Institute of Environmental Sciences, and others.[40] In the years following *Galileo*, director Huang Zuolin would go on to draw an even more direct equivalence between theater artists, specifically, and scientists. In the late 1980s, he claims to have spent years advocating for exploring the question of "dramatists becoming more scientific" (戏剧家科学化) and even argued that dramatists should be admitted to the National Scientists Association.[41] At a time when science and technology reigned supreme—and when the theater world was facing new pressures and competition from the rapid rise of film and television—the move to relate science and theater borrowed the authority of the former to bolster the legitimacy of the latter.

Indeed, the production of *Galileo* and the reintroduction of Brecht seem to have spurred a trend toward belief in the "supremacy of science" (科学至上) in the Chinese theater world of the 1980s. Ke Zunke 柯遵科, a Chinese scholar of the philosophy of science and technology, has critiqued precisely this trend, arguing that translating Brecht's calls for a "theater of a scientific age" into a definition of theater *as* science involved something of a misinterpretation.[42] Noting Huang Zuolin's use of phrases such as "dramatists becoming more scientific," "the scientific nature of Brecht" (布莱希特的科学性), "theater is not only an art, but also a science" (戏剧不但是艺术，也是科学), and "theater must fight on behalf of science" (戏剧为科学而战), Ke sees a connection between Huang's understanding of Brecht and the spread of an ideological "scientism" (科学主义) in the theater world and beyond.[43] Certainly, to Ke's point, Brecht was not an unequivocal advocate of science; in fact, he famously critiqued "science for science's sake" as equivalent to, and as equally anathema as, "art for art's sake." Moreover, *Galileo* and its several versions chart Brecht's increasing skepticism toward scientific exploration over time. Brecht wrote the first version of *Galileo* in November 1938, but revised it several times between then and the end of his life in 1956.[44] Developments in nuclear science in the 1930s–1940s and the dropping of atomic bombs on Hiroshima and Nagasaki made clear to him the perils of a pure science that takes no responsibility for its effect on human society. The final version of the play accordingly revised the character of Galileo so as to argue that, as Peter D. Smith writes, "the commitment of science to its delusions of neutrality was untenable in the nuclear age, when the destruction of life itself had become a real possibility."[45] It therefore would indeed be a misinterpretation and oversimplification to use *Galileo* as support for the reification of science.

However, such a facile misinterpretation of Brecht's nuanced relationship to science and technology by either Huang Zuolin or translator Ding Yangzhong seems unlikely, given that both were well versed in Brechtian theory and familiar with his plays. Huang had first attempted to promote Brecht's work in the PRC in the late 1950s to early 1960s, most famously with a poorly received production of *Mother Courage and Her Children*, whereas Ding had studied in East Germany in the late 1950s and even attended the Berliner Ensemble performance of *Galileo* (in 1957).[46] Furthermore, Huang was actively involved in international artistic and scholarly activities throughout the 1980s, making him conversant in the latest scholarship on Brecht. In the same essay wherein he advocates making theater more scientific, for example, Huang cites an address by Japanese director and theorist Senda Koreya 千田是也 (1904–94), given at an international Brecht conference in 1986, in which Senda touches on Brecht's interest in the sciences. In the address, Senda affirms Brecht's general interest in the relationship between theater and science, but argues that Brecht's method can help to resolve the problems wrought by a science that "threatens to destroy humanity by means of nuclear power and chemical weapons."[47] Here, Senda captures a central issue in Brecht's theory and practice: his ambivalence toward the technologies that resulted from scientific experimentation, and especially the political co-optation of those technologies—what Smith has termed the distinction between "pure science" and "lethal technology."[48] On one hand, Brecht was fascinated by the idea of the "new science" inaugurated by Galileo as an epochal change toward principles that aligned with Marxist philosophy. He saw a parallel between the new science's rejection of an Aristotelian worldview and his own rejection of Aristotelian drama; David Roberts has even argued that Brecht conceived of his epic theater as drama in a Galilean vein, which would constitute a "Copernican turning point" away from past Aristotelian conventions.[49] On the other hand, he was captivated by, but uneasy with, the industrial-technological advances of his age.[50] Huang's citation of Senda suggests that he was well aware of these complexities within Brecht's theoretical and dramaturgical engagement with science and technology, past and present.

Far from reifying science, then, it is precisely the fraught relationship between science and technology embedded in Brechtian thought that helps to illuminate Huang Zuolin's repeated insistence on the scientific nature of the theater and the significance of the 1979 China Youth Art Theater production of *Galileo*. In fact, the key to understanding Huang's promotion of theater and science lies not in his interpretation of Brecht's dramaturgical treatment of the natural sciences, but rather in a specific analogy that Huang draws when making his claim that theater artists are scientists. Referring to the speech quoted in the opening of this chapter, Huang states: "Professor Qian [Xuesen] has said that architects are simultaneously scientists and artists, from now on the Literature and Arts Association should admit them to participate. I support this completely, but I want to add a phrase, which is: theater artists are simultaneously artists and scientists, they should strive to be admitted to the Scientists Association."[51] Architects, notably, work in the applied sciences; they combine artistic design with the engineering of the material world, not the exploration of the nature of the universe. In Huang's analogy, then, theater artists parallel architects in that they too combine engineering—of words on the page, bodies in performance, and sets, lights, and special effects onstage—with an artistic vision. In other words, it is the technological application of their respective crafts that makes each group "scientists." It therefore might be more apt to argue that Huang's vision in fact positions theater as a *techno*science and in doing so captures the Brechtian ambivalences of this modern condition.

As depicted by Brecht, Galileo too is as much a technological innovator as he is a natural scientist, and *Life of Galileo* is riddled with references to the complicated relationship between pure and applied science.[52] For instance, the play begins with the arrival of a technological novelty—a telescope—from the Netherlands, which Galileo improves upon and repurposes toward scientific observation of the heavens, in order to try to prove (experimentally) the controversial theories of Copernicus. As Patricia Anne Simpson notes, "Galilei turns to technology to make unalienable, incontrovertible truths available to the senses. The use of technology to aid the senses, particularly the faculty of sight, raises questions about the nature of signification."[53] The technology of the telescope has implications, then, for the play's portrayal of the nature of scientific truth and the relationship of technology to that truth. From this, the metaphor of the telescope can be extended to the work of the theater itself and the role of theater artists as Galileo-esque technoscientists. Like a telescope, the theater becomes the tool that focuses the audience's attention on specific issues or histories, while also framing them with its specific lens; by using this tool, theater artists have the power to simultaneously reveal inalienable truths and raise questions about perception and signification.

Indeed, questions about the nature of signification were *the* questions plaguing Chinese society—and especially the theater—in the wake of the Cultural Revolution. The entire sign system of the Maoist regime had collapsed, and belief in the human senses, which had been so easily co-opted, was severely shaken. The theater had been especially complicit in the creation and promulgation of the Maoist sign system, due to the *yangbanxi* epitomizing the ideology of the period and in their role as a technology of revolutionary transformation. The task of theater in the post-Mao era was thus to disentangle itself from the zealous religiosity of revolution and reposition itself as an objective, yet still artistic, tool of the age of science and technology.[54] Or, as Roberts says of Brecht: "The secularization of the theatre require[d] that art relinquish its religious functions and take on the functions of science."[55] Chinese theater was in need of its own Copernican turning point, away from the Cultural Revolution and toward a new theater of technoscience. Rather than deluding its audiences, theater would now function like Galileo's telescope, helping them to see and make their own rational judgments about what was happening onstage. In other words, the production of *Galileo* and Huang Zuolin's theater-as-science theory may be read as attempts to shift theater from a revolutionary medium to a revelatory one, in an era where reason and reform, rather than revolution, were now touted as the engines of social, political, and economic change.

## Theater as Technoscience: From Learning to Research, from Life to Laboratory

The concept of theater as science—or rather, theater as technoscience—also surfaced in broader efforts to promote scientific-style research and development in areas of stage technology. This involved a shift in the way such technologies were conceptualized, as well as in the playwriting and production research processes. One central aspect of the technoscientific shift that shaped the theater in this period was a terminological change that emphasized not only "stage technology," or *wutai jishu*, but also "stage technoscience," or *wutai keji*. While the term *keji* had long been in parlance, the specific connection of the term to theater theory and practice did not take place until this particular moment in the immediate post-Mao era.[56] Nor does the concept of *keji* come close to completely replacing the older terminology. However, its increased use in relation to the theater does signal an expansion of the understanding of stage technology and an effort to connect the technical, material parameters of the stage to loftier ideas about advanced science and technology, especially in their official roles as drivers of modernization and economic development.

These terminological and conceptual shifts were reflected in the naming of institutions and in the nature of their research projects, such as the China Institute of Stage Science and Technology Research (中国舞台科学技术研究所) founded by the Ministry of Culture in July 1978.[57] The Institute was tasked with conducting research and consulting on technical topics, including scenography, stage technology, and architectural and mechanical regulations; evaluating work in these areas done by other organizations; and facilitating international exchange. It also published a journal entitled *Stage Design and Technology* (舞台美术与技术) during 1981–83.[58] The journal carried a range of articles, from theoretical treatises and scholarly research to production reviews and technical guides. It was oriented around the idea that scenography deserved more attention as a legitimate field of research and creativity, especially because of its relationship to science and reliance on technology. As the preface to the journal's inaugural issue states, "Scenography has a more extensive, closer, and more direct connection to the natural sciences than any other artistic area, therefore advances in natural sciences and technology also directly influence the creation of scenography."[59] The goal of the journal was to call attention to these close connections and propel collaboration between scenography and technoscience.

Along with the relatively narrow research mandate of the Institute of Stage Science and Technology Research, there was also a broader movement to reposition—and legitimize—stage design and technology as areas of academic study akin to the natural sciences. A number of new publications on stage design and technology were distributed by important institutions, including the Department of Science and Technology of the Ministry of Culture (文化部科技局).[60] The nature of these publications demonstrates a departure from earlier handbooks and technical manuals. Whereas the keyword of the preceding decades was the Maoist ideal of "studying" (学习)

and many materials were framed as simple "how-to" guides for amateurs, the publications from the 1980s tend to emphasize scientific-style "research" (研究) and professionalized knowledge. This shift can be seen even in the titling of books published during this period. The Fine Arts Association and the Beijing branch of the Dramatists Association, for instance, published the *Selected Materials on Scenography and Design in the Capital* (首都舞台美术设计资料选) in 1981—the word "materials" (資料) is one often used to refer to documents collected for historical or academic purposes.[61] Likewise, *Scenography Research* (舞台美术研究) by *xiqu* scholar Gong Hede 龚和德 uses the word for scholarly and experimental research—*yanjiu* 研究—directly in its title.[62] And while some volumes still framed their contents as the personal experience of the authors or of wider appeal, or both, more and more were aimed at theater professionals and scholars.

High-level interest in the science and technology of theater was demonstrated further by Ministry of Culture delegations sent on foreign study trips, such as one group dispatched to North Korea from July 4–25, 1978. During the trip, a group of fourteen theater and film architects, technicians, and designers toured performance venues and cinemas in the Democratic People's Republic of Korea. While the trip's ostensible purpose was to survey the architecture of these venues, the delegation included two scenic designers and technicians, Li Chang and Chen Zhi, who had been involved in both consulting on theater construction and authoring seminal texts on theater technology in the 1950s. The report submitted upon the delegation's return accordingly featured significant discussion of the mechanical and technical outfitting of North Korean theaters, and the team published a book that included as much detail on the theaters' technical apparatus as on their architectural components.[63] As Lu Xiangdong has noted, many of the components observed in North Korea were unheard of in Cultural Revolution–era Chinese theater spaces.[64] This contrast, in particular, helped to spur renewed interest in stage technology research and development, as well as a return of the "technology worship" of the 1950s.

Another influential study trip, to the United States and England, took place in 1980. Whereas the North Korea trip seemed to demonstrate that PRC stage technology lagged behind its near neighbor, the US–England tour introduced its delegates to a wider range of theatrical trends and developments (including, but not limited to, theater architecture and stage technology). Although this delegation did not include any designers or technicians, upon their return, actor Ying Ruocheng 英若诚 (1929–2003) published reflections on his trip that included details of theater architecture, scenography, lighting, and set changes that he had observed abroad.[65] He even viewed architectural and spatial shifts as drivers of change: "Due to all manner of changes in theaters and stages, the creation of the script, acting, directing, scenography, etc. all have experienced great shifts. As reflected in the performance, the most important elements are truth and naturalness, subtlety and refinement, and direct audience interaction."[66] Significantly, Ying draws connections not only between infrastructural changes and the creative process but also to the resulting performance aesthetics and how the audience was engaged. Overall, these foreign trips enabled Chinese theater artists to observe concrete advances in stage technology itself and a broad range of applications. They also made it clear that more sophisticated equipment or innovative spatial arrangements did not necessarily correspond to theatrical styles that flaunted their technologies.

Study trips, as well as the resurgence of access to foreign journals and publications, contributed to theater designers and technicians' perceptions of a technological lag in the capacities of Chinese theater venues, which they blamed squarely on the Cultural Revolution. As Liu Xu 柳絮, a member of the China Institute of Stage Science and Technology Research, notes, the 1960s to early 1970s were a period of particularly fast-paced technological development around the world, including in areas related to theater—and it was precisely during this period that the PRC essentially stopped the clock on its own scientific and technological progress.[67] Recent scholarship, as noted in chapter 4, has demonstrated that the Cultural Revolution was not quite as devoid of science as once assumed and that the post-Mao narrative to this effect served the political interests of the Reform Era regime. Nonetheless, the idea of a Cultural Revolution–driven scientific and technological gap was commonly repeated at this time and proved a powerful motivation for scientific and theatrical researchers alike.

Thus, although many theater troupes did not have the economic means to pursue significant technical advancements until later in the Reform Era, the late 1970s and early 1980s saw the development and spread of new technologies (many of which had already become predominant in foreign theaters in the preceding decades). For example, the first computer-controlled lighting board in the PRC was installed in the Hangzhou Theater (杭州剧场) at the end of 1979.[68] Shanghai Youth Huaju Troupe (上海青年话剧团) lighting designer Yuan Huashui 袁华水 (b. 1954) also describes the successful invention, by the lighting research department of the Shanghai Theatre Academy (上海戏剧学院), of a long-throw spotlight that used xenon bulbs as its lighting source.[69] He notes a shift from the resistance dimmers used in the 1960s to the newer SCR dimmers and electronic control boards in the 1980s. In previous decades, theater technicians had been able to engineer rudimentary dimming devices themselves, such as the saltwater and dial dimmers, and locally produced semiconductor-based SCR dimmers had even been innovated in the 1970s as part of *yangbanxi* popularization efforts. By the 1980s, however, SCR dimmers provided an important point of intersection between stage technology and broader R&D efforts, as growing the domestic semiconductor industry (especially in Shanghai) became a strategic priority.[70] Localized, grassroots innovation thus both presaged and eventually gave way to professionalized and sophisticated research and engineering, resulting in more widespread application of advanced stage technologies.

As the research efforts at Shanghai Theater Academy show, discussion and implementation of "stage science and technology" not only took place at the national level but also at provincial and local institutions. Provincial theaters, for instance, were important sites for research activities. The Shanxi Province Huaju Troupe (山西省话剧团) established a Stage Science and Technology Small Group (舞台科技小组) and hosted a conference on "stage science and technology" in the late spring of 1978. According to a brief article on the conference in *People's Theater*, the gathering was directly inspired by the National Conference on Science of March 1978.[71] One important topic of discussion was how to target avenues for development in key areas of stage technology. Lighting control systems, for instance, could exchange outdated dimmers for the newer SCR-based technology and better lamps, while sets, props, and costumes could experiment with new plastic and polymer materials. The meeting promoted the idea that all amateur and professional literature and arts troupes in the province should begin to "study science, use science, and apply both domestic and foreign technology onstage" in the service of the Four Modernizations.[72] However, even given the wide reach of these mandates, there was nonetheless an overall shift from emphasis on grassroots technological innovation to institutionally sponsored research and development. This parallels the broader shifts from Maoist visions of science and technology to Deng Xiaoping–era technoscience.

Chinese theater's technoscientific shift even bled into areas that rely less directly on stage technology, like acting. As early as the 1950s, the idea of Konstantin Stanislavski's (1863–1938) acting method as a "system" (体系) had appealed to the industrial-technology-driven ethos of the Seventeen Years period. Stanislavksi then fell out of favor at the time of the Sino-Soviet split, only to reemerge in the post-Mao period as the catalyst for development of a more rigorous and systematic approach to actor training. For example, a 1978 conference held by the faculty of the Shanghai Theater Academy—also a central site for stage technology research—began with the goal of reevaluating Stanislavski's acting and directing methods in relation to Chinese theater and answering the criticisms leveled against them during the Cultural Revolution.[73] One of the results of the conference, however, was a push to reform and systematize training programs for *huaju* actors. A series of articles by acting instructors, published in the journal *Theater Arts* (戏剧艺术), outlines the parameters of such a system: actors should receive training in physical theater, as well as text and voice, and learn to adapt the basic skills of "sister arts" (姐妹艺术) such as *xiqu* and ballet for *huaju* performance.[74] The articles themselves are quite technical, calling to mind the strict training programs required for the study of Chinese *xiqu* forms, acrobatics, and ballet. Yet while the architects of this training program do advocate borrowing individual exercises or patterns of movement from other performing arts, they strongly decry the mechanistic importation of entire training systems and the conventionalization (程式化) of forms like *jingju* and *kunqu* 崑曲 (Kun opera). Instead, through training, the body is to be reconfigured as a "highly dynamic and efficient tool for artistic creativity."[75] This essentially involves conceiving of the actor as an engineer who, once provided the proper training, techniques, and methods, will be able to give full expression to any character in any script. This process is articulated in a set of phrases repeated several times throughout these articles: design, organize, embody (设计, 组织, 体现). The reformed approach to performer training thus reflects a highly technical—or, to use the authors' own phrasing, a highly "scientific"—conceptualization of the actor's task.

Beyond this, there was also interest (albeit less widespread) in theories that connected theater even more closely to cutting-edge fields of technology. One example can be found in the work of Robert Cohen, whose *Acting Power* (first published in 1978) famously argued for envisioning the acting process as a cybernetic system. Cohen derives his definition of cybernetics from its early use to describe the "teleological . . . mechanisms" best suited to advancing computer science. For Cohen, cybernetic thinking is fundamentally future-oriented and contradistinctive to deterministic thinking, which he sees as past-oriented.[76] In acting, this aligns cybernetics with a goal-driven approach to character, whereas a deterministic approach focuses more on motivation and clear cause-and-effect chains.[77] In practice, this cybernetic, goal-oriented approach entails creating a "feedback loop" in which actors repeatedly seek information from each other and respond accordingly.[78] Cohen's work was introduced to Chinese audiences in the mid-1980s by an article in the journal *Drama Studies* (戏剧学系), in which author Li Xing 李醒 both describes Cohen's core concepts and argues that they are aligned with the fundamentals of the Stanislavski system.[79] Cohen's cybernetic approach to acting also dovetails with the widespread impact of new information systems and technologies in the 1980s, as described by Xiao Liu, wherein "high-end scientific studies in the areas of information and AI research interacted and intersected with the dissemination of scientific knowledge through popular science journals and with popular imaginations in fiction and films that reflected on the social consequences of new technologies."[80] As demonstrated by the above case, the "information fantasies" analyzed by Liu also took on a visceral incarnation in acting practice aligned with cybernetics and communications theories.

The systematization of performer training and acting cybernetics can be linked more broadly to what Shepherd-Barr has called, in a different context, a "scientificization" of theater. Even the increased interest in Brechtian theater, discussed above, contributed to this trend. As Shepherd-Barr has noted, Brecht was one of many European or American theater artists in the twentieth century whose theories of performance took inspiration from scientific models.[81] In fact, many of these thinkers, including Stanislavski, Appia, Meyerhold, Grotowksi, Peter Brook, Augusto Boal, and Harley Granville-Barker, were translated, discussed, and admired by Chinese theater artists of the late 1970s to the early 1980s, and some had also been influential much earlier (see, for example, discussion of Appia and Meyerhold in chapter 1). This is not to suggest that Chinese theater artists were merely imitating foreign sources, however. Rather, they were part of an ongoing, transnational circulation of ideas and practices, and during the Reform Era, this did involve, to a certain extent, adapting ideas from foreign thinkers. Appropriation of these systems, like their original articulations, furthermore borrowed "the aura of authority vested in science"—as well as the aura of the renewed authority vested in *foreign* sources—to legitimize theatrical pursuits.[82] At the same time, in the case of the PRC, this scientificization was inextricable from technologization and parallel emphasis on research into more advanced lighting, stage mechanics, and theater control systems. It is therefore more accurate to speak of a "technoscientific" shift, rather than only a scientificization, in Chinese theater of this period. Through this shift, theater became akin to a laboratory not of pure science, but rather of the application of scientific principles and theories.

## *Atoms and Love*: Remediating the History of Chinese Science and Technology

The premiere of *Atoms and Love* in April 1980 took the merging of theater and technoscience one step further by representing a modern laboratory onstage. Also inspired by the Four Modernizations, *Atoms and Love* centers on a fictionalized account of scientists working on China's first atomic bomb in the 1960s. The play was based on fieldwork done in national defense science institutes (国防科研) by its coauthors, Li Weixin 李维新, Zheng Bangyu 郑邦玉, Li Yonggui 李永贵, and Zhou Liguo 周立国.[83] Its prologue scene begins shortly after the fall of the Gang of Four, in 1976, and depicts the return of fictional female scientist Ye Jieshan 叶洁珊 to the nuclear test site where she had worked in her youth, more than a decade earlier. The bulk of the play's action unfolds in flashbacks, interspersed with brief cuts to the present, as Ye narrates the events that took place in her lab leading up to China's first successful atomic bomb detonation and the subsequent imprisonment of her colleague He Ziyuan 何梓沅 during the Cultural Revolution. In other words, the play is a dramatization of the labor that took place behind the scenes of one of the PRC's greatest scientific and technological triumphs, as well as the ideological fallout of the Mao era.

Act 1, which begins after Ye Jieshan's present-day opening scene, starts with her arrival at a nuclear weaponry research site in summer 1963. In a nod to the secrecy of national defense, the stage directions refer to the site only as "a certain nuclear weapons institute" (某核武器研究所); historically, the main nuclear design research facilities were euphemistically termed the "Ninth Academy" (or "Ninth Institute").[84] The timing of act 1 sets the play's action into motion at the height of the PRC's historical nuclear drama. The PRC had identified building a nuclear weapons program as a strategic priority as early as the mid-1950s, but initially relied on sending scientists abroad for training and on technology transfer from the Soviet Union. Research progress and even the construction of suitable research facilities then were slowed by the aftermath of the Great Leap Forward and political tensions surrounding the Sino-Soviet split. The Sino-Soviet nuclear partnership collapsed completely with the withdrawal of Soviet experts from the PRC in 1960–61, leaving Chinese scientists and technicians to reverse-engineer many of the techniques and technologies related to nuclear weapons on their own. In other words, they had to apply the ethos of homegrown technology to one of the most complicated, and dangerous, scientific and engineering challenges—building an atomic bomb. By summer 1963, they had made significant progress on their own in the necessary areas of producing fissionable material, bomb design, and component manufacture. The first act of *Atoms and Love* depicts these final moments of research and design, with pressure mounting on He Ziyuan's lab to complete one last essential technical component: the bomb initiator (in the play called the "igniter" [点火装置]).[85] The initiator sits at the very core of a nuclear bomb and, under pressure, releases a stream of neutrons into the bomb's core that kickstarts the primary nuclear explosion; without it, the bomb cannot detonate.

The second act of the play follows the scientists to a nuclear weapons test site in the summer of 1964. Historically, research did move to the Lop Nur Nuclear Weapons Test Base (in Xinjiang) in the summer of 1964, in anticipation of a fall 1964 detonation test. The precise location of the test base was, however, a closely guarded matter of national security. Accordingly, the play does not reveal the precise date or location of act 2. It depicts the scientists' work to refine techniques for measuring the results of the upcoming nuclear test and then successfully conducting the test. A fictionalized phone call directly from Premier Zhou Enlai legitimizes the endeavor. Meanwhile, He Ziyuan ends the act estranged from his fiancée, medical researcher Xiao Yuping 肖羽屏, after he fails to show up for the encampment's group wedding ceremony. (Reviews of the play critiqued the romantic plotline as underdeveloped and, indeed, it functions primarily as a foil for demonstrating how He Ziyuan places his dedication to science above his personal life.) Act 3 then focuses on the suffering of the scientists during the Cultural Revolution. Finally, act 4 sees He Ziyuan released from prison and rehabilitated. Interstitial scenes throughout return the audience to the "present" of 1976, and a brief epilogue concludes the play amid the successful test launch of a new nuclear missile in the post-Mao era.

*Atoms and Love* thus follows in the same vein as *Galileo* by embracing theater's potential as a mediating technology for the history of a scientific experiment, wherein questions and contradictions related to that history could play out and be presented to the audience for evaluation. The mode of remediation in *Galileo*, however, remained analogical, with the history of Renaissance science and technology paralleling the Chinese case. With *Atoms and Love*, remediation hit even closer to home, on multiple levels. First, the main event depicted would have been familiar and immediately recognizable to most audience members. The research and development of the Chinese atomic bomb was a closely guarded matter of national security, but the successful test on October 16, 1964 was a widely publicized and highly celebrated event.[86] One anecdote even relates how some of the first members of the public to learn of the test were members of the cast of the song-and-dance epic *The East Is Red*, who had just finished a performance in the Great Hall of the People. As described by John Lewis and Xue Litai in their history of China's atomic project:

> By chance, thousands of actors and actresses had gathered in the Great Hall of the People after a performance of the musical extravaganza *The East Is Red* to meet the nation's central leaders. At 4:00 in the afternoon, they were greeted by Zhou Enlai. The premier gestured for silence and announced, "Comrades, Chairman Mao has asked me to tell you the good news. Our country's first atomic bomb has been successfully detonated!" At first the crowd remained silent, even stunned. Then the cheering began. . . . A few hours later, Radio Beijing began releasing the news to the world.[87]

This particular event is not depicted in the play, but the "detonation" onstage (indicated by flashes of light and sound effects in the stage directions) might recall for audience members their experience of hearing the news on the radio and seeing photographs of the mushroom cloud in newspapers and the *People's Pictorial* (人民画报). The play even includes a subplot involving the researchers taking and developing photographs of the detonation, which invokes the specific history of media representation of the bomb and the visual medium through which average citizens would have seen evidence of its success.

On another level, the general experience of heroic effort and unjust persecution also remediated the Cultural Revolution experience of many Chinese, just as had the story of Galileo. Like much of the scar literature produced at this time, *Atoms and Love* depicts the persecution of intellectuals as unwarranted and works toward the rehabilitation of scientists, in particular, by emphasizing their contributions to nation and knowledge alike. This remediation operates, however, by taking significant liberties in its depiction of the details of the lives and work of scientists. It is a work of "science fiction" in the same sense that Eric Bentley used to describe Brecht's *Galileo*, which likewise plays rather fast and loose with the details of the historic Galileo Galilei's life and the philosophical significance of his discoveries.[88] Yet the main characters in *Atoms and Love* are not historical individuals, but fictionalized composites of scientists whom the authors met or learned about while doing fieldwork research for the play. The "old scientist" (老科学家) character Xiao Bochen 肖博琛, for instance, parallels a true story that the authors relate in an essay about their playwriting process: that of a foreign-trained scientist who was overexposed to radiation while studying in the United States and hid his condition upon his return, in order to continue to contribute to the national project.[89] Xiao, however, also represents the many scientists who were trained abroad and then patriotically returned after the founding of the PRC in 1949—only to be criticized for their foreign expertise and persecuted during the Cultural Revolution. As the character of Party Secretary Wang reminds Xiao in a scene taking place in 1963, Premier Zhou Enlai referred to scientists like Xiao as "national treasures" (国粹); yet, in the following act, Xiao is beaten to death by Red Guards.

Through characters like Xiao and He Ziyuan, *Atoms and Love* reflects the extreme dissonance experienced by scientists as a collective and, at the same time, transforms the individual scientist into a "type" in a manner reminiscent of socialist realist typicality. This use of typicality echoes the dramaturgy of the *yangbanxi* (and socialist realism more generally), but eschews the extremes of positive and negative characterization promoted by Cultural Revolution dramatic theory. Rather than being paragons of virtue, clear victims of foreign oppression, or counterrevolutionary forces, the scientists in *Atoms and Love* are flawed heroes and victims of overzealous violence (like Xiao) or incorrect charges (like He Ziyuan)—not dissimilar to the dialectical heroism of Brecht's Galileo. He Ziyuan, for example, is accused of being a spy and counterrevolutionary, then imprisoned on the basis of false evidence—a photograph on the back of which he had absentmindedly worked out some equations related to his lab's experiments. His detractors claim that he was using the photograph to smuggle out scientific secrets. However, if anything, he demonstrates the heroic ideal of a scientist by working constantly, sidelining his personal relationships, and even knowingly overexposing himself to radiation in order to ensure the success of his team's experiments. His character flaws surface in his private life, not in his work ethic or politics. The stories of Xiao Bochen and He Ziyuan demonstrate theater's power to rewrite traumatic history, in a way that attempts to rehabilitate the unjustly persecuted while also reasserting the value of scientific advances made under politically oppressive circumstances.

In addition, much like the telescope scenes in *Galileo*, the play focuses not on the pure scientific principles behind nuclear developments, but rather on specific technologies necessary to the successful application of that science. In scene after scene, the characters in *Atoms and Love* are depicted as engaged with highly technical matters: chemically engineering the bomb's initiator, developing a sensor to measure the initiation process, reading and analyzing experiment results. In fact, these and other "technical issues" (技术问题)—— as critic Shen Yi terms them—posed one of the greatest challenges to the writing and reception of the play.[90] As the playwrights themselves note, they encountered a host of unfamiliar technical terms and topics when conducting fieldwork for the play. Self-professed "science illiterates" (科盲), they realized that they could not write about scientists and technicians without a working knowledge of science, so they turned to science popularization primers and returned twice to the labs, spending time interviewing scientists and even participating in experiments.[91] Through these activities, the nature of theater artists' interaction with the knowledge production process shifted once again, to involve consumption of scientific knowledge and actual participation in scientific research.

Beyond the basic difficulty of learning enough science to write a play about scientists, the playwrights and producing theater company also faced the challenge of conveying scientific and technical details to a lay audience— many of whom had had years of basic education interrupted by the Cultural Revolution. Several reviews of the production raise this issue, describing the "technical issues" involved in nuclear science and experimentation as "enough to make one's head ache" and a potential "shackle" (束缚) that the production had escaped.[92] A conversation between He Ziyuan and Ye Jieshan in act 1 demonstrates the playwrights' solution to this problem and one of the play's central dramaturgical characteristics: a curious combination of precision and imprecision, through the marriage of highly technical topics with more vague references. After yet another in a series of failed experiments, Ye suggests returning to an idea that He had previously proposed:

YE JIESHAN: Old He, could you try out that pressurization plan that you were working on before?

HE ZIYUAN: Tell me what you're thinking.

YE JIESHAN: I've looked over the pressurization plan that you originally came up with, which relied on the lab equipment that we actually have. It was researched in great detail, discussed at length, and the experimental method was also quite concrete. At the meeting to debate it, no one could find any flaws. At the time, it was temporarily put aside out of consideration for the dangers of the [radiation] dosage. If we could solve that problem now, could we give it a try?[93]

The dialogue skillfully manages to further the plot via a potential technical solution to the protagonist's main obstacle of failed experiments, without fully explaining what the specific solution entails. Indeed, the words in the term "pressurization plan" (加压方案) are intelligible to the lay audience member insofar as they are clear and recognizable—literally, the words mean "add pressure plan/case"—yet anyone unfamiliar with nuclear science or weapons research would be hard pressed to explain precisely what those terms mean in the context of an atomic bomb initiator design. Instead, they convey a certain scienticity and level of technicality, but neither overwhelm the audience with unfamiliar details nor reveal classified information.

This balance of concrete, accurate information and fuzzier, fictional detail also carries over into the play's reworking of historical fact. Much of the progress described in fictional detail in the play matches historical research into China's nuclear weapons program. For instance, the exchange above references, in general terms, the actual experience of the team working on the Chinese atomic bomb initiator conducting more than two hundred failed experiments before the lead scientist, Wang Fangding 王方定 (b. 1928), produced the stable polonium compound needed to initiate a successful nuclear reaction.[94] Even such details as complaints about poor working conditions hampering research or a technician suffering severe radiation exposure after a lab accident are reflected in the dramatic text.[95] However, there are slight inaccuracies in the play's dating. For example, the final stages of the initiator development in act 1 purportedly take place in the summer of 1963. In the play, the scientists are still struggling with the initiator when they learn that their colleagues in the explosive assembly lab have completed a successful test detonation. Historically, Chinese technicians had already developed and tested the initiator component described in the play by the end of 1962; the tests that took place in the summer and fall of 1963 involved combining the initiator component with the explosive assembly.[96] It is possible that the playwrights, who relied primarily on fieldwork interviews (essentially oral history), may not have had access to precise dates or may have misunderstood the experimental chronology; it is also possible that some of the details were still classified information at the time of the play's composition.

Regardless of the cause, the effect of this slight inaccuracy is that the play's dramaturgical approach to historical detail parallels its imprecise representation of technoscientific detail. In relation to theater's function as a mediating technology for technoscience and history, however, this is not necessarily a problem; rather, such fuzziness may actually help to make both science and history more intelligible to audiences. Moreover, in order to achieve this level of accessibility, *Atoms and Love* ultimately relies on techniques that will now seem familiar to the reader: an emphasis on *tu* technologies and the blending of *xu* (empty) and *shi* (solid) elements.[97] He Ziyuan's pressurization plan is, after all, nothing more than using preexisting equipment in an innovative way to meet a technical challenge. Yet the underlying ethos of self-reliance and homegrown solutions is here translated into the highest levels of science and engineering—and shown to succeed (unlike the infamous smelting of backyard steel during the Great Leap Forward). In a similar vein, pairing technical details with vague terms, or historical precision with vagueness, might be seen as yet another iteration of attempts to balance the virtual and the concrete. Here, the ideological implications fade, but the consequences for enhanced audience engagement remain.

## Staging Science without Realism

In each play, the presence of deeply historical technologies, like Galileo's telescope, and advanced contemporary equipment, like nuclear defense laboratory systems, raises the question once again of how such technologies were represented in the material world of the theater. As noted above, both *Galileo* and *Atoms and Love* were widely acclaimed for their scenography. Performance reviews and broader articles on the scenic design of the period often use both as examples of innovation. Yet, as these sources reveal, neither production ostentatiously capitalized on advances in stage technology, nor did they prioritize verisimilitude in their representation of scientific labs and technologies onstage. Paradoxically, widespread interest and research into new technologies, like the SCR-based dimmer and alternative materials for set construction, did not correspond to the immediate or obvious application of such technologies in plays about science and technology. Instead, both *Galileo* and *Atoms and Love* garnered attention for their more suggestive and nonillusionistic (非幻觉行) use of sets, lights, and stage space.

In the case of *Galileo*, especially, the move away from using advanced technologies to create a believable replica of the real world took direct inspiration from Brechtian theory and aesthetics. According to the scenographer for the production, Xue Dianjie 薛殿杰 (b. 1937), both Brecht's general writing about stage elements and his specific "production guidelines" for *Galileo* influenced Xue's scenic design. Most important of these were Brecht's notes that "the stage setting should not make the audience believe that they are situated in a medieval Italian room or in the Vatican. The audience had to be convinced that they are in a theatre" and that "the performance should enable

Fig. 5.2. Set design for production of *Life of Galileo* by the China Youth Art Theater in 1980 by Xue Dianjie, depicting Galileo using a telescope to observe the night sky. Source: Wang Shizhi and Li Guangchen, eds., *Shoudu wutai meishu sheji ziliao xuan* (Beijing: Zhongguo xiju jia xuehui Beijing fenhui, 1981).

the audience to 'adopt an attitude of astonishment, a critical, discriminating attitude.'"[98] In order to create this heightened awareness of theatricality, Xue created a unit set featuring a raked platform, "cloth-walls" with cut-out windows and doors, and small painted screens hung against the backdrop (fig. 5.2). The walls were constructed with natural-colored fabric and metal poles, with cut-outs in the cloth explicitly revealing the framework. The screens also had exposed metal rods, ropes, and knots. Both Xue and the play's codirectors likened the use of these screens to the type of curtains commonly used in Chinese *xiqu* stage decoration.[99] The screens, they believed, would read as obviously related to *xiqu* to Chinese audience members, and thereby both fulfill Brecht's desire to remind audiences that they were in a theater and also suggest a strong connection between Brechtian and traditional Chinese theater aesthetics. Location changes were indicated by changing the screens, furniture, and decorations. A typically Brechtian white wash lit the stage, enabling the audience to see the movements of actors and stagehands alike. Xue also borrowed the Berliner Ensemble technique of hanging a white half-curtain near the front of the stage and projecting scene titles/summaries onto the curtain before each scene.

At first glance, the plain white wash and simplified use of projections, in particular, seem an almost antitechnological choice in the context of the

Four Modernizations and the Chinese theater world's otherwise keen interest in advancing "stage science and technology." Discussions among theater designers and technicians at this time often brought up lighting and projected backdrops as specific examples of areas in which recent technological advances had been particularly significant for the theater. For example, as noted above, Chinese lighting designers, technicians, and researchers were especially interested in the development of better lighting control systems and high-powered units. A bright white wash might benefit from higher-intensity bulbs but would not require complex lighting levels and cues or long-throw spotlights: it would remain at the same, evenly lit level throughout each scene. Backdrop projections were also a well-developed and commonly used technology in PRC theater by the late 1970s.[100] The sole prior production of a Brechtian play in the PRC—Huang Zuolin's 1959 production of *Mother Courage*—had even used backdrop projections.[101] In *Galileo*, though, the backdrop was painted with a diagram of the celestial bodies, and projection was used only for thematic intertitles.

The quasi-Brechtian scenography in *Galileo*, however, did not represent an all-out rejection of sophisticated stage technology, but rather a shift toward an increasingly critical reflection on the use of technology for theatrical illusion. Indeed, the production of *Galileo* catalyzed a conversation on theater aesthetics that would become a defining debate in Chinese theater in the 1980s and whose terms are still frequently invoked to this today. The debate centered on the issue of theatrical realism, or rather, what it meant to "write reality" (*xieshi*) onstage. As in the Seventeen Years period, the term *xieshi* often was set in opposition to the idea of "writing meaning" (*xieyi*) and a more abstract, suggestive aesthetics. Huang Zuolin had long been a proponent of *xieyi* aesthetics, as had other directors and playwrights invested in combining the Euro-American realist tradition with Chinese *xiqu*. Likewise, the goal of some previous scenographers—and their use of stage technology—had been to achieve a balance of *xu* and *shi*, of virtual and concrete, onstage. Yet, in retrospect, most *huaju* directors, designers, playwrights, and theorists came to see the first several decades of *huaju* as having been dominated by an overly "illusionistic" (幻觉性) mode of *xieshi* aesthetics. In contrast, *Galileo*'s strength lay, as Gong Hede writes, in "creating nonillusionistic artistic truth."[102] The pursuit of artistic truth in turn paralleled the pursuit of scientific truth represented in the play and implied by Huang Zuolin's idea of theater-as-science.[103] The production thus represented a growing concern among Chinese theater artists with the broader question of how to create an "artistic truth" (艺术的真实) onstage and, even more fundamentally, how to define "artistic truth" and "theatrical truth" (戏剧的真实) in an era when ideological "truth" had been turned on its head.

Essays reflecting on these questions demonstrate an understanding of both theatrical illusionism and the creation of artistic truth onstage as simultaneously theoretical, historical, and technical. Writing for *Stage Design and Technology*, for instance, Hu Miaosheng roots the aesthetic idealization of verisimilitude in a history of technological and scientific developments from the Renaissance to nineteenth-century realism and naturalism: "The proscenium stage, perspective [as in the artistic term], stage machinery, and all kinds of special stage effects made scenographers obsessed with developing the techniques of stage illusion."[104] *Galileo* scenic designer Xue Dianjie makes a similar, but more general, connection between scenography and developments in architecture and technology: "Common theater history knowledge tells us, changes in theater architecture and advances in stage technology equipment influence epochal shifts in performance form, and determine the different features of each different era's scenographic creation."[105] This historical-technical process was seen to apply to China as well, especially in the Reform Era, but with two important caveats. First, the veneration of illusionism had arrived in China belatedly, in the early twentieth century, when many European theater artists (like Edward Gordon Craig) were already launching an anti-illusionist revolution. Second, traditional Chinese *xiqu* had separately developed its own non-illusionist techniques and aesthetics, which parallel and combine well with the more experimental strains of twentieth-century European and US theater.

At a time when "borrowing from the West" was back in fashion, the historical connection to bourgeois stage technologies and European naturalism no longer sounded an ideological death knell for illusionism. Rather, it was the fine line between illusion and delusion, as well as the highly romanticized vision of reality that had dominated the stage in the heyday of Soviet socialist realist influence, that troubled Chinese theater artists who had survived the Cultural Revolution. Here again, the slippage from a true to false representation had much to do with the material world of the theater and how the world onstage was produced by designers and technicians. As described by Xue, scenographic illusionism is defined by the materials and techniques used to try to convince the audience that any stage replica is the real thing. He cites the example of a city wall constructed with a soft flat: "although the city wall is usually framed with wood and bound with cloth, the stage-hands always try their best to hide the materials so as to create an illusion of a 'real' brick-built city wall."[106] This act of concealing deludes those watching, which Xue sees as a deliberate attempt to "confuse the audience."[107] Hu Miaosheng goes one step further to point out the multiple possible Chinese translations of "illusion"—in addition to the most common term *huanjue* (幻觉), it might be translated in the sense of a "misconception" (错觉) or even "mistake" (错误).[108] Against this deception, Hu promotes an aesthetics that acknowledges the medium-specific limitations of the theater and embraces simplification (单纯化), conventionalization, and stylization (风格化).[109] In other words, a suppositional theater, à la both Brecht and Chinese *xiqu*, circumvents deceit by privileging techniques that constantly remind the audience: this is theater.

The scenography for *Atoms and Love* continued in this quasi-Brechtian vein, with many commentators perceiving an aesthetic similarity between the play and *Galileo*. Hu Miaosheng, for instance, also references *Atoms and Love* in his discussions of *xieyi* aesthetics; a roundtable discussion of the play, published in *People's Theater*, likewise spoke of how "in terms of stage design, [the play] fundamentally changed illusionistic design methods, and fully used projections and small props to create the stage environment and atmosphere."[110] On a practical level, the production's non-illusionistic configuration of stage space was driven by the need to move quickly between multiple locations, as was the case with *Galileo* and many of the plays discussed in previous chapters. Absent a revolving stage, scenic designer Ji Xiaoqiu 冀晓秋 (b. 1931) relied on large set props and projections to create different environments: the interior of an airplane, a car in motion, scientists' homes, several different lab spaces, a nuclear launch site.[111] The lab spaces and nuclear launch site posed a particularly interesting problem, as these are spaces that loom large in the imagination of the average layperson, but are not public locations, and the stage directions offer little description (figs. 5.3 and 5.4). Most scenes begin with a simple note on the location, such as "a lab in a certain nuclear research institute" for act 1, scene 2. As with the scientific knowledge behind the play's action, a process of demystification and familiarization was required to make the lab space legible for audiences, yet the precise details were left to the designer. Ji Xiaoqiu addressed this by foregrounding defining technologies, such as lab equipment, monitoring screens, instrument panels—all items that would clearly indicate scientific experiment, but without necessarily needing to function. The set design also bears a striking resemblance to other contemporaneous visual depictions of nuclear science, most notably the 1980 film *Death Ray on Coral Island* (珊瑚岛上的死光), adapted from Tong Enzheng's 童恩正 (1935–97) popular science fiction story of the same name (fig. 5.5). The

Fig. 5.3. Collage of renderings for the set design of *Atoms and Love*, with the nuclear scientists' lab top center and the launch site control room bottom right. Source: Wang Shizhi and Li Guangchen, eds., *Shoudu wutai meishu sheji ziliao xuan* (Beijing: Zhongguo xiju jia xuehui Beijing fenhui, 1981).

similarities suggest the collapsing of timelines, with the near past history of Chinese science and technology mapping onto the near futures imagined by science fiction. They furthermore demonstrate theater's ongoing participation in a mediascape that shaped the popular imagination of science and technology, which became all the more important as mass science transitioned to high tech.

Even as *Atoms and Love* worked to familiarize scientific spaces and

Fig. 5.4. Production photograph of scene set in the launch site control room. Source: *Yuanzi yu aiqing* [lianhuanhua] (Beijing: Zhonggo xiju chubanshe, 1980), 77.

align science past with projections of the near future, it also deployed non-illusionistic techniques in a more defamiliarizing mode. One of the most frequently noted elements of the production's scenic design was Ji Xiaoqiu's innovative use of stage projections. The style and techniques for backdrop projection that had been developed in the mid-1960s were perfected for use in the *yangbanxi*, and were seen as ubiquitous by the late 1970s. However, in *Atoms and Love*, Ji used projections not in lieu of painted backdrops, but rather for a range of scenographic effects. To begin, the script calls for the projection of the play's title during the transition between its prologue and act 1, just as its diegetic world begins to flash back to the events of 1963. This single scripted use of a projected title evokes both Brechtian projections and almost pointedly references the cinematic quality of the play's structure. It marks acts 1–4 as a kind of a play-within-a-play, or a film within a play; combined with the clear framing device of Ye Jieshan beginning to narrate the historical events, this signals the constructedness of her story and its multiple levels of mediation. Therefore, even though the projected titles are not indicated throughout the play as they might be in a fully Brechtian production, they nonetheless contribute to a feeling of theatricality, or even metatheatricality.

Fig. 5.5. Control room scene from *Death Ray on Coral Island* film (Shanghai dianying zhipianchang, dir. Zhang Hongmei, 1980).

In performance, projections were also used for specific scenic elements throughout the play, with their most noted application during He Ziyuan's imprisonment scenes in act 3. These scenes take place in a "cowshed," or makeshift Cultural Revolution prison, and the projections significantly diverged from realism to instead create nonillusionistic markers of atmosphere. A giant projected cobweb, for instance, covered one corner of the cyc; when He Ziyuan works late into the night, continuing his scientific calculations even after long days of forced hard labor, handwritten equations appeared across the stage. Veteran director Shu Qiang 舒强 (Jiang Shuqiang 蒋树强, 1915–99) described his response to these application of projection in largely positive terms, with one caveat:

> The performance form was very fresh. . . . The scenic design did not make large set pieces, projections were used in an innovative way, with both *xu* and *shi*, very rich and colorful. The problem was that the scenic objects made by the projections were not of the same style: some were very concrete, some were very abstract—there were even some expressionistic things, which was not easy to understand.[112]

Shu's complaint that the projections were difficult to comprehend demonstrates that elements of *Atoms and Love* were alienating to some of its viewers, despite efforts to the contrary, and that the sense of alienation stemmed specifically from the defamiliarized use of a recognizable stage technology. This defamiliarization operated in contradistinction to (and perhaps represented a rejection of) the technological fantasy of the preceding decades, with abstract projections as the near complete opposite of the *tu* revolving stage.

To return to the topic of stage technology per se, then, what *Atoms and Love* illustrates is a new approach that prioritizes expanding and diversifying the application of existing technologies, alongside research and development of new, more advanced equipment and techniques. This diversification in turn created more space for a variety of theatrical forms and styles to coexist, as opposed to the aesthetic narrowing of the Cultural Revolution. As Xue Dianjie writes:

> In a certain sense, scenographic creativity is restricted by the developmental level of industrial technologies and material conditions, like architectural arts and crafts . . . [but] on the level of craft, the technological level of stage equipment and materials can contribute many more possibilities to our scenographic creativity, which certainly will influence whether or not our scenographic creativity styles and forms will become more diverse.[113]

Xue goes on to illustrate his point with the example of using a revolving stage to create innovative artistic effects, rather than simply to reduce the time of scene changes. We might think of the use of projections in both *Galileo* and *Atoms and Love* in a similar vein: the two productions use the technology to different ends, and neither does so in a style at all akin to the mainstream mode of projected backdrops. As these two productions illustrate, technological advancement led to a diversification of theatrical styles, which enabled more abstract and evocative uses of stage technology, as well as more agency for the individual artist.

The emphasis on critical evaluation and application of stage technology—and as a goal of artistic praxis more generally—also meant that no single approach became a new orthodoxy. The "technology worship" of 1950s theater may have resurfaced, but as seen from the designs for *Galileo* and *Atoms and Love*, it did not in all cases transform into an unqualified celebration of ostentatious technology. Indeed, some critics even voiced concerns about the negative effects of too much technology onstage. Writing about a national scenography exhibition held at the National Art Museum (中国美术馆) in Beijing, for example, Wang Ren 王韧 and Huang Su 黃甦 simultaneously praise the innovative spirit of scenic design and caution against it:

> Another hallmark of the development of scenographic creative work has been the continuous introduction of new successes in science and technology. For the past thirty years, a number of new kinds of equipment, new techniques, and new materials have continuously strengthened and heightened the expressive means and artistic quality of scenography.[114]

Wang and Huang go on to describe several of these innovations, including the use of projections and lighting effects, but also express concern that the application of such technologies is pure spectacle—as they put it, "curiosity for curiosity's sake."[115] Similarly, director Xu Xiaozhong, writing in 1982, complains that technology has become a crutch for poor technique, wherein "directors often use visual and aural artistic tricks to bury the actor's performance. Actors are 'buried up to the teeth' in human technologies, like thick makeup and microphones (even miniature microphones that they wear on their bodies)."[116] These comments reveal a set of competing impulses at work in the theater world. On the one hand, there was a desire to align the historical narrative of technical theater, especially scenography, with the ethos of techoscientific innovation that was officially promoted in the Reform Era. On the other hand, there is the sense that technologies of the stage, even traditional ones like makeup, could obscure the actor's performance. To complete theater's transformation from a revolutionary to a revelatory medium, therefore, required adopting and eschewing technology in equal parts.

Ultimately, Chinese theater's engagement with stage technology in the early Reform Era represents both continuities with and departures from previous periods. The underlying importance of the relationship among technics, politics, and aesthetics persisted, as did the perceived importance of specific technologies and techniques like lighting dimmers, revolving stages, and backdrop projections. Dialogue with Western theories that had been formative in the early and mid-twentieth century and with theorists, like Appia and Stanislavski, was renewed, with other representatives of the "scientificization" of theater added to the conversation. Simultaneously, a heightened emphasis on science and technology as driving forces of modernization shifted the discourse from stage technology to stage technoscience and brought about a closer alignment between the theater and the scientific laboratory. This was reflected in the narratives and characters represented onstage, as well as in the research process for playwriting, producing plays, and stage technology itself. Both the plays and the debates studied in this chapter presaged the broader ideological and cultural shift to come in the last decades of the twentieth century, when the previous emphasis on socialist modernization would give way to an obsession with high-tech innovation. The latter preoccupation would become a driving force in both Chinese society and Chinese art in the decades to come. However, at the same time, productions of the plays and the discourse surrounding them also offered an interpretation of theater-as-technoscience that emphasized artistic agency in the application of stage technology and required the rational engagement of audience members.

The obvious target of critique, in both the theory and practice of early post-Mao theater, was the aesthetics of the previous era, especially the *yangbanxi*. The "model works" of the Cultural Revolution had deployed sophisticated stage technologies—especially lighting and backdrop projections—in the service of what was in hindsight considered a twisted, destructive version of Maoist ideology and misguided attempts to control the artistic process and audience experience. Simplifying and revealing the stage apparatus was thus, most immediately, a rejection of the *yangbanxi* and theater's association with the radical politics of the Cultural Revolution. More fundamentally, it paralleled the general trend of this period to reject the utopianism of the entire high socialist period, from the early days of the CCP through the enthusiastic first decades of the PRC and the fervor of the Cultural Revolution. In retrospect, the technological fantasies and socialist utopianism of theater from the 1950s seemed to be "illusionistic" in the negative sense of illusion as misleading, or even a form of Marxian false consciousness. Discussions thus invoked many of the same terms as debates of the 1950s–1960s—such as *xieyi* aesthetics versus *xieshi* realism or the *xu/shi* binary—but their meaning had changed. No longer did these terms and concepts primarily link theatrical technology and labor to socialist ideals, national pride, and industrialization. Instead, using these aesthetic tools and their associated technologies to prompt audiences to reflect critically on what goes on behind the scenes, both in theater and in politics, now became central. In other words, lifting the curtain on stage technology transformed into a suggestive, or even metaphorical act—a materialization of the idea of theater itself as a revelatory medium.

# Coda

On July 11, 2012, a production entitled *Thunderstorm 2.0* (雷雨2.0) premiered at the Trojan Horse Theater (木马剧场) in Beijing. Inspired by Cao Yu's 1934 play *Thunderstorm*, this version 2.0 borrowed the language of computer updates and interface enhancements while paring down the play to its bare essentials.[1] Cao Yu's byzantine network of relationships and heavy-handed portrayal of an outdated social structure were replaced by a single love triangle between a man and two women. Onstage, in place of highly realistic scenery behind a fourth wall, were three separate box sets representing three different rooms in an early 1990s Beijing apartment. Even the thunderstorm itself—so essential to the original play and early productions—was transformed into pure metaphor, with not a single thunder, lightning, or rain effect in the entire ninety-minute performance (fig. 6.1).

This curious incidence of a thunderless *Thunderstorm* did not, however, imply a turn away from stage technology or an oversimplification of the complex themes of the original. Instead, director Wang Chong 王翀 (b. 1982) exchanged the now-familiar stage apparatus of lighting and sound effects for a tangle of tripods, video cameras, editing equipment, and cables in full view of the audience. Throughout the production, camera operators moved around the stage alongside the actors, and the images they captured were projected onto a single large screen suspended above the crowded stage. Rather than provoking affective responses in audience members or propelling the play's action forward, the cameras and screen splintered the story and provided a more direct window into the emotional worlds of the play's female characters. Newer technologies of interiority and intimacy replaced the technologies of atmosphere called for by Cao Yu's stage directions (discussed in chapter 2). This gave audience members more agency over their own viewing experience

Fig. 6.1. Publicity photo from 2012 production of *Thunderstorm 2.0*, depicting onstage technical equipment and live-feed video projected on a large screen. Photograph by Yang Ken; courtesy Wang Chong and Théatre du Rêve Expérimental.

and, at times, left them thoroughly confused about the very fundamentals of how to watch such a play.

Ten years later, screens onstage and the mixing of media in live performance have become much more common in forms of Chinese theater that range from the experimental (like *Thunderstorm 2.0*) to large-scale commercial performance to state propaganda. The specific technologies featured in these performances have likewise transitioned from being unprecedented (and at high risk of failure) to ubiquitous. The use of LED screens in performance provides one example of this shift: when film director Zhang Yimou 张艺谋 (b. 1950) unfurled a 473-meter-long LED scroll at the Opening Ceremony of the 2008 Beijing Summer Olympics, the entire world marveled. When he repeated and enhanced the feat for the 2022 Beijing Winter Olympics Opening Ceremony by covering an entire stadium floor with LED panels, global audiences barely blinked. Even in the PRC, where news coverage celebrated the production's technical ingenuity more loudly than elsewhere, the basic concept no longer felt novel. Equally advanced uses of screens could also be found, for example, in the commercial tourist production titled *Village Opera of Lu Town* (鲁镇社戏) that had opened the previous year. Situated within a theme park dedicated to revered modern writer Lu Xun 鲁迅 (1881–1936), *Village Opera of Lu Town* not only featured forty-four large LED panels, but suspended them above the stage and moved them into different configurations throughout the performance.[2] This production was only the latest in an entirely new genre, called real-scene landscape performances (山水实景演出), that has gained popularity throughout the country in the past two decades and often features spectacular uses of cutting-edge stage technology. Director Wang Chong and his theater collective, Théâtre du Rêve Expérimental (薪传实验剧团), have also moved into new territory with increasingly bold political commentary in work like *The Revolutionary Model Play 2.0* (样板戏 2.0, 2015) and *Made in China 2.0* (2020/2023), as well as a fully virtual version of *Waiting for Godot* in April 2020 that responded directly to COVID-19 lockdowns. Wang Chong is now one of several in a "new generation" of Chinese avant-garde directors who routinely experiment with different modes of intermediality onstage.[3]

Contemporary Chinese theater trends thus underscore both the continued importance of theatrical technicity and the legacies of the specific cases explored throughout this book. On one level, Wang Chong's *Thunderstorm 2.0* seems to reinforce the importance of historical genealogy and canon through its intertextual engagement with Cao Yu's *Thunderstorm*. *Thunderstorm* remains one of the most important *huaju* plays of the twentieth century; as both a prominent playwright and later head of the Beijing People's Art Theater, Cao Yu played a central role in the development of Chinese theater from the 1930s to the 1990s. Yet the importance of stage technology demonstrated by this study also suggests that even the most canonical dramatic texts cannot be thought of only as texts, and adaptation too must be considered in relation to technicity. In other words, later performances and new plays inspired by *Thunderstorm* exist in dialogue with both the original text and the history of how it has been staged. With *Thunderstorm* in the BPAT repertoire, for example, there exists a practice of literally "re-producing" (复排) the play in accordance with a previous stage version, which became popular in the

1950s. This concept of re-producing relies on copying the technical elements of that 1950s production, designed by Chen Yongxiang 陈永祥 (1925–2013), Song Yin 宋垠 (1924–2014), and Guan Zaisheng 关哉生 (1907–75): set, lighting, sound, costumes, makeup, special effects, and even the actors' blocking, gestures, and character interpretation. Wang Chong's *Thunderstorm 2.0*, in contrast, works in opposition to the practice of re-producing. As Wang has stated in an interview: "I am not satisfied with the fact that *Hamlet* can be performed in endless ways, but there is only one way to do *Thunderstorm*."[4] With more differences than similarities, Wang's *Thunderstorm 2.0* thus must be viewed both in terms of its technological innovations and as an intervention into a theatrical canon defined by mechanical reproducibility. By taking technics as method, one can understand more fully the extent of Wang's intertextual and inter*technical* engagement with the original play and its many stage productions.

At the same time that it targets Chinese canon and canonicity, Wang's work—like both large-scale commercial performance and the screen-forward aesthetics of Zhang Yimou productions—also clearly operates in conversation with global theatrical trends. Live-feed cameras and large screens onstage, multiple perspectives, and meditations on the relationship between mediation and liveness have become common techniques and themes in experimental work from around the world. Meanwhile, high-tech spectacle sells to popular audiences on Broadway and in Beijing alike. Yet Chinese theater is often left out of critical and scholarly conversations on these topics, and similarities are assumed to be imitative or derivative of "Western" theater.[5] Perhaps in reaction, a trend in the opposite direction also exists: much of the discourse surrounding technological innovation in Chinese performance emphasizes when a particular feat or device is unprecedented or unique, especially relative to similar technologies elsewhere. Articles on the infrastructure of the National Center for the Performing Arts (国家大剧院, or NCPA) in Beijing, for instance, claim that its revolving stage, which can both turn and lift using a combination of electric and hydraulic systems, is the only one of its kind in the country and a rarity even internationally.[6] Contemporary Chinese stage technology and productions that employ high-tech devices thus remain trapped between being denied a legitimate place in a global conversation and a compensatory overemphasis on innovation. As with modern technology in the late Qing dynasty, this tension is one that can be found not only in the theater world but also in discussions on Chinese technology in general.

Here, too, the history of Chinese stage technology suggests an essential corrective to how such global connections are perceived and understood. As this study has shown, there has been a transnational component to modern stage technology since its introduction into China in the late nineteenth century, as well as anxiety about China's level of theatrical artistry and technological development relative to Europe and the United States. The transnational nature of both material technology transfer and knowledge circulation makes foreign points of reference common in the historical record. Throughout the twentieth century, Chinese theater artists continually interacted with foreign theater makers, translated foreign texts on the practical and aesthetic applications of stage technology, and compared their own technical capacities and artistic results to foreign models. Yet the case studies in this book also show that these modes of international engagement were diverse and nuanced, and while sometimes imitative, they were far from derivative of or lesser than their foreign counterparts (even when the technology itself was technically less sophisticated). Instead, Chinese theater artists drew inspiration from personal encounters with the foreign, found ways to relate foreign texts to local contexts, adapted foreign technologies to the conditions and materials available to them, and treated foreign models with admiration and skepticism in equal parts. This is true of theater artists worldwide, but Chinese theater artists stand out for their ingenuity and how they acknowledge (and at times evade) cross-cultural politics in even the most technical innovations.

This can be seen especially clearly in the midcentury movement to create homegrown (*tu*) technology discussed in chapter 3, which presages the way theater artists—and "makers" more generally—engage with technology on a hyperlocal scale today.[7] Homegrown technology of the 1950s–1960s was rooted in Maoist ideology and a desire for national self-sufficiency, but the ethos of localized innovation was born long before Mao came to power and persists well into the high-tech twenty-first century. In another Théâtre du Rêve Expérimental piece titled *Ghosts 2.0* (群鬼 2.0, 2014), for instance, cameras on tripods fed live-capture footage to a time-stamped four-by-four matrix projected onto a large screen. The image evoked the look of a classic closed-circuit television video array, which resonated with both global concerns about the ubiquitous monitoring that is characteristic of the digital age and more specific uses of news media control and surveillance technology by PRC authorities.[8] However, this effect was not the original artistic intention, but rather was born of the fact that the CCTV switcher was more easily acquired and less expensive than professional digital video editing and switching equipment. Far from distracting or detracting from the performance, the technical team's ad hoc repurposing of existing technology again added layers of meaning that resonated with the playtext. The actors' blocking, in combination with the CCTV frame, also facilitated a confrontation between them and the political machine: performers frequently walked up to a camera and delivered their lines straight into its lens, demonstrating a full awareness of someone (authorities, audience) watching their every move. Whether a *tu* revolving stage or repurposing of surveillance apparatus, Chinese stage technology repeatedly demonstrates the power of human agency, even when that agency is exerted *within* an ideological apparatus.

On another level, the history of how theater, technology, and politics intersect in China invites observers of contemporary theater to see layers of complexity in what might otherwise appear to be hackneyed narratives. Political theater persists in the PRC today, both in work that is critical of the government (albeit often circuitously, due to censorship) and in lavish government-sponsored productions that celebrate national culture and party history. Zhang Yimou's Olympics Opening Ceremonies have presented versions of the latter to a global audience, but large-scale propaganda performance is omnipresent and has been a part of the CCP playbook since its early days. Recently, multimedia-rich "red history plays" (红色历史剧) have become a top trend in this vein, but they were preceded by productions like *The East Is Red* and Cultural Revolution *yangbanxi* (discussed in chapters 3 and 4) as well as similar epics staged for important party anniversaries.[9] One such epic, entitled *Victory and Peace* (胜利与和平), premiered on the evening of September 3, 2015 in the Great Hall of the People as part of celebrations commemorating the seventieth anniversary of China's victory in the Second Sino-Japanese War. In ninety minutes, more than twenty different vignettes jump disjointedly from gruesome depictions of massacre and destruction (exaggerated by large-scale moving projections); to romanticized ballets of Communist soldiers; to cloying paeans to the present era of peace and prosperity, with happy children singing and a montage of images depicting a diverse Chinese nation in the background.

Like *Thunderstorm 2.0*, the performance of *Victory and Peace* also (intentionally or not) evokes a media genealogy that once again connects politics, aesthetics, and technology. In one particular scene, a large chorus of Chinese laborers appears beneath projected video footage of the Japanese invasion of Manchuria in 1931. Text runs over the historical footage, while a voice-over reads: "Statement by the Communist Party of China on the Brutal Occupation of the Three Northeast Provinces by Japanese Imperialists / The Japa-

Fig. 6.2. Choreography to the lyrics "Roar, Yellow River" (怒吼吧黃河) during the 2015 performance of *Victory and Peace*. Source: CCTV broadcast, *Shengli yu heping: Jinian Kangzhan shengli 70 zhou nian wenyi wanhui*, September 4, 2015, https://youtu.be/Rv-EZXM5kAA, at 21:34.

nese Imperialists have invaded China and are killing more and more Chinese people / Let us have our weapons ready to teach the Japanese aggressors a serious lesson!"[10] With that, the chorus of dancers comes to life, moving in slow motion as the lights shift to illuminate their half-clothed bodies. The background projection cuts to moving images of a raging river. The performers contort their faces and begin to sing stridently, "Roar, Yellow River!" (怒吼吧黃河) (fig. 6.2). Meanwhile, projections spill across the stage and into the auditorium, covering every inch of the walls and ceiling. As the music swells in an operatic register, the audience is fully immersed in the torrents of indignation and revolutionary conviction pouring forth from the stage. On the surface, this vignette seems to be nothing more than a hyperbolic rewriting of historical Chinese resistance against oppression with an ideological veneer; taking technics as method, however, highlights connections between this production and the 1933 Shanghai production of Sergei Tret'iakov's *Roar, China!* (discussed in chapter 1). This scene in *Victory and Peace* does not directly adapt Tret'iakov's narrative; rather, it indirectly echoes the earlier production's use of stage technology to accentuate the play's underlying political message and to galvanize its audiences. This in turn helps to illuminate how the performance works on its audience and calls attention to a historical depth that might not otherwise be apparent from its unnuanced aesthetics.

Contextualizing contemporary performance in relation to the history of Chinese stage technology also demonstrates larger continuities in how theater intersects with scientific and technological development, broadly writ, across seeming historical breaks. In one sense, the death of Mao Zedong and beginning of the Reform Era in the late 1970s did constitute a significant paradigm shift into what is now termed the "postsocialist" period. Likewise, the rise of PRC president and CCP general secretary Xi Jinping has been seen by many as a new historical pivot point, with the current era defined by fast-paced technological advancement alongside increased government control, international tensions, fears of an economic downturn, and moral discipline. Since the late 1970s, the PRC has devoted extensive resources first to "catching up" with global scientific and technological developments of the mid-twentieth century and now to trying to surpass foreign tech giants (especially those based in the United States). As discussed in chapter 5, the theater reflected this national reorientation both by staging plays focused on scientific discovery and by experimenting with stage technology. Similarly, the twenty-first-century ubiquity of multimedia scenography and the construction of state-of-the-art theater spaces with cutting-edge lighting, sound, and special effects equipment correlate closely with how the current regime frames and supports technological growth. At the Nineteenth Party Congress in 2017, for example, President Xi Jinping positioned technological innovation as key to building a socialist nation, calling for the PRC to become a "country of innovators."[11] Innovation, however, has long been essential and was valued even in Cultural Revolution–era *yangbanxi*, as chapter 4 shows, albeit in a much narrower sense. Technology may be more important than ever, but it is not newly important. Technological innovation in contemporary theater therefore should be understood simultaneously as participating in its unique historical moment and in relation to innovations past.

Finally, reconsidering key case studies in modern Chinese theater from the perspective of stage technology demonstrates how theoretical and material engagement with those technologies creates dialectical relationships between associated concepts: fantasy and practicality, control and agency, innovation and failure. From the turn of the twentieth century, Chinese theater artists' use of stage technologies was shaped by the tension between their imagination of what those technologies could do—based on viewing and reading about their use in foreign productions, as well as their translation of foreign textbooks and how-to guides—and the material conditions under which they attempted to produce theater. During the Seventeen Years period, technological fantasy became an increasingly widespread element of theatrical culture. Audiences were asked to imagine the effects of sophisticated stage technologies through vernacular (and more practical) approximations. Perhaps the greatest fantasy offered by modern stage technology, however, was that of control: the idea that electric lighting, revolving sets, or perfectly constructed props could guarantee a politically galvanizing or ideologically appropriate audience response to a play. Yet the cases discussed throughout this book demonstrate that even artists who accepted this concept of the theater repeatedly exercised their own agency in determining *how* stage technology was utilized. Their ingenuity was often in the service of a political or governmental agenda, but their solutions to technical problems could be charmingly idiosyncratic or even hint at the ultimate fallacy of complete control over art and audiences. (It is tempting, for example, to read the use of a simple rubber band to hold batteries in place in *The Red Lantern*'s titular prop as unintentionally mirroring the inner tenuousness of the seemingly well-oiled party machine.) Indeed, the stage technologies discussed in the preceding chapters highlight just how often innovation comes within a hair's breadth of complete system failure. For instance, constructing makeshift lighting dimmers and using electricity to generate lightning effects showcased early twentieth-century Chinese theater technicians' ingenuity, while the not-unlikely failure of these technologies threatened both their operators' personal safety and the longevity of Shanghai's theater venues. For the artists involved in creating theater during the Seventeen Years period and the Cultural Revolution, technological failure was inseparable from ideological failure, in an environment where the latter carried the possibility of persecution or even death.

Here, technology and the theater intersect in one final sense: both seem not only capable of failure, but prone to it. The oft-quoted words of Samuel Beckett—"Try again. Fail again. Fail better."—have served equally as a mantra for Silicon Valley start-up culture and theater artists questing for that ever-elusive combination of artistic and critical success.[12] Drawing on the work of Paul Virilio, Sara Jane Bailes writes in her study of the "poetics of failure" in contemporary US and British performance that "a thing's failure is inevitably summoned to the horizon by virtue of its invention . . . [Yet] whilst indexing the invention of a thing's possible demise, failure is intrinsically linked to the ability to see more and to the expansion of our understanding of an object's properties."[13] Theater, with its originary technicity, always holds the potential for a missed cue or for an actor to go up on a line. This is as true for the simplest shadow puppetry as for a production involving dozens of LED screens. Indeed, the potential for failure is a core component of theater's liveness and what ultimately makes stage technology a part of that liveness, rather than opposed to it. In a society where artistic and political control are both core issues for theater, like modern China, what Bailes says of her case studies is thus all the more significant: "By opening up a discussion of failure, one can begin to interrogate rather than deny the difficulty of stage representation—its weaknesses and dis-ease and what these might indicate—as a space of critical resistance."[14] Many of the productions analyzed in this book may seem far from "a space of critical resistance," with their innovations more often attempting to aid the prevailing ideology than to contest it. Yet the combined and heightened chance of failure in stage technology nonetheless bespeaks both the agency and the courage behind each risk taken.

The scholarly enterprise, too, holds its own potential for failure, but thankfully the happy accident of an unexpected archival find or unforeseen connection often makes research all the richer or points to new directions for future inquiry. Indeed, throughout this book, there are a number of secondary questions that my analysis raises, but does not pursue in all possible directions. First, the materials on which much of this study relies—performance manuals, technical treatises, handbooks for aspiring artists and audiences—connect it to the fields of book history and knowledge production. I do not, however, fully contextualize these theater-specific publications within the history of the publishing industry or fully explore connections with other areas of knowledge production and circulation. How do theater handbooks of the 1950s and early 1960s relate to painting and film projectionist handbooks, for example, or even similar texts in more technical fields of industrial production? What might examining artistic and scientific/technical manuals side by side tell us about what knowledge itself meant during the high socialist period? To pursue this question, in particular, would also lead to further questions about the reception of such manuals: How were they used by everyday readers, especially in milieus outside of large state-sponsored institutions? How did these texts contribute to the lived experience of specific historical moments?

How readers interacted with the textual technologies of manuals and handbooks also connects to this study's repeated invocation of labor and references to human bodies interfacing with technology both onstage and off. Here, too, Chinese theater might contribute to conversations on these issues that are ongoing across multiple fields. What could a study focused on the

Chinese context contribute to our broader understanding of theatrical, or even artistic, labor? Or, within studies of China, how could theatrical labor expand or challenge extant narratives about what labor has meant, first under socialism and then in postsocialist society? In addition, this book has largely not addressed the stage technologies that most directly impact the actor, like body mics or costumes and makeup. Yet in studies of theater and intermediality, for instance, the relationship between actor and technology is often foregrounded. How might a Chinese history of this relationship parallel or diverge from the trends articulated in this book, which is not anthropocentric in that way? How might other topics that center the human, such as institutional histories and actor training programs, shed further light on how and why innovations in theater architecture, scenography, lighting, sound, and so on occurred? And once again, what do Chinese cases add to broader theorizations of human–technology interaction, which are still too often rooted in European and US case studies and contexts?

Finally, this book's core argument for the importance of thinking theater through technicity also opens up new directions for research related to medium specificity and medium ontology. One example of this lies in the many connections between theater and film that arise throughout the study. Many of the theater artists who appear here in relation to their work onstage also worked in film. Yuan Muzhi, for instance, is referenced as the editor of *Play* and an actor in *Roar, China!* (in chapter 1), then again as the director of films set in 1930s Shanghai (in chapter 3). Specific scenographic techniques, such as projected backdrops, also created technological and aesthetic connections across the two media. Moreover, the very concept of thinking of the stage *as* an apparatus evokes the way that, in film, it is taken as a given that the camera is inseparable from the work of art (even as apparatus theory itself has been complicated and challenged). What would it mean if theater were more often approached with technology and apparatus as starting points, rather than dramatic text, acting, or directing? What new potentials would unfold, and how might our understanding of what theater *is* change with this shift of perspective?

Ultimately, this book affirms the centrality of stage technology within the making of modern Chinese theater, but it also demonstrates how technology matters in unexpected ways. As I have shown, specific stage technologies, such as lighting dimmers, revolving stages, and projections, constitute unlikely points of material connection between the theater and technological modernization, knowledge production, political agendas, and artistic innovation in China. At the same time, however, the many cases studied in this book also subvert our understanding of stage technology and of Chinese theater in surprising ways. Stage technology, after all, exists on a spectrum between two poles. On one end is the spectacular technology that amazes and, in doing so, calls attention to itself. When a stage-sized gunboat breaks apart to become two other set pieces or moving projections wash over the entire theater, the audience applauds the technology itself. On the other end of the spectrum lies technology that at its best goes completely unnoticed by the audience—the rubber band holding batteries inside the functional red lantern, or a makeshift dimmer hidden backstage. Throughout the twentieth century, Chinese theater artists and technicians were engaged with experiments across the whole range of this spectrum, but their ingenuity shines brightest at the latter end. The story of stage technology in modern China, then, is not a teleology of advancements over time. Rather, it is a history of how innovative theater artists, often under extreme conditions, mobilized the tools of the stage to make the impossible possible—if only for a moment.

# Notes

## Introduction

1. "Meiguo Niuyu de Luokexi (Roxy) juyuan zhi wutai dengguang shebei," *Juxue yuekan* 2, nos. 7–8 (1933): n.p.

2. For one example of a member of a court delegation who wrote in detail about impressive technological displays, see Li Gui, *A Journey to the East: Li Gui's A New Account of a Trip around the Globe,* trans. Charles Desnoyers (Ann Arbor: University of Michigan Press, 2004), especially 117–24. On Chinese responses to the Paris Opera, in particular, see Siyuan Liu, *Performing Hybridity in Colonial-Modern China* (New York: Palgrave Macmillan, 2013), 14–15.

3. Historian Xiang Jiqing notes that these various terms were then organized under the umbrella term of *wutai meishu* 舞台美術 (scenography) in the 1950s, although the basic concept entered China in the Republican era (1912–1949). Xian Jiqing, *Minguo shiqi Shanghai wutai yanjiu* (Shanghai: Shanghai renmin chubanshe, 2016), 152–53.

4. Jiao Juyin, "Wutai guang chujiang," *Juxue yuekan* 2, nos. 7–8 (1933): 1–64 [i.e., 167–230], at 1 [i.e., 167]; reprinted in *Jiao Juyin wenji,* vol. 1, ed. Yang Hansheng (Beijing: Wenhua yishu chubanshe, 1986), 61–130, at 61. The idea that the merging of science and technology with art was characteristic of modern theater also has a transnational dimension; similar ideas can be found in seminal texts by Hiram Kelly Moderwell, Kenneth Macgowan, and Sheldon Cheney, which were often cited by Chinese theater artists of the 1930s–1940s. For Cheney, see chap. 1, note 14; for Moderwell, chap. 2, note 74.

5. See, for example, Yu's essay "Theater Art and Scientific Invention" (戲劇藝術與科學發明), which was published as part of his serialized column "My Humble Gift" (欽羨) in the *Morning Post Supplement* (晨報副刊) in 1924 and reprinted in his collected essays in 1927. Chen Dabei also comments on the relationship between advances in theater and sciences in his essays on amateur theater, which were also first serialized by the *Morning Post Supplement* in 1921 and then published as *Amateur Theater* (愛美的戲劇) in 1922. Yu Shangyuan, "Qinxian: Xiju yishu yu kexue faming," *Chenbao fukan* (January 26, 1924), 3–4; reprinted in Yu,

*Xiju lunji* (Shanghai: Beixin shuju, 1927), 233–38. Chen Dabei, *Aimei de xiju* (Beijing: Chenbaoshe, 1922; repr. Shanghai: Shanghai shudian, 1992).

6. W. B. Worthen, *Shakespeare, Technicity, Theatre* (Cambridge: Cambridge University Press, 2020), 10.

7. Fan-Pen Li Chen, *Chinese Shadow Theatre: History, Popular Religion and Women Warriors* (Montreal: McGill–Queen's University Press, 2007), 22. Versions of the anecdote can be found in both the first-century CE *Book of Han* (漢書) and in the earlier (ca. 91 BCE) *Records of the Grand Historian* (史記).

8. Joseph Needham, with Wang Ling and Kenneth Girwood Robinson, *Science and Civilisation in China*, vol. 4: *Physics and Physical Technology*, pt. 1: *Physics* (Cambridge: Cambridge University Press, 1962), 122–23.

9. The term "originary technicity" is most often associated with the work of French philosopher Bernard Stiegler, especially his three-volume work on *Technics and Time* (Stanford: Stanford University Press, 1998–2011); Stiegler, however, builds on ideas drawn from Jacques Derrida and others. Arthur Bradley traces the coining of the term to Derrida; see Bradley, *Originary Technicity: The Theory of Technology from Marx to Derrida* (Basingstoke: Palgrave Macmillan, 2011), 2–3.

10. Chris Salter, *Entangled: Technology and the Transformation of Performance* (Cambridge, MA: MIT Press, 2010), xxxv.

11. Robin Bernstein, *Racial Innocence: Performing American Childhood from Slavery to Civil Rights* (New York: New York University Press, 2011); Andrew Sofer, *The Stage Life of Props* (Ann Arbor: University of Michigan Press, 2003).

12. The debate over mediatization and liveness inaugurated by Philip Auslander and Peggy Phelan in the 1990s has given way to more recent work on multimedia performance and intermediality in performance by scholars such as Bruce Barton, Sarah Bay-Cheung, Freda Chappel, Lars Ellestrom, Chiel Kattenbelt, Jennifer Parker-Starbuck, Irina Rajewsky, and many others.

13. On the absence of "technology" as a concept in premodern China, see, for example, Peter J. Golas, *Picturing Technology in China: From Earliest Times to the Nineteenth Century* (Hong Kong: Hong Kong University Press, 2015), ix.

14. Nan Wang, "Philosophical Perspectives on Technology in Chinese Society," *Technology in Society* 35, no. 3 (2013): 165–71, at 166. See also Francesca Bray, *Technology and Gender: Fabrics of Power in Late Imperial China* (Berkeley: University of California Press, 1997), for a discussion of the relationship between technique and technology.

15. Francesca Bray, "Technics and Civilization in Late Imperial China: An Essay in the Cultural History of Technology," *Osiris* 13 (1998): 11–33, at 20.

16. For Stiegler's discussion of the pros-thesis in relation to the myths of Prometheus and Epimetheus, see Bernard Stiegler, *Technics and Time 1: The Fault of Epimetheus*, trans. Richard Beardsworth and George Collins (Stanford: Stanford University Press, 1998), 192–95.

17. W. B. Worthen, "Shakespearean Technicity," in *The Oxford Handbook of Shakespeare and Performance*, ed. James C. Bulman (Oxford: Oxford University Press, 2017), 321–40, at 321; see also *Shakespeare, Technicity, Theatre*, 28.

18. Worthen, "Shakespearean Technicity," 321.

19. Salter, *Entangled*, xxxiii.

20. Benjamin A. Elman, "Toward a History of Modern Science in Republican China," in *Science and Technology in Modern China, 1880s–1940s*, ed. Jing Tsu and Benjamin A. Elman (Leiden: Brill, 2014), 15–38, at 20–21.

21. On railroads and telegraphs, see, for example, Elisabeth Köll, *Railroads and the Transformation of China* (Cambridge, MA: Harvard University Press, 2019); and Zhou Yongming, *Historicizing Online Politics: Telegraphy, the Internet, and Political Participation in China* (Stanford: Stanford University Press, 2006).

22. Liang Qichao, "On the Relationship between Fiction and the Government of the People," in *Modern Chinese Literary Thought: Writings on Literature, 1893–1945*, ed. and trans. Kirk A. Denton (Stanford: Stanford University Press, 1996), 74–81.

23. Liu, *Performing Hybridity*, 14, 19–30, 38–42.

24. On premodern Chinese theater architecture, see, for example, Che Wenming, *Zhongguo gu xitai diaocha yanjiu* (Beijing: Zhonghua shuju, 2011) and *Zhongguo gudai juchang shi* (Beijing: Shangwu yinshu guan, 2021); Liao Ben, *Zhongguo gudai juchang shi* (Zhengzhou: Zhongzhou guji chubanshe, 1997); and Zhou Yibai, *Zhongguo juchang shi*, 2nd ed. (Changsha: Shangwu yinshua guan, 1940).

25. Liana Chen, *Staging for the Emperors: A History of Qing Court Theatre, 1683–1923* (Amherst, NY: Cambria Press, 2021); Joshua Goldstein, *Drama Kings: Players and Publics in the Re-Creation of Peking Opera, 1870–1937* (Berkeley: University of California Press, 2007); Colin Mackerras, *The Chinese Theatre in Modern Times: From 1840 to the Present Day* (Amherst: University of Massachusetts Press, 1975).

26. In the nineteenth century, the palace maintained its own theater troupe. At times, civilian actors and musicians were invited to perform at court; during other periods, they were banned. For a discussion of changes in how palace troupe management shifted throughout the nineteenth century, see Chen, *Staging for the Emperors*, 50–59.

27. Chen, *Staging for the Emperors*, 39–76.

28. Wei Bingbing, "Semicolonialism and Urban Space: Architectural Transformation of Chinese Theaters in Late Qing Shanghai, 1860s–1900s," *Chinese Historical Review* 17, no. 2 (2010): 166–92, at 169. The first teahouse-style theaters in Shanghai were the Fragrance-Filled Courtyard (滿庭芳) and Red Laurel (丹桂) theaters. Such theaters went by a variety of names, including "tea garden" (茶園), "play garden" (戲園), "song hall" (歌館), and "play hall" (戲館). Other important urban venues included lineage associations (會館/堂會), which were civil and commercial institutions composed of members connected through place of origin, dialect spoken, or surname. See also Andrea Goldman, *Opera and the City: The Politics of Culture in Beijing, 1770–1900* (Stanford: Stanford University Press, 2012), 67; Goldstein, *Drama Kings*, 60–61.

29. Xu Peng, "Hearing the Opera: 'Teahouse Mimesis' and the Aesthetics of Noise in Early *Jingju* Recordings, 1890s–1910s," *CHINOPERL: Journal of Chinese Oral and Performing Literature* 36, no. 1 (2017): 1–21; Zhang Zhen, "Teahouse,

Shadowplay, Bricolage: *Laborer's Love* and the Question of Early Chinese Cinema," in *Cinema and Urban Culture in Shanghai, 1922–1943*, ed. Yingjin Zhang (Stanford: Stanford University Press, 1999), 27–50.

30. Gaslight was first installed in Shanghai's foreign concession in 1864. The Lanxin Theater featured performances primarily by the Amateur Dramatic Club of Shanghai, which comprised mostly British expatriate actors. Amateur theatricals in Shanghai began as early as 1850 and were originally housed in makeshift warehouse spaces known as "godown" theaters. Liu, *Performing Hybridity*, 34; J. H. Haan, "Thalia and Terpsichore on the Yangtze: A Survey of Foreign Theatre and Music in Shanghai, 1850–1865," *Journal of the Hong Kong Branch of the Royal Asiatic Society* 29 (1989), 158–251.

31. Xian, *Minguo shiqi Shanghai wutai yanjiu*, 181.

32. Sources differ on the first use of electricity in a Shanghai theater. Xian Jiqing gives the date as 1884, but Liao Ben cites a *Shenbao* article from 1886 to argue that electric lights were used in *xiyuan* well before the twentieth century. See Xian, *Minguo shiqi Shanghai wutai yanjiu*, 183–84; Liao, *Zhongguo gudai juchang shi*, 159–60.

33. Concrete references to *dengcaixi* date as early as the late Ming dynasty, but they attained new levels of popularity and sophistication during the Qing dynasty after the performance style was absorbed into the palace theater repertoire. Jia Zhigang, *Zhongguo jindai xiqu shi (shang), 1840–1911* (Beijing: Wenhua yishu chubanshe, 2011), 339–40.

34. Goldstein describes the implications of the shift from teahouse to playhouse as a site of *jingju* performance, especially in relation to acting technique, repertoire, and actor–audience relationship. See Goldstein, *Drama Kings*, 55–88.

35. Goldstein, *Drama Kings*, 76–79.

36. Revolving *set pieces*, however, had been used in *dengcaixi* much earlier. These were described as akin to early forms of film projection, like the zoetrope (or "running-horse light" [走馬燈] in Chinese), or Muybridge strips. Xu Xingjie and Cai Shicheng, eds., *Shanghai jingju zhi* (Shanghai: Shanghai wenhua chubanshe, 1999), 296; cited in Xian, *Minguo shiqi Shanghai wutai yanjiu*, 166.

37. The earliest *kabuki* revolving stages (*mawari-butai* 廻り舞台) developed in the early eighteenth century and were made by placing a revolving disk on top of a normal stage; later innovations involved cutting a circular section out of the main stage and positioning stagehands underneath to rotate it during performances. This latter innovation is credited to playwright Namiki Shōzō 並木正三 (1730–73), in 1758. Li Chang provides only the surname for the technician involved in installing the New Stage mechanism, noting that the connection was made through the immensely popular *kabuki* actor Ichikawa Sadanji II 市川左團次 (1880–1940). Li Chang, *Yong bu luomu* (Beijing: Zhongguo xiju chubanshe, 2012), 7. On Japanese revolving stages, see James R. Brandon and Samuel L. Leiter, *Kabuki Plays on Stage*, vol. 2: *Villainy and Vengeance, 1773–1799* (Honolulu: University of Hawai'i Press, 2002), 4; Julia A. Iezzi, "Architecture and Stage of Traditional Asian Theatre: Japan," in *The Routledge Handbook of Asian Theatre*, ed. Siyuan Liu (New York: Routledge,

2016), 231–35, at 232; Chad Randl, *Revolving Architecture: A History of Buildings That Rotate, Swivel, and Pivot* (New York: Princeton Architectural Press, 2008), 28–30; Uzuhiko Tsuboi, "Historical Development of Revolving Stages of Theaters Invented in Japan—Improvement by Adoption of European Culture," *Proceedings of the International Conference on Business and Technology Transfer* 1 (2002): 207–12, at 207–8.

38. The First Stage was damaged by fire soon after opening. "Wei fen yiqian zhi Beijing Diyi Wutai," *Shenbao*, June 13, 1914, 6.

39. Soon after, the technology spread throughout Europe and across the Atlantic. The Liberty Theatre in Oakland, CA, and the New Theatre in New York, for instance, installed revolving stages in 1909. For an earlier history of revolving stages, see Harold M. Priest, "Marino, Leonardo, Francini, and the Revolving Stage," *Renaissance Quarterly* 35, no. 1 (1982): 36–60.

40. Kenneth Macgowan, *The Theatre of Tomorrow* (New York: Boni & Liveright, 1921), 38; Hiram K. Moderwell, *The Theatre of To-day* (New York: John Lane Co., 1914), 39–40.

41. Tsuboi, "Historical Development of Revolving Stages," 209.

42. The first use of gaslight in a theater took place in 1804, at the Lyceum Theatre in London, with the technology first used for the house rather than onstage. Gaslit stages soon followed, with the Lyceum, Drury Lane, and Covent Garden leading the way in 1817–18. The Savoy initially opened in October 1881 with electric light in the house and gaslight onstage; the first performance to use electricity to light the stage took place on December 28, 1881. Frederick Penzel, *Theatre Lighting before Electricity* (Middletown, CT: Wesleyan University Press, 1978), 35; 40. See also Gösta M. Bergman, *Lighting in the Theatre* (Totowa, NJ: Rowman and Littlefield, 1977), 252–63; Terence Rees, *Theatre Lighting in the Age of Gas* (London: Society for Theatre Research, 1978), 6–11.

43. Wolfgang Schivelbusch, *Disenchanted Night: The Industrialization of Light in the Nineteenth Century* (Berkeley: University of California Press, 1988), 199.

44. Schivelbusch, *Disenchanted Night*, 201.

45. Schivelbusch, *Disenchanted Night*, 23, 25.

46. Rees, *Theatre Lighting in the Age of Gas*, ix.

47. Ulf Otto, "Enter Electricity: An Allegory's Stage Appearance between Verité and Varieté," *Centaurus* 57, no. 3 (2015): 192–211, at 193.

48. Jia, *Zhongguo jindai xiqu shi (shang)*, 340.

49. Jia, *Zhongguo jindai xiqu shi (shang)*, 340.

50. Xian, *Minguo shiqi Shanghai wutai yanjiu*, 173–77. In English, see Nancy Rao, "Li Xuefang Meets Mei Lanfang: Cantonese Opera's Significant Rise in Shanghai and Beyond," *CHINOPERL: Journal of Chinese Oral and Performing Literature* 39, no. 2 (2020): 151–81.

51. In the late nineteenth century, some *kabuki* theaters also adopted elements of Western theater architecture, such as the proscenium arch. See Iezzi, "Architecture and Stage: Japan," 232–33.

52. *Jiguan bujing* were especially popular in *dengcaixi* and serialized *jingju* performed from the 1910s onward. See Xian, *Minguo shiqi Shanghai wutai yanjiu*,

165–80; Wei Bingbing, "The Bifurcated Theater: Urban Space, Opera Entertainment, and Cultural Politics in Shanghai, 1900s–1930s" (PhD diss., Department of History, National University of Singapore, 2013), 178–86.

53. For use of special effects in court theater, see Chen, *Staging for the Emperors*; Wilt Idema, "Performances on a Three-Tiered Stage: Court Theatre during the Qianlong Era," in *Ad Seres et Tungusos: Festscrift für Martin Gimm zu seinem 65 am 21 Mai 1995*, ed. Lutz Bieg, Erling von Mende, and Martina Siebert (Weisbaden: Harrassowitz, 2000), 201–19.

54. See discussions in Xu, "Hearing the Opera," 6–12, and Zhang, "Teahouse, Shadowplay, Bricolage," 32–33.

55. Huang Changyong, "Shanghai: The Road to a Modern Performing Arts City," *TDR: The Drama Review* 65, no. 2 (2021): 150–66, at 150–51.

56. On these topics, see, for example, Goldman, *Opera and the City*; Goldstein, *Drama Kings*; Colin Mackerras, ed., *Chinese Theater: From Its Origins to the Present Day* (Honolulu: University of Hawai'i Press, 1983); Wei, "Bifurcated Theater"; Xiaoqing Ye, *Ascendant Peace in the Four Seas: Drama and the Qing Imperial Court* (Hong Kong: Chinese University of Hong Kong Press, 2012).

57. Joseph W. Esherick, "Ten Theses on the Chinese Revolution," *Modern China* 21, no. 1 (1995): 45–76, at 45.

58. The phrase that Mao initially used was "to start a revolution in technology"; later speeches and texts use the exact phrase *jishu geming*. See Mao Zedong, "Geming de zhuanbian he dang zai guodu shiqi de zongluxian," in *Mao Zedong wenji*, 8 vols. (Beijing: Renmin chubanshe, 1999), 6:316. Cited in Pan Fang, "Mao Zedong lun kexue jishu yu jishu geming—jinian Mao Zedong danchen 120 zhou nian," in *Mao Zedong yu Zhonghua minzu weida fuxing: Jinian Mao Zedong tongshi tansheng 120 zhou nian xueshu yantaohui lunwen ji (shang)* (Beijing: Zhongyang wenxian chubanshe, 2014); https://www.dswxyjy.org.cn/n1/2019/0228/c423718-30948362.html

59. In terms of historical periodization, the term "high socialist period" refers to when Mao Zedong rose to power and served as the central leader of the CCP, from the early 1940s to his death in 1976.

60. Related targets included building 896 cinemas and establishing 5,279 projection teams. *First Five-Year Plan for the Development of the National Economy of the People's Republic of China in 1953–1957 (Illustrated)* (Beijing: Foreign Languages Press, 1956), n.p.

61. The New Culture Movement (新文化運動) critiqued classical Chinese culture and social structures, and advocated basing a new national culture on democracy, science, vernacular literature, women's literature, and new modes of education. Many of the key figures in the New Culture Movement were also keenly interested in the arts as a component of national culture. The May Fourth Movement (五四運動) grew out of both the New Culture Movement and student protests that took place on May 4, 1919 in response to the proposed Treaty of Versailles. There is a vast body of scholarship on these two movements, in both Chinese and English. See, for example, Vera Schwarcz, *The Chinese Enlightenment: Intellectuals and the*

*Legacy of the May Fourth Movement of 1919* (Berkeley: University of California Press, 1986).

62. See chapter 2 of this study for a discussion of realism and theater technology. On literary realism, see, for example, Marston Anderson, *The Limits of Realism: Chinese Fiction in the Revolutionary Period* (Berkeley: University of California Press, 1990); David Der-wei Wang, *Fictional Realism in Twentieth-Century China: Mao Dun, Lao She, Shen Congwen* (New York: Columbia University Press, 1992).

63. "On New Democracy" was written in January 1940 and published in *Chinese Culture* (中國文化). Mao Zedong, "On New Democracy," in *Selected Works of Mao Tse-tung*, 5 vols. (Beijing: Foreign Languages Press, 1965), 2:339–84, at 2:339; 2:380–82.

64. Vladimir Lenin, "Party Organisation and Party Literature," in Lenin, *Collected Works*, 45 vols. (Moscow: Progress Publishers, 1965), 10:44–49, https://www.marxists.org/archive/lenin/works/1905/nov/13.htm. Original published in *Novaya Zhizn*, no. 12 (November 13, 1905).

65. Mao Zedong, "Zai Yan'an wenyi zuotanhui shang de jianghua," in *Mao Zedong xuanji*, 2nd ed., 4 vols. (Beijing: Renmin chubanshe, 1991), 3:847–79; Mao, "Talks at the Yan'an Conference on Literature and Art," trans. Bonnie S. McDougall, in *Mao Zedong's "Talks at the Yan'an Conference on Literature and Art": A Translation of the 1943 Text with Commentary* (Ann Arbor: University of Michigan Center for Chinese Studies, 1980), 55–86, at 75; see also 98n173 on different phrasing of "cog and screw" between the 1943/1944 and 1953/1966 versions.

66. As D. W. Fokkema has noted, Mao's famous invocation of Lenin seizes upon the image of the revolutionary machine and sidesteps Lenin's cautions against the application of a mechanical system for the creation of Communist Party literature. D. W. Fokkema, *Literary Doctrine in China and Soviet Influence, 1956–1960* (The Hague: Mouton, 1965), 9; Lenin, "Party Organization and Party Literature," 44–49.

67. Important exceptions include Christin Essin, *Working Backstage: A Cultural History and Ethnography of Technical Theater Labor* (Ann Arbor: University of Michigan Press, 2021) and the essays in Elizabeth A. Osborne and Christine Woodworth, eds., *Working in the Wings: New Perspectives on Theatre History and Labor* (Carbondale: Southern Illinois University Press, 2015).

68. The rehearsal process at state-sponsored institutions in the PRC from the mid-1950s onward is an exception to this general rule. At institutions like the Beijing People's Art Theater, most production teams include a "scene recorder" (场记) whose job it is to keep detailed records of rehearsals and meetings.

69. Lewis Mumford, *Technics and Civilization* (New York: Harcourt, Brace, 1934), 6.

70. Kuan-Hsing Chen, *Asia as Method: Toward Deimperialization* (Durham: Duke University Press, 2010). See also the special issue edited by Carlos Rojas on "Method as Method" of *Prism: Theory and Modern Chinese Literature* 16, no. 2 (2019).

71. Xiaomei Chen, *Staging Chinese Revolution: Theater, Film, and the Afterlives*

*of Propaganda* (New York: Columbia University Press, 2016) and *Performing the Socialist State: Modern Chinese Theater and Film Culture* (New York: Columbia University Press, 2023); Xing Fan, *Staging Revolution: Artistry and Aesthetics in Model Beijing Opera during the Cultural Revolution* (Hong Kong: Hong Kong University Press, 2018); Goldstein, *Drama Kings*; Liu, *Performing Hybridity*; Ma Junshan, *Yanju zhiye hua yundong yanjiu* (Beijing: Renmin wenxue chubanshe, 2007).

72. Goldstein, *Drama Kings*, 5.

73. Weihong Bao, *Fiery Cinema: The Emergence of an Affective Medium in China, 1915–1945* (Minneapolis: University of Minnesota Press, 2015); Andrew F. Jones, *Yellow Music: Media Culture and Modernity in the Chinese Jazz Age* (Durham: Duke University Press, 2001); Laikwan Pang, *The Distorting Mirror: Visual Modernity in China* (Honolulu: University of Hawai'i Press, 2007); Zhang Zhen, *An Amorous History of the Silver Screen: Shanghai Cinema, 1896–1937* (Chicago: University of Chicago Press, 2005).

74. Leo Marx, "Technology: The Emergence of a Hazardous Concept," *Technology and Culture* 51, no. 3 (2010): 561–77.

### Chapter 1

1. This chapter follows sources from the 1930s, such as *Liangyou Pictorial* (良友畫報), in using "Hung King Theater" as the English translation of the performance venue name. See, for example, the photo captions published alongside Zheng Boqi, "*Nuhou ba, Zhongguo! de yanchu*," *Liangyou huabao*, no. 81 (1933): 14.

2. For an archive of reprinted primary and secondary materials, performance history, and genealogy of the play's development, see Chiu Kun-liang, *Renmin nandao meicuo ma? "Nuhou ba, Zhongguo!", Teliejiyakefu yu Meiyehede* (Taipei: INK Publishing, 2013). In English, see Mark Gamsa, "Sergei Tret'iakov's *Roar, China!* between Moscow and China," *Itinerario* 36, no. 2 (2012): 91–108; and Walter Meserve and Ruth Meserve, "The Stage History of *Roar China!* Documentary Drama as Propaganda," *Theatre Survey* 21, no. 1 (1980): 1–13.

3. Gamsa, "Sergei Tret'iakov's *Roar, China!*," 93. Gamsa notes that the play was inspired by the execution of two boatmen in Wanxian in June 1924 following the mob killing of American salesman Edwin C. Hawley, but that a better documented incident in August–September 1926 involving the shelling of the town, which is now known as the "Wanxian Incident," heightened the contemporary relevance of Tret'iakov's play.

4. The name of the American merchant varies; he is called "Halei" or "Huolai" (Hawley) in the Chinese translations, but "Ashlay" in the English translation. My descriptions of the play focus on those major plot points/characterizations that are common across scripts and draw primarily on the Chinese translations published between 1929 and 1935, as well as the 1931 British translation by F. Polianovska and Barbara Nixon. Director Ying Yunwei notes that they consulted all available editions (including the English and Japanese translations) and several of the play's Chinese translators for the 1933 production in Shanghai. However, the production script itself is no longer extant. See Ying Yunwei, "*Nuhou ba Zhongguo shangyan*

jihua," *Xi* 1, no. 1 (1933): 56–59, at 56. For a detailed discussion of the many translations of Tret'iakov's play, see Gamsa, "Sergei Tret'iakov's *Roar, China!*"

5. See introduction, note 61.

6. On the development of theater and theater reform throughout China in the early twentieth century, see Fu Jin, *Zhongguo ershi shiji xiju shi*, vol. 1 (Beijing: Zhongguo shehui kexue chubanshe, 2017).

7. See Leo Ou-fan Lee, *Shanghai Modern: The Flowering of a New Urban Culture in China, 1930–1945* (Cambridge, MA: Harvard University Press, 1999).

8. Xian, *Minguo shiqi Shanghai wutai yanjiu*, 73. For discussions of the development of performance spaces and theatrical design in Beijing and Shanghai during the Republican era (1911–49), see also Li Chang, "Zhongguo jindai huaju wutai meishu piantan—cong Chunliu she dao wu Chongqing de wutai meishu," in *Zhongguo huaju shiliao ji*, ed. Zhongguo yishu yanjiuyuan huaju yanjiusuo (Beijing: Wenhua yishu chubanshe, 1987), 252–308.

9. Architectural historian Lu Xiangdong argues that one major factor propelling the theater construction boom of the 1920–1930s was the return of Chinese students from architecture programs in Europe and the United States. Lu Xiangdong, *Zhongguo xiandai juchang de yanjin: Cong da wutai dao da juyuan* (Beijing: Zhongguo jianzhu gongye chubanshe, 2009), 44.

10. On the Great World entertainment complex, see Liang Shen, "'The Great World': Performance Supermarket," *TDR: The Drama Review* 50, no. 2 (2006): 97–116.

11. Chen's series of essays appeared as a stand-alone volume in 1922. A reprint is available in the Republic of China Series (民國叢書) issued by Shanghai shudian. Chen, *Aimei de xiju*.

12. Liu, *Performing Hybridity in Colonial-Modern China*, 8. On Chen Dabei and translation, see also Annelise Finegan Wasmoen, "Translational Stages: Chinese Theatrical Modernism" (PhD diss., Department of Comparative Literature, Washington University in St. Louis, 2021).

13. Chen, *Aimei de xiju*, 13.

14. Chen, *Aimei de xiju*, 11. Sheldon Cheney (1886–1980) was an important theater critic who wrote several highly influential theater history books in the 1910s–1920s and founded *Theatre Arts Magazine*. Notably, Cheney was an advocate of an antirealist "new stagecraft" and "art theatre," as well as being involved in the Little Theater movement in the United States. See Dorothy Chansky, *Composing Ourselves: The Little Theatre Movement and the American Audience* (Carbondale: Southern Illinois University Press, 2004), 7. Emerson Gifford Taylor (1873–1932) was an American novelist and essayist who also wrote a book called *Practical Stage Direction for Amateurs: A Handbook for Amateur Actors and Managers* (New York: E. P. Dutton & Co., 1916; repr. 1923). William Lyon Phelps (1865–1943) was a professor of English at Yale University whose scholarly work primarily focused on novels, but he also wrote on dramatists and published *The Twentieth Century Theatre: Observations on the Contemporary English and American Stage* (New York: Macmillan, 1918).

15. Chen, *Aimei de xiju*, 199–201; quote 201.

16. See introduction, note 5. On Yu Shangyuan and the role of cosmopolitanism in shaping modern Chinese drama, see Man He, "Backstaging Modern Chinese Theatre: Cosmopolitan Intellectuals, Grassroots Amateurs, and Cultural Institutions, 1910s–1940s" (Ann Arbor: University of Michigan Press, forthcoming).

17. Yu, *Xiju lunji*, 233–51.

18. The first *huaju*-related periodical was the *New Drama Magazine* (新劇雜誌), which began publication in May 1914. In the realm of *xiqu*, Tang Xueying has argued that the first theater journal proper in China was *Twentieth-Century Stage* (二十世紀大舞台), which published its first issue in 1904, and Catherine Vance Yeh has also discussed the rise of entertainment tabloids in the late 1890s–1920s. Li Xiao, *Shanghai huaju zhi* (Shanghai: Baijia chubanshe, 2002): 328; Tang, *Minguo chuqi Shanghai xiqu yanjiu* (Beijing: Beijing daxue chubanshe, 2012), 87; Yeh, "A Public Love Affair or a Nasty Game? The Chinese Tabloid Newspaper and the Rise of the Opera Singer as Star," *European Journal of East Asian Studies* 2, no. 1 (2003): 13–51.

19. For example, a precise keyword search for these four terms in the National Index to Chinese Newspapers and Periodicals (全國報刊索引, or QGBKSY) collectively yields eleven results for 1920–29, twenty-nine results for 1930–39, and thirty-eight for 1940–49 (last updated May 13, 2022). A "fuzzy" search yields even higher results, but the relevance of the included articles declines. With approximately 50,000 Chinese and English periodicals and newspapers from the late Qing (1833–1911) and Republican periods (1911–49), this database offers a robust data set for this era. Cross-checks of other databases and nonperiodical sources corroborates these basic statistics, and although a more comprehensive statistical analysis would be useful, it is beyond the methodological scope of the present study.

20. Liu, *Performing Hybridity*, 175–76. As Kay Li notes, sources conflict on the date of this production; her research into advertisements dates its first performance to October 16, 1920. Kay Li, "*Mrs. Warren's Profession* in China: Factors in Cross-Cultural Adaptations," *Shaw* 25 (2005): 201–20, at 202.

21. Song Baozhen, *Zhongguo huaju yishu shi*, vol. 2, ed. Tian Benxiang (Nanjing: Jiangsu fenghuang jiaoyu chubanshe, 2016), 345.

22. Xian, *Minguo shiqi Shanghai wutai yanjiu*, 241; Song, *Zhongguo huaju yishu shi*, 2:345.

23. Ouyang Shanzun, "Tan Zhongguo wutai de dengguang yanbian," *Xiju*, no. 50 (1988): 23–27, at 24.

24. Ouyang, "Tan Zhongguo wutai de dengguang yanbian," 24–25.

25. *Juxue yuekan* 2, nos. 7–8 (1933).

26. Jiao, "Wutai guang chujiang," 1–64 [i.e., 167–230].

27. The article in question was dictated by Cheng and transcribed by Liu Shouhe 劉守鶴 and Tong Jingyin 佟靜因. The second half of the article was published in a later issue of the same journal. Cheng Yanqiu, "Huaju daoyan guankui," *Juxue yuekan* 2, nos. 7–8 (1933): 1–52 [i.e. 79–150], at 46–50.

28. Liu, *Performing Hybridity*, 176.

29. Man He discusses these influential figures and the schools, training pro-

grams, and other institutions they founded in "Backstaging Modern Chinese Theatre."

30. Teaching staff included Zheng Boqi 鄭伯奇, Feng Naichao 馮乃超, Ye Chen 葉沉, Xu Xingzhi 許幸之, Shen Qiyu 沈起予, Tao Jingsun 陶晶孫, Wang Yiliu 王一榴, Mao Zhilin 毛之麟, and Bao Mingqiang 鮑銘強. Li, *Shanghai huaju zhi*, 124–25.

31. Michel Hockx, *Questions of Style: Literary Societies and Literary Journals, 1911–1937* (Leiden: Brill, 2003), 86–117.

32. Gu Jianchen, "Xiao wutai gexin diyi sheng," *Shenbao*, April 17, 1926, 2. Lu Jingruo 陸鏡若 (1885–1915), a key member of the Spring Willow Society (春柳社), likely encountered Craig's work much earlier, while in Japan, through Osanai Kaoru 小山內薰 (1881–1928), who was "strongly attracted to Craig's ideas" and translated "The Art of the Theatre: The First Dialogue" into Japanese in 1908. Liu, *Performing Hybridity*, 99.

33. Reinhardt, a prominent director of German-language theater in the early decades of the twentieth century, emigrated to Hollywood when the Nazis came to power. The Chinese-language article mentioned here is entitled "The Theater in Max Reinhardt's Eyes," with authorship attributed to Reinhardt himself and translation to one "R.D." No source text is mentioned. See Max Reinhardt, "Laiyinhate yan zhong zhi juyuan," *Xiandai xiju* 1, no. 2 (1929): 1–5; Ma Yanxiang [Ni Yi, pseud.], "Wutai dengguang lüetan," *Xiandai xiju* 1, no. 2 (1929): 111–16, at 112.

34. "Zhongguo zuoyi xijujia lianmeng zuijin xingdong gangling," *Wenxue daobao*, nos. 6–7 (October 23, 1931): 31–32, at 31.

35. Ping Liu, "The Left-Wing Drama Movement in China and Its Relationship to Japan," trans. Krista Van Fleit Hang, *positions: east asia cultures critique* 14, no. 2 (2006): 449–66, at 461.

36. Zhao Mingyi, "Guanyu zuoyi xijujia lianmeng" [1957], reprinted in *Zhongguo zuoyi xijujia lianmeng shiliao ji*, ed. Wenhuabu dangshi ziliao zhengji gongzuo weiyuanhui (Beijing: Zhongguo xiju, 1991), 28–39, at 31; Hu Xingliang, "Lun Zhongguo xiandai 'puluo xiju,'" *Xiju wenxue*, no. 11 (1996): 35–43. According to Chinese theater scholar Hu Xingliang, the main theorists of proletarian theater (普羅戲劇 or 無產階級戲劇) were Feng Naichao, Shen Qiyu, and Ye Chen, who were all members of the Creation Society (創造社) and emphasized the importance of revolutionary spirit, class, and struggle to creating theater for the masses. See Hu, "Lun Zhongguo xiandai 'puluo xiju,'" 38; Feng Naichao, "Zhongguo xiju yundong de kuxin," *Chuangzao yuekan* 2, no. 2 (1928): 1–15; Shen Qiyu, "Yishu yundong de genben gainian," *Chuangzao yuekan* 2, no. 3 (1928): 1–7; Ye Chen [Shen Yichen, pseud.], "Yanju yundong de jiantao," *Chuangzao yuekan* 2, no. 6 (1929): 28–36.

37. Some forms used included portable theaters (移動劇場), touring public performances (巡迴公演), and the campus theater movement (學校劇運動).

38. Liu, *Performing Hybridity*; Liang Luo, *The Avant-Garde and the Popular in Modern China: Tian Han and the Intersection of Performance and Politics* (Ann Arbor: University of Michigan Press, 2014).

39. Li, *Shanghai huaju zhi*, 330. As Chinese theater scholar Ma Junshan has noted, lighting equipment at this point had to be imported, which made it expensive and difficult to acquire. Ma Junshan, "Yanju zhiyehua yundong yu Zhongguo huaju wutai meishu de chengshou," *Xiju yishu*, no. 4 (2005): 44–53, at 45.

40. Ma [Ni, pseud.], "Wutai dengguang lüetan," 112.

41. For a brief overview of Appia's lighting theory, see Richard C. Beacham, "Introduction," in *Adolphe Appia: Texts on Theatre*, ed. and trans. Richard C. Beacham (New York: Routledge, 1993), 1–14, at 5; see also Beacham, *Adolphe Appia: Artist and Visionary of the Modern Theatre* (New York: Routledge, 2013).

42. See, for example, Ai Junjie [Shi, pseud.], "Zai tan wutai zhaoming," *Sanliujiu huabao*, no. 68 (1936): 12; Li Puyuan, *Xiju jifa jianghua* (Shanghai: Zhengzhong shuju, [1936] 1947), 108; Wu Renzhi, "Wutai guang: Disan jie dengguang yu jing," *Juchang yishu*, no. 6 (1939): 15–16, at 15; Xiang, *Wutai secai xue*, 52.

43. Cheng, "Huaju daoyan guankui," 47.

44. There were a number of terms used for "dimmer" in the 1930s, including the English term itself. For instance, Cheng Yanqiu calls the dimmer a "*biandianqi* 變燈器," or literally "light-changing device"; He Mengfu, writing in 1936, translates the term as "*jieguangqi* 節光器"; Ouyang Shanzun uses the English term "dimmer" as well as the Chinese translation "*andengqi* 暗燈器." Cheng, "Huaju daoyan guikan," 46; He Mengfu, Wutai zhaoming (Shanghai: Shangwu yinshu guan, 1936), 39; Ouyang Shanzun, "Dianqi jian: Zui jiandan de 'dimmer' de zuofa," Xi 1, no. 1 (1933): 40–43.

45. Ouyang, "Dianqi jian," 43.

46. Weihong Bao, "The Art of Control: Hong Shen, Behavioral Psychology, and the Technics of Social Effects," *Modern Chinese Literature and Culture* 27, no. 2 (2015): 249–97.

47. Jiao, "Wutai guang chujiang," 5–6.

48. Film's reliance on the science of optics was likewise used to position the medium as distinctly modern and "scientific," ironically often in distinction to theater. For a discussion of Republican-era film and scientism, see chap. 1 in Jason McGrath, *Chinese Film: Realism and Convention from the Silent Era to the Digital Age* (Minneapolis: University of Minnesota Press, 2022), especially 61–66.

49. Xiang, *Wutai secai xue*, 62.

50. Wu Renzhi, "Wutai guang: Diyi jie fan lun wutaiguang de zuoyong," *Juchang yishu*, no. 1 (1938): 9–11, at 11.

51. Zhang Geng, "Wei guanzhong de xiju jianghua: shiyi, wutai dengguang he xiaoguo," *Shenghuo zhishi* 1, no. 12 (1936): 606–8, at 607.

52. Bao, "Art of Control"; Bao, *Fiery Cinema*.

53. Robert Crane notes that it was voted most popular play of the year by Moscow audiences. See Crane, "Between Factography and Ethnography: Sergei Tretyakov's *Roar, China!* and Soviet Orientalist Discourse," in *Text & Presentation 2010*, ed. Kiki Gounaridou (Jefferson, NC: McFarland, 2011), 41–53, at 41.

54. For the most complete listing of productions compiled to date, see Chiu, *Renmin nandao meicuo ma?*, 299–304.

55. See, for example, "'*Roar, China!*' in Moscow," *Manchester Guardian*, December 14, 1926, 9.

56. Crane, "Between Factography and Ethnography," 47–48.

57. "Watery Grave Snug and Warm in 'Roar, China'," *New York Herald Tribune*, November 16, 1930, H2.

58. Baird Leonard, "Theatre," *Life* 96, no. 2506 (November 14, 1930): 16–17, at 16.

59. See Tao Jingsun, "'Roar Chinese' juqing lüeshu," *Lequn zhoukan* 1, no. 4 (1929): 152–53; Tian Han, "*Nuhou ba, Zhongguo!*," *Nanguo zhoukan* 9 (1929): 445–50; Tian Han, "*Nuhou ba, Zhongguo!* (xu)," *Nanguo zhoukan* 10 (1929): 491–504. The Chinese translations were published in *Mass Literature and Arts* (大眾文藝), *Contradiction Monthly* (矛盾月刊), and *Amusement for the Masses* (群樂). A further translation by Pan Jienong was published as a stand-alone volume in 1935, with photographs and set design drawings from the 1933 production. See Sergei Tret'iakov, *Nuhou ba, Zhongguo!*, trans. Pan Jienong (Shanghai: Liangyou zong gongsi, 1935).

60. Chiu details the reception of *Roar, China!* in China throughout *Renmin nandao meicuo ma?*

61. For a list of both successful and failed Chinese performances, see Ge Fei, "*Nuhou ba Zhongguo!* yu 1930 niandai zhengzhi xuanchuan ju," *Yishu pinglun* 10 (2008): 23–28, at 28. For an extensive discussion of the multimedia circulation of text and image related to *Roar, China!*, see Xiaobing Tang, "Echoes of *Roar, China!* On Vision and Voice in Modern Chinese Art," *positions: east asia cultures critique* 14, no. 2 (2006): 467–94.

62. Ouyang Yuqian, "*Nuhou ba Zhongguo* zai Guangdong shangyan ji," *Xiju* 2, no. 2 (1930): 108–9.

63. The "Eight Immortals Bridge" is used as a landmark in advertisements for the Hung King Theater. For discussion of the theater's location, along with maps and descriptions of the surrounding theater clusters in Republican Shanghai, see Xian, *Minguo shiqi Shanghai wutai yanjiu*, 50–55.

64. "Huangjin da xiyuan kaimu shengkuang," *Xinwen bao*, February 2, 1930, 4.

65. Huang Jinrong was a police officer in the French Concession and notorious figure in Shanghai's underworld, with close connections to the notorious Green Gang. He owned several theaters and other entertainment establishments. See Brian G. Martin, *The Shanghai Green Gang: Politics and Organized Crime, 1919–1937* (Berkeley: University of California Press, 1996), 37–39, 64–78.

66. The article continues to extol additional characteristics of the theater, such as the use of preassigned, numbered seating as in Western-style theaters. Yi Bie, "Huangjin da xiyuan zhi xin jihua," *Jin gangzuan*, May 30, 1929.

67. Xian, *Minguo shiqi Shanghai wutai yanjiu*, 124–25; Li, *Shanghai huaju zhi*, 45–49.

68. Ying, "*Nuhou ba Zhongguo* shangyan jihua," 58. Ying Yunwei titles his essay a *shangyan jihua* 上演計畫, which might be translated as "performance plan" or

"staging plan." However, an article from the journal *Juchang yishu*, originally published in 1939 and reprinted in the volume *Xiju meixue lunji*, uses the English word "design" as a translation for *jihua* in this context, so I have adopted the translation "production design" in an attempt to approximate contemporaneous understanding of the term. See Gu Zhongyi, "Daoyan shu gailun di san zhang: Shangyan jihua de jiben yuanze (weiwan)," *Juchang yishu*, no. 8 (1939): 10–12, at 10.

69. Zhang Yunqiao, "Ying Yunwei he huaju *Nuhou ba, Zhongguo!*," *Shanghai tan* no. 7 (1995): 38–39, at 38.

70. Bi Bo, "Kan *Nuhou ba, Zhongguo!* zhi hou," *Shanhu* 3, no. 9 (1933): 4–7, at 6.

71. Zhang, "Ying Yunwei he huaju *Nuhou ba, Zhongguo!*," 38.

72. Ying, "*Nuhou ba Zhongguo* shangyan jihua," 59. Even though he uses the English word "spotlight," Ying likely did not refer to the high wattage, long-throw spotlights today used to follow individual performers with a sharp circle of light. Rather, the term denotes single-bulb lighting units used to create focused areas of light onstage. See also He, *Wutai zhaoming*, 29.

73. Ouyang, "Tan Zhongguo wutai dengguang de yanbian," 25.

74. The term *qiangjing* would have been new to its readers, given that the term does not commonly appear in print until the mid-1930s. Text searches of the digitized *Shenbao*, for example, show the term first used in that newspaper in 1935, in reference to *Roar, China!* For an example of historiography that lists *Roar, China!* as the first *huaju* production in China to attempt a blackout quick change with no curtain, see Li, *Shanghai huaju zhi*, 94.

75. Zhang, "Ying Yunwei he huaju *Nuhou ba, Zhongguo!*," 38–39.

76. Christin Essin, *Stage Designers in Early Twentieth-Century America: Artists, Activists, Cultural Critics* (New York: Palgrave Macmillan, 2012), 95–96.

77. The episode of the boy's suicide was one of the most acclaimed moments in the Meyerhold Theater production, but is curiously abbreviated in the translated Chinese scripts published around the time of the Theater Society production. In Pan Jienong's translation, for example, the stage directions describing the suicide are cut, leaving only the sudden discovery of the already-deceased boy and the commotion surrounding the discovery of his body. The lines about the camera, however, remain intact. See Sergei Tret'iakov, *Roar, China! An Episode in Nine Scenes*, trans. F. Polianovska and Barbara Nixon (London: Martin Lawrence, 1931), 76; Tret'iakov, *Nuhou ba, Zhongguo!*, 112.

78. Tret'iakov, *Roar, China!*, 85.

79. Tang, "Echoes of *Roar, China!*," 482.

80. As points of comparison, other advertisements on the same page of *Shenbao* as *Roar, China!*'s list prices of six jiao or one to one-and-a-half yuan for daytime screenings of Noel Coward's film *Cavalcade* at the Nanjing Grand (南京大戲院), but a tiered ticketing scheme of only two *jiao* to eight *jiao* for another theater performance, *The New Case of a Body in a Trunk* (新箱尸案) at the Hong Kong Grand Theater (香港大戲院). "Nuhou ba, Zhongguo!" (and surrounding ads), *Shenbao*, September 15, 1933, 7; on ticket sales, see Ying, "*Nuhou ba Zhongguo!* shangyan jihua," 58.

81. "Shanghai guohuo gongsi," *Shenbao*, September 15, 1933, 21.
82. San Wen, *"Nuhou ba Zhongguo!," Shiri tan* 5 (1933): 13.
83. Ren Yuren, "Ping *Xi*," *Xi* 1, no. 2 (1933): 15–16, at 15; Yuan Muzhi, "Liang ji kongshou juan—jidian shengming," *Xi* 1, no. 2 (October 1933): 21.
84. Yuan Muzhi, "Wei xiju yundong qiantu dasuan," *Xi* 1, no. 1 (1933): 1.
85. Ying, *"Nuhou ba Zhongguo!* shangyan jihua."
86. One review of the publication notes the significance of its documentation of production details and compares this practice to many other theater societies, whose performances are unfortunately "lost" as soon as the curtain closes because they do not publish or preserve similar documents. Ren, "Ping *Xi*," 16.
87. Bertolt Brecht, "The Modern Theatre Is the Epic Theatre," in *Brecht on Theatre: The Development of an Aesthetic*, trans. and ed. John Willet (London: Methuen Drama, 1964), 37.
88. Sergei Eisenstein, "Montage of Attractions: For *Enough Stupidity in Every Wiseman*," trans. Daniel Gerould, *TDR: The Drama Review* 18, no. 1 (1974): 77–85.
89. Sergei Tret'iakov, "The Theater of Attractions [1924]," trans. Kristin Romberg, *October*, no. 118 (Fall 2006): 19–26, at 23; italics per the original.
90. "Xiju xiao congshu," *Shenbao*, October 16, 1936, 7. The authors and editors of these volumes were largely Beijing-based theater educators and theorists, but the series was published by the Shanghai Commercial Press and advertised in *Shenbao*, which suggests wide distribution.
91. Zhang, "Wei guanzhong de xiju jianghua," 606.

## Chapter 2

1. *Foggy Chongqing*, originally titled *The Whip* (鞭), was retitled for its premiere: Song Zhidi, *Bian* (Chongqing: Shenghuo shudian, 1940), 2–3; Song Zhidi, *Wu Chongqing* (Beijing: Zhongguo xiju chubanshe, 1957), 2–3.
2. Fu Jin, *A History of Chinese Theatre in the 20th Century II*, trans. Qiang Zhang (New York: Routledge, 2021), 125–27.
3. Bao, *Fiery Cinema*, 319; Peter Sloterdijk, *Terror from the Air*, trans. Amy Patton and Steve Corcoran (Los Angeles: Semiotext(e), 2009), 9.
4. For recent histories that complicate the origin story of modern Chinese drama, see, for example, Liu, *Performing Hybridity in Colonial-Modern China*.
5. As Xiaomei Chen notes, however, Hu Shih's play was not actually the first experiment in realist dramaturgy by a Chinese playwright; Hong Shen, for instance, wrote a play called *The Pear Seller* (賣栗人) in 1915. Xiaomei Chen, "Introduction," in *The Columbia Anthology of Modern Chinese Drama*, ed. Xiaomei Chen (New York: Columbia University Press, 2010), 1–55, at 4, 47; Hu Shi, *The Main Event in Life*, trans. Edward M. Gunn, in *Columbia Anthology of Modern Chinese Drama*, ed. Chen, 57–65.
6. This is not to imply that playwrights of the 1920s were less significant due to the length or genre of their work. A number of important Chinese *huaju* play-

wrights such as Tian Han, Hong Shen, Bai Wei 白薇 (Huang Zhang 黄彰, 1894–1987), and Ding Xilin 丁西林 (1893–1974) wrote, published, and staged early work in the 1920s. On Tian Han's early work, for example, see Luo, *The Avant-Garde and the Popular in Modern China*. On Hong Shen, see "Hong Shen and the Modern Mediasphere in Republican-Era China," ed. Kirk A. Denton, special issue, *Modern Chinese Literature and Culture* 27, no. 2 (2015). On female playwright Bai Wei, see, for example, Hiu Man Keung, "The Private Stage: A Study on Chinese Printed Drama by Bai Wei and Yuan Changying, 1922–1936" (PhD diss., Department of Asian Studies, University of Edinburgh, 2020); Haiping Yan, *Chinese Women Writers and the Feminist Imagination, 1905–1948* (London: Routledge, 2006), 100–134. On Ding Xilin, see John B. Weinstein, "Ding Xilin and Chen Baichen: Building a Modern Theater through Comedy," *Modern Chinese Literature and Culture* 20, no. 2 (2008): 92–130; R. A. Herd and Zhang Jian, "Wildean Echoes in the Plays of Ding Xilin," *Modern Chinese Literature and Culture* 22, no. 1 (2010): 162–96.

7. In *Amateur Drama*, this second chapter includes subsections on the relationship between theater troupe and script, standards for script selection, appropriate length, and morality. Chen, *Aimei de xiju*, 27–58.

8. Xiang Peiliang, *Juben lun* (Shanghai: Shangwu yinshu guan, 1936).

9. Chen Baichen and Dong Jian date the so-called Golden Age of modern drama from 1937 to 1949, from the onset of the Second Sino-Japanese War to the end of the Chinese Civil War and founding of the People's Republic of China. Chen Baichen and Dong Jian, *Zhongguo xiandai xiju shigao, 1899–1949* (Beijing: Zhongguo xiju chubanshe, 2008), 283. More recent scholarship, however, tends to prefer periodization less dependent on dates of political-historical significance. In her introduction to the *Columbia Anthology of Modern Chinese Drama*, Xiaomei Chen dates the arrival of the Golden Age of *huaju* to the publication of Cao Yu's *Thunderstorm* in 1934. Chen, "Introduction," 11.

10. On wartime drama in occupied Shanghai, see chap. 3 of Edward Gunn, *Unwelcome Muse: Chinese Literature in Shanghai and Peking, 1937–1945* (New York: Columbia University Press, 1980), 109–50, and Gunn, "Shanghai's 'Orphan Island' and the Development of Modern Drama," in *Popular Chinese Literature and Performing Arts in the People's Republic of China, 1949–1979*, ed. Bonnie S. McDougall (Berkeley: University of California Press, 1984), 36–53.

11. Chang-tai Hung, *War and Popular Culture: Resistance in Modern China, 1937–1945* (Berkeley: University of California Press, 1994), 50.

12. Hung, *War and Popular Culture*, 54.

13. Hung, *War and Popular Culture*, 50, 62.

14. Chen Baichen and Dong Jian list more than a hundred representative scripts from this period. Chen and Dong, *Zhongguo xiandai xiju shigao*, 301–7.

15. These are modern classics in the sense that these plays and playwrights have become part of the literary canon via critical and scholarly attention, anthologization, and so forth and also continue to be key pieces in the theatrical repertoire. *Thunderstorm, Under Shanghai Eaves, It's Only Spring,* and *Return on a Snowy Night*, for example, are all included in the *Columbia Anthology of Modern Chinese Drama*. Several of the plays written by Cao Yu, Wu Zuguang, and Guo Moruo during this

time have also become repertoire staples of major state-sponsored theaters such as the Beijing People's Art Theater since the 1950s.

16. The book of lectures was published in 1940, but the preface is dated 1938. Yu Shangyuan et al., *Zhanshi xiju jiangzuo* (Chongqing: Zhengzhong shuju, 1940). Similarly, the publication dates for individual volumes of the "Wartime Theater Theory" series vary, but the series preface is dated 1939. For *The Performance Handbook*, see Song Zhidi et al., *Yanju shouce* (Chongqing: Shanghai zazhi gongsi, 1939).

17. Zhao Qingge, *Bianju fangfa lun* (Chongqing: Duli chubanshe, 1942).

18. Wan Jiabao [Cao Yu, pseud.], "Bianju shu," in *Zhanshi xiju jiangzuo*, ed. Yu Shangyuan et al. (Chongqing: Zhengzhong shuju, 1940), 36–50.

19. Man He, "*Juren* (Men and Women of Theatre) in the Confucian Temple: Technics, Prompts, and Plays to Serve the Nation, 1934–1945," *Asian Theatre Journal* 38, no. 1 (2021): 245–74, at 250–51.

20. Hong Shen, *Dianying xiju de bianju fangfa* ([Shanghai?]: Zhengzhong shuju, 1935). Reprinted in *Hong Shen wenji* (Beijing: Zhongguo xiju chubanshe, 1959), 3:261–389.

21. Xia Yan seems to have published the same essay earlier as "On Relief from the Script Famine" (論劇本荒的救濟), in two issues of *Chinese Art World Pictorial* (中國藝壇畫報) in 1939.

22. Xia Yan, "Juben de chuangzuo," *Qingnian xiju* 1, no. 1 (1940): 2.

23. Xia Yan, "Juben de chuangzuo," 2.

24. Ma, *Yanju zhiye hua yundong yanjiu*, 5–10.

25. Ma, *Yanju zhiye hua yundong yanjiu*, 22.

26. Ma, *Yanju zhiye hua yundong yanjiu*, 33.

27. In his chapter on the professionalization of playwrights, Ma Junshan writes of Chen Baichen, Li Jianwu, Wu Tian 吳天 (1912–89), Wu Zuguang, You Ling 於伶 (Ren Xigui 任錫圭, 1907–97), Zhou Yibai 周貽白 (1900–1977), and others that they all "wrote for performance, wrote for theater troupes, and playwrights' fees were a main source of their livelihood." Ma, *Yanju zhiye hua yundong yanjiu*, 22.

28. These changes also spurred a movement of film industry personnel to the theater. Edward Gunn argues that the embargo on foreign films in Shanghai during this period led many theater venues to shift to offering theatrical performances, and that the theater was censored less stringently than film under the Japanese occupation. Edward Gunn, "Shanghai's 'Orphan Island,'" 48–49.

29. On the relationship between realism and epistemology, see, for example, Peter Button's discussion of Cai Yi in *Configurations of the Real in Chinese Literary and Aesthetic Modernity* (Leiden: Brill, 2009) and chap. 1 of Roy Bing Chan's *The Edge of Knowing: Dreams, History, and Realism in Modern Chinese Literature* (Seattle: University of Washington Press, 2017), 11–38.

30. Marston Anderson, *The Limits of Realism: Chinese Fiction in the Revolutionary Period* (Berkeley: University of California Press, 1990), 56.

31. Ge Yihong, for example, discusses the restrictions imposed by theaters, as well as the dramaturgical limits of time and space. Ge Yihong, "Lun Kangzhan zhong de juben chuangzuo," *Xin yanju* 1, no. 1 (1938): 18–20, at 20.

32. Randy Barbara Kaplan, "Planting the Seeds of Theatrical Realism in China:

Tian Han's Contributions to Modern Chinese Drama, 1920–1929," *World Literature Today* 62, no. 1 (1988): 55–61, at 57.

33. J. I. Crump, *Chinese Theater in the Days of Kublai Khan* (Ann Arbor: Center for Chinese Studies, University of Michigan, 1990); Min Tian, "Stage Directions in the Performance of Yuan Drama," *Comparative Drama* 39, nos. 3–4 (2005–6): 397–443.

34. As Rolston notes, very early twentieth-century *jingju* publications were often sparing in their inclusion of stage directions, but the printing of substantive editions increased over time. David L. Rolston, *Inscribing Jingju/Peking Opera: Textualization and Performance, Authorship and Censorship of the "National Drama" of China from the Late Qing to the Present* (Leiden: Brill, 2021), 539–43.

35. Bess Rowen, "Undigested Reading: Rethinking Stage Directions through Affect," *Theatre Journal* 70, no. 3 (2018): 307–26, at 312–13; quote 313. See also Rowen, *The Lines between the Lines: How Stage Directions Affect Embodiment* (Ann Arbor: University of Michigan Press, 2021).

36. Rowen, "Undigested Reading," 312.

37. Kay Li, *Bernard Shaw and China: Cross-Cultural Encounters* (Gainesville: University Press of Florida, 2007), 6–8. On the New Culture Movement, see chap. 1, note 60.

38. Recent scholarship complicates this standard interpretation of the event, which is based largely on a few influential reviews and reflections by leading theater artists. Kay Li, for instance, reexamines the supposedly poor box-office numbers and highlights the production's innovations in staging and advertising. See Li, *Bernard Shaw and China*, 76–114. For details on the production, see also Wendi Chen, "The First Shaw Play on the Chinese Stage: The Production of *Mrs. Warren's Profession* in 1921," *Shaw* 19 (1999): 99–118.

39. Li, *Bernard Shaw and China*, 116.

40. Joseph S. M. Lau, *Ts'ao Yü, the Reluctant Disciple of Chekhov and O'Neill: A Study in Literary Influence* (Hong Kong: Hong Kong University Press, 1970).

41. On the May Fourth Movement, see introduction, note 61. Scholars have argued that *Thunderstorm* was directly influenced by—or at least is in dialogue with—plays such as *Hippolytus*, *Phèdre*, and *Desire under the Elms*, as well as Ibsen's *A Doll's House* and *Ghosts* and Alexander Ostrovsky's *The Storm*.

42. Cao Yu, "Leiyu," *Wenxue jikan* 1, no. 3 (1934): 161–244, at 222.

43. This comment is in fact made in an epilogue to *Sunrise*, which was not included in the original serialization of the play but was published in the edition of the play included in the author's 1936 collected drama: Cao Yu, "*Richu* ba," in *Richu*, vol. 2 of *Cao Yu xiju ji* (Shanghai: Wenhua shenghuo chubanshe, [1936] 1946), 2:i–xxxii, at xi; Chen and Dong, *Zhongguo xiandai xiju shigao*, 263n1. Texts consulted were the 1943 reissue—*Leiyu*, vol. 1 of *Cao Yu xiju ji* (Shanghai: Wenhua shenghuo chubanshe, [1936] 1943)—and a reprint of the *Sunrise* epilogue in his complete works: "*Richu* ba," in *Cao Yu quanji*, ed. Tian Benxiang and Li Yijun (Shijiazhuang: Huashan wenyi chubanshe, 1996), 1:380–97.

44. Thunder, lightning, and rain all fall under the category of "stage effects"

(舞台效果) and were frequently discussed in contemporaneous technical theater publications.

45. Cao Yu did have acting experience from his years at Nankai Elementary School (南開中學), well-known for its drama curriculum and for educating many important figures, such as Zhou Enlai.

46. Wang Ling, "Wutai xiaoguo de zhifa," *Xiandai yanju* 1, no. 1 (1934): 31–32. This was not the only way to create flashes of light onstage. Later articles suggest a visual effect more specific to lightning (閃電) could be created by cutting the shape of a bolt of lightning into a wooden box, painting the box black, and installing a light bulb inside the box. When illuminated briefly, the bolt would then appear to flash. See, for example, Huang Cun, "Wutai xiaoguo san (lei, dian)," *Zongyi: Meishu xiju dianying yinyue banyue kan* 1, no. 3 (1948): 5.

47. Cao, "*Richu* ba," 2:xi.

48. Cao, *Leiyu*, in *Cao Yu xiju ji*, 1:244–45. The translation is taken from Cao Yu, *Thunderstorm*, trans. Wang Tso-liang and A. C. Barnes, rev. Charles Qianzhi Wu, in *Columbia Anthology of Modern Chinese Drama*, ed. Chen, 227–352, at 319. The *Anthology* translation adds sections from the original 1934 *Wenxue jikan* script that had been redacted from the 1956 version on which the 1958 Liang and Barnes translation is based. However, a comparison shows that the 1934 original did not include this particular block of stage directions; they were included in the 1936 (1943 reissue) and later editions.

49. See, for example, Cao Yu, *Richu*, vol. 2 of *Cao Yu xiju ji* (Shanghai: Wenhua shenghuo chubanshe, [1936] 1946), 2:241–42. *Sunrise* was serialized in *Wenji yuekan* in 1936 and published as a stand-alone volume in the same year.

50. Cao, *Richu*, 319, 325.

51. Cao, *Richu*, 328.

52. For example, He Mengfu specifically notes abrupt lighting shifts (as well as expense) as problems of slider or dial dimmers. He, *Wutai zhaoming*, 39–40.

53. See, for example, Linda McJannet, *The Voice of Elizabethan Stage Directions: The Evolution of a Theatrical Code* (Newark: University of Delaware Press; London: Associated University Presses, 1999); Sarah Dustagheer and Gillian Woods, eds., *Stage Directions and Shakespearean Theatre* (London: Bloomsbury Arden Shakespeare, 2018).

54. Their changes may reflect contemporaneous court performances more than the original performance practices of the earlier period during which the *zaju* were composed. Min, "Stage Directions," 398, 404.

55. Cao Yu goes on to disparage the use of effects merely for spectacle and to attract the audience, which he sees as the antithesis of "serious" theater. Cao Yu, "*Richu* di san mu fuji," in *Cao Yu quanji*, ed. Tian and Liu, 1:378–79. Originally published in *Wenji yuekan*, no. 5 (1936).

56. On the curriculum at the National School of Drama, see chap. 4 in He Man, "Backstaging Modern Chinese Theatre: Cosmopolitan Intellectuals, Grassroots Amateurs, and Cultural Institutions, 1910s–1940s" (forthcoming, University

of Michigan Press); for an example of an article that uses Cao Yu as a model, see Tu Kelin, "Guanyu juben de chuangzuo gaibian he fanyi," *Zhongguo qingnian* 1, no. 2 (1943): 44–46.

57. Li Chang, "Zhongguo jindai huaju wutai meishu piantan," 282.

58. "Lane houses" (弄堂房子) or "alley houses" are a well-known feature of Shanghai's urban architecture, and their close confines feature prominently in many films, novels, short stories, and plays from and set in early twentieth-century Shanghai. On lane houses, see Jie Li, *Shanghai Homes: Palimpsests of Private Life* (New York: Columbia University Press, 2015).

59. See, for example, the 1957 edition, which includes a small photograph of the set on the page describing the play's opening setting. While it was common practice to include images from the production in published scripts, the placement of the image on the same page as the stage directions is unusual. A line drawing of the set also appears alongside the stage directions in the play's English translation in the *Columbia Anthology*. Xia Yan, *Shanghai wuyan xia* (Beijing: Zhongguo xiju chubanshe, 1957), 2; Xia Yan, *Under Shanghai Eaves*, trans. George Hayden, in *Columbia Anthology of Modern Chinese Drama*, ed. Chen, 397–447, at 398.

60. My translation, based on the 1939 Chinese-language edition, with reference to George Hayden's translation. Xia Yan, *Shanghai wuyan xia* (Shanghai: Xiandai xiju chubanshe, 1939), 4–5; Xia, *Under Shanghai Eaves*, trans. Hayden, 399.

61. Xia, *Shanghai wuyan xia*, 56; *Under Shanghai Eaves*, trans. Hayden, 420.

62. Xia, *Shanghai wuyan xia*, 3; *Under Shanghai Eaves*, trans. Hayden, 398–99.

63. See, for example, "Shanghai juyishe chongyan *Shanghai wuyan xia*," *Xinwen bao*, November 13, 1940, and Shi Ling, "Guan *Shanghai wuyan xia*," *Li bao*, July 18, 1940.

64. "Shanghai juyishe chongyan *Shanghai wuyan xia*."

65. "Xia Yan yaoqiu *Shanghai wuyan xia* zhengge fangzi shangtai," *Tie bao*, August 2, 1937. Xia's preface to the 1937 printing of the play confirms that he did write the play *for* the Amateur Experimental Theater Troupe. However, the Second Sino-Japanese War began a few days before their scheduled performance, forcing them to cancel. See Xia Yan, "Zixu," in *Xiayan xiju yanjiu ziliao shang*, ed. Hui Lin (Beijing: Zhongguo xiju chubanshe, 1980), 15–16, at 15. Originally published in *Shanghai wuyan xia* (Shanghai: Xiju shidai chubanshe, 1937), 1–3.

66. Xia's comment, written in the mid-1950s, has obvious political undertones. Xia Yan, "Tan *Shanghai wuyan xia* de chuangzuo," in *Xia Yan xiju yanjiu ziliao (shang)*, ed. Hui Lin (Beijing: Zhongguo xiju chubanshe, 1980), 20–26, at 20–21.

67. For example, some theater troupes formed partnerships with foreign organizations in order to gain access to theater spaces in Shanghai's foreign concessions, where the Japanese regime had less control. Fu, *A History of Chinese Theatre in the 20th Century II*, 105–6.

68. He Mengfu, "Zhe yidai (dumuju)," *Kangzhan wenyi* 4, nos. 5–6 (1939): 151.

69. He, *Wutai zhaoming*, 39–40.

70. Yang Zeping, "Ji kangzhan zhong de da houfang ying ju ren He Mengfu," *Wenshi zazhi* 5 (2014): 29–30, at 29. The drama department in which He Mengfu

studied was first established at the National Beijing Academy of the Arts in 1925 (see chapter 1). The school changed its name to the Peking University Academy of the Arts in 1928.

71. The troupes included the Mingxing Experimental Little Theater (明星 實驗小劇場), Amateur Theater Society, and the Amateur Experimental Theater Troupe.

72. Yang, "Ji Kangzhan zhong de da houfang ying ju ren He Mengfu," 29–30, at 29.

73. H. K. Moderwell was an important figure in the American Little Theatre Movement who, along with Sheldon Cheney, advocated "art theatre" and anti-realist scenography. (See Chansky, *Composing Ourselves*, 7, 72–73.) Moderwell's volume is notable for its description of the modern theater as a "gathering of . . . forces"—similar to the concept of theater as a "synthetic art" (綜合的藝術) that became popular in Chinese theater theory of this period—and for foregrounding its mechanical and design aspects such as stage equipment, scenery, color, and lighting (including references to Craig, Appia, and Reinhardt). Moderwell, *The Theatre of To-day*; H. K. Moderwell [Modewei], *Jindai de xiju yishu* (Chengdu: Juyi chubanshe, 1941).

74. Tim Shao-Hung Teng, "Murderous Shadows, Terrifying Air: *Dr. Caligari* in China," *Journal of Chinese Cinemas* 14, no. 3 (2020): 223–41, at 225, 237.

75. Teng, "Murderous Shadows," 225. See also Bao, *Fiery Cinema*, 26–27.

76. Edna Tow, "The Great Bombing of Chongqing and the Anti-Japanese War, 1937–1945," in *The Battle for China: Essays on the Military History of the Sino-Japanese War of 1937–1945*, ed. Mark Peattie, Edward J. Drea, and Hans van de Ven (Stanford: Stanford University Press, 2011), 256–82, at 256–57.

77. See especially chap. 6 in Bao, *Fiery Cinema*, 317–74.

78. See Tan Gang, "Living Underground: Bomb Shelters and Daily Lives in Wartime Chongqing (1937–1945)," *Journal of Urban History* 43, no. 3 (2017): 383–99.

79. During World War II, navigating in thick cloud or fog cover was a significant challenge for the relatively new technology of military aircraft. Several nations invested in military science and technology experiments that attempted to solve this problem. For a discussion of wartime experiments with fog and their connection to contemporary Japanese visual art, see Yuriko Furuhata, "The Fog Medium: Visualizing and Engineering the Atmosphere," in *Screen Genealogies: From Optical Device to Environmental Medium*, ed. C. R. Buckley, Rüdiger Campe, and Francesco Casetti (Amsterdam: Amsterdam University Press, 2019), 187–213.

80. Chongqing residents spent much of the time in the countryside or in bunkers during the months of April-October, so theater troupes utilized the foggy season of October-April for performances. Chu Fu-sung notes high levels of engagement, with some 300,000 total audience members for twenty plays in the 1943–44 season. Chu Fu-sung, "Wartime Chinese Literature," in *China after Seven Years of War*, ed. Hollington K. Tong (New York: Macmillan, 1945), 125–47, at 134, 139.

81. Zhang Wujun, "Chongqing wu yu Zhongguo Kangzhan wenxue," *Xinan daxue xuebao (shehui kexue ban)* 35, no. 2 (2009): 162–65.

82. Song Shi, *Song Zhidi yanjiu ziliao* (Beijing: Jiefangjun wenyi chubanshe, 1987), 473. After participating in leftist and national salvation drama activity in Shanghai for much of the 1930s, Song Zhidi traveled with the Shanghai Theater Salvation Association (上海戲劇界救亡協會) in 1937 and then went from Wuhan to Chongqing in 1938. He remained in Chongqing until 1945, with the exception of a period in Hong Kong between January 1941 and May 1942 following the New Fourth Army Incident.

83. Constantine Tung, "Experience and Conviction in China's Wartime Drama, 1937–1945," in *La Littérature chinoise au temps de la guerre de résistance contre le Japon (de 1937 à 1945): Colloque international* (Paris: Éditions de la Fondation Singer-Polignac, [1982]), 377–94, at 383.

84. Chen and Dong, *Zhongguo xiandai xiju shigao*, 364.

85. Song, *Wu Chongqing*, 2–3.

86. Song, *Wu Chongqing*, 3.

87. Gernot Böhme, *Atmospheric Architectures: The Aesthetics of Felt Spaces*, ed. and trans. Anna-Christina Engels-Schwarzpaul (London: Bloomsbury Academic, 2017), 69, 14–17. In a later chapter, Böhme also writes specifically on the relationship between staging and atmospheres.

88. Böhme, *Atmospheric Architectures*, 28.

89. Drew Campbell, *Technical Theater for Nontechnical People*, 2nd ed. (New York: Allworth, 2004), 62–66.

90. A number of popular science periodicals, such as *Scientific China* (科學的中國) and *Science Pictorial* (科學畫報) published brief descriptions of dry ice and its uses for cooling systems, making ice cream, and so forth in 1935–36. Around the same time, there are also articles about the use of dry ice in seeding clouds to create rain.

91. "You ganbing zaocheng ganwu," *Kexue de Zhongguo* 9, no. 9 (1937): 786.

92. See Furuhata, "Fog Medium," 195–96.

93. He, *Wutai zhaoming*, 33–35.

94. The use of the term "line" (路線) here parallels the CCP political rhetoric of the "mass line" (群眾路線), which would continue to be used throughout the Maoist era. Zhang Geng, "Juben chuangzuo wenti," *Shilun congkan* no. 4 (1939): 142–46, at 145.

95. Bao, "Art of Control," 289.

96. Hong Shen, "Xiju de tuji"; qtd. in Li Chang, "Zhongguo jindai huaju wutai meishu piantan," 293.

97. Hong Shen, *Xiju daoyan de chubu zhishi* (Shanghai: Zhongguo wenhua fuwu chubanshe, 1943); reprinted in *Hong Shen wenji* (Beijing: Zhongguo xiju chubanshe, 1959), 3:389–510; quote 3:460.

98. For Hong Shen, eschewal of specific areas of stage technology also did not necessarily mean a less technical approach to other areas of the theater, such as acting. See Man He, "*Juren* (Men and Women of Theatre) in the Confucian Temple," 245–74, at 249–51.

99. Song Zhidi, "Xiju yu xuanchuan (daixu)," in *Yanju shouce*, ed. Song Zhidi et al. (Chongqing: Shanghai zazhi gongsi, 1939), iii–vi, at iv; He Mengfu, "Jiangzuo: Di qi jiang wutai zhuangzhi," *Shehui jiaoyu fudao* 1 (1943): 107–14, at 113.

100. See Brian James DeMare, *Mao's Cultural Army: Drama Troupes in China's Rural Revolution* (Cambridge: Cambridge University Press, 2015).

## Chapter 3

1. The word *changxiangqu* 畅想曲 in the Chinese title is a musical term used to translate the "fantasia" or "caprice" of Western European composition (for which *huanxiangqu* 幻想曲 is more commonly used). Here, I use "fantasia" to accord with the discussion of fantasy throughout the chapter. The word "rhapsody" is often used in the English the title of this play, and its contemporaneous film adaptation had the English release title *Ballad of the Ming Tombs Reservoir*; https://www.imdb.com/title/tt5820664/releaseinfo?ref_=ttspec_sa_2

2. Tian Han, "*Shisanling shuiku changxiangqu*," *Juben*, no. 8 (1958): 38–77. The film adaptation of the play (dir. Jin Shan, 1958) recently has attracted more scholarly attention than the play itself; see, for example, Ying Qian, "When Taylorism Met Revolutionary Romanticism: Documentary Cinema in China's Great Leap Forward," *Critical Inquiry* 46, no. 3 (2020): 578–604; and chap. 1 in Paola Iovene, *Tales of Futures Past: Anticipation and the Ends of Literature in Contemporary China* (Stanford: Stanford University Press, 2014), 20–24.

3. Cheng Yuangong, "Guanxin Beijing chengshi jianshe," in *Zhou Enlai yu Beijing* (Beijing: Zhongyang chubanshe, 1998), 38; qtd. in Wang Jun, *Chengji* (Beijing: Shenghuo dushu xinzhi sanlian shudian, 2003), 38; qtd. and trans. in Jianfei Zhu, *Architecture of Modern China: A Historical Critique* (London: Routledge, 2009), 81.

4. See, for example, Baichun Zhang, Jiuchun Zhang, and Fang Yao, "Technology Transfer from the Soviet Union to the People's Republic of China: 1949–1966," *Comparative Technology Transfer and Society* 4, no. 2 (2006): 105–67.

5. See, for example, Mao Zedong, "On New Democracy," 2:339–84, at 2:339; 2:380–82.

6. "Talks at the Yan'an Conference on Literature and Art," 55–86. For analysis of how Mao's "cultural army" was mobilized, especially using regional dramatic forms as propaganda, see DeMare, *Mao's Cultural Army*.

7. Kuai Dashen and Rao Xianlai, *Xin Zhongguo wenhua guanli tizhi yanjiu* (Shanghai: Shanghai renmin chubanshe, 2010), 107.

8. BPAT was established under the purview of the Beijing municipal government; China Youth Art Theater was a national-level troupe under the Ministry of Culture. For an overview of the reorganization of the arts under the PRC, see chap. 10 in Colin Mackerras, *The Chinese Theatre in Modern Times, from 1840 to the Present Day* (Amherst: University of Massachusetts Press, 1975). For ethnography detailing the effects of PRC policies for performing artists, see chap. 4 of Francesca R. Sborgi Lawson, *The Narrative Arts of Tianjin: Between Music and Language* (Burlington, VT: Ashgate, 2011), 23–30.

9. For a discussion of ambiguities in directives and the difficulty of implementing reforms on provincial and local levels, see Brian James DeMare, "Drama from Beijing to Long Bow: Reforming Shanxi Stages in Socialist China," in *Rethinking Chinese Socialist Theaters of Reform: Performance Practice and Debate in the Mao Era*, ed. Xiaomei Chen, Tarryn Li-Min Chun, and Siyuan Liu (Ann Arbor: University of Michigan Press, 2021), 187–215.

10. Zhou Enlai had participated in theater performances in his youth at Nankai Elementary School in Tianjin, and, perhaps partly due to his personal interest in the arts, he took an active role in the reform of China's cultural field. The speech quoted here was delivered at the at the First All-China Literature and Arts Workers Representatives Meeting, mentioned above. Zhou Enlai, "Zai Zhonghua quanguo wenxue yishu gongzuozhe daibiao dahui shang de zhengzhi baogao," *Zhou Enlai xuan ji* (Beijing: Renmin chubanshe, 1980), 356–57.

11. Siyuan Liu, *Transforming Tradition: The Reform of Chinese Theater in the 1950s and Early 1960s* (Ann Arbor: University of Michigan Press, 2021), 30–31.

12. Fu Jin, *Xin Zhongguo xiju shi, 1949–2000* (Changsha: Hunan meishu chubanshe, 2002), 10; Liu, *Transforming Tradition*, 42–97; Bonnie S. McDougall and Kam Louie, *The Literature of China in the Twentieth Century* (New York: Columbia University Press, 1997), 292.

13. Kuai and Rao, *Xin Zhongguo wenhua guanli tizhi yanjiu*, 113, 121.

14. See, for example, chap. 4 in Chang-tai Hung, *Politics of Control: Creating Red Culture in the Early People's Republic of China* (Honolulu: University of Hawai'i Press, 2021), 84–108.

15. The festival took place during August 5–19, 1951, and following its conclusion, the troupe toured East Germany, Hungary, Poland, the Soviet Union, Romania, Bulgaria, Czechoslovakia, Austria, and Albania. The centerpiece of the tour was a production of *The White-Haired Girl* (白毛女), but performances also included excerpts from *jingju*, Xinjiang and Tibetan ethnic minority dance, acrobatics, vocal solos and choral pieces, and instrumental performances on the *pipa* and violin, among others. The troupe totaled 222 members. Shi Yajuan, ed., *Dang women zai ci xiangju: Zhongguo qingnian wengongtuan chufang 9 guo yi nian ji* (Beijing: Wenhua yishu chubanshe, 2004), 487–95.

16. Li Chang et al., *Juchang yu wutai jishu* (Wuhan: Zhongnan renmin wenxue yishu chubanshe, 1954).

17. Li Chang and Qi Mudong, "Houji," in Li Chang et al., *Juchang yu wutai jishu*, 75.

18. "Internal study document" was a fairly common designation during the early PRC. In this case, the audience for the lectures themselves included members of several prominent Beijing-based, state-sponsored theater troupes, and the same groups plus party members or officials working in cultural areas would have been likely readers of the published version. Zhongguo xijujia xiehui weiyuanhui, ed., *Wutai meishu gongzuo jingyan jianjie (neibu xuexi ziliao)* (Beijing: Zhongguo xijujia xiehui yishu weiyuanhui, 1957).

19. *Xin yanju*, vol. 1 (Beijing: Tianxia chubanshe, 1951). The preface notes that

it was first published in Shanghai in May 1937, then in Wuhan and Chonqing; the print run ended in 1940.

20. A common title format literally announces the books as "how-to" guides, as in *Zenme yang paixi he yanxi?* [How to rehearse and perform plays?] (Shenyang: Liaoning renmin chubanshe, 1956).

21. This quote comes from the brief content description (内容提要) included alongside publication information in most PRC-published books. People's Press (人民出版社) publication houses were established in the early 1950s at both the national level (in Beijing) and in each province. Zhang Yaoqing, *Wutai meishu rumen* (Shenyang: Liaoning renmin chubanshe, 1956), n.p.

22. A number of scholars have also discussed the promotion of amateur activities in fields such as writing, music, theater, and fine art. See, for example, Julia F. Andrews, *Painters and Politics in the People's Republic of China, 1949–1979* (Berkeley: University of California Press, 1994); Laurence Coderre, *Newborn Socialist Things: Materiality in Maoist China* (Durham: Duke University Press, 2021); Fokkema, *Literary Doctrine in China*; Colin Mackerras, *Amateur Theatre in China 1949–1966* (Canberra: Australian National University Press, 1973); Bonnie S. McDougall, ed., *Popular Chinese Literature and the Performing Arts in the People's Republic of China, 1949–1979* (Berkeley: University of California Press, 1984).

23. As Mackerras notes, there is reason to doubt the veracity of these numbers, but even if dramatically inflated, the fact of their publication suggests that there were at least attempts to promote amateur theater and that quantitative increase was of importance to party leadership. On the other hand, given the difficulty of accurately calculating the true number of workers and peasants engaged in everyday dramatic activity, it is also possible that these seemingly inflated statistics are actually underreporting the extent to which amateur theater had permeated Chinese society by the end of the 1950s. Mackerras, *Amateur Theatre*, 8–10.

24. For a report on Great Leap theatrical activities issued in fall 1958, see "Yuejin! Yuejin! Zai yuejin!—Xiju jie Dayuejin zongshu," *Xiju bao* 11 (1958): 29–30.

25. Shanghai renmin yishu juyuan, "Shanghai renmin yishu juyuan zenme yang zou qunzhong luxian kaizhan chuangzao huodong," in *Xiju gongzuo yuejin jingyan xuanji* (Shanghai: Shanghai wenyi chubanshe, 1958), 27–32, at 32.

26. In Chinese, the terms *kexue* 科学 (science) and *jishu* 技术 (technology) are often used as a composite term, abbreviated as *keji* 科技 (science and technology, or technoscience). The neologism first appeared in newspapers and periodicals in the 1920s and widely in publications of the 1950s, but initially was rarely used in theater-related discourse. See chapter 5 for a discussion of the use of *keji* in relation to theater technology.

27. See, for example, Chenshu Zhou, *Cinema Off Screen: Moviegoing in Socialist China* (Oakland: University of California Press, 2021), 83–89; Jie Li, *Cinematic Guerrillas: Maoist Propaganda as Spirit Mediumship* (New York: Columbia University Press, 2023), especially chap. 2, "Mobile Projectionists and the Things They Carried."

28. Nicolai Volland, *Socialist Cosmopolitanism: The Chinese Literary Universe, 1945–1965* (New York: Columbia University Press, 2017), 109–12, quote at 111.

29. On the use of literature and the arts for propaganda before and after 1949, see, for example, Xiaomei Chen, *Acting the Right Part: Political Theater and Popular Drama in Contemporary China, 1966–1996* (Honolulu: University of Hawai'i Press, 2002), and Chen, *Staging Chinese Revolution*; DeMare, *Mao's Cultural Army*; David Holm, *Art and Ideology in Revolutionary China* (Oxford: Clarendon Press, 1991); Chang-tai Hung, *Mao's New World: Political Culture in the Early People's Republic* (Ithaca: Cornell University Press, 2017) and *Politics of Control*.

30. Sigrid Schmalzer, *The People's Peking Man: Popular Science and Human Identity in Twentieth-Century China* (Chicago: University of Chicago Press, 2008), 63.

31. For a multifaceted discussion of party–state control of culture during this period, see Hung, *Politics of Control*.

32. In relation to theater and dance, in particular, see, for example, the essays in Chen, Chun, and Liu, eds., *Rethinking Chinese Socialist Theaters of Reform*.

33. Schmalzer, *People's Peking Man*, 56.

34. For background on these campaigns, see, for instance, Roderick MacFarquhar, *The Hundred Flowers Campaign and the Chinese Intellectuals* (New York: Praeger, 1960). For a recent critical reevaluation, see Dayton Lekner, "A Chill in Spring: Literary Exchange and Political Struggle in the Hundred Flowers and Anti-Rightist Campaigns of 1956–1958," *Modern China* 45, no. 1 (2019): 37–63.

35. Mao Zedong, "Be Activists in Promoting the Revolution" (October 7, 1957), in *Selected Works of Mao Tse-tung*, 5:483–97, at 489; qtd. in Schmalzer, *People's Peking Man*, 119.

36. Some interpretations of this period argue that the "Hundred Flowers" campaign was a political maneuver designed to identify and purge political enemies. See, for example, Roderick MacFarquhar, *Origins of the Cultural Revolution*, vol. 1: *Contradictions among the People, 1956–1957* (New York: Columbia University Press, 1974).

37. Tian Han, in turn, would be persecuted during the Cultural Revolution. Rudolf Wagner, *The Contemporary Chinese Historical Drama: Four Studies* (Berkeley: University of California Press, 1990), 4–5. For additional discussion of how the Hundred Flowers campaign and Anti-Rightist Movement affected the theater world, see Maggie Greene, *Resisting Spirits: Drama Reform and Cultural Transformation in the People's Republic of China* (Ann Arbor: University of Michigan Press, 2019), 66–73; and Liu, *Transforming Tradition*.

38. Huang opposed the Three Gorges Dam project on the Yangtze River for environmental reasons. See chap. 1 in Judith Shapiro, *Mao's War against Nature: Politics and the Environment in Revolutionary China* (Cambridge: Cambridge University Press, 2001), 21–66.

39. For discussion of how the "class politics of scientific knowledge" played out in the relationship between science and superstition, see Schmalzer, *People's Peking Man*, 113–36, quotes at 114, 119.

40. Shen Yan, "'Da yuejin' yu shehui zhuyi wutuobang xiju," *Wenyi yanjiu*, no. 8 (2013): 95–102, at 98. There were notably few "science plays" written before 1949 or during the Seventeen Years period, but many plays (and films) feature industrial

and agricultural technologies. Key exceptions include *Fascist Bacillus* (法西斯细菌, 1944) by Xia Yan; *Peking Man* (北京人, 1940) by Cao Yu, which features a paleontologist character; and *The Young Generation* (年轻的一代, 1963) by Chen Yun 陈耘 and Xu Jingxian 徐景贤, which focuses on geologists. See Xiaomei Chen, "'Playing in the Dirt': Plays about Geologists and Memories of the Cultural Revolution and the Maoist Era," *China Review* 5, no. 2 (2005): 65–95; Chen, *Performing the Socialist State: Modern Chinese Theater and Film Culture* (New York: Columbia University Press, 2023), 202–48.

41. Tian Han, "Yi gaodu shehui zhuyi ganjin zhengqu xiju chuangzuo da fengshou," *Juben* 4 (1958): 2–6.

42. According to Tian Han, the theater companies were engaged in a quota-setting competition; the China Youth Art Theater, for instance, upped their promised script production from 110 to 366 after hearing of the numbers pledged by BPAT. Tian Han, "Yi gaodu shehui zhuyi ganjin zhengqu xiju chuangzuo da fengshou," *Juben*, no. 4 (1958): 2–3.

43. Shanghai renmin yishu juyuan, "Shanghai renmin yishu juyuan zenme yang zou qunzhong luxian kaizhan chuangzao huodong," 32. The dating in this article is unclear; numbers may refer either to plays already performed by the time the article was published or to a target to be performed by the end of the year.

44. Iovene, *Tales of Futures Past*, 21. The topic of "red" vs. "expert" was widely discussed in the theater world at this time. See, for example, a record of discussions held by the China Youth Art Theater in May 1958, published in *Theater Gazette*: "Qingyi taolun hong zhuan wenti," *Xiju bao*, no. 10 (1958): 23–24.

45. Iovene, *Tales of Futures Past*, 21.

46. Li Zhiyan, "Huaju *Shisanling shuiku changxiangqu* chuangzuo jishi," *Qingyi*, no. 1 (1993), repr. in *Tian Han chuangzuo ceji* (Chengdu: Sichuan wenyi chubanshe, 1994), 118–29, at 124.

47. Li, "Huaju *Shisanling shuiku changxiangqu* chuangzuo jishi," 128.

48. Li, "Huaju *Shisanling shuiku changxiangqu* chuangzuo jishi," 128.

49. Wei Qixuan, "Xiang Sulian xiju xuexi: Tian Han tongzhi tan quan Sulian juhui yanguan gan," *Juben*, no. 2 (1958): 81–85, at 82.

50. Li Zhiyan, "Huaju *Shisanling shuiku changxiangqu* chuangzuo jishi," 128–29.

51. Zhang Fuji, "Jieshao Qingyi chuangzao de tu zhuantai," *Zhongguo xiju*, no. 15 (1958): 35–36.

52. Zhang, "Jieshao Qingyi chuangzao de tu zhuantai," 35.

53. Sun Haoran, "Guanju zatan," *Xiju bao*, no. 16 (1958): 31–33, at 32.

54. Sun, "Guanju zatan," 32; Fang Chu, "Tan huaju *Shisanling shuiku changxiangqu*," *Zhongguo xiju*, no. 13 (1958): 35.

55. Xu Xiaozhong, "Guanyu 'zhuantai' de yi feng xin," in *Daoyan yishu lun* (Beijing: Wenhua yishu chubanshe, 2017), 455–59, at 459. This piece is undated, but Xu references several of his productions from the late 1950s and 1960s as support for his theories of the revolving stage; the ideas expressed are therefore contemporaneous with the China Youth Art Theater production discussed.

56. Xu, "Guanyu 'zhuantai' de yi feng xin," 455, 459.

57. Wei, "Xiang Sulian xiju xuexi," 82. See chap. 5, note 103 for a discussion of the term *yishu zhenshi* 艺术真实.

58. Wei, "Xiang Sulian xiju xuexi," 82.

59. Wei, "Xiang Sulian xiju xuexi," 82.

60. Liang Luo, "The Experimental and the Popular in Chinese Socialist Theater of the 1950s," in *Rethinking Chinese Socialist Theaters*, ed. Chen Xiaomei, Chun, and Liu, 135–61, at 137.

61. "Wei xiju yishu chuangzao geng hao de jishu tiaojian," *Xiju bao*, no. 10 (1960): 15–16, at 15. See also Sun Shifeng, "Meishu gongchang ye yao dagao jishu geming," *Shanghai xiju*, no. 4 (1960): 39. *Theater Gazette* was a publication of the Chinese Dramatists Association and thus often reflects official ideology.

62. For a discussion of the mixture of industrial and traditional aesthetics in the film adaptation of *Fantasia*, see Qian, "When Taylorism Met Revolutionary Romanticism," 594.

63. Zhang, "Jieshao Qingyi chuangzao de tu zhuantai," 35.

64. "Jishu geming, biandi kaihua," *Xiju bao*, no. 10 (1960): 16–18.

65. Sigrid Schmalzer, *Red Revolution, Green Revolution: Scientific Farming in Socialist China* (Chicago: University of Chicago Press, 2016), 37.

66. Schmalzer, *Red Revolution, Green Revolution*, 34.

67. Zhou, *Cinema Off Screen*, 89.

68. "Jishu geming, biandi kaihua," 17.

69. Tian Han, "*Shisanling shuiku changxiangqu*," *Juben*, no. 8 (1958): 38–77, at 70. Amateur theater handbooks from this period describe various techniques for stage smoke, such as pouring hot water onto quicklime, that is, calcium oxide, 生石灰, to create cooking steam. Quicklime/calcium oxide is involved in a form of steel production, demonstrating yet another level on which theatrical production was materially tied to industrial production. Li Tianshun and Wang Shiwei, *Jianyi wutai xiaoguo* (Tianjin: Hebei renmin chubanshe, 1959), 19.

70. Iovene, *Tales of Futures Past*, 23.

71. Mo Yan was a *huaju* playwright and director born in Fushan, Shandong Province, and is *not* the same person as Nobel-winning novelist Mo Yan 莫言 (Guan Moye 管谟业, b. 1955). For the original script, see Shen Ximeng, Mo Yan, and Lü Xingchen, "*Nihongdeng xia de shaobing*," *Juben*, no. 2 (1963): 2—41.

72. Tang notes that according to *Xiju bao* (no. 184 [April 1964]: 30–31), *Sentinels* was performed by fifty-three different troupes around the country. Yomi Braester provides slightly different figures, perhaps covering a longer time frame, noting that the play was staged by more than a hundred troupes around the country, as well as in North Korea, Vietnam, and Albania. Xiaobing Tang, *Chinese Modern: The Heroic and the Quotidian* (Durham: Duke University Press, 2000), 167n13; Yomi Braester, *Painting the City Red: Chinese Cinema and the Urban Contract* (Durham: Duke University Press, 2010), 83.

73. For the harrowing details of the Great Leap Forward, see, for example, Frank Dikötter, *Mao's Great Famine: The History of China's Most Devastating Catastrophe, 1958–1962* (New York: Walker, 2010); Roderick MacFarquhar, *The Origins of the Cultural Revolution*, vol. 2: *The Great Leap Forward, 1958–1960* (New

York: Columbia University Press, 1983); Yang Jisheng, *Tombstone: The Great Chinese Famine, 1958–1962*, ed. Edward Friedman, Guo Jian, and Stacy Mosher, trans. Stacy Mosher and Guo Jian (New York: Farrar, Straus and Giroux, 2013).

74. The Beijing People's Art Theater, for instance, produced seventeen plays in 1958, ten in 1959, eleven in 1960, then only three plays in 1961 and six in 1962. "Jumu huigu," Beijing renmin yishu juyuan, https://www.bjry.com/play/class ic.html

75. For more on how this period of liberalization affected *xiqu* reform and organization, see Liu, *Transforming Tradition*, 63; for a case study of how these political and policy shifts affected repertoire, see Greene, *Resisting Spirits*.

76. Schmalzer, *Red Revolution, Green Revolution*, 39.

77. Tang, *Chinese Modern*, 166.

78. See chap. 2 in Braester, *Painting the City Red*, 56–94.

79. Shen et al., "Nihongdeng xia de shaobing," 6. Like many highly popular and officially sanctioned plays of this period, *The White-Haired Girl* was also adapted across different theater genres and attained its most iconic iteration as a ballet during the Cultural Revolution. Schmalzer notes that the popular *xin geju* 新歌剧 (new music drama) version of the play was developed as part of an antisuperstition drive that also emphasized the usefulness of "modern" medical science. Schmalzer, *Peking Man*, 58; on *The White-Haired Girl* and *xin geju*, see Max L. Bohnenkamp, "Neither Western Opera, nor Old Chinese Theater: The Modernist 'Integrated Art-Form' and the Origins of the Maoist 'New Music-Drama,'" in *Rethinking Chinese Socialist Theaters of Reform*, 34–60, and "Turning Ghosts into People: *The White-Haired Girl*, Revolutionary Folklorism, and the Politics of Aesthetics in Modern China" (PhD diss., Department of East Asian Languages and Civilizations, University of Chicago, 2014).

80. Shen et al., "Nihongdeng xia de shaobing," 7.

81. Guo Moruo, for instance, "warned that the modern metropolises, especially Shanghai, where new literature and art were created, were in essence extensions of foreign countries, their residents 'rather separated from the great contemporary life in China.'" Qtd. in Liu, *Transforming Tradition*, 16.

82. Liang Luo, for example, gives examples of theater troupes performing *The Legend of the White Snake* in the early 1950s being criticized for using lighting and scenery to attract audiences. Luo, "Experimental and the Popular," 142. See also Liu's discussion of the restriction of "vulgar gimmicks" in *xiqu* performance in chap. 2 of *Transforming Tradition*, 107–9.

83. Braester, *Painting the City Red*, 87.

84. The neon signage advertised Royal Brand typewriters. Chen Dahua et al., *Nihongdeng zhizao jishu yu yingyong* (Beijing: Zhongguo qinggongye chubanshe, 1997), 6. See also "Neon Timeline," Neonsigns.hk (online interactive exhibition), curated by Aric Chen and Tobias Berger, M+ Museum (Hong Kong), last updated June 30, 2014, https://www.neonsigns.hk/neon-timeline/?lang=en

85. Christoph Ribbat, *Flickering Light: A History of Neon*, trans. Anthony Mathews (London: Reaktion Books, 2013), 7–8, 23–24.

86. Chen Dahua et al., *Nihongdeng zhizao jishu yu yingyong*, 7.

87. Lee, *Shanghai Modern*, 3–4.

88. For a discussion of Yuan Muzhi's use of the same sequence in *Street Angel* and the earlier film *City Scenes* (aka *Scenes of City Life*), see Mariagrazia Costantino, "'City Lights' and the Dream of Shanghai," in *Revealing/Reveiling Shanghai: Cultural Representations from the Twentieth and Twenty-First Centuries*, ed. Lisa Bernstein and Chu-chueh Cheng (Albany: State University of New York Press, 2020), 53–82.

89. Zhang Yingjin, ed., *Cinema and Urban Culture in Shanghai, 1922–1943* (Stanford: Stanford University Press, 1999), 169.

90. Braester, *Painting the City Red*, 87.

91. "Neon Timeline," https://www.neonsigns.hk/neon-timeline/?lang=en. There are also multiple reports of (mostly minor) neon signage fires in Shanghai newspapers from the 1930s. See, for example, "Nanking Road Neon-Sign Catches Fire," *North China Daily News*, November 29, 1935, 13.

92. Cao Yongjiu and Li Yuzeng, *Wutai shiyong xiaoguo* (Shenyang: Liaoning renmin chubanshe, 1957), 68. The content description on the front inside cover of the book notes that the techniques are drawn from experience with both professional and amateur theater troupes, but the target audience is urban and rural amateur troupes.

93. He Qun, "Wutai shang nihongdeng de zuofa," *Xiju bao*, no. 8 (1963): 37.

94. Hanchao Lu, *Beyond the Neon Lights: Everyday Shanghai in the Early Twentieth Century* (Berkeley: University of California Press, 1999), 336n40.

95. Fengzi, "Huaju wutai shang de xin shouhuo—tuijian huaju *Nihongdeng xia de shaobing*," *Renmin ribao*, March 10, 1963, 5. See also Fengzi, "Shaobing xunli—Beijing wutai shang *Nihongdeng xia de shaobing* mantan," *Beijing ribao*, June 21, 1963, repr. in *"Nihongdeng xia de shaobing" zhuanji*, ed. Nanjing shifan xueyuan zhongwen xi (Nanjing: Nanjing shifan xueyuan, 1979), 210–19.

96. Mo Yan, "*Nihongdeng xia de shaobing* de daoyan gousi," *Xiju bao*, no. 4 (1963): 15–21, at 19.

97. Mo Yan, "*Nihongdeng xia de shaobing* de daoyan gousi," 18.

98. See, for example, Ge Hede, "Dengxia shuqing—tan *Nihongdeng xia de shaobing* de meishu sheji," *Guangming ribao*, March 13, 1963, repr. *"Nihongdeng xia de shaobing" zhuanji*, ed. Nanjing shifan xueyuan zhongwen xi (Nanjing: Nanjing shifan xueyuan, 1979), 299–304, at 302; Gui Zhongsheng, "Qiantan *Nihongdengxia de shaobing* wutai meishu sheji," *Renmin ribao*, March 17, 1963; and Hu Miaosheng, "Jianlun wutai meishu de xu yu shi," *Renmin xiju*, no. 11 (1978): 21–28; 31, at 25, which was also published with the title "Wutai meishu de xu yu shi" in *Xiju yishu*, no. 1 (1978): 41–57; 122.

99. Tina Lu, *Persons, Roles, and Minds: Identity in "Peony Pavilion" and "Peach Blossom Fan"* (Stanford: Stanford University Press, 2001), 124.

100. Stephen Owen, *Readings in Chinese Literary Thought* (Boston: Brill, 1996), 5–6.

101. Lu, *Persons, Roles, and Minds*, 124.

102. As Jason McGrath has noted, there is an interesting slippage between the

terms *xunixing* and *jiadingxing*. "Suppositionality" is typically the translation for *jiadingxing*, but Haiping Yan, for instance, also translates *xunixing* as "suppositionality." See Jason McGrath, "Suppositionality, Virtuality, and Chinese Cinema," *boundary 2* 49, no. 1 (2022): 263–92, at 269–70; Haiping Yan, "Theatricality in Classical Chinese Drama," in *Theatricality*, ed. Tracy C. Davis and Thomas Postlewait (Cambridge: Cambridge University Press, 2003), 65–89, at 66–67.

103. Li Ruru, *The Soul of Beijing Opera: Theatrical Creativity and Continuity in the Changing World* (Hong Kong: Hong Kong University Press, 2010), 160.

104. Initially a term borrowed from the Japanese to refer to the magic lantern, *huandeng* by the 1960s referred to a wide range of projection technologies that encompassed single slides and film strips made of different materials, as well as either electric or nonelectric lighting sources. For a history of *huandeng* in relation to cinema, see Zhou, *Cinema Off Screen*, 83–89.

105. Xia Yan, "*Sai Jinhua*," *Wenxue* 6, no. 4 (1936): 553–90, at 554.

106. Fan, *Staging Revolution*, 208.

107. He Mengfu, *Wutai zhaoming*, 33–34.

108. For example, a stage effects handbook from 1957 describes how to use projections to make it appear to be snowing onstage. See Shao Chongfei, *Tantan wutai xiaoguo de zhizuo yu shiyong* (Beijing: Beijing chubanshe, 1957), 44. On the use of projected surtitles, see Li Hanfei, "Da hao zimu," *Xiju bao*, no. 20 (1959): 20; Yin Shucun, "Yao renzhen gao hao huandeng zimu," *Shanghai xiju* 1 (1960): 55. Surtitles are helpful in making the poetic aria lyrics of *xiqu* more intelligible to audience members, especially when troupes perform in a dialect different from that spoken by their audience members.

109. Liu Lu, "Huaju wutai meishu chuangzuo wenti de tantao," *Xiju bao*, no. 7 (1956): 28–31, at 29.

110. Here, the term *paoyun deng* is not to be confused with the dance genre of *yunwu* 云舞 (local to parts of Anhui Province), which is sometimes also referred to as *paoyun deng*.

111. Ou Zaixin, *Wutai huandeng yishu* (Beijing: Zhongguo xiju chubanshe, 1992), 3–4. *Wutai huandeng yishu* was not published until 1992, but the preface cited is dated 1980, and Ou writes that he began work on the book in the early 1970s.

112. Lü Dekang, "Jieshao liangzhong wutai dengying chenjing jishu," *Xiju bao*, no. 6 (1963): 35–38, at 35.

113. Lü, "Jieshao liangzhong wutai dengying chenjing jishu," 35.

114. Shanghai shiyan gejuyuan dengguangzu, "Zai wutai shang shiyong huandeng de chubu jingyan," *Shanghai xiju*, no. 2 (1960): 30–32, at 30.

115. Mo Yan, "Daoyan gousi," 18.

116. See, for example, "Ba hao xi song dao nongcun qu," *Xiju bao*, no. 9 (1965): 2–3; Bian Ji, "Shangshan xiaxiang yan haoxi," *Xiju bao*, no. 10 (1965): 41–42.

117. Shanghai shiyan gejuyuan dengguangzu, "Zai wutai shang shiyong huandeng de chubu jingyan," 31.

118. For a discussion of *The East Is Red* in relation to the concept of "red classics" and the creative process behind the production, see Chen, *Staging Chinese Revolution*, 235–45.

119. Chen, *Staging Chinese Revolution*, 244.

120. Qinghua daxue tumu jianzhu xi juyuan jianzhu sheji zu, *Zhongguo huitang juchang jianzhu* (Beijing: Qinghua daxue tumu jianzhu xi, 1960), 33.

121. Li Yegan and Han Libo, "Canjia *Dongfanghong* wutai meishu gongzuo de tihui," *Renmin ribao*, October 15, 1964, 5; Liu Lu, "Wutai meishu de geming yu chuangxin," *Renmin ribao*, October 11, 1964, 4; Tong Benyi, "*Dongfanghong* de houtai gongzuo," *Renmin ribao*, October 15, 1964, 5.

122. Li and Han, "Canjia *Dongfanghong* wutai meishu gongzuo de tihui," 5.

123. Li and Han, "Canjia *Dongfanghong* wutai meishu gongzuo de tihui," 5.

124. Liu Mingxiu, *Wutai huandeng he teji* (Yichang: Hubei renmin chubanshe, 1980), 1; Ou Zaixin, *Wutai huandeng yishu*, 4.

125. Tina Mai Chen, "Mobile Film Projection in Socialist and Post-Socialist China," China Policy Institute Blog, May 8, 2015; Jie Li, "Cinematic Guerrillas in Mao's China," *Screen* 61, no. 2 (2020): 207–29, and *Cinematic Guerrillas*; Zhou, *Cinema Off Screen*.

126. Zhou, *Cinema Off Screen*, 89.

127. Zhou, *Cinema Off Screen*, 92.

128. Shanghai shiyan gejuyuan dengguangzu, "Zai wutai shang shiyong huandeng de chubu jingyan," 30.

129. "Beijing wutai meishu gongzuozhe zuotan—wutai meishu ruhe bianyu shangshan xiaxiang," *Xiju bao*, no. 11 (1965): 41–42, at 42.

130. Liu Rui, "Santou juguangdeng he santou huandeng," *Xiju bao*, no. 11 (1965): 42.

131. Schmalzer mentions slide shows in relation to science dissemination in the 1950s; Schmalzer, *People's Peking Man*, 69–70; Jie Li also discusses the use of slide shows during the Socialist Education Movement in *Cinematic Guerrillas*.

132. Ou Zaixin, for instance, devotes significant sections of his first two chapters to the problem of distortion. Ou Zaixin, *Wutai huandeng yishu*, 1–37.

## Chapter 4

1. Zhongguo jingju tuan, *Geming xiandai jingju "Hongdeng ji" (yijiu qiling nian [1970] wu yue yanchuben)* (Beijing: Renmin chubanshe, 1972), 335.

2. On the semiotics of *The Red Lantern* in particular, see chap. 4 in Yomi Braester, *Witness against History: Literature, Film, and Public Discourse in Twentieth-Century China* (Stanford: Stanford University Press, 2003), 106–27.

3. This was not new to the Cultural Revolution, but accentuated; see discussion of bourgeois entertainment vs. revolutionary art in chapter 3.

4. Chen, *Acting the Right Part*, 119–20.

5. Coderre, *Newborn Socialist Things*, 162.

6. There is a large body of scholarship on *yangbanxi* film. See note 14 for gen-

eral studies that include film, as well as Chris Berry, "Every Colour Red? Colour in the Films of the Cultural Revolution Model Stage Works," *Journal of Chinese Cinemas* 6, no. 3 (2012): 233–46, and Berry, "Red Poetics: The Films of the Chinese Cultural Revolution Revolutionary Model Operas," in *The Poetics of Chinese Cinema*, ed. Gary Bettinson and James Udden (New York: Palgrave Macmillan, 2016), 29–49; Kristine Harris, "Re-makes/Re-models: *The Red Detachment of Women* between Stage and Screen," *Opera Quarterly* 26, nos. 2–3 (2010): 316–42; Jason McGrath, "Cultural Revolution Model Opera Films and the Realist Tradition in Chinese Cinema," *Opera Quarterly* 26, nos. 2–3 (2010): 342–76.

7. For background on Cultural Revolution history and politics, see, for example, Roderick MacFarquhar, *The Origins of the Cultural Revolution*, vols. 1–3 (New York: Columbia University Press, 1974–99); MacFarquhar and Michael Schoenhals, *Mao's Last Revolution* (Cambridge, MA: Belknap Press of Harvard University Press, 2006).

8. Theater also functioned as a powerful metaphor for both politics and everyday life during the Cultural Revolution. See, for example, Ban Wang, *The Sublime Figure of History: Aesthetics and Politics in Twentieth-Century China* (Stanford: Stanford University Press, 1997); and Tuo Wang, *The Cultural Revolution and Overacting: Dynamics between Politics and Performance* (Lanham, MD: Lexington Books, 2014).

9. For discussions of the actual impact of the Cultural Revolution on scientific inquiry vs. how the period has been addressed in the historical narrative, see, for example, Darryl E. Brock and Chunjuan Nancy Wei, "Introduction: Reassessing the Great Proletarian Cultural Revolution," in *Mr. Science and Chairman Mao's Cultural Revolution: Science and Technology in Modern China*, ed. Chunjuan Nancy Wei and Darryl E. Brock (Lanham, MD: Lexington Books, 2013), 1–40; and Sigrid Schmalzer, "On the Appropriate Use of Rose-Colored Glasses: Reflections on Science in Socialist China," *Isis* 98, no. 3 (2007): 571–83.

10. See Fang Lizhi, *The Most Wanted Man in China: My Journey from Scientist to Enemy of the State*, trans. Perry Link (New York: Henry Holt, 2016).

11. Brock and Wei, "Introduction," 23.

12. Li Ruru, *The Soul of Beijing Opera*, 121–22.

13. Wagner, *Contemporary Chinese Historical Drama*, 136–37.

14. See Braester, *Witness against History*; Chen, *Acting the Right Part*, 73–158; Paul Clark, *The Cultural Revolution: A History* (Cambridge: Cambridge University Press, 2008); Coderre, *Newborn Socialist Things*; Fan, *Staging Revolution*; Barbara Mittler, *A Continuous Revolution: Making Sense of Cultural Revolution Culture* (Cambridge, MA: Harvard University Press, 2016); Laikwan Pang, *The Art of Cloning: Creative Production during China's Cultural Revolution* (New York: Verso, 2017).

15. Pang, *Art of Cloning*, 84.

16. See, for instance, Sigrid Schmalzer's critique of negative post-1976 historical narratives and discussion of evidence that complicates the narrative. Schmalzer, "On the Appropriate Use of Rose-Colored Glasses," 576–83.

17. See, for example, the essays in Wei and Brock, eds., *Mr. Science and Chairman Mao's Cultural Revolution.*

18. Pang, *Art of Cloning,* 84.

19. Pang, *Art of Cloning,* 91.

20. Joel Andreas, *Rise of the Red Engineers: The Cultural Revolution and the Origins of China's New Class* (Stanford: Stanford University Press, 2009).

21. Andrea Bardin and Giovanni Carrozzini, "Organizing Invention through Technical Mentality: Simondon's Challenge to the 'Civilisation of Productivity,'" *Culture and Organization* 23, no. 1 (2017): 26–33, at 29; see also Gilbert Simondon, "Technical Mentality," trans. Arne De Boever, *Parrhesia* 7, nos. 2–3 (2009): 17–27. http://parrhesiajournal.org/parrhesia07/parrhesia07.pdf

22. The designation of the eight official *yangbanxi* took place in November 1966 at the Proletarian Cultural Revolution Meeting for the Circle of Literature and Art in the Capital, followed by two editorials published in the *People's Daily* and *Red Flag* (红旗) on May 31, 1967, that introduced the concept and individual works more broadly. Fan, *Staging Revolution,* 72.

23. Jiang Qing was born Lan Shuming 李淑蒙 and took the stage name Lan Ping 藍蘋 when she worked as an actor in her youth. After marrying Mao, she had stepped back from an active role in both politics and the theater until 1963. For a discussion of the development of the *yangbanxi* with particular attention to Jiang Qing's role in the process, see chap. 2 in Chen, *Acting the Right Part,* 73–121.

24. Jiang Qing, "On the Revolution in Peking Opera (Tan Jingju geming)," trans. Jessica Ka Yee Chan, *Opera Quarterly* 26, nos. 2–3 (2010): 455–59; Jiang Qing, "Tan jingju geming: Yijiu liusi nian qi yue jingju xiandai xi guanmo yanchu renyuan de zuotanhui shang de jianghua," *Renmin ribao,* May 10, 1967, 1.

25. Ellen Judd argues that the *yangbanxi* troupes also provided a model for the social organization of professionalized arts. See Judd, "Prescriptive Dramatic Theory of the Cultural Revolution," in *Drama in the People's Republic of China,* ed. Constantine Tung and Colin Mackerras (Albany: State University of New York Press, 1987), 94–118, at 94.

26. For a detailed discussion of the scripting process of the *yangbanxi,* see Fan, *Staging Revolution,* chap. 5.

27. Jiang, "On the Revolution in Peking Opera," 457; "Tan jingju geming," 1.

28. Richard King, "Typical People in Typical Circumstances," in *Words and Their Stories: Essays on the Language of the Cultural Revolution,* ed. Ban Wang (Leiden: Brill, 2010), 185–204.

29. Raymond Williams, *Marxism and Literature* (Oxford: Oxford University Press, 2009), 102.

30. For a detailed discussion of both, see Judd, "Prescriptive Drama Theory," 101–5.

31. Jiang Deming, "Qianchui bailian jingyi qiujing—ji jingju *Hongdeng ji* zaidu yanchu," *Renmin ribao,* October 13, 1964, 2.

32. Clark, *Cultural Revolution,* 127–28; cited in Berry, "Every Colour Red?," 234.

33. *Beijing ribao,* May 11, 1970, 3.

34. Fan, *Staging Revolution*, 201.

35. Fan, *Staging Revolution*, 201–2.

36. Lu, *Zhongguo xiandai juchang de yanjin*, 100.

37. Julia F. Andrews notes a similar technical shift in the visual arts. She specifically cites the year 1953 as marking "an important transition from a rigid emphasis on popularized subjects and forms to the administration of art as a professional, specialized undertaking" and attributes this change to a nationwide interest in Soviet technology. Andrews, *Painters and Politics in the People's Republic of China*, 110.

38. Li, "Xuexi jiejian Ouzhou xianjin de wutai meishu gongzuo," 108, 111.

39. "Shoudu juchang jiancheng," *Xiju bao*, no. 11 (1955): 42–43. In addition to the written records of the events leading up to the construction of the Capital Theater, documents such as a list of technical requirements for the theater are preserved in the BPAT Theater Museum.

40. From August 1949 to the end of 1958, there were some 11,527 advisors from the USSR and other foreign countries in China advising on a range of projects, from industry and economics to education and culture. Kuai and Rao, *Xin Zhongguo wenhua guanli tizhi yanjiu*, 142; "Shoudu juchang jiancheng."

41. Jiang Yibing, "Guanghui de yingxiong xingxiang, zhanxin de wutai meishu—xuexi geming xiandai jingju *Hongdeng ji* wutai meishu de tihui," *Beijing ribao*, May 16, 1970, 3.

42. Shu Haoqing, "Yiqie wei le suzao wuchan jieji yingxiong xingxiang—xuexi *Zhiqu weihushan* wutai meishu zhaji," *Renmin ribao*, October 28, 1969, 3. The importance of environmental details has also been noted by Xing Fan, based on her interviews with the scenic and lighting designers involved with the *yangbanxi*. Fan, *Staging Revolution*, 198–208.

43. For an in-depth discussion of typicality, including its role in Cultural Revolution artistic theory, see King, "Typical People in Typical Circumstances."

44. Zhongguo jingju tuan, *Geming xiandai jingju "Hongdeng ji"* (Shanghai: Shanghai wenhua chubanshe, 1968), 3.

45. Zhongguo jingju tuan, *Geming xiandai jingju "Hongdeng ji" (yijiu qiling nian [1970] wu yue yanchuben)*. For a published English translation of this work, see Weng Ouhong and A Jia, *The Red Lantern* [1970], rev. China Peking Opera Troupe, trans. Brenda Austin and John B. Weinstein, in *The Columbia Anthology of Modern Chinese Drama*, ed. Xiaomei Chen (New York: Columbia University Press, 2010), 732–68.

46. Shanghai jingju tuan *Zhiqu Weihushan* juzu, *Geming xiandai jingju "Zhiqu Weihushan" (yijiu qiling nian [1970] qi yue yanchuben)* (Beijing: Renmin chubanshe, 1971), 367.

47. Shanghai jingju tuan *Zhiqu Weihushan* juzu, *Geming xiandai jingju "Zhiqu Weihushan"*, 367–68.

48. Shanghai jingju tuan *Haigang* zu, *Geming xiandai jingju "Haigang" (yijiu qi'er nian [1972] yi yue yanchuben)* (Beijing: Renmin wenxue chubanshe, 1974), 26; 41–47.

49. Shanghai jingju tuan *Haigang* zu, *Geming xiandai jingju "Haigang"*, 344.

50. Some scholars translate this as "red, smooth, and luminescent." See Jiehong Jiang, *Burden or Legacy: From the Chinese Cultural Revolution to Contemporary Art* (Hong Kong: Hong Kong University Press, 2007), 20; Richard King et al., *Art in Turmoil: The Chinese Cultural Revolution, 1966–76* (Vancouver: University of British Columbia Press, 2010), xi.

51. Braester, *Witness against History*, 121–27.

52. Shanghai jingju tuan *Zhiqu Weihushan* juzu, *Geming xiandai jingju "Zhiqu Weihushan"*, 360.

53. For opening scene choreography, see Shanghai jingju tuan *Haigang* zu, *Geming xiandai jingju "Haigang"*, 225–32.

54. Tina Mai Chen, "The Human–Machine Continuum in Maoism: The Intersection of Soviet Socialist Realism, Japanese Theoretical Physics, and Chinese Revolutionary Theory," *Cultural Critique* no. 80 (Winter 2012): 151–82, at 155.

55. Pang, *Art of Cloning*, 124, referencing Chen, "Human–Machine Continuum"; see esp. 163–64.

56. Costumes and makeup are arguably also key components of this experience, but are beyond the scope of this chapter. See Rosemary A. Roberts, *Maoist Model Theatre: The Semiotics of Gender and Sexuality in the Chinese Cultural Revolution (1966–1976)* (Leiden: Brill, 2010).

57. Shu, "Yiqie wei le suzao wuchan jieji yingxiong xingxiang," 3.

58. Fan, *Staging Revolution*, 256. For additional analysis of this moment, see Barbara Mittler, "Cultural Revolution Model Works and the Politics of Modernization in China: An Analysis of *Taking Tiger Mountain by Strategy*," *World of Music* 45, no. 2 (2003): 53–81, at 66.

59. Ren Yi, "Shengse zhuangli, qingjing jiaorong—xuexi *Hongse niangzi jun* wutai meishu de tihui," *Beijing ribao*, October 10, 1970, 3.

60. Ren Yi, "Manhuai jiqing hui hongtu—xuexi *Hongse niangzi jun* wutai meishu zhaiji," *Renmin ribao*, August 28, 1970.

61. The genealogy of this phrase can be traced to early Chinese poetics, including discussions of the relationship between the poet and his environment in Liu Xie's 劉勰 sixth-century treatise *The Literary Mind and the Carving of Dragons* (文心雕龍). Other antecedents include the concepts of "emotion within scenery, scenery within emotion" (情中景，景中情) articulated by seventeenth-century scholar Wang Fuzhi 王夫之 in his *Notes on Poetry from the Ginger Studio* (薑齋詩話) and Wang Guowei's 王國維 discussion of "the realm of meaning" (意境) in his 1910 *Notes on Poetry for the Human Realm* (人間詞話).

62. For example, one piece, written by filmmaker and critic Gao Honghu 高鴻鵠, discusses the relationship of scenery and emotion in the film version of the model opera *Raid on the White Tiger Regiment* (奇袭白虎团); another, written under the pseudonym Xiao Qiu 小丘, uses *On the Docks* to do the same. Gao Honghu, "Ji qing yu jing, qing jing jiao rong," *Renmin ribao*, October 22, 1972, 4; Xiao Qiu, "Jing he qing—yishu bianzhengfa xuexi zaji," *Renmin ribao*, January 6, 1973, 4.

63. Fang Yun, *Geming yangbanxi xuexi zhaji* (Shanghai: Shanghai renmin chubanshe, 1974), 113. According to Ellen Judd, "Fang Yun" is a pseudonym for a writ-

ing group organized by close associates of Jiang Qing, and the theorizations put forward in this treatise were somewhat controversial at the time. Judd, "Prescriptive Dramatic Theory," 96.

64. Li Zehou, *The Chinese Aesthetic Tradition*, trans. Maija Bell Samai (Honolulu: University of Hawai'i Press, 2010), 152–53, quote 152.

65. Xiao, "Jing he qing."

66. Jia Xian, "The Past, Present and Future of Scientific and Technical Journals of China," *Learned Publishing* 19, no. 2 (2006): 134.

67. A large number of technical materials circulated in this manner. (See Zhongguo banben tushuguan, ed., *Quanguo neibu faxing tushu zong mu* [Beijing: Zhonghua shuju, 1988].) The same can be said for foreign literature and films, which were famously available for high-level cadres but not to the masses. Handwritten copies of banned and suspect texts also circulated. See, for example, Lena Henningsen, "Literature of the Cultural Revolution," in *Routledge Handbook of Modern Chinese Literature*, ed. Ming Dong Gu with Tao Feng (New York: Routledge, 2019), 423–34, at 426–31; Kong Shuyu, "For Reference Only: Restricted Publication and Distribution of Foreign Literature during the Cultural Revolution," *Journal of Chinese Contemporary Art* 1, no. 2 (2002): 76–85; Yang Jian, *Mudi yu yaolan: Wenhua dageming zhong de dixia wenxue* (Beijing: Zhaohua chubanshe, 1993).

68. The term *zhaji* 札记 can be translated as "reading notes," but the articles entitled with this phrase are typically responses to either live performances or the filmed *yangbanxi*. "Viewing notes" therefore more fully conveys the sense in which the term is used.

69. This trend was not limited to the Cultural Revolution, but the shift of publication venue from specialist journals to major newspapers is significant. The term used for scenography in Cultural Revolution sources, *wutai meishu* 舞台美术, typically refers collectively to sets (布景), lighting (灯光), and costumes and makeup (化妆服装, or 人物造型 [lit. "character molding"]). While the English term "scenography" sometimes more narrowly refers to scenic design, here it is used in its more capacious sense to refer to all design elements that structure the visual, experiential, and spatial composition of a performance.

70. The Shu Haoqing article cited in note 42, for example, was reprinted at least twice in the collections *Xuexi geming yangbanxi, puji geming yangbanxi*, vol. 1 (n.p., 1970), and *Geming yangbanxi chuangzuo jingyan* (Nanchang: Jiangxi renmin chubanshe, 1972).

71. Coderre, *Newborn Socialist Things*, 151–53. Coderre also comments on the investment in standardization indicated by these guides.

72. Pang, *Art of Cloning*, 96.

73. The term *yanchuben* 演出本 is used for both simplified scripts and for the longer production bibles discussed in this chapter. Publication formats also included simplified scripts, performance editions, sheet music (staff notation), main melody music (simple notation), and pictorials. Li Song, ed., *Yangbanxi biannian shi houbian* (Taipei: Xiuwei zixun keji, 2012), 275.

74. Pang, *Art of Cloning*, 91, citing Liu Gao and Shi Feng, eds., *Xin Zhongguo chuban wushinian jishi* (Beijing: Xinhua chubanshe, 1999), 128.

75. The term "promptbook" or "show bible" typically refers to the stage manager's copy of the script, which contains detailed notations on blocking, lighting, sound, and special effects cues, prop sheets, set drawings, and other documents essential to running the production. Promptbooks are not typically reproduced or published for wide readership. In this chapter, I call into question the previous terming of these *yangbanxi* texts as "production manuals," so have opted to refer to them instead as "production bibles" in order to emphasize both their relationship to performance and their capacious content.

76. Zhongguo jingju tuan, *Geming xiandai jingju "Hongdeng ji"*, 323–57.

77. Clark, *Chinese Cultural Revolution*, 123–34.

78. Clark, *Chinese Cultural Revolution*, 87; Shi Yonggang, Liu Qiongxiong, and Xiao Yifei, eds., *Geming yangbanxi: 1960 niandai de hongse geju* (Beijing: Zhongguo fazhan chubanshe, 2012), 48. Pang and Coderre follow similar lines of interpretation, respectively linking the publication of *yangbanxi* materials to a broader culture of copying and the molding (塑造) of amateur bodies into revolutionary heroes. Pang, *Art of Cloning*, 91–102; Coderre, *Newborn Socialist Things*, 150.

79. See, for example, "Dianshi jilupian *Zhiqu weihushan Hongdeng ji* paicheng," *Jiefangjun bao*, July 31, 1970.

80. King, "Typical People in Typical Circumstances," 200; see also Williams, *Marxism and Literature*, 101–3.

81. Gazetteers are available from the Wanfang Data New China Local Gazetteers database.

82. For more nuanced discussions of the meaning and role of the "amateur" in *yangbanxi* performance, see Laurence Coderre, "Breaking Bad: Sabotaging the Production of the Hero in the Amateur Performance of *Yangbanxi*," in *Listening to China's Cultural Revolution: Music, Politics, and Cultural Continuities*, ed. Paul Clark, Laikwan Pang, and Tsan-Huang Tsai (Basingstoke: Palgrave Macmillan, 2016), 65–83; and Ellen Judd, "China's Amateur Drama: The Movement to Popularize the Revolutionary Model Operas," *Bulletin of Concerned Asian Scholars* 15, no. 1 (1983): 30–31.

83. Zhang Zhennan, ed., *Shuangyashan xiqu zhi* (n.p., 1989), 131.

84. "Jinan shi jingjutuan yanchu geming xiandai jingju *Shajiabang*," *Dazhong ribao*, February 14, 1972, 3.

85. "Zuo hao puji geming yangbanxi de gongzuo," *Renmin ribao*, July 15, 1970.

86. Zhang Lijun's work shows that peasant household theater troupes (庄户剧团) had attempted to perform the *yangbanxi* as early as 1966, years before the official campaign to popularize the *yangbanxi* began in 1970. Zhang Lijun, "*Yangbanxi*" zai xiangtu Zhongguo de jieshou meixue yanjiu (Beijing: Renmin chubanshe, 2014), 73.

87. Anqiu xian jingju tuan, "Shenru gongnongbing, zhuanyi lizudian," *Shandong wenyi*, no. 6 (January 1972): 12–16, at 13.

88. Xinjun, "Xuexi *Chusheng de Taiyang* wutai meishu de tihui," *Renmin xiju*, no. 6 (1976): 20–21.

89. Fang, *Geming yangbanxi xuexi zhaji*, 117.

90. Coderre, "Breaking Bad," 72; McGrath, "Cultural Revolution Model Opera Films," 344.

91. *Lanzhou xiqu zhi* (Lanzhou: Lanzhou xiqu zhi bianweihui, 1993), 27.

92. The specific piece of equipment was a silicon-controlled rectifier (SCR) dimmer, a now common type of solid-state dimmer that allows for better control and smoother shifts between different lighting levels. For further discussion of semiconductor-based dimmers, see chap. 5. "Kekonggui wutai tiaoguang," *Keji jianbao*, no. 1 (January 1971): 26. Reprinted from *Kunming keji* (1971), 16.

93. "Kekonggui wutai tiaoguang."

94. Anqiu xian jingju tuan, "Shenru gongnongbing, zhuanyi lizudian," 13.

95. "Quxian Mao Zedong sixiang wenyi xuanchuandui shenru shanqu puji geming yangbanxi," *Renmin ribao*, September 27, 1970.

96. "Zai douzheng zhong jianchi puji geming yangbanxi—Zhongguo renmin jiefangjun Shanghai jingbei qu moubu yeyu xuanchuandui diaocha," in *Yizhi chang dao gongchan zhuyi—Gongnongbing puji geming yangbanxi diaocha baogao*, ed. Shanghai shifan daxue Zhongwen xi gongnongbing xueyuan diaocha xiaozu (Shanghai: Shanghai renmin chubanshe, 1975), 74–85.

97. "Zai douzheng zhong jianchi puji geming yangbanxi," 84.

## Chapter 5

1. Qian Xuesen, "Kexue jishu xiandaihua yiding yao daidong wenxue yishu xiandaihua," *Wutai meishu yu jishu* 1 (1981): 4–8.

2. For two perspectives on these trends in Chinese theater of the 1980s-1990s, see, for example, Xiaomei Chen, *Occidentalism: A Theory of Counter-Discourse in Post-Mao China*, 2nd ed. (Lanham, MD: Rowman and Littlefield, 2002), and Claire Conceison, *Significant Other: Staging the American in China* (Honolulu: University of Hawai'i Press, 2004).

3. The General Political Department Huaju Troupe is based in Beijing and is one of many performing arts troupes affiliated with the PRC military. It formed in March 1951 out of several propaganda troupes that had been active during the Second Sino-Japanese War and the Chinese Civil War. The troupe's military affiliation may help to explain why they were permitted to perform a play that involved reference to classified topics like nuclear arms development; although the nuclear tests of the 1960s were public knowledge and widely celebrated, many details of the development process were not. For a history of the General Political Department Huaju Troupe, see Zhongguo yishu yanjiuyuan huaju yanjiusuo, ed. *Junlü xiju zhi hua: Zongzheng huajutuan de chuangzuo daolu* (Beijing: Zhongguo xiju chubanshe, 1993), 257–78.

4. Deng Xiaoping, "Speech at the Opening Ceremony of the National Conference on Science," in *Selected Works of Deng Xiaoping: vol. 2, 1975–1982* (Beijing: Foreign Language Press, 1984), 101–16; Deng Xiaoping, "Zai Quanguo kexue dahui kaimu shi shang de jianghua," in *Deng Xiaoping wenxuan*, vol. 2, 2nd ed. (Beijing: Renmin chubanshe, 1994), 85–100.

5. Merle Goldman and Denis Fred Simon, "Introduction: The Onset of Chi-

na's New Technological Revolution," in *Science and Technology in Post-Mao China*, edited by Denis Fred Simon and Merle Goldman (Cambridge, MA: Harvard University Press, 1989), 1–20, at 9.

6. The Four Modernizations were also promoted by Zhou Enlai in 1963, in the wake of the Great Leap Forward; although he was in poor health by the mid-1970s and passed away in January 1976, Zhou influenced the initial revival of the policy in 1975. His reputation as a moderate counterpart to Chairman Mao and his historic support of the policy simultaneously helped to legitimize the policy and to enable the party of the late 1970s to portray its embrace of the Four Modernizations as a step away from Mao's more radical policies.

7. For a detailed discussion of the waves of ideological and policy change related to science in the immediate post-Mao years, see H. Lyman Miller, *Science and Dissent in Post-Mao China: The Politics of Knowledge* (Seattle: University of Washington Press, 1996), 69–75.

8. Xiaowen Xu, "Early Modern Drama: Hong Shen, Ouyang Yuqian, Xia Yan," in *The Routledge Handbook of Modern Chinese Literature*, ed. Ming Dong Gu (New York: Routledge, 2019), 183–93.

9. Hu Shuhe, *Cao Yu pingzhuan* (Beijing: Zhongguo xiju chubanshe, 1994), 347–50.

10. Chen, *Acting the Right Part*, 160.

11. BPAT produced revivals (复排) of 1950s stagings of *Thunderstorm* in 1979 and *Sunrise* in 1981. "Jumu huigu," *Beijing renmin yishu juyuan*, http://www.bjry.com/play/1972-1981.html

12. For an overview of post–Cultural Revolution developments in Chinese theater, see, for example, Constantine Tung, "Introduction: Tradition and Experience of the Drama of the People's Republic of China," in *Drama in the People's Republic of China*, ed. Constantine Tung and Colin Mackerras (Albany: State University of New York Press, 1987), 1–27, at 13–20; and Haiping Yan, "Theater and Society: An Introduction to Contemporary Chinese Drama," in *Theater and Society: An Anthology of Contemporary Chinese Drama*, ed. Haiping Yan (Armonk, NY: M. E. Sharpe, 1998), ix–xlvii.

13. For introductory discussions of scar literature and root-seeking literature, see, for example, Sabina Knight, "Scar Literature and the Memory of Trauma," in *The Columbia Companion to Modern Chinese Literature*, ed. Kirk A. Denton (New York: Columbia University Press, 2016), 293–98, and Mark Leenhouts, "Culture against Politics: Root-Seeking Literature," in *Columbia Companion to Modern Chinese Literature*, ed. Denton, 299–306.

14. As discussed in chapter 4, many periodicals ceased publication for extended periods during the Cultural Revolution, and the overall number of books published for the general public decreased dramatically. For discussion of postdramatic theater, see Hans-Thies Lehmann, *Postdramatic Theatre*, trans. Karen Jürs-Munby (London: Routledge, 2006).

15. During the 1980s, the term "exploration" was used widely to describe a variety of new directions taken in dramatic literature and theatrical performance; some

scholars, like Rossella Ferrari, have argued for the use of the term "avant-garde" (先锋) to describe Chinese experimental theater of the 1980s; Rosella Ferrari, *Pop Goes the Avant-Garde: Experimental Theatre in Contemporary China* (London: Seagull, 2012). There is a robust body of scholarship in both Chinese and English on experimental theater of the 1980s. In addition to Ferrari, see, for example, Chen Jide, *Zhongguo dangdai xianfeng xiju, 1979–2000* (Beijing: Beijing xiju chubanshe, 2004); Zhang Zhongnian, ed., *Zhongguo shiyan xiju* (Shanghai: Shanghai renmin chubanshe, 2009).

16. Colin Mackerras, "Modernization and Contemporary Chinese Theatre: Commercialization and Professionalization," in *Drama in the People's Republic of China*, ed. Tung and Mackerras, 181–212.

17. Andreas, *Rise of the Red Engineers*, quote 214.

18. At the same time, this also brought concerns of overcommercialization and the commodification of art. Mackerras discusses these concerns in the context of the early 1980s, but the debate would come to a head in the 1990s as the performing arts began to face even stronger competition from mediatized forms of entertainment like television. Mackerras, "Modernization and Contemporary Chinese Theatre," 202–3.

19. On scientist plays, see Chen, *Performing the Socialist State*, 202–48.

20. Hui Faye Xiao, "Science and Poetry: Narrativizing Marital Crisis in Reform-Era Rural China," *Modern Chinese Literature and Culture* 23, no. 2 (2011): 146–74, at 151–52; Guo Moruo, "Kexue de chuntian—zai Quanguo kexue dahui bimushi shang de jianghua," *Renmin ribao*, April 1, 1978, 3.

21. See, for example, Hua Li, *Chinese Science Fiction during the Post-Mao Cultural Thaw* (Toronto: University of Toronto Press, 2021); Rui Kunze, "Displaced Fantasy: Pulp Science Fiction in the Early Reform Era of the People's Republic of China," *East Asian History* 41 (August 2017): 25–40; Rudolf G. Wagner, "Lobby Literature: The Archaeology and Present Functions of Science Fiction in China," in *After Mao: Chinese Literature and Society, 1978–1981*, ed. Jeffrey C. Kinkley (Cambridge, MA: Council on East Asian Studies, Harvard University, 1985), 17–62.

22. Ke Zunke, "Bei lishi kongzhi de huaju: *Jialilüe zhuan* de kexue chuanbo yanjiu," *Kexue wenhua pinglun* 2, no. 6 (2005): 41–54, at 52.

23. Hu Miaosheng, "Cong *Cai Wenji* zhi *Jialilüe zhuan*—Lun wutai meishu de xieyi xing," *Xiju yishu*, no. 2 (1981): 48–61; Luan Guanhua, "Jie hou fuxing de jingxiang—'Shoudu wutai meishu sheji zhanlan' guangan," *Renmin xiju*, no. 1 (1981): 33–34.

24. Chen, *Occidentalism*, 53–54.

25. A similar series of oppositions appears in other publicity for and reviews of the play. Ding Yangzhong, "Bulaixite he ta de *Jialilüe zhuan*," *Renmin xiju*, no. 3 (1979): 32–34, at 34.

26. Chen, *Occidentalism*, 53; Li Jiayao, "Di jiushi yi ge xi de chenggong yanchu—Zuolin daoyan *Jialilüe zhuan* ceji," *Shanghai xiju*, no. 3 (1979): 31–32; Shouhua Qi, *Adapting Western Classics for the Chinese Stage* (New York: Routledge, 2019), 35.

27. Huang Zuolin, "Zhuiqiu kexue xuyao teshu de yonggang—wei Bulaixite de *Jialilüe zhuan* shouci zai Zhongguo shangyan er zuo," *Wenyi yanjiu* no. 1 (1979): 121–27, at 125.

28. "Zhongguo qingnian yishu juyuan zhunbei shangyan *Jialilüe zhuan*," *Renmin xiju*, no. 1 (1979): 15.

29. Guo Moruo, "Kexue de chuntian." Huang's daughter, Huang Shuqin 黄 蜀芹, also relates the *Galileo* production directly to the national conference in her memoir. Huang Shuqin, *Dongbian guangying du hao—Huang Shuqin yanjiu wenji* (Beijing: Zhongguo dianying chubanshe, 2002), 7; qtd. in Gu Chunfang, *Ta de wutai: Zhongguo xiju nü daoyan chuangzuo yanjiu* (Shanghai: Shanghai yuandong chubanshe, 2011), 68.

30. Huang, "Zhuiqiu kexue xuyao teshu de yonggang," 127. Brecht addresses his idea of "theater for a scientific age" perhaps most directly in his "Short Organum for the Theatre." See Brecht, "A Short Organum for the Theatre," in *Brecht on Theatre: The Development of an Aesthetic*, ed. and trans. John Willett (London: Metheun Drama, 1964), 179–205, at 179–80.

31. Chen Yong, "The Beijing Production of *Life of Galileo*," trans. Adrian Hsia, Tak-Wai Wong, and Antony Tatlow, in *Brecht and East Asian Theatre: The Proceedings of a Conference on Brecht in East Asian Theatre*, ed. Antony Tatlow and Tak-wai Wong (Hong Kong: Hong Kong University Press, 1982), 88–95, at 89.

32. Chen, "Beijing Production of *Life of Galileo*," 92–93.

33. Kirsten Shepherd-Barr, *Science on Stage: From Doctor Faustus to Copenhagen* (Princeton: Princeton University Press, 2006), 25.

34. Huang, "Zhuiqiu kexue xuyao teshu de yonggang," 123.

35. Huang, "Zhuiqiu kexue xuyao teshu de yonggang," 125; Fredrich Engels, "Introduction," in *Socialism: Utopian and Scientific*, trans. Edward Aveling (London: S. Sonnenschein & Co., 1892), xx.

36. Reviews and scholarship have emphasized a strong parallel between the story of *Galileo* translator Ding Yangzhong, who worked on his translation while imprisoned during the Cultural Revolution, and Galileo himself. See, for example, Qi, *Adapting Western Classics*, 34.

37. Chen, *Occidentalism*, 55; Lin Kehuan, "Bianzheng de xiju xingxiang: Lun Jialilüe xingxiang," *Xiju yishu luncong*, no. 1 (1979): 220–25, at 224; see also Lin Kehuan, "Lüe tan *Jialilüe zhuan*," *Juben*, no. 7 (1979): 94–96, at 96; Zhang Li, "Shi weiren, ke ye shi zuiren," *Renmin xiju*, no. 6 (1979): 39–42.

38. Chen, *Occidentalism*, 54–55.

39. Chen, *Occidentalism*, 54; see also Chen, *Acting the Right Part*, 302.

40. Chen Yong, "Beijing Production of *Life of Galileo*," 95; see also Chen, *Occidentalism*, 55.

41. These remarks were first made in a report circulated to the Shanghai Theater Academy after Huang attended a meeting of the International Brecht Society in 1987. Huang Zuolin, "Guoji Bulaixite xuehui di qi jie yantaohui de ganshou," in *Wo yu xieyi xijuguan* (Beijing: Zhongguo xiju chubanshe, 1990), 261.

42. Although she does not accuse Huang or Chen of misinterpreting Brecht,

Xiaomei Chen has noted that the production also ran counter to Brecht's "alienation effect" in that it caused the post–Cultural Revolution Chinese audience to *identify* with Galileo's experiences of persecution and betrayal. Ke, "Bei lishi kongzhi de huaju," 52; Chen, *Acting the Right Part,* 302.

43. Ke, "Bei lishi kongzhi de huaju," 52.

44. Ralph Manheim and John Willett, "Introduction," in *Life of Galileo,* ed. John Willett and Ralph Manheim (New York: Arcade, 1994), vi–xxii, at xix.

45. Peter D. Smith, *Metaphor and Materiality: German Literature and the World-View of Science, 1780–1955* (Oxford: Legenda, 2000), 277–78.

46. Qi, *Adapting Western Classics,* 34.

47. Senda Korea [*sic*], "Greetings from Japan to the International Brecht Society," *Brecht Yearbook* 14 (1989): 5–6, at 6

48. See chap. 6 in Smith, *Metaphor and Materiality,* 265–318.

49. David Roberts, "Brecht and the Idea of a Scientific Theatre," *Brecht Yearbook* 13 (1987): 41–59, at 42.

50. R. G. Davis provides one example of Brecht's simultaneous praise of and uneasiness about science and technology in "Brecht / Science / Ecology," *Brecht Yearbook* 23 (1997): 80–83, at 81.

51. Huang, "Guoji Bulaixite xuehui di qi jie yantaohui de ganshou," 261. Huang refers here to Qian, "Kexue jishu xiandaihua," cited in note 1.

52. The idea of "pure" versus "applied" science is itself a problematic binary, and one that is very much collapsed in the Chinese term *keji,* or technoscience, and problematized by Brecht's work. See, for example, the discussion in Smith, *Metaphor and Materiality,* 265–318.

53. Patricia Anne Simpson, "Revolutionary Reading: The Circulation of Truth in Brecht's *Leben des Galilei,*" *Brecht Yearbook* 15 (1990): 165–85, at 170.

54. For one approach to culture and religiosity during the Cultural Revolution, see discussion of propaganda as a "revolutionary spirit medium" in Jie Li, *Cinematic Guerrillas.*

55. Roberts, "Brecht and the Idea of a Scientific Theatre," 45.

56. Keyword searches for the phrase "舞台科技" in the National Index to Chinese Newspapers and Periodicals select databases for the period 1833–1949, for instance, yielded no results. Similarly, in a subject search for the same term in the CNKI periodicals database, which includes journals published in the 1950s–1960s, the earliest result dates to 1975. Neither of these search methods is exhaustive, but the lack of results relative to the representativeness of the database sets suggests that the term was not commonly used before the mid to late 1970s.

57. The Institute later became the China Institute of Arts, Science, and Technology (中国艺术科技研究所, or CASTI). Today, CASTI is under the Ministry of Culture and Tourism. It conducts research in a number of areas related to theater technology, digital arts, art materials, and research popularization. See its official website: https://www.casti.org.cn

58. Yi Ke, "Yu gaige kaifang tong pin gongzheng sui shidai dachao zhulang qianxing—qingzhu Zhongguo yishu keji yanjiusuo jiansuo 40 zhou nian," *Zhong-*

*guo wenhua bao*, January 8, 2019, https://www.casti.org.cn/casti/xwzx02/201901
/ee3d88c93e2846ff82a08540837e750a.shtml, accessed May 10, 2022. For other
examples of China Institute of Arts Science and Technology publications, see, for
example, Gansu gongye daxue jixie yi xi, "*Zhongguo juchang jianzhu sheji guifan he
Wutai jixie jishu guifan* wancheng chugao," *Gansu gongye daxue xuebao* no. 3 (1985):
55.

59. Li Chao, "Yao zhongshi wutai meishu zhe men xueke: Dai fakanci," *Wutai
meishu yu jishu* 1 (1981): 1–3, at 2.

60. Li Chang, "Wutai meishu de duoyang hua," *Zhongguo xiju nianjian 1982*,
ed. Zhongguo xiju nianjian bianji bu (Beijing: Zhongguo xiju chubanshe, 1982),
16–19, at 16.

61. Wang Shizhi and Li Guangchen, eds., *Shoudu wutai meishu sheji ziliao xuan*
(Beijing: Zhongguo xiju jia xiehui beijing fenhui, 1981). To be sure, there are also
examples of theater publications that use the terms "research" and "materials" from
the 1950s, but the general trends prioritized learning from the masses and amateur
knowledge.

62. Gong Hede, *Wutai meishu yanjiu* (Beijing: Zhongguo xiju chubanshe,
1987).

63. Xu Hongzhuang, ed., *Chaoxian juchang yingyuan ziliao ji* (Beijing: Wenhuabu juchang yingyuan jianzhu daibiao tuan, 1978).

64. Lu Xiangdong, *Zhongguo xiandai juchang de yanjin*, 186.

65. On Ying Ruocheng, see Ying Ruocheng and Claire Conceison, *Voices
Carry: Behind Bars and Backstage during China's Revolution and Reform* (Lanham,
MD: Rowman and Littlefield, 2009).

66. Ying Ruocheng, "Xifang huaju biaoyan de xin faxian," *Renmin xiju*, no. 11
(1980): 45–48, at 46.

67. Liu Xu, "Jiji kaizhan wenyi lingyu zhong de kexue jishu yanjiu," *Wutai meishu yu jishu* 1 (1981): 25–28, at 25.

68. Liu, "Jiji kaizhan wenyi lingyu zhong de kexue jishu yanjiu," 26.

69. Yuan Huashui, "Jinnian lai wutai zhaoming jishu de fazhan," *Shanghai xiju*,
no. 3 (1983): 61. The silicon-controlled rectifier–based dimmer, also called a thyris-
tor dimmer, is a form of solid-state dimmer that controls light with a semiconductor and alternating current. The first solid-state dimmer was invented in 1959 by
Joel S. Spira, whose company Lutron Electronics quickly popularized the dimmer
for household use.

70. See Denis Fred Simon and Detlef Rehn, *Technological Innovation in China:
The Case of the Shanghai Semiconductor Industry* (Cambridge, MA: Ballinger, 1988).

71. Cai Fangyun, "Shanxi sheng zhaokai jutuan wutai keji huiyi," *Renmin xiju*,
no. 7 (1978): 89.

72. Cai, "Shanxi sheng zhaokai jutuan wutai keji huiyi."

73. Conference proceedings were published in the inaugural issue of the journal *Theatre Arts*, which began as a quarterly. It is now one of the leading academic
theater publications in the PRC. Xiju yishu yanjiu shi and Biaoyan xi biaoyan
jiaoyan zu, "Guanyu Sitannisilafusiji tixi de taolun," *Xiju yishu* no. 1 (1978): 9–28.

74. Liu Zifen et al., "Huaju yanyuan xingti xunlian (xuyan)," *Xiju yishu* no. 2 (1978): 52–57; "Huaju yanyuan xingti xunlian (yi) jigong," *Xiju yishu* no. 3 (1978): 51–65; "Huaju yanyuan xingti xunlian (er) wutai jineng," *Xiju yishu* no. 1 (1979): 100–102; "Huaju yanyuan xingti xunlian (xu)," *Xiju yishu* no. 2 (1979): 106–9.

75. Liu Zhifen et al., "Huaju yanyuan xingti xunlian (xuyan)," 56.

76. Robert Cohen, *Acting Power: The 21st Century Edition* [1st ed., *An Introduction to Acting*, 1978] (London: Routledge, 2013), 31.

77. Cohen, *Acting Power*, 30–31.

78. Cohen, *Acting Power*, 34.

79. Li Xing, "Kongzhi lun, xinxi lun yu xiju biaoyan," *Xiju xuexi*, no. 3 (1984): 43–51, at 45. Li Xing's argument anticipates the points made in an article published three decades later, in which Tom Scholte characterizes the Stanislavski system of acting as "proto-cybernetic." See Tom Scholte, "Proto-Cybernetics in the Stanislavski System of Acting: Past Foundations, Present Analyses and Future Prospects," *Kybernetes* 44, nos. 8–9 (2015): 1371–79.

80. Xiao Liu, *Information Fantasies: Precarious Mediation in Postsocialist China* (Minneapolis: University of Minnesota Press, 2019), 32.

81. Shepherd-Barr, *Science on Stage*, 38.

82. Shepherd-Barr, *Science on Stage*, 38.

83. Li Weixin, Zheng Bangyu, Li Yonggui, and Zhou Liguo, "*Yuanzi yu aiqing,*" *Juben*, no. 4 (1980): 4–37.

84. During the first several decades of the PRC, important military and defense-related government ministries were titled by number rather than by reference to their specific mandates. The Ninth Academy, or Northwest Nuclear Weapons Research and Design Academy (in Qinghai Province), was one of two main nuclear research and design facilities in the 1950s–1960s. The other was the Beijing Nuclear Weapons Research Institute. John Wilson Lewis and Xue Litai, *China Builds the Bomb* (Stanford: Stanford University Press, 1988), 140–41.

85. A more common term for this component seems to be "detonator" (引爆装置) although the Chinese translation for the US National Ignition Facility, which studies new methods for initiating nuclear fusion reactions, does use the term *dianhuo zhuangzhi*. The way that the play describes the "igniter" and how it functions match the functions of a bomb initiator in a typical "implosion design" for a nuclear bomb; the fact that this component was historically difficult for PRC scientists to perfect also maps onto the action of the play. For a basic description of nuclear detonation, see Wisconsin Project on Nuclear Arms Control, "Nuclear Weapons Primer," https://www.wisconsinproject.org/nuclear-weapons/#implosion; accessed May 10, 2022. For a source contemporaneous to the play, see Wu Yigong, Zhang Shufa, Zhong Weilun, and Zhou Liansheng, *He wuqi* (Beijing: Zhanshi chubanshe, 1979), 44–45.

86. The January issue of the popular full-color *People's Pictorial* (人民画报), for instance, carried three full-color photographs of the nuclear test and a reprint of the official announcement of its success.

87. Lewis and Xue, *China Builds the Bomb*, 189.

88. Eric Bentley, "Introduction: The Science Fiction of Bertolt Brecht," in *Galileo*, trans. Charles Laughton (New York: Grove Press, 1966), 7–42.

89. Both the making-of story and the play also contain the curious detail of the character taking pills composed of dried centipedes (蜈蚣), which are used in traditional Chinese medicine to dissipate toxins and relieve pain. Li et al., "Yuanzi yu aiqing," 12; Li Weixin, Zheng Bangyu, Li Yonggui, and Zhou Liguo, "Cong shenghuo dao zhuti," *Juben*, no. 4 (1980): 38–40, at 39.

90. Shen Yi, "You yi de tansuo—*Yuanzi yu aiqing* guan hou," *Juben*, no. 5 (1980): 93–96, at 93.

91. Li et al., "Cong shenghuo dao zhuti," 38.

92. Shen, "You yi de tansuo," 93; Zhao Cheng, "Kegui de xianshen jingshen—huaju *Yuanzi yu aiqing* guan hou," *Renmin ribao*, April 26, 1980, 8.

93. Li et al., "*Yuanzi yu aiqing*," 8.

94. Lewis and Xue, *China Builds the Bomb*, 157–58.

95. Lewis and Xue, *China Builds the Bomb*, 157–58.

96. Lewis and Xue, *China Builds the Bomb*, 159–60.

97. See chapter 3 for a discussion of the genealogies and different connotations of these terms.

98. Xue Dianjie, "Stage Design for Brecht's *Life of Galileo*," trans. Tak-Wai Wong, in *Brecht and East Asian Theatre: The Proceedings of a Conference on Brecht in East Asian Theatre*, ed. Antony Tatlow and Tak-Wai Wong (Hong Kong: Hong Kong University Press, 1982), 72–86, at 72. The text to which Xue refers seems to be Brecht's essay, "Building Up a Part: Laughton's Galileo," which includes a list of nine points related to the play's staging. See Bertolt Brecht, "Building Up a Part: Laughton's Galileo," in *Life of Galileo*, trans. John Willett, ed. John Willett and Ralph Manheim (New York: Arcade, 1994), 131–38, at 136–38.

99. Xue, "Stage Design for Brecht's *Life of Galileo*," 81.

100. Liu Xu even goes so far as to suggest that Chinese versions of this technology had been influential beyond China. Liu, "Jiji kaizhan wenyi lingyu zhong de kexue jishu yanjiu," 25.

101. Gong Boan, "First Performance of Brecht's Dramatic Work in China—the Production of *Mother Courage* and Its Stage Design," trans. Ping-Leung Chan, in *Brecht and East Asian Theatre*, ed. Tatlow and Wong, 65–71, at 69; see also plate 7 following Gong's essay, labeled "Backdrop projection."

102. Gong Hede, "Chuangzao fei huanjue zhuyi de yishu zhenshi—huaju *Jialilüe zhuan* wutai meishu xinshang," *Xiju yishu luncong* 1 (1979): 226–33, at 226.

103. The slight difference of term used by Huang and Gong for "scientific truth" (科学真理 or 科学的真理) and "artistic truth" (艺术真实) is important. Both *zhenli* 真理 and *zhenshi* 真实 can be translated as "truth," but the former implies the truth of a scientific principle, while the latter implies the truth as reality. The phrase *yishu zhenshi* 艺术真实 therefore may also be translated as "artistic reality." For theater artists, the key point was that artistic truth could be created by reflecting a truer version of reality onstage, but that this reality was not necessarily tied to realism (in either the nineteenth-century European sense or as deformed via Mao-era socialist realism).

104. Hu Miaosheng, "Wutai meishu de jiadingxing," *Wutai meishu yu jishu* 1 (1981): 10–20, at 10.

105. Xue Dianjie, "Baituo huanjue zhuyi shufu, dadan yunyong wutai jiadingxing," *Wutai meishu yu jishu* 1 (1981): 20–24, at 21.

106. Xue, "Stage Design for Brecht's *Life of Galileo*," 78.

107. Xue, "Stage Design for Brecht's *Life of Galileo*," 82.

108. Hu, "Cong *Cai Wenji* zhi *Jialilüe zhuan*," 50.

109. Hu, "Wutai meishu de jiadingxing," 17.

110. Hu, "Cong *Cai Wenji* dao *Jialilüe zhuan*," 52–53; "Tansuo huaju yanchu de xin xingshi—*Yuanzi yu aiqing* zuotanhui xiaoji," *Renmin xiju*, no. 5 (1980): 15–17, at 15.

111. Ji Xiaoqiu is a painter and scenic designer from Liaoning Province who worked in the scenic design departments of the PLA General Political Department *wengongtuan* and *huaju* troupe for most of her career. She also was a member of the scenic design team for the epic *Song of the Revolution* (中国革命之歌), staged in 1984 for the thirty-fifth anniversary of the founding of the PRC.

112. "Tansuo huaju yanchu de xin xingshi," 15.

113. Xue Dianjie, "Baituo huanjue zhuyi shufu," 21.

114. Wang Ren and Huang Su, "Wutai meishu: Zai tansuo yu chuangzuo zhong qianjin," *Xiju bao*, no. 1 (1983): 3–7, at 6.

115. Wang and Huang, "Wutai meishu," 5.

116. Xu Ziaozhong, "Ba ziji de xingshi fuyu ziji de guannian," in *Xu Xiaozhong daoyan yishu yanjiu*, ed. Lin Yinyu (Beijing: Zhongguo xiju chubanshe, 1991), 384.

### Coda

1. For my previous work on Wang Chong and *Thunderstorm 2.0*, see Tarryn Li-Min Chun, "Spoken Drama and Its Doubles: *Thunderstorm 2.0* by Wang Chong and Théâtre du Rêve Expérimental," *TDR: The Drama Review* 63, no. 3 (2019): 155–63; Chun, "Wang Chong and the Theatre of IMMEDIACY: Technology, Performance, and Intimacy in Crisis," *Theatre Survey* 62, no. 3 (2021): 295–321.

2. The number of screens was noted widely in show publicity and social media reviews as one of the production's main innovations. See, for example, WORLDSHOW (@worldshow1), "44 kuai ping? 44 ben shu? Ruhe gouzao *Luzhen shexi* zhe bu daxing shijing yinghuaju?" WeChat, June 2, 2021, https://mp.weixin.qq.com /s/N-aXZlgtYMXEIKlijlIDZw. On *Village Opera of Lu Town*, see also Kirk Denton and Yichun Xu, "Lu Town: Theme Parks and the Commodification of Literary Culture in China," *Cultural History* 11, no. 2 (2022): 148–80, at 171–74.

3. Xi Muliang and Annie Feng, "Chinese Directors: The New Generation," *Critical Stages/Scènes Critiques*, no. 18 (December 2018), https://www.critical-stag es.org/18/chinese-directors-the-new-generation/

4. Chen Ran, "*Leiyu 2.0* dianfu Cao Yu," *Xin Jing bao* (July 12, 2012): C10, http://epaper.bjnews.com.cn/html/2012-07/12/content_355641.htm?div=0

5. Important exceptions exist in the work of theater journals with a specifically international framework, like *Critical Stages/Scènes Critiques* or *Theatre*

*Research International (TRI)* and recent projects like the Transmedia Arts Seminar at metaLAB (at) Harvard, cochaired by Magda Romanska and Hana Worthen (later, Ramona Mosse).

6. Zheng Rongjian, "Guojia da juyuan de dixia 'moshu shi,'" *Zhongguo yishu bao*, April 18, 2012, http://www.cflac.org.cn/ys/xwy/201204/t20120418_134386 .htm

7. On the "maker movement" in contemporary China, see Silvia Lindtner, *Prototype Nation: China and the Contested Promise of Innovation* (Princeton: Princeton University Press, 2020).

8. Chun, "Wang Chong and the Theatre of Immediacy," 301–2.

9. On major historical works performed in honor of national anniversaries such as *The East Is Red* (1964; see chap. 3), *Song of the Chinese Revolution* (1984), and *The Road to Revival* (复兴之路, 2009), see Chen, *Staging Chinese Revolution*, 235–86; Chen, "Performing the 'Red Classics': From *The East Is Red* to *The Road to Revival*," in *Red Legacies in China: Cultural Afterlives of the Communist Revolution*, ed. Jie Li and Enhua Zhang (Cambridge, MA: Harvard University Asia Center Publications, 2016), 151–83.

10. "Nuhou ba, Huang he," at 19:24, in *Shengli yu heping: Jinian Kangzhan shengli 70 zhou nian wenyi wanhui*, CCTV, September 3, 2015; video, 1:39:58, https://youtu.be/Rv-EZXM5kAA?t=1164, accessed May 10, 2022.

11. Xi Jinping, "Full Text of Xi Jinping's Report at 19th CPC National Congress: 'Secure a Decisive Victory in Building a Moderately Prosperous Society in All Respects and Strive for the Great Success of Socialism with Chinese Characteristics for a New Era,'" Nineteenth National Congress of the Communist Party of China, October 18, 2017; *Xinhua News*, November 4, 2017, https://www.chinad aily.com.cn/china/19thcpcnationalcongress/2017-11/04/content_34115212.htm

12. Mark O'Connell, "The Stunning Success of 'Fail Better': How Samuel Beckett Became Silicon Valley's Life Coach," *Slate*, January 29, 2014, https://slate .com/culture/2014/01/samuel-becketts-quote-fail-better-becomes-the-mantra-of -silicon-valley.html

13. Sara Jane Bailes, *Performance Theatre and the Poetics of Failure: Forced Entertainment, Goat Island, Elevator Repair Service* (London: Routledge, 2011), 11.

14. Bailes, *Performance Theatre*, 12–13.

# Bibliography

## Databases

China Academic Journals Full-text Database. 中国知网. (CNKI, or CAJ)
Chinamaxx Digital Libraries. 中文集献. (Chinamaxx)
Dacheng Old Journals Full-text Database. 大成老旧刊全文数据库. (Dacheng Database)
Duxiu Database. 读秀. (Duxiu)
*Jiefangjun bao* Digital Archive (by East View). 解放军报.
National Index to Chinese Newspapers and Periodicals. 全国报刊索引. (QGBKSY, or CNBKSY)
New China Local Gazetteers (by Wanfang Data). 中国新方志库.
*Renmin ribao* Digital Archive 1946–2023. 人民日报图文数据库 1946–2023. (RMRB Database)
*Shenbao* Digital Archive. 申報全文數據庫. (Shenbao Database)

## Frequently Cited Periodicals

| | | |
|---|---|---|
| *Beijing ribao* | 北京日报 | *Beijing Daily* |
| *Guangming ribao* | 光明日报 | *Guangming Daily* (Shanghai) |
| *Jiefangjun bao* | 解放军报 | *People's Liberation Daily* |
| *Juben* | 剧本 | *Drama Monthly* |
| *Renmin ribao* | 人民日报 | *People's Daily* |
| *Renmin xiju* | 人民戏剧 | *People's Theater* |
| *Shanghai xiju* | 上海戏剧 | *Shanghai Theater* |
| *Shenbao* | 申報 | *Shanghai News* |
| *Wutai meishu yu jishu* | 舞台美术与技术 | *Stage Design and Technology* |
| *Xiju bao* | 戏剧报 | *Theater Gazette* |
| *Xiju yishu* | 戏剧艺术 | *Theatre Arts* |

## Works Cited

Ai Junjie 艾俊階 [Shi 時, pseud.]. "Zai tan wutai zhaoming" 再談舞台照明 [Another discussion of stage lighting]. *Sanliujiu huabao* 三六九畫報, no. 68 (1936): 12. QGBKSY.

Anderson, Marston. *The Limits of Realism: Chinese Fiction in the Revolutionary Period.* Berkeley: University of California Press, 1990.

Andreas, Joel. *Rise of the Red Engineers: The Cultural Revolution and the Origins of China's New Class.* Contemporary Issues in Asia and the Pacific. Stanford: Stanford University Press, 2009.

Andrews, Julia F. *Painters and Politics in the People's Republic of China, 1949–1979.* Berkeley: University of California Press, 1994. http://ark.cdlib.org/ark:/13030 /ft6w1007nt/

Anqiu xian jingju tuan 安丘县京剧团 [Anqiu County Jingju Troupe]. "Shenru gongnongbing, zhuanyi lizudian" 深入工农兵，转移立足点 [Go to the workers, peasants and soldiers, shift your stance]. *Shandong wenyi* 山东文艺, no. 6 (January 1972): 12–16. CNKI.

Appia, Adolphe. *Adolphe Appia: Texts on Theatre.* Edited and translated by Richard C. Beacham. London: Routledge, 1993.

"Ba hao xi song dao nongcun qu" 把好戏送到农村去 [Send good plays to the countryside]. *Xiju bao*, no. 9 (1965): 2–3. CNKI.

Bailes, Sara Jane. *Performance Theatre and the Poetics of Failure: Forced Entertainment, Goat Island, Elevator Repair Service.* London: Routledge, 2011.

Bao, Weihong. "The Art of Control: Hong Shen, Behavioral Psychology, and the Technics of Social Effects." *Modern Chinese Literature and Culture* 27, no. 2 (2015): 249–97. https://doi.org/10.5749/minnesota/9780816681334.001.0001

Bao, Weihong. *Fiery Cinema: The Emergence of an Affective Medium in China, 1915–1945.* Minneapolis: University of Minnesota Press, 2015.

Bardin, Andrea, and Giovanni Carrozzini. "Organising Invention through Technical Mentality: Simondon's Challenge to the 'Civilisation of Productivity.'" *Culture and Organization* 23, no. 1 (2017): 26–33.

Beacham, Richard C. *Adolphe Appia: Artist and Visionary of the Modern Theatre.* New York: Routledge, 2013.

Beacham, Richard C. "Introduction: Adolphe Appia, 1862–1928." In *Adolphe Appia: Texts on Theatre*, edited and translated by Richard C. Beacham, 1–14. New York: Routledge, 1993.

"Beijing wutai meishu gongzuozhe zuotan—wutai meishu ruhe bianyu shangshan xiaxiang" 北京舞台美术工作者座谈—舞台美术如何便于上山下乡 [Beijing scenography workers forum—How scenography facilitates the Down to the Countryside Movement]. *Xiju bao*, no. 11 (1965): 41–42. CNKI.

Bentley, Eric. "Introduction: The Science Fiction of Bertolt Brecht." In *Galileo*, translated by Charles Laughton; edited by Eric Bentley, 7–42. New York: Grove Press, 1966.

Bergman, Gösta M. *Lighting in the Theatre.* Totowa, NJ: Rowman and Littlefield, 1977.

Bernstein, Robin. *Racial Innocence: Performing American Childhood from Slavery to Civil Rights*. New York: New York University Press, 2011.

Berry, Chris. "Every Colour Red? Colour in the Films of the Cultural Revolution Model Stage Works." *Journal of Chinese Cinemas* 6, no. 3 (2012): 233–46. https://doi.org/10.1386/jcc.6.3.233_1

Berry, Chris. "Red Poetics: The Films of the Chinese Cultural Revolution Revolutionary Model Operas." In *The Poetics of Chinese Cinema*, edited by Gary Bettinson and James Udden, 29–49. East Asian Popular Culture. New York: Palgrave Macmillan, 2016. https://doi.org/10.1057/978-1-137-55309-6_3

Bi Bo 碧波. "Kan *Nuhou ba, Zhongguo!* zhi hou" 看「怒吼吧, 中國！」之後 [After watching *Roar, China!*]. *Shanhu* 珊瑚 3, no. 9 (1933): 4–7. QGBKSY.

Bian Ji 卞驥. "Shangshan xiaxiang yan haoxi" 上山下乡演好戏 [Performing good shows during the Down to the Countryside Movement]. *Xiju bao*, no. 10 (1965): 41–42. CNKI.

Böhme, Gernot. *Atmospheric Architectures: The Aesthetics of Felt Spaces*. Edited and translated by Anna-Christina Engels-Schwarzpaul. London: Bloomsbury Academic, 2017.

Bohnenkamp, Max L. "Neither Western Opera, nor Old Chinese Theater: The Modernist 'Integrated Art-Form' and the Origins of the Maoist 'New Music-Drama.'" In *Rethinking Chinese Socialist Theaters of Reform*, edited by Chen, Chun, and Liu, 34–60. Ann Arbor: University of Michigan Press, 2021.

Bohnenkamp, Max L. "Turning Ghosts into People: *The White-Haired Girl*, Revolutionary Folklorism, and the Politics of Aesthetics in Modern China." PhD diss., Department of East Asian Languages and Civilizations, University of Chicago, 2014.

Bradley, Arthur. *Originary Technicity: The Theory of Technology from Marx to Derrida*. Basingstoke: Palgrave Macmillan, 2011.

Braester, Yomi. *Painting the City Red: Chinese Cinema and the Urban Contract*. Asia-Pacific: Culture, Politics, and Society. Durham: Duke University Press, 2010.

Braester, Yomi. *Witness against History: Literature, Film, and Public Discourse in Twentieth-Century China*. Stanford: Stanford University Press, 2003.

Brandon, James R., and Samuel L. Leiter. *Kabuki Plays on Stage*, vol. 2: *Villainy and Vengeance, 1773–1799*. Honolulu: University of Hawai'i Press, 2002.

Bray, Francesca. "Technics and Civilization in Late Imperial China: An Essay in the Cultural History of Technology." *Osiris* 13 (1998): 11–33. https://doi.org/10.1086/649278

Bray, Francesca. *Technology and Gender: Fabrics of Power in Late Imperial China*. Berkeley: University of California Press, 1997.

Brecht, Bertolt. "Building Up a Part: Laughton's Galileo." In *Life of Galileo*, translated by John Willett, edited by John Willett and Ralph Manheim, 131–38. New York: Arcade, 1994.

Brecht, Bertolt. "The Modern Theatre Is the Epic Theatre." In *Brecht on Theatre: The Development of an Aesthetic*, edited and translated by John Willett, 33–42. London: Methuen Drama, 1964.

Brecht, Bertolt. "A Short Organum for the Theatre." In *Brecht on Theatre: The Development of an Aesthetic*, edited and translated by John Willett, 179–205. London: Methuen Drama, 1964.

Brock, Darryl E., and Chunjuan Nancy Wei. "Introduction: Reassessing the Great Proletarian Cultural Revolution." In *Mr. Science and Chairman Mao's Cultural Revolution*, edited by Wei and Brock, 1–40. Lanham, MD: Lexington Books, 2013.

Button, Peter. *Configurations of the Real in Chinese Literary and Aesthetic Modernity*. Ideas, History, and Modern China. Leiden: Brill, 2009.

Cai Fangyun 蔡方云. "Shanxi sheng zhaokai jutuan wutai keji huiyi" 山西省召开剧团舞台科技会议 [Shanxi Province holds meeting on stage technology in theatre troupes]. *Renmin xiju*, no. 7 (1978): 89. CNKI.

Campbell, Drew. *Technical Theater for Nontechnical People*. 2nd ed. New York: Allworth, 2004.

Cao Yongjiu 曹永久 and Li Yuzeng 李玉增. *Wutai shiyong xiaoguo* 舞台实用效果 [Practical effects for the stage]. Shenyang: Liaoning renmin chubanshe, 1957. Chinamaxx.

Cao Yu 曹禺. *Leiyu* 雷雨 (*Thunderstorm*). *Wenxue jikan* 文學季刊 1, no. 3 (1934): 161–244. QGBKSY.

Cao Yu 曹禺. *Leiyu* 雷雨 (*Thunderstorm*). Vol. 1 of *Cao Yu xiju ji* 曹禺戲劇集 [Collected drama of Cao Yu]. Shanghai: Wenhua shenghuo chubanshe, [1936] 1943. Chinamaxx.

Cao Yu 曹禺. *Richu* 日出 (*Sunrise*). Vol. 2 of *Cao Yu xiju ji* 曹禺戲劇集 [Collected drama of Cao Yu]. Shanghai: Wenhua shenghuo chubanshe, [1936] 1946. Chinamaxx.

Cao Yu 曹禺. "*Richu* ba" 日出跋 [Epilogue to *Sunrise*]. In *Richu* 日出 (*Sunrise*), i–xxxii. Vol. 2 of *Cao Yu xiju ji* 曹禺戲劇集 [Collected drama of Cao Yu]. Shanghai: Wenhua shenghuo chubanshe, [1936] 1946. Chinamaxx.

Cao Yu 曹禺. "*Richu* ba" 日出跋 [Epilogue to *Sunrise*]. In *Cao Yu quanji* 曹禺全集 [Complete works of Cao Yu], 7 vols., edited by Tian Benxiang 田本相 and Li Yijun 李一军, 1:380–97. Shijiazhuang: Huashan wenyi chubanshe, 1996.

Cao Yu 曹禺. "*Richu* di san mu fuji" 《日出》第三幕附记 [Addendum to act 3 of *Sunrise*]. In *Cao Yu quanji* 曹禺全集 [Complete works of Cao Yu], edited by Tian Benxiang 田本相 and Li Yijun 李一军, 1:378–79. Shijiazhuang: Huashan wenyi chubanshe, 1996. Originally published in *Wenji yuekan*, no. 5 (1936).

Cao Yu 曹禺. *Thunderstorm*. Translated by Wang Tso-liang and A. C. Barnes [1958], revised by Charles Qianzhi Wu. In *Columbia Anthology of Modern Chinese Drama*, edited by Chen, 227–352. New York: Columbia University Press, 2010.

Chan, Roy Bing. *The Edge of Knowing: Dreams, History, and Realism in Modern Chinese Literature*. Seattle: University of Washington Press, 2017.

Chansky, Dorothy. *Composing Ourselves: The Little Theatre Movement and the American Audience*. Theater in the Americas. Carbondale: Southern Illinois University Press, 2004.

Che Wenming 车文明. *Zhongguo gu xitai diaocha yanjiu* 中国古代戏台调查研究 [Fieldwork research on ancient stages of China]. Beijing: Zhonghua shuju, 2011.

Che Wenming 车文明. *Zhongguo gudai juchang shi* 中国古代剧场史 [A history of ancient stages in China]. Beijing: Shangwu yinshu guan, 2021.

Chen Baichen 陈白尘 and Dong Jian 董建. *Zhongguo xiandai xiju shigao, 1899–1949* 中国现代戏剧史稿, 1899–1949 [History of modern Chinese drama, 1899–1949]. Beijing: Zhongguo xiju chubanshe, 2008.

Chen Dabei 陳大悲. *Aimei de xiju* 愛美的戲劇 [Amateur theater]. Beijing: Chen-baoshe, 1922. Reprinted in Minguo congshu 民國叢書 [Republic of China series]. Shanghai: Shanghai shudian, 1992. Chinamaxx.

Chen Dahua 陈大华, Yu Bing 于冰, He Kaixian 何开贤, and Cai Zuquan 蔡祖泉. *Nihongdeng zhizao jishu yu yingyong* 霓虹灯制造技术与应用 [The manufacturing technology and application of neon lights]. Beijing: Zhongguo qinggongye chubanshe, 1997. Duxiu.

Chen, Fan-Pen Li. *Chinese Shadow Theatre: History, Popular Religion and Women Warriors*. Montreal: McGill–Queen's University Press, 2007.

Chen Jide 陈吉德. *Zhongguo dangdai xianfeng xiju, 1979–2000* 中国当代先锋戏剧, 1979–2000 [Contemporary avant-garde theater in China]. Beijing: Beijing xiju chubanshe, 2004.

Chen, Kuan-Hsing. *Asia as Method: Toward Deimperialization*. Durham: Duke University Press, 2010.

Chen, Liana. *Staging for the Emperors: A History of Qing Court Theatre, 1683–1923*. Cambria Sinophone World Series. Amherst, NY: Cambria Press, 2021.

Chen Ran 陈然. "*Leiyu 2.0 dianfu Cao Yu*"《雷雨2.0》颠覆曹禺 [*Thunderstorm 2.0* subverts Cao Yu]. *Xin Jing Bao* 新京报, July 12, 2012, C10. http://epaper.bjnews.com.cn/html/2012-07/12/content_355641.htm?div=0

Chen, Tina Mai. "The Human–Machine Continuum in Maoism: The Intersection of Soviet Socialist Realism, Japanese Theoretical Physics, and Chinese Revolutionary Theory." *Cultural Critique*, no. 80 (Winter 2012): 151–82. https://doi.org/10.5749/culturalcritique.80.2012.0151

Chen, Tina Mai. "Mobile Film Projection in Socialist and Post-Socialist China." China Policy Institute Blog, May 8, 2015. https://theasiadialogue.com/2015/05/08/enduring-themes-of-propaganda-mobile-film-projection-in-socialist-and-post-socialist-china/

Chen, Wendi. "The First Shaw Play on the Chinese Stage: The Production of *Mrs. Warren's Profession* in 1921." *Shaw* 19 (1999): 99–118.

Chen, Xiaomei. *Acting the Right Part: Political Theater and Popular Drama in Contemporary China, 1966–1996*. Honolulu: University of Hawai'i Press, 2002.

Chen, Xiaomei, ed. *The Columbia Anthology of Modern Chinese Drama*. Weatherhead Books on Asia. New York: Columbia University Press, 2010.

Chen, Xiaomei. "Introduction." In *The Columbia Anthology of Modern Chinese Drama*, edited by Xiaomei Chen, 1–55. New York: Columbia University Press, 2010.

Chen, Xiaomei. *Occidentalism: A Theory of Counter-Discourse in Post-Mao China*. 2nd ed. Lanham, MD: Rowman and Littlefield, 2002.

Chen, Xiaomei. "Performing the 'Red Classics': From *The East Is Red* to *The Road to Revival*." In *Red Legacies in China: Cultural Afterlives of the Communist Revo-*

*lution*, edited by Jie Li and Enhua Zhang, 151–83. Cambridge, MA: Harvard University Asia Center Publications, 2016.

Chen, Xiaomei. *Performing the Socialist State: Modern Chinese Theater and Film Culture*. New York: Columbia University Press, 2023.

Chen, Xiaomei. "'Playing in the Dirt': Plays about Geologists and Memories of the Cultural Revolution and the Maoist Era." *China Review* 5, no. 2 (2005): 65–95.

Chen, Xiaomei. *Staging Chinese Revolution: Theater, Film, and the Afterlives of Propaganda*. New York: Columbia University Press, 2016.

Chen, Xiaomei, Tarryn Li-Min Chun, and Siyuan Liu, eds. *Rethinking Chinese Socialist Theaters of Reform: Performance Practice and Debate in the Mao Era*. Ann Arbor: University of Michigan Press, 2021.

Chen Yong. "The Beijing Production of *Life of Galileo*." Translated by Adrian Hsia, Tak-Wai Wong, and Antony Tatlow. In *Brecht and East Asian Theatre*, edited by Tatlow and Wong, 88–95. Hong Kong: Hong Kong University Press, 1982.

Cheng Yanqiu 程硯秋. "Huaju daoyan guankui" 話劇導演管窺 [A close look at drama directing]. *Juxue yuekan* 劇學月刊 2, nos. 7–8 (1933): 1–64. Dacheng Database.

Cheng Yanqiu 程硯秋. "Huaju daoyan guankui (xu)" 話劇導演管窺 (續) [A close look at drama directing (cont'd)]. *Juxue yuekan* 劇學月刊 2, no. 10 (1933): 1–38.

Cheng Yuangong 成元功. "Guanxin Beijing chengshi jianshe" 关心北京城市建设 [On Beijing's urban development]. In *Zhou Enlai yu Beijing* 周恩来与北京 [Zhou Enlai and Beijing]. Beijing: Zhongyang chubanshe, 1998.

Chiu Kun-Liang 邱坤良. *Renmin nandao meicuo ma? "Nuhou ba, Zhongguo!", Teliejiyakefu yu Meiyehede* 人民難道沒錯嗎?《怒吼吧, 中國》·特列季亞科夫與梅耶荷德 [Were the people right? *Roar, China!*, Tret'iakov, and Meyerhold]. Taipei: INK Publishing, 2013.

Chu Fu-sung. "Wartime Chinese Literature." In *China after Seven Years of War*, edited by Hollington K. Tong, 125–47. New York: Macmillan, 1945.

Chun, Tarryn Li-Min. "Spoken Drama and Its Doubles: *Thunderstorm 2.0* by Wang Chong and Théâtre du Rêve Expérimental." *TDR: The Drama Review* 63, no. 3 (2019): 155–63.

Chun, Tarryn Li-Min. "Wang Chong and the Theatre of IMMEDIACY: Technology, Performance, and Intimacy in Crisis." *Theatre Survey* 62, no. 3 (2021): 295–321.

Clark, Paul. *The Chinese Cultural Revolution: A History*. Cambridge: Cambridge University Press, 2008.

Clark, Paul, Laikwan Pang, and Tsan-Huang Tsai, eds. *Listening to China's Cultural Revolution: Music, Politics, and Cultural Continuities*. Chinese Literature and Culture in the World. Basingstoke: Palgrave Macmillan, 2016.

Coderre, Laurence. "Breaking Bad: Sabotaging the Production of the Hero in the Amateur Performance of *yangbanxi*." In *Listening to China's Cultural Revolution*, edited by Clark, Pang, and Tsai, 65–83. Chinese Literature and Culture in the World. Basingstoke: Palgrave Macmillan, 2016.

Coderre, Laurence. *Newborn Socialist Things: Materiality in Maoist China*. Durham: Duke University Press, 2021.

Cohen, Robert. *Acting Power: The 21st Century Edition.* [1st ed., *Acting Power: An Introduction to Acting*, 1978.] London: Routledge, 2013.

Conceison, Claire. *Significant Other: Staging the American in China.* Honolulu: University of Hawai'i Press, 2004.

Costantino, Mariagrazia. "'City Lights' and the Dream of Shanghai." In *Revealing/Reveiling Shanghai: Cultural Representations from the Twentieth and Twenty-First Centuries,* edited by Lisa Bernstein and Chu-chueh Cheng, 53–82. Albany: State University of New York Press, 2020.

Crane, Robert. "Between Factography and Ethnography: Sergei Tretyakov's *Roar, China!* and Soviet Orientalist Discourse." In *Text & Presentation 2010,* edited by Kiki Gounaridou, 41–53. Jefferson, NC: McFarland, 2011.

Crump, J. I. *Chinese Theater in the Days of Kublai Khan.* Ann Arbor: Center for Chinese Studies, University of Michigan, 1990.

Davis, R. G. "Brecht / Science / Ecology." *Brecht Yearbook* 23 (1998): 80–83.

DeMare, Brian James. "Drama from Beijing to Long Bow: Reforming Shanxi Stages in Socialist China." In *Rethinking Chinese Socialist Theaters of Reform,* edited by Chen, Chun, and Liu, 187–215. Ann Arbor: University of Michigan Press, 2021.

DeMare, Brian James. *Mao's Cultural Army: Drama Troupes in China's Rural Revolution.* Cambridge Studies in the History of the People's Republic of China. Cambridge: Cambridge University Press, 2017.

Deng Xiaoping. "Speech at the Opening Ceremony of the National Conference on Science." In *Selected Works of Deng Xiaoping,* vol. 2, *1975–1982,* 101–16. Beijing: Foreign Languages Press, 1984.

Deng Xiaoping 邓小平. "Zai Quanguo kexue dahui kaimu shi shang de jianghua" 在全国科学大会开幕式上的讲话 [Speech at the opening ceremony of the National Science Conference]. In *Deng Xiaoping wenxuan* 邓小平文选, vol. 2, 2nd ed., 85–100. Beijing: Renmin chubanshe, 1994.

Denton, Kirk A., ed. *The Columbia Companion to Modern Chinese Literature.* New York: Columbia University Press, 2016.

Denton, Kirk A., ed. "Hong Shen and the Modern Mediasphere in Republican-Era China." Special issue, *Modern Chinese Literature and Culture* 27, no. 2 (2015).

Denton, Kirk A., and Yichun Xu. "Lu Town: Theme Parks and the Commodification of Literary Culture in China." *Cultural History* 11, no. 2 (2022): 148–80.

"Dianshi jilupian *Zhiqu Weihushan Hongdeng ji* paicheng" 电视纪录影片《智取威虎山》《红灯记》拍成 [TV documentaries *Taking Tiger Mountain by Strategy* and *The Red Lantern* filmed successfully]. *Jiefangjun bao,* July 31, 1970. https://dlib.eastview.com/browse/doc/14029860

Dikötter, Frank. *Mao's Great Famine: The History of China's Most Devastating Catastrophe, 1958–1962.* New York: Walker, 2010.

Ding Yangzhong 丁扬忠. "Bulaixite he ta de *Jialiliie zhuan*" 布莱希特和他的《伽利略传》[Brecht and his *Life of Galileo*]. *Renmin xiju,* no. 3 (1979): 32–34. CNKI.

Dustagheer, Sarah, and Gillian Woods, eds. *Stage Directions and Shakespearean Theatre.* London: Bloomsbury Arden Shakespeare, 2018.

Eisenstein, Sergei. "Montage of Attractions: For *Enough Stupidity in Every Wiseman*." Translated by Daniel Gerould. *TDR: The Drama Review* 18, no. 1 (1974): 77–85. https://doi.org/10.2307/1144865

Elman, Benjamin A. "Toward a History of Modern Science in Republican China." In *Science and Technology in Modern China, 1880s–1940s*, edited by Jing Tsu and Benjamin A. Elman, 15–38. Leiden: Brill, 2014.

Engels, Frederick [Friedrich]. "Introduction." In *Socialism: Utopian and Scientific*, translated by Edward Aveling, v–xxxix. London: S. Sonnenschein & Co., 1892. Hathitrust Digital Library. https://hdl.handle.net/2027/uc1.31175000213051

Esherick, Joseph W. "Ten Theses on the Chinese Revolution." *Modern China* 21, no. 1 (1995): 45–76.

Essin, Christin. *Stage Designers in Early Twentieth-Century America: Artists, Activists, Cultural Critics*. New York: Palgrave Macmillan, 2012.

Essin, Christin. *Working Backstage: A Cultural History and Ethnography of Technical Theater Labor*. Ann Arbor: University of Michigan Press, 2021.

Fan, Xing. *Staging Revolution: Artistry and Aesthetics in Model Beijing Opera during the Cultural Revolution*. Hong Kong: Hong Kong University Press, 2018.

Fang Chu 方楚. "Tan huaju *Shisanling shuiku changxiangqu*" 谈话剧十三陵水库畅想曲 [On *Fantasia of the Ming Tombs Reservoir*]. *Zhongguo xiju*, no. 13 (1958): 35. CNKI.

Fang Lizhi. *The Most Wanted Man in China: My Journey from Scientist to Enemy of the State*. Translated by Perry Link. New York: Henry Holt, 2016.

Fang Yun 方耘. *Geming yangbanxi xuexi zhaji* 革命样板戏学习札记 [Notes on studying the *yangbanxi*]. Shanghai: Shanghai renmin chubanshe, 1974.

Feng Naichao 冯乃超. "Zhongguo xiju yundong de kuxin" 中國戲劇運動的苦心 [The painstaking efforts of the Chinese theater movement]. *Chuangzao yuekan* 創造月刊 2, no. 2 (1928): 1–12. QGBKSY.

Fengzi 风子 [Feng Fengzi 封风子]. "Huaju wutai shang de xin shouhuo—tuijian huaju *Nihongdeng xia de shaobing*" 话剧舞台上的新收获—推荐话剧《霓虹灯下的哨兵》 [A new harvest on the spoken drama stage—Recommending the spoken drama *Sentinels under the Neon Lights*]. *Renmin ribao*, March 10, 1963. RMRB Database.

Fengzi 风子 [Feng Fengzi 封风子]. "Shaobing xunli—Beijing wutai shang *Nihongdeng xia de shaobing* mantan" '哨兵'巡礼—北京舞台上《霓虹灯下的哨兵》漫谈 [The *Sentinels'* Parade—Random thoughts on *Sentinels under the Neon Lights*]. *Beijing ribao*, June 21, 1963. Reprinted in *"Nihongdeng xia de shaobing" zhuanji*, edited by Nanjing shifan xueyuan zhongwen xi, 210–19. Nanjing: Nanjing shifan xueyuan, 1979. Chinamaxx.

Ferrari, Rossella. *Pop Goes the Avant-Garde: Experimental Theatre in Contemporary China*. Enactments. London: Seagull, 2012.

*First Five-Year Plan for the Development of the National Economy of the People's Republic of China in 1953–1957 (Illustrated)*. Beijing: Foreign Languages Press, 1956.

Fokkema, D. W. *Literary Doctrine in China and Soviet Influence, 1956–1960*. The Hague: Mouton, 1965.

Fu Jin. *A History of Chinese Theatre in the 20th Century II*. Translated by Qiang Zhang. China Perspectives. New York: Routledge, 2021.

Fu Jin 傅谨. *Xin Zhongguo xiju shi, 1949–2000* 新中国戏剧史1949–2000 [A history of drama in the People's Republic of China, 1949–2000]. Changsha: Hunan meishu chubanshe, 2002.

Fu Jin 傅谨. *Zhongguo ershi shiji xiju shi* 中国二十世纪戏剧史 [A history of Chinese drama in the twentieth century], vol. 1. Beijing: Zhongguo shehui kexue chubanshe, 2017.

Furuhata, Yuriko. "The Fog Medium: Visualizing and Engineering the Atmosphere." In *Screen Genealogies: From Optical Device to Environmental Medium*, edited by Craig Buckley, Rüdiger Campe, and Francesco Casetti, 187–213. Amsterdam: Amsterdam University Press, 2019.

Gamsa, Mark. "Sergei Tret'iakov's *Roar, China!* between Moscow and China." *Itinerario* 36, no. 2 (2012): 91–108. https://doi.org/10.1017/S0165115312000587

Gang, Tan. "Living Underground: Bomb Shelters and Daily Lives in Wartime Chongqing (1937–1945)." *Journal of Urban History* 43, no. 3 (2017): 383–99. https://doi.org/10.1177/0096144215579056

Gansu gongye daxue jixie yi xi 甘肃工业大学机械一系 [Department of Mechanical Engineering, Gansu University of Technology]. "*Zhongguo juchang jianzhu sheji guifan he Wutai jixie jishu guifan* wancheng chugao"《中国剧场建筑设计规范》和《舞台机械技术规范》完成初稿 [First drafts of *Specifications for Theater Design in China* and *Specifications for Stage Machinery* completed]. *Gansu gongye daxue xuebao* 甘肃工业大学学报, no. 3 (1985): 55. CNKI.

Gao Honghu 高鸿鹄. "Ji qing yu jing, qing jing jiao rong" 寄情于景, 情景交融 [Transmitting sentiment through scenery, the blending of scenery and sentiment]. *Renmin ribao*, October 22, 1972, 1. RMRB Database.

Ge Fei 葛飞. "*Nuhou ba Zhongguo!* yu 1930 niandai zhengzhi xuanchuan ju"《怒吼吧，中国！》与 1930 年代政治宣传剧 [*Roar, China!* and 1930s political propaganda productions]. *Yishu pinglun* 艺术评论 10 (2008): 23–28. CNKI.

Ge Hede 葛和德. "Dengxia shuqing—tan *Nihongdeng xia de shaobing* de meishu sheji" 灯下抒情—谈《霓虹灯下的哨兵》的美术设计 [Lyricism under the lights—On scenic design in *Sentinels under the Neon Lights*]. *Guangming ribao*, March 13, 1963. Reprinted in *"Nihongdeng xia de shaobing" zhuanji*, edited by Nanjing shifan xueyuan zhongwen xi, 299–304. Nanjing: Nanjing shifan xueyuan, 1979. Chinamaxx.

Ge Yihong 葛一虹. "Lun Kangzhan zhong de juben chuangzuo" 論抗戰中的劇本創作 [On playwriting during the War of Resistance]. *Xin yanju* 新演劇 1, no. 1 (1938): 18–20.

Golas, Peter J. *Picturing Technology in China: From Earliest Times to the Nineteenth Century*. Hong Kong: Hong Kong University Press, 2015.

Goldman, Andrea S. *Opera and the City: The Politics of Culture in Beijing, 1770–1900*. Stanford: Stanford University Press, 2012.

Goldman, Merle, and Denis Fred Simon. "Introduction: The Onset of China's New Technological Revolution." In *Science and Technology in Post-Mao China*, edited by Simon and Goldman, 1–20. Harvard Contemporary China Series. Cambridge, MA: Harvard University Press, 1989.

Goldstein, Joshua. *Drama Kings: Players and Publics in the Re-Creation of Peking Opera, 1870–1937*. Berkeley: University of California Press, 2007.

Gong Boan. "First Performance of Brecht's Dramatic Work in China—The Production of *Mother Courage* and Its Stage Design." Translated by Ping-Leung Chan. In *Brecht and East Asian Theatre*, edited by Tatlow and Wong, 65–71. Hong Kong: Hong Kong University Press, 1982.

Gong Hede 龚和德. "Chuangzao fei huanjue zhuyi de yishu zhenshi—huaju *Jialilüe zhuan* wutai meishu xinshang" 创造非幻觉主义的艺术真实—话剧《伽利略传》舞台美术欣赏 [Creating a nonillusionistic artistic truth—Scenography in *Life of Galileo*]. *Xiju yishu luncong* 戏剧艺术论丛, no. 1 (1979): 226–33.

Gong Hede 龚和德. *Wutai meishu yanjiu* 舞台美术研究 [Scenography research]. Beijing: Zhongguo xiju chubanshe, 1987.

Greene, Maggie. *Resisting Spirits: Drama Reform and Cultural Transformation in the People's Republic of China*. China Understandings Today. Ann Arbor: University of Michigan Press, 2019.

Gu Chunfang 顾春芳. *Ta de wutai: Zhongguo xiju nü daoyan chuangzuo yanjiu* 她的舞台：中国戏剧女导演创作研究 [Her stage: A study on productions by female Chinese directors]. Shanghai: Shanghai yuandong chubanshe, 2011.

Gu Jianchen 谷劍塵. "Xiao wutai gexin diyi sheng" 笑舞台革新第一聲 [On the first sounds of innovation at Xiao Theater]. *Shenbao*, April 17, 1926, 2. Shenbao Database.

Gu Zhongyi 顾仲彝. "Daoyan shu gailun di san zhang: Shangyan jihua de jiben yuanze (weiwan)" 導演術概論：第三章：上演計劃的基本原則 (未完) [A brief discussion on directing: Chapter Three: Fundamental principles of production design (to be cont'd)]. *Juchang yishu* 劇場藝術, no. 8 (1939): 10–12. QGBKSY.

Gui Zhongsheng 桂中生. "Qiantan *Nihongdengxia de shaobing* wutai meishu sheji" 浅谈《霓虹灯下的哨兵》舞台美术设计 [Brief talk on the scenic design of *Sentinels under the Neon Lights*]. *Renmin ribao*, March 17, 1963. RMRB Database.

Gunn, Edward [M.]. "Shanghai's 'Orphan Island' and the Development of Modern Drama." In *Popular Chinese Literature and Performing Arts in the People's Republic of China, 1949–1979*, edited by McDougall, 36–53. Studies on China. Berkeley: University of California Press, 1984.

Gunn, Edward [M.]. *Unwelcome Muse: Chinese Literature in Shanghai and Peking, 1937–1945*. New York: Columbia University Press, 1980.

Guo Moruo 郭沫若. "Kexue de chuntian—zai Quanguo kexue dahui bimushi shang de jianghua" 科学的春天—在全国科学大会闭幕式上的讲话 [Springtime for science—Speech at the National Science Conference closing ceremony]. *Renmin ribao*, April 1, 1978. RMRB Database.

Haan, J. H. "Thalia and Terpsichore on the Yangtze: A Survey of Foreign Theatre and Music in Shanghai, 1850–1865." *Journal of the Hong Kong Branch of the Royal Asiatic Society* 29 (1989): 158–251. https://www.jstor.org/stable/23890817

Harris, Kristine. "Re-makes/Re-models: *The Red Detachment of Women* between Stage and Screen." *Opera Quarterly* 26, nos. 2–3 (2010): 316–42. https://doi.org/10.1093/oq/kbq015

He, Man. "Backstaging Modern Chinese Theatre: Cosmopolitan Intellectuals, Grassroots Amateurs, and Cultural Institutions, 1910s–1940s." Ann Arbor: University of Michigan Press, forthcoming.

He, Man. "*Juren* (Men and Women of Theatre) in the Confucian Temple: Technics, Prompts, and Plays to Serve the Nation, 1934–1945." *Asian Theatre Journal* 38, no. 1 (2021): 245–74. https://doi.org/10.1353/atj.2021.0012

He Mengfu 賀孟斧. "Jiangzuo: Di qi jiang wutai zhuangzhi" 講座: 第七講 舞台裝置 [Lecture: No. 7 stage installations]. *Shehui jiaoyu fudao* 社會教育輔導 1 (1943): 107–14. QGBKSY.

He Mengfu 賀孟斧. *Wutai zhaoming* 舞台照明 [Stage lighting]. Xiju xiao congshu 戲劇小叢書 [Drama series]. Shanghai: Shangwu yinshu guan, 1936.

He Mengfu 賀孟斧. "Zhe yidai (dumuju)" 這一代 (独幕剧) [This era (one-act play)]. *Kangzhan wenyi* 抗戰文藝 4, nos. 5–6 (1939): 151–55. QGBKSY.

He Qun 賀群. "Wutai shang nihongdeng de zuofa" 舞台上霓虹灯的做法 [Ways to produce neon lights onstage]. *Xiju bao*, no. 8 (1963): 37. CNKI.

Henningsen, Lena. "Literature of the Cultural Revolution." In *Routledge Handbook of Modern Chinese Literature*, edited by Ming Dong Gu, with Tao Feng, 423–34. New York: Routledge, 2019.

Herd, R. A., and Zhang Jian. "Wildean Echoes in the Plays of Ding Xilin." *Modern Chinese Literature and Culture* 22, no. 1 (2010): 162–96.

Hockx, Michel. *Questions of Style: Literary Societies and Literary Journals in Modern China, 1911–1937*. China Studies. Leiden: Brill, 2003.

Holm, David. *Art and Ideology in Revolutionary China*. Oxford: Clarendon, 1991.

Hong Shen 洪深. *Dianying xiju de bianju fangfa* 電影戲劇的編劇方法 [Methods for writing film and theater scripts]. [Shanghai?]: Zhengzhong shuju, 1935. Reprinted in *Hong Shen wenji* 洪深文集, 3:261–389. Beijing: Zhongguo xiju chubanshe, 1959.

Hong Shen 洪深. *Xiju daoyan de chubu zhishi* 戲劇導演的初步知識 [Introductory knowledge for theater directors]. Shanghai: Zhongguo wenhua fuwu chubanshe, 1943. Reprinted in *Hong Shen wenji* 洪深文集, 3:389–510. Beijing: Zhongguo xiju chubanshe, 1959.

Hu Miaosheng 胡妙胜. "Cong *Cai Wenji* zhi *Jialilüe zhuan*—Lun wutai meishu de xieyi xing" 从《蔡文姬》至《伽利略传》—论舞台美术的写意性 [From *Cai Wenji* to *Life of Galileo*—"Writing meaning" in scenography]. *Xiju yishu*, no. 2 (1981): 48–61. CNKI.

Hu Miaosheng 胡妙胜. "Jian lun wutai meishu de xu yu shi" 简论舞台美术的虚与实 [A brief discussion of the "empty" and the "solid" in scenography]. *Renmin xiju*, no. 11 (1978): 21–28, 31. CNKI. Also published as "Wutai meishu de xu yu shi" 舞台美术的虚与实 [The "empty" and the "solid" in scenography]. *Xiju yishu*, no. 1 (1978): 41–57, 122. CNKI.

Hu Miaosheng 胡妙胜. "Wutai meishu de jiadingxing" 舞台美术的假定性 [Suppositionality in scenography]. *Wutai meishu yu jishu* 1 (1981): 10–20. Chinamaxx.

Hu Shi. *The Main Event in Life*. Translated by Edward M. Gunn. In *Columbia Anthology of Modern Chinese Drama*, edited by Chen, 57–65. New York: Columbia University Press, 2010.

Hu Shuhe 胡叔和. *Cao Yu pingzhuan* 曹禺评传 [A critical biography of Cao Yu]. Beijing: Zhongguo xiju chubanshe, 1994.

Hu Xingliang 胡星亮. "Lun Zhongguo xiandai 'puluo xiju'" 论中国现代'普罗戏剧' [On modern proletarian drama in China]. *Xiju wenxue* 戏剧文学, no. 11 (1996): 35–43. CNKI.

Huang Changyong. "Shanghai: The Road to a Modern Performing Arts City." *TDR: The Drama Review* 65, no. 2 (2021): 150–66.

Huang Cun 黄村. "Wutai xiaoguo san (lei, dian)" 舞台效果三 (雷, 電) [Stage effects 3 (thunder, lightning)]. *Zongyi: Meishu xiju dianying yinyue banyue kan* 綜藝：美術戲劇電影音樂半月刊 1, no. 3 (1948): 5. QGBKSY.

Huang Shuqin 黃蜀芹. *Dongbian guangying du hao—Huang Shuqin yanjiu wenji* 东边光影独好—黄蜀芹研究文集 [Light and shadow in the East: Collected research on Huang Shuqin]. Beijing: Zhongguo dianying chubanshe, 2002.

Huang Zuolin 黃佐临. "Guoji Bulaixite xuehui di qi jie yantaohui de ganshou" 国际布莱希特学会第七届研讨会的感受 [Reflections on the Seventh Annual Conference of the International Brecht Society]. In *Wo yu xieyi xijuguan* 我与写意戏剧观. Beijing: Zhongguo xiju chubanshe, 1990.

Huang Zuolin 黃佐临. "Zhuiqiu kexue xuyao teshu de yonggan—wei Bulaixite de *Jialilüe zhuan* shouci zai Zhongguo shangyan er zuo" 追求科学需要特殊的勇敢—为布莱希特的《伽俐略传》首次在中国上演而作 [Pursuing science requires exceptional courage—on the debut of Brecht's *Life of Galileo* in China]. *Wenyi yanjiu* 文艺研究 no. 1 (1979): 121–27. CNKI.

"Huangjin da xiyuan kaimu shengkuang" 黃金大戲院開幕盛況 [The grand opening of the Hung King Theater]. *Xinwen bao* 新聞報, February 2, 1930. QGBKSY.

Hung, Chang-tai. *Mao's New World: Political Culture in the Early People's Republic*. Ithaca: Cornell University Press, 2017.

Hung, Chang-tai. *Politics of Control: Creating Red Culture in the Early People's Republic of China*. Honolulu: University of Hawai'i Press, 2021.

Hung, Chang-tai. *War and Popular Culture: Resistance in Modern China, 1937–1945*. Berkeley: University of California Press, 1994.

Idema, Wilt. "Performances on a Three-Tiered Stage: Court Theatre during the Qianlong Era." In *Ad Seres et Tungusos: Festscrift für Martin Gimm zu seinem 65 am 21 Mai 1995*, edited by Lutz Bieg, Erling von Mende, and Martina Siebert, 201–19. Opera Sinologica. Weisbaden: Harrassowitz, 2000.

Iezzi, Julie A. "Architecture and Stage of Traditional Asian Theatre: Japan." In *The Routledge Handbook of Asian Theatre*, edited by Siyuan Liu, 231–34. New York: Routledge, 2016.

Iovene, Paola. *Tales of Futures Past: Anticipation and the Ends of Literature in Contemporary China*. Stanford: Stanford University Press, 2014.

Jia Zhigang 贾志刚. *Zhongguo jindai xiqu shi (shang), 1840–1911* 中国近代戏曲史（上）, *1840–1911* [A modern history of Chinese opera (vol. 1), 1840–1911]. Beijing: Wenhua yishu chubanshe, 2011.

Jiang Deming 姜德明. "Qianchui bailian jingyi qiujing—ji jingju *Hongdeng ji* zaidu yanchu" 千锤百炼 精益求精—记京剧《红灯记》再度演出 [Striving for perfection—A record of the reperformance of *The Red Lantern*]. *Renmin ribao*, October 13, 1964. RMRB Database.

Jiang Jiehong, ed. *Burden or Legacy: From the Chinese Cultural Revolution to Contemporary Art*. Hong Kong: Hong Kong University Press, 2007.

Jiang Qing. "On the Revolution in Peking Opera (Tan Jingju geming)." Translated by Jessica Ka Yee Chan. *Opera Quarterly* 26, nos. 2–3 (2010): 455–59.

Jiang Qing 江青. "Tan jingju geming: Yijiu liusi nian qi yue zai jingju xiandai xi guanmo yanchu renyuan de zuotanhui shang de jianghua" 谈京剧革命：一九六四年七月在京剧现代戏观摩演出人员的座谈会上的讲话 [On the revolution in Peking Opera: Speech from the plenary discussion with performers after the Modern Peking Opera Trial Performance Convention, July 1964]. *Renmin ribao*, May 10, 1967, 1. RMRB Database.

Jiang Yibing 江一兵. "Guanghui de yingxiong xingxiang, zhanxin de wutai meishu—xuexi geming xiandai jingju *Hongdeng ji* wutai meishu de tihui" 光辉的英雄形象，崭新的舞台美术—学习革命现代京剧《红灯记》舞台美术的体会 [Glorious images of heroes, brand new scenography—Lessons learned from studying the revolutionary modern Beijing opera *The Red Lantern*]. *Beijing ribao*, May 16, 1970, 3.

Jiao Juyin 焦菊隐. "Wutai guang chujiang" 舞台光初講 [A preliminary discussion of stage lighting]. *Juxue yuekan* 劇學月刊 2, nos. 7–8 (1933): 1–64 [i.e., 167–230]. Reprinted in *Jiao Juyin wenji*, vol. 1 焦菊隐文集 第一卷 [Collected works of Jiao Juyin], edited by Yang Hansheng, 1:61–130. Beijing: Wenhua yishu chubanshe, 1986. Chinamaxx.

"Jinan shi jingjutuan yanchu geming xiandai jingju *Shajiabang*" 济南市京剧团演出革命现代京剧《沙家浜》 [Jinan Municipal Beijing Opera Troupe performs the revolutionary modern Beijing opera *Shajiabang*]. *Dazhong ribao* 大众日报, February 14, 1972.

"Jishu geming, biandi kaihua" 技术革命，遍地开花 [Technological revolution blossoms everywhere]. *Xiju bao*, no. 10 (1960): 16–18. CNKI.

Jones, Andrew F. *Yellow Music: Media Culture and Modernity in the Chinese Jazz Age*. Durham: Duke University Press, 2001.

Judd, Ellen. "China's Amateur Drama: The Movement to Popularize the Revolutionary Model Operas." *Bulletin of Concerned Asian Scholars* 15, no. 1 (1983): 26–35. https://doi.org/10.1080/14672715.1983.10404863

Judd, Ellen. "Prescriptive Dramatic Theory of the Cultural Revolution." In *Drama in the People's Republic of China*, edited by Tung and Mackerras, 94–118. Albany: State University of New York Press, 1987.

"Jumu huigu" 剧目回顾 [Past repertoire]. Beijing renmin yishu juyuan 北京人民艺术剧院 [Beijing People's Art Theater]. 2007. https://www.bjry.com/play/classic.html (accessed May 10, 2022).

Kaplan, Randy Barbara. "Planting the Seeds of Theatrical Realism in China: Tian Han's Contributions to Modern Chinese Drama, 1920–1929." *World Literature Today* 62, no. 1 (1988): 55–61. https://doi.org/10.2307/40144010

Ke Zunke 柯遵科. "Bei lishi kongzhi de huaju: *Jialilüe zhuan* de kexue chuanbo yanjiu" 被历史控制的话剧：《伽利略传》的科学传播研究 [Spoken drama controlled by history: The transmission of science in *Life of Galileo*]. *Kexue wenhua pinglun* 科学文艺评论 2, no. 6 (2005): 41–54. CNKI.

"Kekonggui wutai tiao guang" 可控硅舞台调光 [Silicon-controlled rectifier stage lighting dimmer]. *Keji jianbao* 科技简报, no. 1 (January 1971): 26. CNKI. Reprinted from *Kunming keji* 昆明科技 (1971), 16.

Keung, Hiu Man. "The Private Stage: A Study on Chinese Printed Drama by Bai Wei and Yuan Changying, 1922–1936." PhD diss., Department of Asian Studies, University of Edinburgh, 2020. https://hdl.handle.net/1842/36654

King, Richard. "Typical People in Typical Circumstances." In *Words and Their Stories: Essays on the Language of the Cultural Revolution*, edited by Ban Wang, 185–204. Handbook of Oriental Studies. Leiden: Brill, 2010.

King, Richard, with Ralph C. Croizier, Shengtian Zheng, and Scott Watson, eds. *Art in Turmoil: The Chinese Cultural Revolution, 1966–76.* Contemporary Chinese Studies. Vancouver: University of British Columbia Press, 2010.

Kinkley, Jeffrey C., ed. *After Mao: Chinese Literature and Society, 1978–1981.* Harvard East Asian Monographs. Cambridge, MA: Council on East Asian Studies, Harvard University, 1985.

Knight, Sabina. "Scar Literature and the Memory of Trauma." In *Columbia Companion to Modern Chinese Literature*, edited by Denton, 293–98. New York: Columbia University Press, 2016.

Köll, Elisabeth. *Railroads and the Transformation of China.* Cambridge, MA: Harvard University Press, 2019.

Kong Shuyu. "For Reference Only: Restricted Publication and Distribution of Foreign Literature during the Cultural Revolution." *Journal of Chinese Contemporary Art* 1, no. 2 (2002): 76–85.

Kuai Dashen 蒯大申 and Rao Xianlai 饶先来. *Xin Zhongguo wenhua guanli tizhi yanjiu* 新中国文化管理体制研究 [A study of the cultural management system in new China]. Shanghai: Shanghai renmin chubanshe, 2010.

Lanzhou xiqu zhi bianweihui 兰州戏曲志编委会 [Lanzhou Drama Gazetteer Editorial Board], ed. *Lanzhou xiqu zhi* 兰州戏曲志 [Lanzhou drama gazetteer]. Lanzhou: [Lanzhou xiqu zhi bianweihui], 1993.

Lau, Joseph S. M. *Ts'ao Yü, the Reluctant Disciple of Chekhov and O'Neill: A Study in Literary Influence.* Hong Kong: Hong Kong University Press, 1970.

Lawson, Francesca R. Sborgi. *The Narrative Arts of Tianjin: Between Music and Language.* SOAS Musicology Series. Burlington, VT: Ashgate, 2011.

Lee, Leo Ou-fan. *Shanghai Modern: The Flowering of a New Urban Culture in China, 1930–1945.* Cambridge, MA: Harvard University Press, 1999.

Leenhouts, Michael. "Culture against Politics: Root-Seeking Literature." In *Columbia Companion to Modern Chinese Literature*, edited by Denton, 299–306. New York: Columbia University Press, 2016.

Lehmann, Hans-Thies. *Postdramatic Theatre.* Translated by Karen Jürs-Munby. London: Routledge, 2006.

Lekner, Dayton. "A Chill in Spring: Literary Exchange and Political Struggle in the Hundred Flowers and Anti-Rightist Campaigns of 1956–1958." *Modern China* 45, no. 1 (2019): 37–63. https://doi.org/10.1177/0097700418783280

Lenin, Vladimir Il'ich. "Party Organization and Party Literature." In Lenin, *Col-*

*lected Works*, 45 vols., 10:44–49. Moscow: Progress Publishers, 1965. http://www
.marxists.org/archive/lenin/works/1905/nov/13.htm

Leonard, Baird (Leola). "Theatre." *Life* 96, no. 2506 (November 14, 1930): 16–17.

Lewis, John Wilson, and Xue Litai. *China Builds the Bomb*. ISIS Studies in International Policy. Stanford: Stanford University Press, 1988.

Li Chang 李畅. "Wutai meishu de duoyang hua" 舞台美术的多样化 [The diversification of scenography]. In *Zhongguo xiju nianjian 1982* 中国戏剧年鉴 1982 [1982 Chinese theater yearbook], edited by Zhongguo xiju nianjian bianji bu 中国戏剧年鉴编辑部 [Chinese theater yearbook editing department], 16–19. Beijing: Zhongguo xiju chubanshe, 1982.

Li Chang 李畅. "Xuexi jiejian Ouzhou xianjin de wutai meishu gongzuo" 学习借鉴欧洲先进的舞台美术工作 [Learning and borrowing from advanced European stage work]. In *Dang women zai ci xiangju: Zhongguo qingnian wengongtuan chufang 9 guo yi nian ji*, edited by Shi Yajuan, 108–11. Beijing: Wenhua yishu chubanshe, 2004.

Li Chang 李畅. *Yong bu luomu* 永不落幕 [The curtain never falls]. Beijing: Zhongguo xiju chubanshe, 2012.

Li Chang 李畅. "Zhongguo jindai huaju wutai meishu piantan—cong Chunliu she dao wu Chongqing de wutai meishu" 中国近代话剧舞台美术片谈—从春柳社到雾重庆的舞台美术 [Scenography in modern Chinese drama—From Spring Willow Society to Foggy Chongqing]. In *Zhongguo huaju shiliao ji* 中国话剧史料集 [Collected historical materials of Chinese spoken drama], edited by Zhongguo yishu yanjiuyuan huaju yanjiusuo 中国艺术研究院话剧研究所 [Chinese Academy of Arts Institute of Spoken Drama], 252–308. Beijing: Wenhua yishu chubanshe, 1987.

Li Chang 李畅 and Qi Mudong 齐牧冬. "Houji" 后记 [Afterword]. In *Juchang yu wutai jishu*, edited by Li Cheng et al., 75. Wuhan: Zhongnan renmin wenxue yishu chubanshe, 1954.

Li Chang 李暢, Qi Mudong 齊牧冬, et al. *Juchang yu wutai jishu* 劇場與舞台技術 [Theater and stage technology]. Wuhan: Zhongnan renmin wenxue yishu chubanshe, 1954.

Li Chao 李超. "Yao zhongshi wutai meishu zhe men xueke: Dai fakanci" 要重视舞台美术这门学科：代发刊词 [Valuing scenography as an area of study: Foreword (to the first issue)]. *Wutai meishu yu jishu* 1 (1981): 1–3.

Li Gui. *A Journey to the East: Li Gui's A New Account of a Trip around the Globe*. Translated by Charles Desnoyers. Ann Arbor: University of Michigan Press, 2004.

Li Hanfei 李汉飞. "Da hao zimu" 打好字幕 [Put up the subtitles well]. *Xiju bao*, no. 20 (1959): 20. CNKI.

Li, Hua. *Chinese Science Fiction during the Post-Mao Cultural Thaw*. Toronto: University of Toronto Press, 2021.

Li Jiayao 李家耀. "Di jiushiyi ge xi de chenggong yanchu—Zuolin daoyan *Jialilüe zhuan* ceji" 第九十一个戏的成功演出—佐临导演《伽俐略传》侧记 [Successful performance of the 91st play—A by-the-side record of (Huang) Zuolin directing *Life of Galileo*]. *Shanghai xiju*, no. 3 (1979): 31–32. CNKI.

Li, Jie. "Cinematic Guerrillas in Mao's China." *Screen* 61, no. 2 (2020): 207–29. https://doi.org/10.1093/screen/hjaa017

Li, Jie. *Cinematic Guerrillas: Maoist Propaganda as Spirit Mediumship.* New York: Columbia University Press, 2023.

Li, Jie. *Shanghai Homes: Palimpsests of Private Life.* Global Chinese Culture. New York: Columbia University Press, 2015.

Li, Kay. *Bernard Shaw and China: Cross-Cultural Encounters.* Florida Bernard Shaw Series. Gainesville: University Press of Florida, 2007.

Li, Kay. "*Mrs. Warren's Profession* in China: Factors in Cross-Cultural Adaptations," *Shaw* 25 (2005): 201–20.

Li Men 李門. *Zen'yang zuzhi yeyu huaju yanchu* 怎样组织业余话剧演出 [How to organize amateur spoken drama performance]. Guangzhou: Guangdong renmin chubanshe, 1956.

Li Puyuan 李朴圜. *Xiju jifa jianghua* 戲劇技法講話 [Lecture on theater techniques]. Shanghai: Zhengzhong shuju, [1936] 1947.

Li Ruru. *The Soul of Beijing Opera: Theatrical Creativity and Continuity in the Changing World.* Hong Kong: Hong Kong University Press, 2010.

Li Song 李松, ed. *Yangbanxi biannian shi houbian*「樣板戲」編年史後篇 [A chronicle of model opera of the Chinese Cultural Revolution, vol. 2]. Taipei: Xiuwei zixun keji, 2012.

Li Tianshun 李天顺 and Wang Shiwei 王世伟. *Jianyi wutai xiaoguo* 简易舞台效果 [Simple stage effects]. Tianjin: Hebei renmin chubanshe, 1959. Chinamaxx.

Li Weixin 李维新, Zheng Bangyu 郑邦玉, Li Yonggui 李永贵, and Zhou Liguo 周立国. "Cong shenghuo dao zhuti" 从生活到主题 [From life to theme]. *Juben*, no. 4 (1980): 38–40. CNKI.

Li Weixin, Zheng Bangyu, Li Yonggui, and Zhou Liguo. "*Yuanzi yu aiqing*" 原子与爱情 [*Atoms and love*]. *Juben*, no. 4 (1980): 4–37. CNKI.

Li Xiao 李晓. *Shanghai huaju zhi* 上海话剧志 [Shanghai drama gazetteer]. Shanghai: Baijia chubanshe, 2002.

Li Xing 李醒. "Kongzhi lun, xinxi lun yu xiju biaoyan" 控制论，信息论与戏剧表演 [Cybernetics, information theory, and theater performance]. *Xiju xuexi* 戏剧学系, no. 3 (1984): 43–51. CNKI.

Li Yegan 李也甘 and Han Libo 韩林波. "Canjia *Dongfanghong* wutai meishu gongzuo de tihui" 参加《东方红》舞台美术工作的体会 [Our experience participating in scenography work on *The East Is Red*]. *Renmin ribao*, October 15, 1964. RMRB Database.

Li Zehou. *The Chinese Aesthetic Tradition.* Translated by Maija Bell Samei. Honolulu: University of Hawai'i Press, 2010.

Li Zhiyan 黎之彦. "Huaju *Shisanling shuiku changxiangqu* chuangzuo jishi" 话剧《十三陵水库畅想记》创作纪实 [A record of the creative process behind *Fantasia of the Ming Tombs Reservoir*]. *Qingyi* 青艺, no. 1 (1993). Reprinted in *Tian Han chuangzuo ceji* 田汉创作侧记 [Notes from alongside Tian Han's creative work], 118–29. Chengdu: Sichuan wenyi chubanshe, 1994. Chinamaxx.

Liang Qichao. "On the Relationship between Fiction and the Government of the

People." In *Modern Chinese Literary Thought: Writings on Literature, 1893–1945*, edited and translated by Kirk A. Denton, 74–81. Stanford: Stanford University Press, 1996.

Liao Ben 廖奔. *Zhongguo gu dai juchang shi* 中国古代剧场史 [A history of ancient Chinese stages]. Zhengzhou: Zhongzhou guji chubanshe, 1997.

Lin Kehuan 林克欢. "Bianzheng de xiju xingxiang: Lun Jialilüe xingxiang" 辩证的戏剧形象：论伽利略形象 [Dialectical theater image: On the image of Galileo]. *Xiju yishu luncong* 戏剧艺术论丛, no. 1 (1979): 220–25.

Lin Kehuan 林克欢. "Lüe tan *Jialilüe zhuan*" 略谈《伽利略传》[A brief talk on *Life of Galileo*]. *Juben*, no. 7 (1979): 94–96; 40. CNKI.

Lindtner, Silvia M. *Prototype Nation: China and the Contested Promise of Innovation*. Princeton Studies in Culture and Technology. Princeton: Princeton University Press, 2020.

Liu Gao 刘杲 and Shi Feng 石峰, eds. *Xin Zhongguo chuban wushinian jishi* 新中国出版五十年纪事 [Record of fifty years of publishing in new China]. Beijing: Xinhua chubanshe, 1999.

Liu Lu 刘露. "Huaju wutai meishu chuangzuo wenti de tantao" 话剧舞台美术创作问题的探讨 [An exploration of issues in scenography creative work]. *Xiju bao*, no. 7 (1956): 28–31. CNKI.

Liu Lu 刘露. "Wutai meishu de geming yu chuangxin" 舞台美术的革命与创新 [The revolution and innovation of stage art]. *Renmin ribao*, October 11, 1964. RMRB Database.

Liu Mingxiu 刘铭秀. *Wutai huandeng he teji* 舞台幻灯和特技 [Stage projection and special effects]. Yichang: Hubei renmin chubanshe, 1980. Chinamaxx.

Liu, Ping. "The Left-Wing Drama Movement in China and Its Relationship to Japan." Translated by Krista Van Fleit Hang. *positions: east asia cultures critique* 14, no. 2 (2006): 449–66. https://doi.org/10.1215/10679847-2006-009

Liu Rui 刘锐. "Santou juguangdeng he santou huandeng" 三头聚光灯和三头幻灯 [Three-lens focus lights and three-lens projectors]. *Xiju bao*, no. 11 (1965): 42–43. CNKI.

Liu, Siyuan. *Performing Hybridity in Colonial-Modern China*. Palgrave Studies in Theatre and Performance History. New York: Palgrave Macmillan, 2013.

Liu, Siyuan. *Transforming Tradition: The Reform of Chinese Theater in the 1950s and Early 1960s*. Ann Arbor: University of Michigan Press, 2021.

Liu, Xiao. *Information Fantasies: Precarious Mediation in Postsocialist China*. Minneapolis: University of Minnesota Press, 2019.

Liu Xu 柳絮. "Jiji kaizhan wenyi lingyu Zhong de kexue jishu yanjiu" 积极开展文艺领域中的科学技术研究 [Carrying out urgent scientific research in the fields of literature and the arts]. *Wutai meishu yu jishu* 1 (1981): 25–28.

Liu Zhifen 刘芷芬, Yao Jiazheng 姚家征, Fan Yisong 范益松, Ding Gennan 丁根南, and Xu Zhong 徐忠. "Huaju yanyuan xingti xunlian (er) wutai jineng" 话剧演员形体训练：（二）舞台技能 [Physical training for spoken drama actors: (2) Stage skills]. *Xiju yishu*, no. 1 (1979): 100–102. CNKI.

Liu Zhifen 刘芷芬, Yao Jiazheng 姚家征, Fan Yisong 范益松, Ding Gennan 丁

根南, and Xu Zhong 徐忠. "Huaju yanyuan xingti xunlian (xu)" 话剧演员形体训练(续) [Physical training for spoken drama actors (continued)]. *Xiju yishu*, no. 2 (1979): 106–9. CNKI.

Liu Zhifen 刘芷芬, Yao Jiazheng 姚家征, Fan Yisong 范益松, Ding Gennan 丁根南, and Xu Zhong 徐忠. "Huaju yanyuan xingti xunlian (xuyan)" 话剧演员形体训练(序言) [Physical training for spoken drama actors (prologue)]. *Xiju yishu*, no. 2 (1978): 52–57. CNKI.

Liu Zhifen 刘芷芬, Yao Jiazheng 姚家征, Fan Yisong 范益松, Ding Gennan 丁根南, and Xu Zhong 徐忠. "Huaju yanyuan xingti xunlian (yi) jigong" 话剧演员形体训练(一) 基功 [Physical training for spoken drama actors: (1) Foundations]. *Xiju yishu*, no. 3 (1978): 51–65. CNKI.

Lü Dekang 吕德康. "Jieshao liangzhong wutai dengying chenjing jishu" 介绍两种舞台灯影衬景技术 [Introducing two types of stage light-and-shadow outline technology]. *Xiju bao*, no. 6 (1963): 35–38. CNKI.

Lu, Hanchao. *Beyond the Neon Lights: Everyday Shanghai in the Early Twentieth Century*. Berkeley: University of California Press, 1999.

Lu, Tina. *Persons, Roles, and Minds: Identity in "Peony Pavilion" and "Peach Blossom Fan."* Stanford: Stanford University Press, 2001.

Lu Xiangdong 卢向东. *Zhongguo xiandai juchang de yanjin: Cong da wutai dao da juyuan* 中国现代剧场的演进: 从大舞台到大剧院 [On the evolution of modern theaters in China: A history from grand stage to grand theater]. Beijing: Zhongguo jianzhu gongye chubanshe, 2009.

Luan Guanhua 栾冠华. "Jie hou fuxing de jingxiang—'Shoudu wutai meishu sheji zhanlan'" guangan 劫后复兴的景象—《首都舞台美术设计展览》观感 [The postdisaster revival—Viewing the "Beijing Scenography Exhibition"]. *Renmin xiju*, no. 1 (1981): 33–34. CNKI.

Luo, Liang. *The Avant-Garde and the Popular in Modern China: Tian Han and the Intersection of Performance and Politics*. Ann Arbor: University of Michigan Press, 2014.

Luo, Liang. "The Experimental and the Popular in Chinese Socialist Theater of the 1950s." In *Rethinking Chinese Socialist Theaters of Reform*, edited by Chen, Chun, and Liu, 135–61. Ann Arbor: University of Michigan Press, 2021.

Ma Junshan 马俊山. *Yanju zhiye hua yundong yanjiu* 演剧职业化运动研究 [Research on the theater professionalization movement]. Beijing: Renmin wenxue chubanshe, 2007.

Ma Junshan 马俊山. "Yanju zhiye hua yundong yu huaju wutai yishu de zhengti hua" 演剧职业化运动与话剧舞台艺术的整体化 [The theater professionalization movement and integration in spoken drama artistry]. *Wenyi zhengming* 文艺争鸣, no. 4 (2004): 45–52. CNKI.

Ma Junshan 马俊山. "'Yanju zhiye hua yundong' yu Zhongguo huaju wutai meishu de chengshou" 演剧职业化运动与中国话剧舞台美术的成熟 [The theater professionalization movement and the maturation of Chinese spoken drama scenography]. *Xiju yishu*, no. 4 (2005): 44–53.

Ma Yanxiang 馬彥祥 [Ni Yi 尼一, pseud.]. "Wutai dengguang lüetan" 舞台燈光

略談 [A brief introduction to stage lighting]. *Xiandai xiju* 現代戲劇 1, no. 2 (1929): 111–16. QGBKSY.

MacFarquhar, Roderick. *The Hundred Flowers Campaign and the Chinese Intellectuals*. New York: Praeger, 1960.

MacFarquhar, Roderick. *Origins of the Cultural Revolution*, vol. 1: *Contradictions among the People, 1956–1957*. New York: Columbia University Press, 1974.

MacFarquhar, Roderick. *The Origins of the Cultural Revolution*, vol. 2: *The Great Leap Forward, 1958–1960*. New York: Columbia University Press, 1983.

MacFarquhar, Roderick. *The Origins of the Cultural Revolution*, vol. 3: *The Coming of the Cataclysm, 1961–1966*. New York: Columbia University Press, 1999.

MacFarquhar, Roderick, and Michael Schoenhals. *Mao's Last Revolution*. Cambridge, MA: Belknap Press of Harvard University Press, 2006.

Macgowan, Kenneth. *The Theatre of Tomorrow*. New York: Boni & Liveright, 1921.

Mackerras, Colin. *Amateur Theatre in China 1949–1966*. Contemporary China Papers. Canberra: Australian National University Press, 1973.

Mackerras, Colin, ed. *Chinese Theater: From Its Origins to the Present Day*. Honolulu: University of Hawai'i Press, 1983.

Mackerras, Colin. *The Chinese Theatre in Modern Times: From 1840 to the Present Day*. Amherst: University of Massachusetts Press, 1975.

Mackerras, Colin. "Modernization and Contemporary Chinese Theatre: Commercialization and Professionalization." In *Drama in the People's Republic of China*, edited by Tung and Mackerras, 181–212. Albany: State University of New York Press, 1987.

Manheim, Ralph, and John Willett. "Introduction." In *Life of Galileo*, edited by John Willett and Ralph Manheim, vi–xxii. New York: Arcade, 1994.

Mao Zedong. "Be Activists in Promoting the Revolution" (October 9, 1957). In *Selected Works of Mao Tse-tung*, 5 vols., 5:483–97. Beijing: Foreign Languages Press, 1965.

Mao Zedong 毛泽东. "Geming de zhuanbian he dang zai guodu shiqi de zongluxian" 革命的转变和党在过渡时期的总路线 [Shifts in revolution and the Party's general line during the transition period]. *Mao Zedong wenji* 毛泽东文集, 8 vols., 6:315–17. Beijing: Renmin chubanshe, 1999.

Mao Zedong. "On New Democracy." In *Selected Works of Mao Tse-tung*, 5 vols., 2:339–84. Beijing: Foreign Languages Press, 1965.

Mao Zedong. "Talks at the Yan'an Conference on Literature and Art." Translated by Bonnie S. McDougall. In *Mao Zedong's "Talks at the Yan'an Conference on Literature and Art": A Translation of the 1943 Text with Commentary*, 55–86. Michigan Papers in Chinese Studies. Ann Arbor: University of Michigan Center for Chinese Studies, 1980.

Mao Zedong 毛泽东. "Zai Yan'an wenyi zuotanhui shang de jianghua" 在延安文艺座谈会上的讲话 [Talks at the Yan'an Forum on Literature and Art]. In *Mao Zedong xuanji* 毛泽东选集, 2nd ed., 4 vols., 3:847–79. Beijing: Renmin chubanshe, 1991.

Martin, Brian G. *The Shanghai Green Gang: Politics and Organized Crime, 1919–1937*. Berkeley: University of California Press, 1996.

Marx, Leo. "Technology: The Emergence of a Hazardous Concept." *Technology and Culture* 51, no. 3 (2010): 561–77. https://doi.org/10.1353/tech.2010.0009

McDougall, Bonnie S., ed. *Popular Chinese Literature and the Performing Arts in the People's Republic of China, 1949–1979.* Studies on China. Berkeley: University of California Press, 1984.

McDougall, Bonnie S., and Kam Louie. *The Literature of China in the Twentieth Century.* New York: Columbia University Press, 1997.

McGrath, Jason. *Chinese Film: Realism and Convention from the Silent Era to the Digital Age.* Minneapolis: University of Minnesota Press, 2022.

McGrath, Jason. "Cultural Revolution Model Opera Films and the Realist Tradition in Chinese Cinema." *Opera Quarterly* 26, nos. 2–3 (2010): 343–76. https://doi.org/10.1093/oq/kbq016

McGrath, Jason. "Suppositionality, Virtuality, and Chinese Cinema." *boundary 2* 49, no. 1 (2022): 263–92. https://doi.org/10.1215/01903659-9615487

McJannet, Linda. *The Voice of Elizabethan Stage Directions: The Evolution of a Theatrical Code.* Newark: University of Delaware Press; London: Associated University Presses, 1999.

Meserve, Walter J., and Ruth I. Meserve. "The Stage History of *Roar China!* Documentary Drama as Propaganda." *Theatre Survey* 21, no. 1 (1980): 1–13. https://doi.org/10.1017/S004055740000764X

Miller, H. Lyman. *Science and Dissent in Post-Mao China: The Politics of Knowledge.* Seattle: University of Washington Press, 1996.

Mittler, Barbara. *A Continuous Revolution: Making Sense of Cultural Revolution Culture.* Harvard East Asian Monographs. Cambridge, MA: Harvard University Press, 2016.

Mittler, Barbara. "Cultural Revolution Model Works and the Politics of Modernization in China: An Analysis of *Taking Tiger Mountain by Strategy.*" *World of Music* 45, no. 2 (2003): 53–81.

Mo Yan 漠雁. "*Nihongdeng xia de shaobing* de daoyan gousi"《霓虹灯下的哨兵》的导演构思 [Directorial concept for *Sentinels under the Neon Lights*]. *Xiju bao*, no. 4 (1963): 15–21. CNKI.

Moderwell, Hiram Kelly. *The Theatre of To-day.* New York: John Lane Co., 1914. https://hdl.handle.net/2027/hvd.32044100870484

Moderwell, Hiram Kelly [Modewei 莫德威]. *Jindai de xiju yishu* 近代的戲劇藝術 [The theatre of today]. Chengdu: Juyi chubanshe, 1941.

Mumford, Lewis. *Technics and Civilization.* New York: Harcourt, Brace, & Co., 1934.

Nanjing shifan xueyuan zhongwen xi 南京师范学院中文系 [Nanjing Normal School Chinese Department], ed. "*Nihongdeng xia de shaobing*" zhuanji《霓虹灯下的哨兵》专集 [*Sentinels under the Neon Lights* collected essays]. Zhongguo dandai wenxue ziliao 中国当代文学资料. Nanjing: Nanjing shifan xueyuan, 1979. Chinamaxx.

"Nanking Road Neon-Sign Catches Fire." *North China Daily News*, November 29, 1935, 13. QGBKSY.

Needham, Joseph, with Wang Ling and Kenneth Girwood Robinson. *Science and Civilisation in China*, vol. 4: *Physics and Physical Technology*, pt. I: *Physics*. Cambridge: Cambridge University Press, 1962.

"Neon Timeline." Neonsigns.hk (online interactive exhibition). Curated by Aric Chen and Tobias Berger. M+ Museum (Hong Kong). Last updated June 30, 2014. https://www.neonsigns.hk/neon-timeline/?lang=en

O'Connell, Mark. "The Stunning Success of 'Fail Better': How Samuel Beckett Became Silicon Valley's Life Coach." *Slate*, January 29, 2014. https://slate.com /culture/2014/01/samuel-becketts-quote-fail-better-becomes-the-mantra-of -silicon-valley.html

Osborne, Elizabeth A., and Christine Woodworth, eds. *Working in the Wings: New Perspectives on Theatre History and Labor*. Carbondale: Southern Illinois University Press, 2015.

Otto, Ulf. "Enter Electricity: An Allegory's Stage Appearance between Verité and Varieté." *Centaurus* 57, no. 3 (2015): 192–211. https://doi.org/10.1111/1600-0498 .12091

Ou Zaixin 欧载欣. *Wutai huandeng yishu* 舞台幻灯艺术 [The art of stage projection]. Beijing: Zhongguo xiju chubanshe, 1992. Chinamaxx.

Ouyang Shanzun 歐陽山尊. "Dianqi jian: Zui jiandan de 'dimmer' de zuofa" 電氣間: 最簡單的 dimmer 的作法 [Between the electrics: Simple dimmer methods]. *Xi* 戲 1, no. 1 (1933): 40–43. Dacheng Database.

Ouyang Shanzun 欧阳山尊. "Tan Zhongguo wutai de dengguang yanbian" 谈中国舞台的灯光演变 [On the evolution of Chinese stage lighting]. *Xiju* 戏剧, no. 50 (1988): 23–27.

Ouyang Yuqian 歐陽予倩. "*Nuhou ba Zhongguo!* zai Guangdong shangyan" ji《怒吼罷中國》在廣東上演記 [A record of performing *Roar, China!* in Guangdong]. *Xiju* 戲劇 2, no. 2 (1930): 108–9. QGBKSY.

Owen, Stephen. *Readings in Chinese Literary Thought*. Cambridge, MA: Council on East Asian Studies, Harvard University, 1992.

Pan Fang 潘鈜. "Mao Zedong lun kexue jishu yu jishu geming—jinian Mao Zedong danchen 120 zhou nian" 毛泽东论科学技术与技术革命—纪念毛泽东诞辰120周年 [Mao Zedong on technoscience and technological revolution—Commemorating the 120th anniversary of the birth of Mao Zedong]. In Zhonggong Zhongyang wenxian yanjiushi, Zhongguo zhonggong wenxian yanjiuhui, and Mao Zedong sixiang shengping yanjiu fenhui 中共中央文献研究室, 中国中共文献研究会, 毛泽东思想生平研究分会 eds., *Mao Zedong yu Zhonghua minzu weida fuxing: Jinian Mao Zedong tongshi tansheng 120 zhou nian xueshu yantaohui lunwen ji (shang)* 毛泽东与中华民族伟大复兴: 纪念毛泽东同志诞辰120周年学术研讨会论文集（上）[Mao Zedong and the great rejuvenation of the Chinese nation: Proceedings of an academic conference commemorating the 120th anniversary of Mao Zedong's birth (I)]. Beijing: Zhongyang wenxian chubanshe, 2014. https://www.dswxyjy.org.cn/n1 /2019/0228/c423718-30948362.html

Pang, Laikwan. *The Art of Cloning: Creative Production during China's Cultural Revolution*. London: Verso Books, 2017.

Pang, Laikwan. *The Distorting Mirror: Visual Modernity in China.* Honolulu: University of Hawai'i Press, 2007.

Penzel, Frederick. *Theatre Lighting before Electricity.* Middletown, CT: Wesleyan University Press, 1978.

Phelps, William Lyon. *The Twentieth Century Theatre: Observations on the Contemporary English and American Stage.* New York: Macmillan, 1918.

Priest, Harold M. "Marino, Leonardo, Francini, and the Revolving Stage." *Renaissance Quarterly* 35, no.1 (1982): 36–60.

Qi, Shouhua. *Adapting Western Classics for the Chinese Stage.* New York: Routledge, 2019.

Qian Xuesen 钱学森. "Kexue jishu xiandaihua yiding yao daidong wenxue yishu xiandaihua" 科学技术现代化一定要带动文学艺术现代化 [Modernization in scientific technology should propel modernization in literature and the arts]. *Wutai meishu yu jishu* 1 (1981): 4–8.

Qian, Ying. "When Taylorism Met Revolutionary Romanticism: Documentary Cinema in China's Great Leap Forward." *Critical Inquiry* 46, no. 3 (2020): 578–604. https://doi.org/10.1086/708075

Qinghua daxue tumu jianzhu xi juyuan jianzhu sheji zu 清华大学土木建筑系剧院建筑设计组 [Theater Architectural Design Group, Department of Civil Engineering, Tsinghua University]. *Zhongguo huitang juchang jianzhu* 中国会堂剧场建筑 [Auditorium and theater architecture in China]. Beijing: Qinghua daxue tumu jianzhu xi, 1960.

"Qingyi taolun hong zhuan wenti" 青艺讨论红专问题 [China Youth Art Theater discusses the problem of "Red" vs. "Expert"]. *Xiju bao*, no. 10 (1958): 23–24. CNKI.

"Quxian Mao Zedong sixiang wenyi xuanchuandui shenru shanqu puji geming *yangbanxi*" 衢县毛泽东思想文艺宣传队深入山区普及革命样板戏 [Qu County Mao Zedong Thought Cultural Propaganda Troupe goes to mountain areas to popularize the model works]. *Renmin ribao*, September 27, 1970. RMRB Database.

Randl, Chad. *Revolving Architecture: A History of Buildings That Rotate, Swivel, and Pivot.* New York: Princeton Architectural Press, 2008.

Rao, Nancy. "Li Xuefang Meets Mei Lanfang: Cantonese Opera's Significant Rise in Shanghai and Beyond." *CHINOPERL: Journal of Chinese Oral and Performing Literature* 39, no. 2 (2020): 151–181.

Rees, Terence. *Theatre Lighting in the Age of Gas.* London: Society for Theatre Research, 1978.

Reinhardt, Max. "Laiyinhate yan zhong zhi juyuan" 萊因哈特眼中之劇院 [The theater in Max Reinhardt's eyes]. Translated by R. D. *Xiandai xiju* 現代戲劇 1, no. 2 (1929): 1–5. QGBKSY.

Ren Yi 任毅. "Manhuai jiqing hui hongtu—xuexi *Hongse niangzi jun* wutai meishu zhaji" 满怀激情绘宏图—学习《红色娘子军》舞台美术札记 [Drafting a great plan filled with fervor—Notes on studying the scenography of *The Red Detachment of Women*]. *Renmin ribao*, August 28, 1970. RMRB Database.

Ren Yi 韧宜. "Shengse zhuangli, qingjing jiaorong—xuexi *Hongse niangzi jun* wutai meishu de tihui" 声色壮丽，情景交融—学习《红色娘子军》舞台美术的体会 [Majestic sights and sounds, harmony of scene and emotion—Lessons learned from studying the scenography of *The Red Detachment of Women*]. *Beijing ribao*, October 10, 1970.

Ren Yuren 任于人. "Ping *Xi*" 評「戲」[A review of *Play*]. *Xi* 戲 1, no. 2 (October 1933): 15–16. Dacheng Database.

Ribbat, Christoph. *Flickering Light: A History of Neon*. Translated by Anthony Matthews. London: Reaktion Books, 2013.

"*Roar, China!* in Moscow." *Manchester Guardian*, December 14, 1926.

Roberts, David. "Brecht and the Idea of a Scientific Theatre." *Brecht Yearbook* 13 (1987): 41–59.

Roberts, Rosemary A. *Maoist Model Theatre: The Semiotics of Gender and Sexuality in the Chinese Cultural Revolution (1966–1976)*. Leiden: Brill, 2010.

Rojas, Carlos, ed. "Method as Method." Special issue, *Prism: Theory and Modern Chinese Literature* 16, no. 2 (2019).

Rolston, David L. *Inscribing Jingju/Peking Opera: Textualization and Performance, Authorship and Censorship of the "National Drama" of China from the Late Qing to the Present*. Studies in the History of Chinese Texts. Leiden: Brill, 2021.

Rowen, Bess. *The Lines between the Lines: How Stage Directions Affect Embodiment*. Ann Arbor: University of Michigan Press, 2021.

Rowen, Bess. "Undigested Reading: Rethinking Stage Directions through Affect." *Theatre Journal* 70, no. 3 (2018): 307–26. https://doi.org/10.1353/tj.2018.0057

Rui Kunze. "Displaced Fantasy: Pulp Science Fiction in the Early Reform Era of the People's Republic of China." *East Asian History* 41 (August 2017): 25–40.

Salter, Chris. *Entangled: Technology and the Transformation of Performance*. Cambridge, MA: MIT Press, 2010.

San Wen 三文. "*Nuhou ba Zhongguo!*" 怒吼吧中國! [*Roar, China!*]. *Shiri tan* 十日談 5 (1933): 12–13. QGBKSY.

Schivelbusch, Wolfgang. *Disenchanted Night: The Industrialization of Light in the Nineteenth Century*. Berkeley: University of California Press, 1988.

Schmalzer, Sigrid. "On the Appropriate Use of Rose-Colored Glasses: Reflections on Science in Socialist China." *Isis* 98, no. 3 (2007): 571–83. https://doi.org/10.1086/521159

Schmalzer, Sigrid. *The People's Peking Man: Popular Science and Human Identity in Twentieth-Century China*. Chicago: University of Chicago Press, 2008.

Schmalzer, Sigrid. *Red Revolution, Green Revolution: Scientific Farming in Socialist China*. Chicago: University of Chicago Press, 2016.

Scholte, Tom. "Proto-Cybernetics in the Stanislavski System of Acting: Past Foundations, Present Analyses and Future Prospects." *Kybernetes* 44, nos. 8–9 (2015): 1371–79. https://doi.org/10.1108/K-11-2014-0234

Schwarcz, Vera. *The Chinese Enlightenment: Intellectuals and the Legacy of the May Fourth Movement of 1919*. Berkeley: University of California Press, 1986.

Senda Korea [*sic*]. "Greetings from Japan to the International Brecht Society." *Brecht Yearbook* 14 (1989): 5–6. https://digital.library.wisc.edu/1711.dl/BrechtYearbook

"Shanghai guohuo gongsi" 上海國貨公司 [Shanghai Domestic Products Company]. *Shenbao*, September 15, 1933, 21. Shenbao Database.

Shanghai jingju tuan *Haigang* zu 上海京剧团《海港》组 [Shanghai jingju troupe *On the Docks* team]. *Geming xiandai jingju "Haigang" (yijiu qi'er nian* [1972] *yi yue yanchuben)* 革命现代京剧《海港》(一九七二年一月演出本) [Revolutionary modern Beijing opera *On the Docks* (January 1972 performance edition); full promptbook]. Beijing: Renmin wenxue chubanshe, 1974.

Shanghai jingju tuan *Zhiqu Weihushan* juzu 上海京剧团《智取威虎山》剧组 [Shanghai jingju troupe *Taking Tiger Mountain by Strategy* play team]. *Geming xiandai jingju "Zhiqu Weihushan" (yijiu qiling nian* [1970] *qi yue yanchuben* 革命现代京剧《智取威虎山》(一九七〇年七月演出本) [Revolutionary modern Beijing opera *Taking Tiger Mountain by Strategy* (July 1970 performance edition); full promptbook]. Beijing: Renmin chubanshe, 1971.

"Shanghai juyishe chongyan *Shanghai wuyan xia*" 上海劇藝社重演《上海屋簷下》 [Shanghai Theater Art Society performs *Under Shanghai Eaves*]. *Xinwen bao* 新聞報, November 13, 1940.

Shanghai renmin yishu juyuan 上海人民艺术剧院 [Shanghai People's Art Theater]. "Shanghai renmin yishu juyuan zenme yang zou qunzhong luxian kaizhan chuangzao huodong" 上海人民艺术剧院怎么样走群众路线开展创造活动 [How the Shanghai People's Art Theater followed the mass line to carry out creative activities]. *Xiju gongzuo yuejin jingyan xuanji* 戏剧工作跃进经验选辑 [Selected works from the experience of theater work during the Great Leap Forward], 27–32. Shanghai: Shanghai wenyi chubanshe, 1958. Duxiu.

Shanghai shifan daxue Zhongwen xi gongnongbing xueyuan diaocha xiaozu 上海师范大学中文系工农兵学员调查小组 [Shanghai Normal University Chinese Department Worker-Peasant-Soldier Survey Group], ed. "Zai douzheng zhong jianchi puji geming yangbanxi—Zhongguo renmin jiefangjun Shanghai jingbei qu moubu yeyu xuanchuandui diaocha" 在斗争中坚持普及革命样板戏—中国人民解放军上海警备区某部业余宣传队调查 [Continue to popularize the revolutionary model opera in the midst of struggle—A study of a PLA Shanghai garrison command amateur propaganda troupe]. In *Yizhi chang dao gongchan zhuyi—Gongnongbing puji geming yangbanxi diaocha baogao* 一直唱到共产主义—工农兵普及革命样板戏调查报告 [Singing all the way to communism—Investigative report on the popularization of revolutionary model opera by workers, peasants, and soldiers], 74–85. Shanghai: Shanghai renmin chubanshe, 1975.

Shanghai shiyan gejuyuan dengguangzu 上海实验歌剧院灯光组 [Shanghai Experimental Opera Theater Lighting Group]. "Zai wutai shang shiyong huandeng de chubu jingyan" 在舞台上使用幻灯的初步经验 [First experiences using projections onstage]. *Shanghai xiju*, no. 2 (1960): 30–32.

Shao Chongfei 邵冲飞. *Tantan wutai xiaoguo de zhizuo yu shiyong* 谈谈舞台效果的制作与使用 [A discussion of the production and use of stage effects]. Beijing: Beijing chubanshe, 1957. Chinamaxx.

Shapiro, Judith. *Mao's War against Nature: Politics and the Environment in Revolu-*

*tionary China*. Studies in Environment and History. Cambridge: Cambridge University Press, 2001.

Shen, Liang. "'The Great World': Performance Supermarket." *TDR: The Drama Review* 50, no. 2 (2006): 97–116.

Shen Qiyu 沈起予. "Yishu yundong de genben gainian" 藝術運動的根本概念 [Fundamental principles of arts movements]. *Chuangzao yuekan* 創造月刊 2, no. 3 (1928): 1–7. QGBKSY.

Shen Ximeng 沈西蒙, Mo Yan 漠雁, and Lü Xingchen 吕兴臣. "*Nihongdeng xia de shaobing*" 霓虹灯下的哨兵 [*Sentinels under the Neon Lights*]. *Juben*, no. 2 (1963): 2–41. CNKI.

Shen Yan 申燕. "'Da yuejin' yu shehui zhuyi wutuobang xiju" "大跃进"与社会主义乌托邦戏剧 ["The Great Leap Forward" and socialist utopian drama]. *Wenyi yanjiu* 文艺研究, no. 8 (2013): 95–102. CNKI.

Shen Yi 沈毅. "You yi de tansuo—*Yuanzi yu aiqing* guan hou" 有益的探索—《原子与爱情》观后 [A beneficial exploration—After seeing *Atoms and Love*]. *Juben*, no. 5 (1980): 93–96. CNKI.

*Shengli yu heping: Jinian Kangzhan shengli 70 zhou nian wenyi wanhui* 胜利与和平：纪念抗战胜利70周年文艺晚会 [Victory and peace: An evening of literature and arts celebrating the 70th victory of the War of Resistance against Japan]. CCTV. September 3, 2015. Video, 1:39:58. https://youtu.be/Rv-EZXM5kAA. Accessed May 10, 2022.

Shepherd-Barr, Kirsten. *Science on Stage: From Doctor Faustus to Copenhagen*. Princeton: Princeton University Press, 2006.

Shi Ling 施羚. "Guan *Shanghai wuyan xia*" 觀上海屋簷下 [Watching *Under Shanghai Eaves*]. *Li bao* 力报, July 18, 1940. QGBKSY.

Shi Yajuan 石雅娟, ed. *Dang women zai ci xiangju: Zhongguo qingnian wengongtuan chufang 9 guo yi nian ji* 当我们再次相聚：中国青年文工团出访9国一年记 [Until we meet again: Memories of the China Youth Cultural Troupe touring nine countries in one year]. Beijing: Wenhua yishu chubanshe, 2004.

Shi Yonggang 师永刚, Liu Qiongxiong 刘琼雄, and Xiao Yifei 肖伊绯, eds. *Geming yangbanxi: 1960 niandai de hongse geju* 革命样板戏：1960 年代的红色歌剧 [Revolutionary model works: Red opera in 1960s]. Beijing: Zhongguo fazhan chubanshe, 2012.

"Shoudu juchang jiancheng" 首都剧场建成 [Capital Theater completed]. *Xiju bao*, no. 11 (1955): 42–43.

Shu Haoqing 舒浩晴. "Yiqie wei le suzao wuchan jieji yingxiong xingxiang—xuexi *Zhiqu Weihushan* wutai meishu zhaji" 一切为了塑造无产阶级英雄形象—学习《智取威虎山》舞台美术札记 [All to create the image of the proletarian hero—Notes on studying the scenography of *Taking Tiger Mountain by Strategy*]. *Renmin ribao*, October 28, 1969, 3. Reprinted in *Geming yangbanxi chuangzuo jingyan* 革命样板戏创作经验 [Experiences of creating the revolutionary model works], 133–38. Nanchang: Jiangxi renmin chubanshe, 1972.

Simon, Denis Fred, and Merle Goldman, eds. *Science and Technology in Post-Mao China*. Harvard Contemporary China Series. Cambridge, MA: Harvard University Press, 1989.

Simon, Denis Fred, and Detlef Rehn. *Technological Innovation in China: The Case of the Shanghai Semiconductor Industry*. Cambridge, MA: Ballinger, 1988.

Simondon, Gilbert. "Technical Mentality." Translated by Arne De Boever. *Parrhesia* 7, nos. 2–3 (2009): 17–27. http://parrhesiajournal.org/parrhesia07/parrhesia07.pdf

Simpson, Patricia Anne. "Revolutionary Reading: The Circulation of Truth in Brecht's *Leben des Galilei*." *Brecht Yearbook* 15 (1990): 165–82. https://digital.library.wisc.edu/1711.dl/BrechtYearbook

Sloterdijk, Peter. *Terror from the Air*. Translated by Amy Patton and Steve Corcoran. Los Angeles: Semiotext(e), 2009.

Smith, Peter D. *Metaphor and Materiality: German Literature and the World-View of Science, 1780–1955*. Studies in Comparative Literature. Oxford: Legenda, 2000.

Sofer, Andrew. *The Stage Life of Props*. Ann Arbor: University of Michigan Press, 2003.

Song Baozhen 宋宝珍. *Zhongguo huaju yishu shi* 中国话剧艺术史 [A history of Chinese drama]. 9 vols., vol. 2. Edited by Tian Benxiang 田本相. Nanjing: Jiangsu fenghuang jiaoyu chubanshe, 2016.

Song Shi 宋时. *Song Zhidi yanjiu ziliao* 宋之的研究资料 [Research materials on Song Zhidi]. Beijing: Jiefangjun wenyi chubanshe, 1987.

Song Zhidi 宋之的. *Bian* 鞭 [*The Whip*]. Chongqing: Shenghuo shudian, 1940. Duxiu.

Song Zhidi 宋之的. *Wu Chongqing* 雾重庆 [*Foggy Chongqing*]. Beijing: Zhongguo xiju chubanshe, 1957. Chinamaxx.

Song Zhidi 宋之的. "Xiju yu xuanchuan (daixu)" 戲劇與宣傳（代序）[Drama and propaganda (a preface)]. In *Yanju shouce* 演劇手冊 [Performance handbook], edited by Song Zhidi et al., iii–vi. Chongqing: Shanghai zazhi gongsi, 1939.

Song Zhidi 宋之的, He Mengfu 賀孟斧, Ge Yihong 葛一虹, Zhang Min 章泯, Zhao Yue 趙越, Zhou Yan 周彥, Chen Liting 陳鯉庭, and Zhao Ming 趙明. *Yanju shouce* 演劇手冊 [Performance handbook]. Chongqing: Shanghai zazhi gongsi, 1939.

Stiegler, Bernard. *Technics and Time 1: The Fault of Epimetheus*. Translated by Richard Beardsworth and George Collins. Meridian. Stanford: Stanford University Press, 1998.

Sun Haoran 孙浩然. "Guan ju zatan" 观剧杂谈 [Notes on performances]. *Xiju bao*, no. 16 (1958): 31–33. CNKI.

Su Shifeng 苏石风. "Meishu gongchang ye yao dagao jishu geming" 美术工场也要大搞技术革命 [Art workshops must also engage in technological revolution]. *Shanghai xiju*, no. 4 (1960): 39. CNKI.

Tang, Xiaobing. *Chinese Modern: The Heroic and the Quotidian*. Post-Contemporary Interventions. Durham: Duke University Press, 2000.

Tang Xiaobing. "Echoes of *Roar, China!* On Vision and Voice in Modern Chinese Art." *positions: east asia cultures critique* 14, no. 2 (2006): 467–94.

Tang Xueying 唐雪瑩. *Minguo chuqi shanghai xiqu yanjiu* 民國初期上海戲曲研究 [A study of the Chinese opera in Shanghai during the early period of the Republic of China]. Beijing: Beijing daxue chubanshe, 2012.

"Tansuo huaju yanchu de xin xingshi—*Yuanzi yu aiqing* zuotanhui" xiaoji探索话剧演出的新形式—《原子与爱情》座谈会小记 [Exploring new forms of spoken drama performance—Notes on the symposium on *Atoms and Love*]. *Renmin xiju*, no. 5 (1980): 15–17. CNKI.

Tao Jingsun 陶晶孙. "'Roar Chinese' (Juqing lüeshu)" "Roar Chinese" 剧情略述 ["Roar Chinese"plot summary]. *Lequn zhoukan* 乐群月刊 1, no. 4 (1929): 152–53.

Tatlow, Antony, and Tak-Wai Wong, eds. *Brecht and East Asian Theatre: The Proceedings of a Conference on Brecht in East Asian Theatre*. Hong Kong: Hong Kong University Press, 1982.

Taylor, Emerson Gifford. *Practical Stage Direction for Amateurs: A Handbook for Amateur Actors and Managers*. New York: E. P. Dutton & Co., 1916; repr. 1923.

Teng, Tim Shao-Hung. "Murderous Shadows, Terrifying Air: *Dr. Caligari* in China." *Journal of Chinese Cinemas* 14, no. 3 (2020): 223–41. https://doi.org/10.1080/17508061.2020.1837572

Tian Benxiang 田本相, ed. *Zhongguo huaju yishu shi* 中国话剧艺术史 [A history of Chinese drama]. 9 vols. Nanjing: Jiangsu fenghuang jiaoyu chubanshe, 2016.

Tian Han 田漢. "*Nuhou ba, Zhongguo!*" 怒吼吧, 中國! [*Roar, China!*]. *Nanguo zhoukan* 南國周刊 9 (1929): 445–50. QGBKSY.

Tian Han 田漢. "*Nuhou ba, Zhongguo!* (xu)" 怒吼吧, 中國! (續) [*Roar, China!* cont'd]. *Nanguo zhoukan* 南國周刊 10 (1929): 491–504. QGBKSY.

Tian Han 田汉. "Shisanling shuiku changxiangqu" 十三陵水库畅想曲 [*Ballad* (i.e., *Fantasia*) *of the Ming Tombs Reservoir*]. *Juben*, no. 8 (1958): 38–77. CNKI.

Tian Han 田汉. "Yi gaodu shehui zhuyi ganjin zhengqu xiju chuangzuo da fengshou" 以高度社会主义干劲争取戏剧创作大丰收 [Strive for a bumper crop of theatrical creation through high-level socialism]. *Juben*, no. 4 (1958): 2–6. CNKI.

Tian, Min. "Stage Directions in the Performance of Yuan Drama." *Comparative Drama* 39, nos. 3–4 (2005–6): 397–443. https://doi.org/10.1353/cdr.2005.0018

Tong Benyi 童本一. "*Dongfanghong* de houtai gongzuo"《东方红》的后台工作 [Backstage work on *The East Is Red*]. *Renmin ribao*, October 15, 1964, 5. RMRB Database.

Tow, Edna. "The Great Bombing of Chongqing and the Anti-Japanese War, 1937–1945." In *The Battle for China: Essays on the Military History of the Sino-Japanese War of 1937–1945*, edited by Mark Peattie, Edward J. Drea, and Hans van de Ven, 256–82. Stanford: Stanford University Press, 2011.

Tret'iakov, Sergei. *Nuhou ba, Zhongguo!* 怒吼罷, 中國! [*Roar, China!*]. Translated by Pan Jienong 潘子農. Shanghai: Liangyou zong gongsi, 1935.

Tret'iakov, Sergei. *Roar, China! An Episode in Nine Scenes*. Translated by F. Polianovska and Barbara Nixon. London: Martin Lawrence, 1931.

Tret'iakov, Sergei. "The Theater of Attractions [1924]." Translated by Kristin Romberg. *October*, no. 118 (Fall 2006): 19–26.

Tsuboi, Uzuhiko. "Historical Development of Revolving Stages of Theaters Invented in Japan—Improvement by Adoption of European Culture." *Proceedings of the International Conference on Business & Technology Transfer* 1 (2002): 207–12. https://doi.org/10.1299/jsmeicbtt.2002.1.0_207

Tu Kelin 屠克林. "Guanyu juben de chuangzuo gaibian he fanyi" 關於劇本的創作改編和翻譯 [On the matter of the adaptation and translation of scripts]. *Zhongguo qingnian* 中國青年 1, no. 2 (1943): 44–46. QGBKSY.

Tung, Constantine. "Experience and Conviction in China's Wartime Drama, 1937–1945." In *La Littérature chinoise au temps de la guerre de résistance contre le Japon (de 1937 à 1945): Colloque international*, 377–94. Paris: Éditions de la Fondation Singer-Polignac, [1982].

Tung, Constantine. "Introduction: Tradition and Experience of the Drama of the People's Republic of China." In *Drama in the People's Republic of China*, edited by Tung and Mackerras, 1–27. Albany: State University of New York Press, 1987.

Tung, Constantine, and Colin Mackerras, eds. *Drama in the People's Republic of China*. Albany: State University of New York Press, 1987.

Volland, Nicolai. *Socialist Cosmopolitanism: The Chinese Literary Universe, 1945–1965*. Studies of the Weatherhead East Asian Institute. New York: Columbia University Press, 2017.

Wagner, Rudolf G. *The Contemporary Chinese Historical Drama: Four Studies*. Berkeley: University of California Press, 1990.

Wagner, Rudolf G. "Lobby Literature: The Archaeology and Present Functions of Science Fiction in China." In *After Mao*, edited by Kinkley, 17–62. Harvard East Asian Monographs. Cambridge, MA: Council on East Asian Studies, Harvard University, 1985.

Wan Jiabao 萬家寶 [Cao Yu 曹禺, pseud.]. "Bianju shu" 編劇術 [Playwriting techniques]. In Yu Shangyuan 余上沅 et al., *Zhanshi xiju jiangzuo* 戰時戲劇講座 [Lectures on wartime theater], 36–50. Chongqing: Zhengzhong shuju, 1940.

Wang, Ban. *The Sublime Figure of History: Aesthetics and Politics in Twentieth-Century China*. Stanford: Stanford University Press, 1997.

Wang, David Der-wei. *Fictional Realism in Twentieth-Century China: Mao Dun, Lao She, Shen Congwen*. New York: Columbia University Press, 1992.

Wang Jun 王军. *Chengji* 城记 [A record of the city]. Beijing: Shenghuo dushu xinzhi sanlian shudian, 2003.

Wang Ling 王鈴. "Wutai xiaoguo de zhifa" 舞台效果的製法 [How to produce stage effects]. *Xiandai yanju* 現代演劇 1, no. 1 (1934): 31–32. QGBKSY.

Wang, Nan. "Philosophical Perspectives on Technology in Chinese Society." *Technology in Society* 35, no. 3 (2013): 165–71. https://doi.org/10.1016/j.techsoc.2013.05.001

Wang Ren 王韌 and Huang Su 黃甦. "Wutai meishu: Zai tansuo yu chuangzuo zhong qianjin" 舞台美术：在探索与创造中前进 [Scenography: Advances in exploration and creation]. *Xiju bao*, no. 1 (1983): 3–7. CNKI.

Wang Shizhi 王石之 and Li Guangchen 李光晨, eds. *Shoudu wutai meishu sheji ziliao xuan* 首都舞台美术设计资料选 [Select materials on scenography and design in the capital]. Beijing: Zhongguo xiju jia xiehui beijing fenhui, 1981.

Wang, Tuo. *The Cultural Revolution and Overacting: Dynamics between Politics and Performance*. Lanham, MD: Lexington Books, 2014.

Wasmoen, Annelise Finegan. "Translational Stages: Chinese Theatrical Modernism." PhD diss., Department of Comparative Literature, Washington University in St. Louis, 2021. https://doi.org/10.7936/tzy0-0q83

"Watery Grave Snug and Warm in *Roar, China.*" *New York Herald Tribune*, November 16, 1930.

Wei Bingbing. "The Bifurcated Theater: Urban Space, Opera Entertainment, and Cultural Politics in Shanghai, 1900s–1930s." PhD diss., Department of History, National University of Singapore, 2013. https://scholarbank.nus.edu.sg/handle/10635/49417

Wei Bingbing. "Semicolonialism and Urban Space: Architectural Transformation of Chinese Theaters in Late Qing Shanghai, 1860s–1900s." *Chinese Historical Review* 17, no. 2 (2010): 166–92.

Wei, Chunjuan Nancy, and Darryl E. Brock, eds. *Mr. Science and Chairman Mao's Cultural Revolution: Science and Technology in Modern China.* Lanham, MD: Lexington Books, 2013.

"Wei fen yiqian zhi Beijing Diyi wutai" 未焚以前之北京第一舞臺 [The First Stage in Beijing before it burned down]. *Shenbao*, June 13, 1914, 6. Shenbao Database.

Wei Qixuan 韦启玄. "Xiang Sulian xiju xuexi: Tian Han tongzhi tan quan Sulianju huiyan guangan" 向苏联戏剧学习：田汉同志谈全苏联剧会演观感 [Learning from Soviet theater: Comrade Tian Han discusses impressions of seeing performances at the All-Soviet Drama Conference]. *Juben*, no. 2 (1958): 81–85. CNKI.

"Wei xiju yishu chuangzao geng hao de jishu tiaojian" 为戏剧艺术创造更好的技术条件 [Creating better technical conditions for the dramatic arts]. *Xiju bao*, no. 10 (1960): 15–16. CNKI.

Weinstein, John B. "Ding Xilin and Chen Baichen: Building a Modern Theater through Comedy." *Modern Chinese Literature and Culture* 20, no. 2 (2008): 92–130.

Weng Ouhong 翁偶虹 and A Jia 阿甲. *The Red Lantern* [1970]. Revised by the China Peking Opera Troupe. Translated by Brenda Austin and John B. Weinstein. In *Columbia Anthology of Modern Chinese Drama*, edited by Chen, 732–68. New York: Columbia University Press, 2010.

Williams, Raymond. *Marxism and Literature.* Reprint ed. Marxist Introductions. Oxford: Oxford University Press, 2009.

WORLDSHOW (@worldshow1), "44 kuai ping? 44 ben shu? Ruhe gouzao *Luzhen shexi* zhe bu daxing shijing yinghuaju?" WeChat, June 2, 2021. https://mp.weixin.qq.com/s/N-aXZlgtYMXEIKlijlIDZw

Worthen, W. B. *Shakespeare, Technicity, Theatre.* Cambridge: Cambridge University Press, 2020.

Worthen, W. B. "Shakespearean Technicity." In *The Oxford Handbook of Shakespeare and Performance*, edited by James C. Bulman, 321–40. Oxford: Oxford University Press, 2017.

Wu Renzhi 吳仞之. "Wutai guang: Disan jie dengguang yu jing" 舞臺光：第三節燈光與景 [Stage lighting: Chapter 3, lighting and scenery]. *Juchang yishu* 劇場藝術, no. 6 (1939): 15–16. Dacheng Database.

Wu Renzhi 吳仞之. "Wutai guang: Diyi jie fan lun wutaiguang de zuoyong" 舞臺光：第一節 汎論舞臺光的作用 [Stage lighting: Chapter 1, A general discussion of the uses of stage lighting]. *Juchang yishu* 劇場藝術, no. 1 (1938): 9–11. Dacheng Database.

Wu Yigong 武以功, Zhang Shufa 张树发, Zhong Weilun 仲伟伦, and Zhou Liansheng 周连胜. *He wuqi* 核武器 [Nuclear weapons]. Beijing: Zhanshi chubanshe, 1979. Chinamaxx.

Xi Jinping 习近平. "Full text of Xi Jinping's report at 19th CPC National Congress: 'Secure a Decisive Victory in Building a Moderately Prosperous Society in All Respects and Strive for the Great Success of Socialism with Chinese Characteristics for a New Era.'" Nineteenth National Congress of the Communist Party of China, October 18, 2017; *Xinhua News*, November 4, 2017. https://www .chinadaily.com.cn/china/19thcpcnationalcongress/2017-11/04/content_3411 5212.htm

Xi Muliang and Annie Feng. "Chinese Directors: The New Generation." *Critical Stages/Scènes Critiques* no. 18 (December 2018). https://www.critical-stages.org /18/chinese-directors-the-new-generation/

Xia Yan 夏衍. "Juben de chuangzao" 劇本的創作 [The writing of plays]. *Qingnian xiju* 青年戲劇 1, no. 1 (1940): 2.

Xia Yan 夏衍. "*Sai Jinhua* 賽金花." *Wenxue* 文学 6, no. 4 (1936): 553–90. QGBKSY.

Xia Yan 夏衍. *Shanghai wuyan xia* 上海屋簷下 (*Under Shanghai Eaves*). Shanghai: Xiandai xiju chubanshe, 1939. Dacheng Database.

Xia Yan 夏衍. *Shanghai wuyan xia* 上海屋檐下 (*Under Shanghai Eaves*). Beijing: Zhongguo xiju chubanshe, 1957. Chinamaxx.

Xia Yan 夏衍. "Tan *Shanghai wuyan xia* de chuangzuo" 谈上海屋檐下的创作 [On the creation of *Under Shanghai Eaves*]. In *Xia Yan xiju yanjiu ziliao (shang)* 夏衍戏剧研究资料(上), edited by Hui Lin 会林, 20–26. Beijing: Zhongguo xiju chubanshe, 1980.

Xia Yan. *Under Shanghai Eaves.* Translated by George Hayden. In *Columbia Anthology of Modern Chinese Drama*, edited by Chen, 397–447. New York: Columbia University Press, 2010.

Xia Yan 夏衍. "Zixu" 自序 [Preface]. In *Shanghai wuyan xia* 上海屋簷下 (*Under Shanghai Eaves*), 1–3. Shanghai: Xiju shidai chubanshe, 1937. Reprinted in *Xiayan xiju yanjiu ziliao shang* 夏衍戏剧研究资料上, edited by Hui Lin 会林, 15–16. Beijing: Zhongguo xiju chubanshe, 1980. Chinamaxx.

"Xia Yan yaoqiu *Shanghai wuyan xia* zhengge fangzi shangtai" 夏衍要求'上海屋檐下'整個房子上台 [Xia Yan required an entire house onstage for *Under Shanghai Eaves*]. *Tie bao* 铁报, August 2, 1937.

Xian, Jia. "The Past, Present and Future of Scientific and Technical Journals of China." *Learned Publishing* 19, no. 2 (2006): 133–41. https://doi.org/10.1087/09 5315106776387039

Xian Jiqing 贤骥清. *Minguo shiqi Shanghai wutai yanjiu* 民国时期上海舞台研究 [Research on Shanghai stages in the Republic of China]. Shanghai: Shanghai renmin chubanshe, 2016.

Xiang Peiliang 向培良. *Juben lun* 劇本論 [Script theory]. Xiju xiao congshu 戲劇小叢書 [Drama series]. Shanghai: Shangwu yinshu guan, 1936.

Xiang Peiliang 向培良. *Wutai secai xue* 舞台色彩學 [Color studies for the stage].

Xiju xiao congshu 戲劇小叢書 [Drama series]. Shanghai: Shangwu yinshua guan, 1935.

Xiao, Hui Faye. "Science and Poetry: Narrativizing Marital Crisis in Reform-Era Rural China." *Modern Chinese Literature and Culture* 23, no. 2 (2011): 146–74.

Xiao Qiu 小丘 [pseud.]. "Jing he qing—yishu bianzhengfa xuexi zaji" 景和情—艺术辩证法学习杂记 [Scene and feeling—Notes on studying the dialectics of art]. *Renmin ribao*, January 6, 1973, 4. RMRB Database.

Xiaowen Xu. "Early Modern Drama: Hong Shen, Ouyang Yuqian, Xia Yan." In *The Routledge Handbook of Modern Chinese Literature*, edited by Ming Dong Gu, 183–93. New York: Routledge, 2019.

"Xiju xiao congshu" 戲劇小叢書 [Drama series]. *Shenbao*, October 16, 1936, 7. Shenbao Database.

Xiju yishu yanjiu shi 戏剧艺术研究室 [Theater Arts Research Department] and Biaoyan xi biaoyan jiaoyan zu 表演系表演教研组 [Acting Department Performance Teaching and Research Group]. "Guanyu Sitannisilafusiji tixi de taolun" 关于斯坦尼斯拉夫斯基体系的讨论 [A discussion of the Stanislavsky system of acting]. *Xiju yishu*, no. 1 (1978): 9–28.

Xinjun 欣君 [pseud]. "Xuexi *Chusheng de Taiyang* wutai meishu de tihui" 学习《初生的太阳》舞台美术的体会 [Lessons learned from studying the scenography of *The Rising Sun*]. *Renmin xiju*, no. 6 (1976): 20–21. CNKI.

Xu Hongzhuang 许宏庄, ed. *Chaoxian juchang yingyuan ziliao ji* 朝鲜剧场影院资料集 [North Korean theater and cinema data collection]. Beijing: Wenhuabu juchang jianzhu daibiao tuan, 1978.

Xu Peng. "Hearing the Opera: 'Teahouse Mimesis' and the Aesthetics of Noise in Early *Jingju* Recordings, 1890s–1910s," *CHINOPERL: Journal of Chinese Oral and Performing Literature* 36, no. 1 (2017): 1–21. https://doi.org/10.1080/01937 774.2017.1337693

Xu Xiaozhong 徐晓钟. "Ba ziji de xingshi fuyu ziji de guannian" 把自己的形式赋予自己的观念 [Invest your own form with your own ideas]. In *Xu Xiaozhong daoyan yishu yanjiu* 徐晓钟导演艺术研究 [Director Xu Xiaozhong's artistic research], edited by Lin Yinyu 林荫宇. Beijing: Zhongguo xiju chubanshe, 1991.

Xu Xiaozhong 徐晓钟. "Guanyu 'zhuantai' de yi feng xin" 关于"转台"的一封信 [A letter regarding the "revolving stage"]. In *Daoyan yishu lun* 导演艺术论 [On the art of directing], 455–59. Beijing: Wenhua yishu chubanshe, 2017.

Xu Xingjie 徐幸捷 and Cai Shicheng 蔡世成, eds. *Shanghai jingju zhi* 上海京剧志 [Shanghai Beijing opera gazetteer]. Shanghai: Shanghai wenhua chubanshe, 1999.

Xue Dianjie 薛殿杰. "Baituo huanjue zhuyi shufu, dadan yunyong wutai jiadingxing" 摆脱幻觉主义束缚，大胆运用舞台假定性 [Cast off the constraints of illusionism, boldly use the suppositionality of the stage]. *Wutai meishu yu jishu*, no. 1 (1981): 20–24.

Xue Dianjie. "Stage Design for Brecht's *Life of Galileo*." Translated by Tak-Wai Wong. In *Brecht and East Asian Theatre*, edited by Tatlow and Wong, 72–86. Hong Kong: Hong Kong University Press, 1982.

Yan, Haiping. *Chinese Women Writers and the Feminist Imagination, 1905–1948*. Asia's Transformations. London: Routledge, 2006.

Yan, Haiping, ed. *Theater and Society: An Anthology of Contemporary Chinese Drama*. Asia and the Pacific. Armonk, NY: M. E. Sharpe, 1998.

Yan, Haiping. "Theater and Society: An Introduction to Contemporary Chinese Drama." In *Theater and Society: An Anthology of Contemporary Chinese Drama*, edited by Haiping Yan, ix–xlvii. Asia and the Pacific. Armonk, NY: M. E. Sharpe, 1998.

Yan, Haiping. "Theatricality in Classical Chinese Drama." In *Theatricality*, edited by Tracy C. Davis and Thomas Postlewait, 65–89. Cambridge: Cambridge University Press, 2003.

Yang Jian 杨健. *Mudi yu yaolan: Wenhua dageming zhong de dixia wenxue* 墓地与摇篮：文化大革命中的地下文学 [The cradle and the grave: Underground literature during the Cultural Revolution]. Beijing: Zhaohua chubanshe, 1993.

Yang Jisheng. *Tombstone: The Great Chinese Famine, 1958–1962*. Edited by Edward Friedman, Guo Jian, and Stacy Mosher. Translated by Stacy Mosher and Guo Jian. New York: Farrar, Straus and Giroux, 2013.

Yang Zeping 杨泽平. "Ji kangzhan zhong de da houfang ying ju ren He Mengfu" 记抗战中的大后方影剧人贺孟斧 [Remembering He Mengfu, a man of film and theater at the rear guard of the War of Resistance]. *Wenshi zazhi* 文史杂志, no. 5 (2014): 29–30. CNKI.

Ye Chen 葉沉 [Shen Yichen 沈一沉, pseud.]. "Yanju yundong de jiantao" 演劇運動的檢討 [Self-criticism of the theater movement]. *Chuangzao yuekan* 創造月刊 2, no. 6 (1929): 28–36.

Ye, Xiaoqing. *Ascendant Peace in the Four Seas: Drama and the Qing Imperial Court*. Hong Kong: Chinese University Press, 2013.

Yeh, Catherine Vance. "A Public Love Affair or a Nasty Game? The Chinese Tabloid Newspaper and the Rise of the Opera Singer as Star." *European Journal of East Asian Studies* 2, no. 1 (2003): 13–51. https://doi.org/10.1163/15700615-00201003

Yi Bie 一别. "Huangjin da xiyuan zhi xin jihua" 黃金大戲院之新計劃 [A new plan for the Hung King Theater]. *Jin gangzuan* 金钢钻, May 30, 1929. QGBKSY.

Yi Ke 易轲. "Yu gaige kaifang tong pin gongzheng sui shidai dachao zhulang qianxing—qingzhu Zhongguo yishu keji yanjiusuo jiansuo 40 zhou nian" 与改革开放同频共振随时代大潮逐浪前行—庆祝中国艺术科技研究所建所40周年 [Resonating at the same frequency as opening and reform to move forward following the great waves of the times—Celebrating the 40th anniversary of the founding of the China Institute of Arts Science and Technology]. *Zhongguo wenhua bao* 中国文化报, January 8, 2019.

Yin Shucun 殷曙村. "Yao renzhen gao hao huandeng zimu" 要认真搞好幻灯字幕 [Work hard to produce projected surtitles successfully]. *Shanghai xiju*, no. 1 (1960): 55. CNKI.

Ying Ruocheng 英若城. "Xifang huaju biaoyan de xin faxian" 西方话剧表演的新发现 [New discoveries in Western spoken drama performance]. *Renmin xiju*, no. 11 (1980): 45–48. CNKI.

Ying Ruocheng and Claire Conceison. *Voices Carry: Behind Bars and Backstage during China's Revolution and Reform.* Lanham, MD: Rowman and Littlefield, 2009.

Ying Yunwei 應雲微. "*Nuhou ba Zhongguo!* shangyan jihua" 怒吼吧中國上演計畫 [Production design for *Roar, China!*]. *Xi* 戲 1, no. 1 (1933): 56–59. Dacheng Database.

"You ganbing zaocheng ganwu" 由乾冰造成幹霧 [Using dry ice to create dry fog]. *Kexue de Zhongguo* 科學的中國 9, no. 9 (1937): 786. QGBKSY.

Yu Shangyuan 余上沅. "Qinxian: Xiju yishu yu kexue faming" 欽羨: 戲劇藝術與科學發明 [My humble gift: Theater art and scientific invention]. *Chenbao fukan* 晨報副刊, January 26, 1924, 3–4. Reprinted in Yu Shangyuan, *Xiju lunji*, 233–38.

Yu Shangyuan 余上沅. *Xiju lunji* 戲劇論集 [Drama essays]. Shanghai: Beixin shuju, 1927.

Yu Shangyuan 余上沅 et al. *Zhanshi xiju jiangzuo* 戰時戲劇講座 [Lectures on wartime theater]. Chongqing: Zhengzhong shuju, 1940.

Yuan Huashui 袁华水. "Jinnian lai wutai zhaoming de jishu fazhan" 近年来舞台照明的技术发展 [Recent technological developments in stage lighting]. *Shanghai xiju*, no. 3 (1983): 61. CNKI.

Yuan Muzhi 袁牧之. "Liang ji kongshou quan—ji dian shengming" 兩記空手拳—幾點聲明 [Two punches with empty hands—A few calls (to action)]. *Xi* 戲 1, no. 2 (1933): 21. Dacheng Database.

Yuan Muzhi 袁牧之. "Wei xiju yundong qiantu dasuan" 為戲劇運動前途打算 [Plans for the future of the theater movement]. *Xi* 戲 1, no. 1 (1933): 1. Dacheng Database.

"Yuejin! Yuejin! Zai yuejin!—Xiju jie Dayuejin zongshu" 跃进！跃进！再跃进！—戏剧界大跃进总述 [Leap! Leap! Leap again!—An overview of the theater world during the Great Leap Forward]. *Xiju bao*, no. 11 (1958): 29–30. CNKI.

*Zenme yang paixi he yanxi?* 怎么样排戏和演戏? [How to rehearse and perform plays?]. Shenyang: Liaoning renmin chubanshe, 1956.

Zhang, Baichun, Jiuchun Zhang, and Fang Yao. "Technology Transfer from the Soviet Union to the People's Republic of China: 1949–1966." *Comparative Technology Transfer and Society* 4, no. 2 (2006): 105–67. https://doi.org/10.1353/ctt.2006.0024

Zhang Fuji 张傅吉. "Jieshao Qingyi chuangzao de tu zhuantai" 介绍青艺创造的土转台 [Introducing the China Youth Art Theater homegrown revolving stage]. *Zhongguo xiju*, no. 15 (1958): 35–36. CNKI.

Zhang Geng 張庚. "Juben chuangzuo wenti" 劇本創作問題 [Problems in script composition]. *Shilun congkan* 時論叢刊, no. 4 (1939): 142–46. QGBKSY.

Zhang Geng 張庚. "Wei guanzhong de xiju jianghua: Shiyi, wutai dengguang he xiaoguo" 為觀眾的戲劇講話: 十一 舞台燈光和效果 [Theater talks for the audience: 11, Stage lighting and effects]. *Shenghuo zhishi* 生活知識 1, no. 12 (1936): 606–8. QGBKSY.

Zhang Geng 張庚. *Xiju gailun* 戲劇概論 [Overview of drama]. Xiju xiao congshu 戲劇小叢書 [Drama series]. Shanghai: Shangwu yinshu guan, 1936.

Zhang Li 张黎. "Shi weiren, ke yeshi zuiren" 是伟人，可也是罪人 [A great man, but also a wrongdoer]. *Renmin xiju*, no. 6 (1979): 39–42. CNKI.

Zhang Lijun 张丽军. *"Yangbanxi" zai xiangtu Zhongguo de jieshou meixue yanjiu* "样板戏"在乡土中国的接受美学研究 [Research on the reception aesthetics of the "model works" in rural China]. Beijing: Renmin chubanshe, 2014.

Zhang Wujun 张武军. "Chongqing wu yu Zhongguo Kangzhan wenxue" 重庆雾与中国抗战文学 [Chongqing fog and Chinese literature of the War of Resistance]. *Xinan daxue xuebao (shehui kexue ban)* 西南大学学报（社会科学版）35, no. 2 (2009): 162–65. CNKI.

Zhang Yaoqing 张耀卿. *Wutai meishu rumen* 舞台美术入门 [Introduction to scenography]. Shenyang: Liaoning renmin chubanshe, 1956.

Zhang, Yingjin, ed. *Cinema and Urban Culture in Shanghai, 1922–1943*. Stanford: Stanford University Press, 1999.

Zhang Yunqiao 张云乔. "Ying Yunwei he huaju *Nuhou ba, Zhongguo!*" 应云卫和话剧《怒吼吧，中国！》 [Ying Yunwei and the spoken drama *Roar, China!*]. *Shanghai tan* 上海滩, no. 7 (1995): 38–39. CNKI.

Zhang Zhen. *An Amorous History of the Silver Screen: Shanghai Cinema, 1896–1937*. Chicago: University of Chicago Press, 2005.

Zhang Zhen. "Teahouse, Shadowplay, Bricolage: *Laborer's Love* and the Question of Early Chinese Cinema." In *Cinema and Urban Culture in Shanghai, 1922–1943*, edited by Yingjin Zhang, 27–50. Stanford: Stanford University Press, 1999.

Zhang Zhennan 张震南, ed. *Shuangyashan xiqu zhi* 双鸭山戏曲志 [Shuangyashan drama gazetteer]. N.p., 1989.

Zhang Zhongnian 张仲年, ed. *Zhongguo shiyan xiju* 中国实验戏剧 [Experimental theater in China]. Shanghai: Shanghai renmin chubanshe, 2009.

Zhao Cheng 赵成. "Kegui de xianshen jingshen—huaju *Yuanzi yu aiqing* guan hou" 可贵的献身精神—话剧《原子与爱情》观后 [A valuable spirit of dedication—After seeing the spoken drama *Atoms and Love*]. *Renmin ribao*, April 26, 1980, 8. RMRB Database.

Zhao Mingyi 赵铭彝. "Guanyu zuoyi xijujia lianmeng" 关于左翼戏剧家联盟 [Regarding the League of Left-Wing Dramatists]. [1957]. In *Zhongguo zuoyi xijujia lianmeng shiliao ji* 中国左翼戏剧家联盟史料集 [Collected historical materials of the Chinese League of Left-Wing Dramatists], 28–39, edited by Wenhuabu dangshi ziliao zhengji gongzuo weiyuanhui 文化部党史资料征集工作委员会 [Ministry of Culture Party History Materials Collection Working Committee]. Beijing: Zhongguo xiju chubanshe, 1991.

Zhao Qingge 趙清閣. *Bianju fangfa lun* 編劇方法論 [On playwriting methodology]. Chongqing: Duli chubanshe, 1942.

Zheng Boqi 鄭伯奇. "*Nuhou ba, Zhongguo!* de yanchu" 「怒吼罷，中國！」的演出 [The performance of *Roar, China!*]. *Liangyou huabao* 良友畫報, no. 81 (1933): 14. Dacheng Database.

Zheng Rongjian 郑荣健. "Guojia da juyuan de dixia 'moshu shi'" 国家大剧院的地下"魔术师" [The "magician" underground at the National Center for the Performing Arts]. *Zhongguo yishu bao* 中国艺术报, April 18, 2012. http://www.cflac.org.cn/ys/xwy/201204/t20120418_134386.htm

Zhongguo banben tushuguan 中国版本图书馆 [China Bibliographic Library]. *Quanguo neibu faxing tushu zong mu* 全国内部发行图书总目 [Catalog of internal publications in China]. Beijing: Zhonghua shuju, 1988.

Zhongguo jingju tuan 中国京剧团 [National Beijing Opera Troupe]. *Geming xiandai jingju "Hongdeng ji"* 革命现代京剧红灯记 [Revolutionary modern Beijing opera *The Red Lantern*]. Shanghai: Shanghai wenhua chubanshe, 1968.

Zhongguo jingju tuan 中国京剧团 [National Beijing Opera Troupe]. *Geming xiandai jingju "Hongdeng ji" (yijiu qiling* [1970] *nian yanchuben)* 革命现代京剧红灯记(一九七○年演出本) [Revolutionary modern Beijing opera *The Red Lantern* (May 1970 performance edition); full promptbook]. Beijing: Renmin chubanshe, 1972.

Zhongguo jingju tuan 中国京剧团 [National Beijing Opera Troupe]. *Geming xiandai jingju "Hongdeng ji" (yijiu qiling nian* [1970] *wu yue yanchuben)* 革命现代京剧红灯记(一九七○年五月演出本) [Revolutionary modern Beijing opera *The Red Lantern* (May 1970 performance edition); script and simplified score]. Beijing: Renmin chubanshe, 1970.

"Zhongguo qingnian yishu juyuan zhunbei shangyan" *Jialilüe zhuan* 中国青年艺术剧院准备上演《伽俐略传》[China Youth Art Theater prepares to perform *Life of Galileo*]. *Renmin xiju*, no. 1 (1979): 15. CNKI.

Zhongguo xiju chubanshe bianjibu 中国戏剧出版社编辑部 [China Theater Press Editorial Department], ed. *Nongcun yeyu jutyuan zen'yang datai he jianzhu juchang* 农村业余剧团怎样搭台和建筑剧场 [How rural amateur troupes can put up a stage and construct a theater]. Beijing: Zhongguo xiju chubanshe, 1958.

Zhongguo xiju chubanshe bianjibu 中国戏剧出版社编辑部 [China Theater Press Editorial Department], ed. *Zen'yang zuohao xunhui yanchu* 怎样做好巡回演出 [How to tour a performance]. Beijing: Zhongguo xiju chubanshe, 1958.

Zhongguo xijujia xiehui yishu weiyuanhui 中国戏剧家协会艺术委员会 [Art Committee of Chinese Dramatists Association], ed. *Wutai meishu gongzuo jingyan jianjie (neibu xuexi ziliao)* 舞台美术工作经验简介(内部学习资料) [Introduction to experience working in scenography (internal study document)]. Beijing: Zhongguo xijujia xiehui yishu weiyuanhui, 1957.

Zhongguo yishu yanjiuyuan huaju yanjiusuo 中国艺术研究院话剧研究所 [Chinese Academy of Arts Institute of Spoken Drama]. *Junlü xiju zhi hua: Zongzheng huajutuan de chuangzuo daolu* 军旅戏剧之花：总政话剧团的创作道路 [The flowering of military drama: The creative path of the General Political Department Spoken Drama Troupe]. Beijing: Zhongguo xiju chubanshe, 1993.

"Zhongguo zuoyi xijujia lianmeng zuijin xingdong gangling" 中國左翼戲劇家聯盟最近行動綱領最 [Guiding principles for the recent activities of the Chinese League of Left-Wing Dramatists]. *Wenxue daobao* 文學導報, nos. 6–7 (October 23, 1931): 31–32. QGBKSY. Reprinted in *Zhongguo zuoyi xijujia lianmeng shiliao ji* 中国左翼戏剧家联盟史料集 [Collected historical materials of the Chinese League of Left-Wing Dramatists], 17–19, edited by Wenhuabu dangshi ziliao zhengji gongzuo weiyuanhui 文化部党史资料征集工作委员会 [Ministry of Culture Party History Materials Collection Working Committee]. Beijing: Zhongguo xiju chubanshe, 1991.

Zhou, Chenshu. *Cinema Off Screen: Moviegoing in Socialist China*. Oakland: University of California Press, 2021.

Zhou Enlai 周恩来. "Zai Zhonghua quanguo wenxue yishu gongzuozhe daibiao dahui shang de zhengzhi baogao" 在中华全国文学艺术工作者代表大会上的政治报告（一九四九年七月六日）[Political report at the All-China Literature and Arts Workers Congress (July 6, 1949)]. In *Zhou Enlai xuanji (shang)* 周恩来选集（上）[Selected works of Zhou Enlai, vol. 1], 344–58. Beijing: Renmin chubanshe, 1980.

Zhou Yibai 周貽白. *Zhongguo juchang shi* 中國劇場史 [A history of Chinese theaters]. [1936]. 2nd ed. Changsha: Shangwu yinshua guan, 1940.

Zhou Yongming. *Historicizing Online Politics: Telegraphy, the Internet, and Political Participation in China*. Stanford: Stanford University Press, 2006.

Zhu, Jianfei. *Architecture of Modern China: A Historical Critique*. London: Routledge, 2009.

"Zuo hao puji geming yangbanxi de gongzuo" 做好普及革命样板戏的工作 [Carry out the work of popularizing the revolutionary model works]. *Renmin ribao*, July 15, 1970. RMRB Database.

# Index

acting: cybernetic, 27, 193–94, 269n79; standardization of, 97, 103; styles of, 13, 34, 191; techniques of, 43, 69, 116–17, 192–93, 269n79; and venues, 228n33; in *yangbanxi*, 142, 157, 169
*Acting Power* (Cohen), 193–94
actors: amateur, 106, 160; and atmosphere, 92; and audiences, 34, 228n34; in Cultural Revolution, 144, 171, 180, 193; *jingju*, 15–16, 228n34; and lighting, 14, 41, 43, 140, 157; and new realism, 16; and stagehands, 53, 202; and technology, 8, 14, 34, 55, 94, 114, 115, 123–24, 155, 157, 210, 217, 222; training of, 11–12, 34, 40, 116–17, 193–94, 222
All-China Cultural Administrative Conferences, 103
All-China Federation of Literature and Arts (Wenlian), 102, 109
Amateur Experimental Theater Troupe, 85, 244n65, 245n71
amateur theater (*aimei xiju*): actors in, 106, 160; and Chen Dabei, 5, 33–34, 67, 225n5; and foreign influence, 34, 228n30; and knowledge production, 18, 110–11; manuals for, 25, 106, 107, 108, 110, 160, 252n69, 254n92; *vs.* professionalization, 71; promotion of, 107, 249n23; in Reform Era, 180; in remote venues, 166–72; and scenery

and sentiment, 169; in Shanghai, 228n30; and technology, 24, 26, 106–8, 169, 171–72; and *yangbanxi*, 143, 163, 167–68, 170–71, 262n86
*Amateur Theater* (Chen Dabei), 33–34, 37, 67
Amateur Theater Society, 87
Anderson, Marston, 71
Andreas, Joel, 146, 180
Anqiu County Jingju Troupe, 168, 170
Anti-Rightist Movement (1957), 110
Anti-Spiritual Pollution Campaign (1983), 181
Appia, Adolphe, 3, 14, 37, 41, 42, 43, 194, 210
architecture: as art, 187; foreign influence on, 190–91, 229n51, 233n9; modern theater, 12, 13, 14, 15, 34, 48–49, 222; regulations on, 189; and scenography, 84, 91, 96, 204, 209; and stagecraft, 5, 6–7, 176. *See also* proscenium stages
Artaud, Antonin, 179
*Asia as Method* (Chen Kuan-Hsing), 22
atmosphere: in *Fantasia*, 112–13; and lighting, 85, 87–88; *vs.* mixed media performances, 212; and special effects, 63–66, 154; and stage directions, 74, 90–91, 92, 95; in wartime theater, 89–95

Liang Qichao, 11
*Life Knowledge* (periodical), 60
*Life* magazine, 49
*Life of Galileo* (play; Brecht), 27, 177, 181,
    182–88; and alienation effect, 266n42;
    and *Atoms and Love*, 196, 197, 198;
    projections in, 209; scenography of,
    201–2, 203, 205
lighting technology: and actors, 14,
    41, 43, 140, 157; advances in, 35–36,
    191–92; and atmosphere, 85, 87–88;
    and audiences, 40–44, 58, 59, 157–58;
    and directors, 5, 43, 126–27; and
    electricity, 4, 5, 9–15, 17, 20, 33, 34,
    76–77, 81, 149, 220, 228n32, 229n42;
    experimentation with, 14, 42, 43; in
    *Fantasia*, 112–13; and fog, 93; foreign,
    122, 229n42, 236n39; gaslight, 12,
    14, 228n30, 229n42; and ideology,
    17, 43–44, 61–62; imitation, 124–30;
    and modernization, 10, 11, 12; and
    nonillusionistic scenography, 203; in
    production bibles, 162, 163, 164–65,
    170; publications on, 1–3, 60–61; and
    realism, 14–15, 34, 41; in *Red Lantern*,
    140–41; in remote venues, 166, 169;
    in *Roar, China!*, 28, 49, 59, 238n72;
    and shadows, 6, 87–88; in Shanghai,
    24, 33; in *Under Shanghai Eaves*,
    84–85; and stage directions, 76–77,
    78, 79–80; and technological fantasy,
    126; and *tu* innovation, 117, 170–71,
    192, 220, 243n46; in *xiqu*, 34–35, 61;
    and *yangbanxi*, 151, 152–54, 155. *See also*
    dimmers; neon lights; projections
Lin Kehuan, 184
*Lingering Fog* (play; Lao She), 89
literature: and atmosphere, 88, 122;
    foreign, 253n81, 261n67; Mao on, 101–
    3, 110, 120, 231n66; popular, 107–8;
    in Reform Era, 179; revolutionary,
    18–19, 71–72; root-seeking, 179; scar,
    179, 181, 197; and science, 175, 180, 181,
    192; and social reform, 11, 47, 55, 121,

230n61; typicality in, 147–48, 184–85;
    wartime, 89; *xu* and *shi* in, 127; and
    *yangbanxi*, 161. *See also* manuals;
    periodicals
*Literature and Art News* (newspaper),
    47
Liu, Siyuan, 11, 23, 40
Liu Lu, 131
Liu Xu, 191
Long-Life Theater Troupe, 90
Lu, Tina, 127
Lu Xiangdong, 150, 190, 233n9
Lü Xingchen, 119
Lu Xun, 214
Luan Guanhua, 181
Luo, Liang, 40

Ma Junshan, 23, 70, 236n39, 241n27
Ma Yanxiang, 37, 40
MacFarquhar, Roderick, 143
Macgowan, Kenneth, 225n4
Mackerras, Colin, 11, 107, 180, 249n23
*Made in China 2.0* (play), 214
Man He, 69
manuals: for amateur theater, 25, 106,
    107, 108–9, 160, 252n69, 254n92; for
    audiences, 99, 106, 138, 160; in Cul-
    tural Revolution, 159–66; for direc-
    tors, 69, 95; in early PRC, 105–11;
    on film, 70, 107, 137; and knowledge
    production, 97, 99, 108, 117, 221; for
    the masses, 99–100; on playwriting,
    65, 67, 69, 147; as popular literature,
    107; and professionalization, 71;
    on projections, 131, 134, 255n108; on
    scenography, 69, 106, 108–9, 160; as
    sources, 21–22; on stage technology,
    69; and technological fantasy, 119; on
    theatrical technoscience, 189–90
Mao Dun, 122
Mao Zedong, 110, 128, 154, 230n59; and
    Cultural Revolution, 143, 144, 145;
    death of, 174, 178; and first atomic
    bomb detonation, 197; and Great

tive, 165–66, 172; in literature, 147–48, 184–85; and proletarian theater, 151, 158; and scientists, 198; and stage technology, 165–66; in *yangbanxi*, 147–48, 172

*Uncle Tom's Cabin* (novel; Stowe), 30, 66
*Under Shanghai Eaves* (play; Xia Yan), 25, 65, 68, 70, 91, 240n15; stage directions for, 84–85
United States (US), 220, 222; and early *huaju*, 18, 30, 33, 37, 41; imperialism of, 33, 49; realism in, 73, 203; *Roar, China!* in, 44–45, 46; and science, 178, 194; technology from, 10, 17, 178, 219, 229n39; theater study trips to, 190. *See also* West, the
utopia, socialist, 98, 100, 111–19, 137, 211

venues, 227n28, 228n30; and acting, 228n33; in Beijing, 13, 15, 17, 104–5, 150, 164, 165, 215; for film, 12, 15, 48; in foreign concessions, 244n67; and *jingju*, 228n33; modern, 149–50, 219, 233n9; prices at, 238n80; for *Red Lantern*, 149, 150, 164; remote, 166–72; in Shanghai, 12–14, 28, 32–33, 48–49, 56, 228n37, 237n63; for *yangbanxi*, 149–52, 164–65, 166–72
*Victory and Peace* (epic production), 217–18
*Village Opera of Lu Town* (real-scene landscape performance), 214
Virilio, Paul, 220
Volland, Nicolai, 107, 116

Wagner, Richard, 14, 41
*Waiting for Godot* (play; Beckett), 214
Wan Jiabao. *See* Cao Yu
Wang Chong, 212, 214, 215
Wang Fangding, 200
Wang Ren, 210
Wanxian Incident (1926), 31, 232n3
*War of Resistance Literature and Art* (journal), 85

"Wartime Theater Theory Series," 69
*wenmingxi* (civilized drama), 11, 18, 23, 33; commercialism of, 70; ideology of, 30, 39; original writing for, 66; special effects in, 61
West, the: and amateur theater, 34, 228n30; bourgeois decadence of, 121; and Cultural Revolution, 16–17, 144; and modernization, 10, 15, 23, 34, 73; in New Era, 219; publications from, 191; realism in, 8, 14, 39, 204; in Shanghai, 122, 228n30, 253n81; and socialist utopian plays, 111; stage technologies from, 3, 36–38, 99, 150, 176, 215–16; students returning from, 35, 36–37, 190–91; theater in, 7, 73, 74, 121, 179, 215; and transnational knowledge, 3, 13, 39–48, 62, 194, 216, 225n4; *vs. tu* innovation, 118
*White-Haired Girl, The* (musical), 121, 125, 126, 248n15, 253n79
Wilde, Oscar, 35
*Wilderness, The* (play; Cao Yu), 68
Williams, Raymond, 148
woodblock prints, 55
Worker's Club (Beijing), 150
World War I, 32
Worthen, W. B., 6, 8, 9
"Writing of Plays, The" (Xia Yan), 70
Wu Renzhi, 43
Wu Tian, 241n27
Wu Yonggang, 123
Wu Zuguang, 68, 110, 240n15, 241n27

Xi Jinping, 219
Xia Yan, 88, 94, 96, 131, 244n65; in Cultural Revolution, 178–79; engineering background of, 83–84. See also *Under Shanghai Eaves*
Xiang Peiliang, 43, 60, 67
Xiao, Hui Faye, 180
Xiao Liu, 194
*Xie Yaohuan* (play; Tian Han), 145
Xinhai Revolution (1911–12), 16, 32

Xiong Foxi, 37, 87
Xiong Wei, 112
*xiqu* (sung drama): commercialism of,
12, 70; and Cultural Revolution, 144,
146, 149; *vs. huaju*, 66, 121; lighting
technology in, 34–35, 61; manuals on,
107; nonillusionistic scenography in,
8, 116, 202, 203, 204, 205; periodicals
on, 1, 36, 169–70; as propaganda, 18,
64; and socialist utopian plays, 111,
116; special effects in, 16, 33, 35, 61;
stage directions for, 73; and stage
technology, 3, 7, 15, 34–35, 112, 121, 131;
in teahouse theaters, 12; training for,
193; and *xu* and *shi*, 128–29. See also
*jingju*; *zaju*
*xiyuan* (play garden) performances, 12
*xu* (empty) and *shi* (solid), 127–28, 137,
182, 201, 208, 211
Xu Qu, 85
Xu Xiaozhong, 114–15, 210
Xue Dianjie, 201–2, 204, 205, 209

*Yama Zhao* (play; Hong Shen), 35, 72
*yangbanxi* (*geming yangbanxi*; revolutionary model operas), 139, 140–73,
217, 258nn22–25; acting in, 142, 157,
169; and amateur theater, 143, 163,
167–68, 170–71, 262n86; audiences for,
142, 157–58, 159; characterization in,
147–48, 198; feedback and revision
of, 146–47, 148; and ideology, 143, 152,
188; "learning from," 160–66; and
lighting technology, 151, 152–54, 155,
192; performance editions of, 161;
popularization of, 162–63, 166, 172,
192; projections in, 151, 172, 207; as
propaganda, 26, 121, 145, 172; reaction
against, 176, 178, 211; scripts for, 143,

146–47, 148, 149, 151, 152; stage direc-
tions for, 148, 151–52; standardization
of, 161–62; technological fantasy of,
172–73; theater troupes for, 160–61,
170–71; *tu* technology in, 26, 143, 151,
170–71, 172, 173, 219; venues for, 149–
52, 166–72. *See also* production bibles
Ye Chen, 235n36
Ying Ruocheng, 190–91
Ying Yunwei, 30, 49–52, 58, 89
You Ling (Ren Xigui), 241n27
Yu Shangyuan, 5, 34, 37, 87
Yuan Huashui, 191
Yuan Muzhi, 30, 40, 57, 122, 130, 222
Yuan Shikai, 32
*yueju* (Cantonese opera), 15
Yunnan Provincial Spoken Drama
Troupe, 170

*zaju* (mixed drama), 72–73, 82, 243n54
Zhang Fuji, 117
Zhang Geng, 43–44, 60, 70
Zhang Pengchun, 37
Zhang Yaoqing, 106
Zhang Yimou, 213–14, 215, 217
Zhang Yingjin, 123
Zhang Yunqiao, 49–50, 51–52, 53
Zhao Taimou, 37
Zhen, Zhang, 23
Zheng Bangyu, 195
Zheng Geng, 94
Zhou, Chenshu, 118, 134–35
Zhou Enlai, 16, 101, 147, 197, 264n6; in
*Atoms and Love*, 196, 198; on litera-
ture and arts, 102–3, 248n10
Zhou Liguo, 195
Zhou Xuan, 123
Zhou Yang, 103
Zhou Yibai, 241n27